The Sounds of Early Cinema

EDITED BY
RICHARD ABEL
AND RICK ALTMAN

The Sounds of
Early Cinema

INDIANA UNIVERSITY PRESS

Bloomington and Indianapolis

This book is a publication of

Indiana University Press
601 North Morton Street
Bloomington, IN 47404-3797 USA

http://iupress.indiana.edu

Telephone orders   800-842-6796
Fax orders   812-855-7931
Orders by e-mail   iuporder@indiana.edu

© 2001 by Indiana University Press

The paper used in this publication meets the minimum requirements of American National Standard for Information Sciences—Permanence of Paper for Printed Library Materials, ANSI Z39.48-1984.

Manufactured in the United States of America

Library of Congress Cataloging-in-Publication Data
The sounds of early cinema / edited by Richard Abel and Rick Altman.
     p.   cm.
     Selected papers, rev., of Domitor's four-day Fifth Biennual Conference, hosted by the Motion Picture Division of the Library of Congress, Washington, D.C., during the first week of June 1998.
    Papers in English; includes the original French texts of six papers in the appendix.
    Includes bibliographical references and index.
    ISBN 0-253-33988-X (cloth : alk. paper) — ISBN 0-253-21479-3 (pbk. : alk. paper)
     1. Silent films—History and criticism—Congresses. 2. Motion pictures—Sound effects—Congresses. 3. Motion pictures and music—Congresses.   I. Abel, Richard, date   II. Altman, Rick, date   III. Domitor Conference (5th : 1998 : Library of Congress)
  PN1995.75 .S64 2001
  791.43'024—dc21   2001001470

1 2 3 4 5   06 05 04 03 02 01

Contents

APPENDIXES: ORIGINAL FRENCH TEXTS

Acknowledgments

Domitor, the Motion Picture and Recorded Sound Division of the Library of Congress, and the Center for the Humanities at Drake University provided funding for critical stages of this book's production.

The Executive Committee of Domitor, presided over first by Paolo Cherchi Usai and then by Tom Gunning, offered steadfast encouragement throughout the editing process.

Joan Catapano's strong support was crucial to our contract negotiations with Indiana University Press; Michael Lundell and Jane Lyle ensured that the production process would be efficient and assured; Carol Kennedy achieved an unusual degree of consistency in copyediting the texts of twenty-five different authors; and Lynne Nugent diligently combed through those texts to compile the index.

Introduction
Richard Abel and Rick Altman

No play of the past season has contained a situation more thrilling than the reproduction of a parade of the Ninety-sixth Regiment French Cavalry. The soldiers march to the stirring tune of the "Marseillaise" and the scene stirred the audience to a pitch of enthusiasm that has rarely been equaled by any form of entertainment. The playing of the "Marseillaise" aided no little in the success of the picture. In the sham battle scene the noise and battle din created also added to the wonderful realism of the scene. A political argument and a street scene (children dancing to the strains of a hand-organ) were also excellent specimens of the work of the cinematographe [at Keith's Bijou Theatre].

—Philadelphia Record, 11 August 1896

At the far end [of a nickelodeon on Sixth Avenue, in Manhattan] is situated what might be called the stage. Of course only a sheet is in evidence, which is not suspended from the top as in other places, but embedded in a sort of a wooden frame, surrounded by electric lights, giving the idea of a picture frame before the picture is in. Directly below the screen the entire orchestra is seated. This consists of only a piano and a drum, but it fills the bill.

—Views and Films Index, 25 April 1906

[At a London show] wonderfully realistic effects are introduced. In fact, two men are behind the screen doing nothing else but produce noises corresponding with events happening on the curtain. These effects absolutely synchronise with the movements, so that it is difficult to believe that actual events are not occurring.

—Kinematograph and Lantern Weekly, 24 October 1907

"It has always been my idea," said Mr. Barrow [pianist at Harry Altman's theater, 108th Street and Madison Avenue, in Manhattan], when seen by a FILMS INDEX reporter, "that the pianists who at present furnish the accompaniment for the majority of the picture shows fail to use sufficient judgment in their work. It seems to me as if the prevailing style of musical accompaniment to moving picture films is not the kind which might appeal to the very best class of people. Of course it is very true that the main object for which folks come to the shows is to see the pictures; but, to my way of thinking, the next important factor to good films is good music."

—Views and Films Index, 16 May 1908

Judging by the number of characters it requires, the enormous amount of work produced by the performers [behind the screen] and the particular attention it received from Mr. Dhavrol [manager of the Nationoscope in Montréal], next week's talking picture is going to produce, we believe, a considerable impression, as the theatrical effects we will have a chance to admire in *La Justice de Dieu* [God's Justice] have hardly been seen before.

—*La Presse,* early November 1908

[At the Orpheum, in Chicago] the masterpiece was the Pathé Frères film, "The Violin Maker of Cremona." . . . there the music was soft and appropriate. When Philippo, the poor wounded fiddler, plays a few notes to show that the violin is perfect, the orchestra stops, the violinist only plays a few sweet notes and stops as soon as the bow on the screen stops touching the violin strings.

—*Moving Picture World,* 19 March 1910

We cite these selected remarks from the first fifteen years of cinema's history to suggest how ubiquitous was the presence of sound in the so-called silent cinema, yet how equally diverse it was, from one historical moment and/or exhibition site to another. Until recently, sound (and its absence) has been relatively neglected by historians writing about early cinema, as they have focused on cinema's development as a major mass culture industry, as a popular, sophisticated (and eventually respected) form of story-telling, or as a venue for marketing personalities (from stars to *auteurs*).[1] That lack of attention, together with a growing awareness of sound's significance, prompted Domitor—an international association of historians and archivists devoted to the study of early cinema (prior to 1915)—to make sound the subject of its fifth biannual conference, hosted by the Motion Picture Division of the Library of Congress, Washington, D.C., during the first week of June 1998. That four-day conference drew approximately one hundred people from North America and Europe, presented more than forty papers of varying lengths and daily hour-long roundtable discussions, and capped each day with a rich variety of *son-et-lumière* performances, from magic lantern shows to nickelodeon programs (including illustrated songs as well as films). For publication purposes, the editors (who also served as the conference program committee)[2] have split the papers presented into two groups of revised essays. The present volume contains essays on general theory as applied to film sound, sound practices in production, sound-related exhibition practices (in moving picture shows as well as in other similar cultural venues), film music, and the politics of sound reception. Other essays, specifically devoted to "Global Experiments in Early Synchronous Sound," appeared in a special issue of *Film History* 11.4 (1999).

As conference participants repeatedly insisted, the work collected here hardly can be taken as the culmination of research on sound and early cinema. Rather, along with a 1996 book by Martin Marks and a 1996 article by Rick Altman,[3] both much discussed during the conference, these essays mark the beginning of serious study. Despite the well-worn cliché that the "silent cinema" was rarely silent, participants were still startled, as Ben Brewster put it,[4] to hear about and listen to the sheer diversity of sound(s) and sound/image relations that seemed to characterize early exhibition: barkers and ballyhoos, pianists and "traps" or "effects" players, effects machines and sync-sound apparatuses, lecturers and actors speaking beside or behind the screen, illustrated song performers, and small or large orchestras. Whether instrumental, vocal, or mechanical, sound ranged from the improvised to the preplanned—as in scripts, scores, and cue sheets. And the practice of combining sounds with images differed widely depending on the exhibition venue (the nickelodeon in Chicago versus the summer chautauqua in rural Iowa, the music hall in London or Paris versus the newest cinema "palace" in New York City) as well as the historical moment (a single venue might change radically from, say, 1906 to 1910).

What also struck participants was the multiplicity of theoretical or methodological perspectives needed to more fully come to grips with this diversity. Several essays suggest what could be learned from theorists of visual-audial reproduction to help explain why some sound-image practices flourished while others did not, why some were marketed with much success while others fell flat. Other essays recommend drawing lessons from historians of prior or contemporaneous cultural forms and practices that deployed sound, such as staged dramas, vaudeville programs, magic lantern shows, popular song sheet music, and phonographic cylinders and records. Still others suggest paying attention to the insights of theorists and historians of mass culture about the concerns, interests, and desires (the cultural, social, and ideological expectations) of the new audiences for entertainment at the turn of the last century. All this demonstrates yet again what Noël Burch long ago called the distinctive *otherness* of early cinema, and it also compounds early cinema's configuration as an unusually complex hybrid medium.

The concept of intermediality, invoked by Altman and André Gaudreault, offers an especially useful way to better grasp that configuration, one that also serves to cluster the first series of essays in this volume. Here, intermediality has to be understood as referring to relations both between cinema and other cultural practices and within cinema itself, particularly defined in terms of exhibition.[5] One of several provocative questions the concept raises is whether the diversity of sound-image practices are to be taken as variations on a still-emerging "singularly cinematic theme," to borrow Jeffrey Klenotic's language,[6] or as fundamentally differing forms of media practice (drawing on divergent traditions) that all inhabited the physical and discursive spaces opened up by moving pictures. In other words, focusing on sound in this context forces us to complicate our notion of early cinema as a "cinema of attractions," in which moving pictures co-existed as much as competed with then-current media practices, whose convergence accentuated the appeals for audience response. And that, of course, problematizes the periodization of cinema's early history: in terms of what

Brewster describes as "cinematic ambiance," the crucial point of transition from a "cinema of attractions" to a "narrative cinema" may not be 1907 but rather 1910 or even later. A second question is whether different sound-image practices mediated the unstable relation between film space and theater space (as separate yet overlapping) in different ways and, if so, what effects those mediations may have had for the spectator's experience (social, cultural, cognitive, psychological). Yet a third question, posed most explicitly by Tom Gunning, grows out of specific late-nineteenth-century historical conditions, in which a whole series of apparatuses (fictive as well as material or scientific) aimed to separate the human sensorium into "autonomous" components for analysis and reproduction. Did the different sound-image practices of early cinema, then, tend to maintain and exploit this separation (merely masking the gaps and fissures, so to speak), or did they instead strive to recombine what had been separated and in a variety of ways, so as to produce a "new" form of "wholeness" in mass entertainment?

If a half-dozen essays in this volume "speak to one another" within the context of intermediality, the others explore questions and issues of sound within more familiar, more specific categories. Five essays take up the issue of sound as a significant component of production, either as a neglected historical determinant in the development of film as a story-telling medium, in both North America and Europe, or as part of an experiment in creating hybrid texts of stage and screen elements. These cover a range of genres from melodrama or historical epic to comedy and focus not only on archive prints whose textual elements (especially in terms of editing) seem organized in relation to assumed or imagined sounds but on surviving scenarios and film scripts with explicit notations for sound cues. Another five essays seek to describe and analyze specific instances of sound practices in early cinema exhibition, primarily in North America. These cover a range of venues (chautauquas, music halls, vaudeville houses, nickelodeons, Hale's Tours) and little studied forms of sound (illustrated songs, spoken dialogue, sound effects), sometimes within specific geographical regions. And they raise issues to pursue further: the "national" character of the illustrated songs in United States nickelodeons (especially in contrast to all the French Pathé films shown there), the "reality effect" or "dreamwork" of sound in the synesthetic experience of "cheap amusements," and the relative appeal and value of effects, music, and dialogue as an accompaniment to films.[7] In addition, four essays focus explicitly on the political implications of sound reception in moving picture shows, particularly within a country such as Canada, divided into strongly marked Anglophone and Francophone "imagined communities,"[8] and one of those argues that sound space began to be organized differently in exhibition venues during the transition period between early cinema and the narrative cinema of the middle 1910s.

Because conference participants spoke so highly of the nightly *son-et-lumière* performances, the editors have felt compelled to include in a final section, along with two related essays on film music, several texts devoted to those performances, even if words can only partly re-present the experience.[9] Patrick Loughney, for instance, writes about perhaps the most magical moment of the week: his and David Francis's presentation of the well-known [*Dickson Experimental Sound Film*] in which W. K. L. Dickson plays the violin, resynchronized (by hand and eye) with the audio tape of a newly restored cylinder recording made at the same time, as a test for the original 1895 Edison Kinetophone. Altman details the research and provocative conclusions that led to the University of Iowa Sound Study Group's production and performance of several "exemplary" nickelodeon programs, as "The Living Nickelodeon," and the lively debate that ensued over various questions those programs raised. In what initially served as a complement to Marks's subtle piano performances of surviving scores for several 1912 Kalem films, Herbert Reynolds offers a concise overview of Kalem's film scores (1907–1916), with special attention to those of Walter C. Simon.[10] Finally, the two other essays devoted to film music look closely at the interrelations of theater and cinema in terms of sound-image practices: the one analyzing the unacknowledged impact of musical conventions from melodrama on films, from *The Great Train Robbery* to *'Way Down East*; the other, the divisive effects of the "Negro Theme" or "Motif of Barbarism" in Joseph Carl Breil's score for *The Birth of a Nation*.

Just as this ending section could not cover every performance—perhaps most missed, besides Marks's, are accounts of Ron Magliozzi's presentation of sheet music history and illustrated songs (performed by Bob Kosovsky) and Laura Minici Zotti's magic lantern show using slides and sound notations from the Minici Zotti Collection (Padua, Italy)—so too could this book not include every paper presented or cover all the issues raised during the conference. Yet several should be mentioned, if only to acknowledge their absence and to stimulate further study. As Corey Creekmur, Gary Keller, and Louisa Shein would agree, certainly one issue concerns how sound may have been used—other than in *The Birth of a Nation*—either to exploit or maintain the ethnic and racial differences so flagrantly espoused at the turn of the last century or else to resist or subvert those differences. As John Fullerton and Alison Griffiths would attest, another issue involves how sound worked in relation to nonfiction films, especially if it differed in significant ways from how sound functioned in relation to narrative films. Finally, as Creekmur and Jane Gaines noted, very little work on sound and early cinema has yet been informed by recent queer theory; nor has it, Lauren Rabinovitz pointedly added, been shaped or framed all that much by feminist film theory.

We would hope that what has been said (and left unsaid) in this collection of essays will provoke further dialogue, research, and writing on sound and early cinema. For, in order to better understand cinema's emergence, especially as a cultural practice at the turn of the last century, we first have to recognize that the experience of sound and hearing was no less significant than that of images and seeing.

Because both French and English are the official languages of Domitor, the six French texts translated here by Franck Le Gac and Wendy Schubring also appear in their original language in an appendix.

Notes

1. For informative surveys of recent critical attention to sound and early cinema, see Germain Lacasse, "L'orgue de barbare ou l'indescriptible musique de l'inaudible cinéma," *Iris* 27 (Spring 1999), 49–65; and "This Year's Sound Conferences/Les colloques de l'année en sound studies," *Iris* 27 (Spring 1999), 148–174. An exciting book appeared recently that should contribute immensely to the project initiated by the 1998 Domitor conference and that this volume seeks to share more widely and extend: James Lastra, *Perception, Representation, Modernity: Sound Technology and the American Cinema* (New York: Columbia University Press, 2000).

2. Martin M. Marks served as the third member of the Domitor conference program committee but was unable to participate either in editing the present volume or in contributing an essay.

3. Martin Miller Marks, *Music and the Silent Film* (New York: Oxford University Press, 1997). Rick Altman, "The Silence of the Silents," *Musical Quarterly* 80, no. 4 (Winter 1996), 648–718. In reporting on the 1998 Domitor conference, Donald Crafton offers an extensive critique of Altman, in "Playing the Pictures: Intermediality and Early Cinema Patronage," *Iris* 27 (Spring 1999), 152–162.

4. Ben Brewster, "The Fifth Domitor Conference, Washington, D.C., 1–5 June, 1998," *Domitor Bulletin* 12, no. 2 (July 1998), 4–7.

5. For a slightly different analysis of intermediality, which lays out four sound categories within the context of cinema defined as an *event,* see Rick Altman, "Film Sound—All of It," *Iris* 27 (Spring 1999), 31–48.

6. Email message from Jeffrey Klenotic to Richard Abel, 16 June 1998.

7. For a characteristically astute analysis of recent critical work on the lecturer in early cinema, see Tom Gunning, "The Scene of Speaking: Two Decades of Discovering the Film Lecturer," *Iris* 27 (Spring 1999), 67–79.

8. The term comes from Benedict Anderson's influential book on nationalism, *Imagined Communities: Reflections on the Origin and Spread of Nationalism,* 2nd ed. (London: Verso, 1991).

9. For another account that gives particular attention to the films shown during those performances, see Brian Taves, "Archival Notes," *Cinema Journal* 38, no. 1 (Fall 1998): 115–116. Crafton begins his report on the 1998 Domitor conference with an analysis of the [*Dickson Experimental Sound Film*], in "Playing the Pictures," 152.

10. A substantially longer essay that develops Reynolds's oral presentation at the Domitor conference, one that analyzes with exceptional thoroughness the music, lectures, and effects produced by Kalem for many of its films, appears in *Film History* 12, no. 4 (2000).

Part One: *A Context of Intermediality*

1 Early Phonograph Culture and Moving Pictures
Ian Christie

It has long been recognized that the phonograph provided a prototype for the whole family of late-nineteenth-century spatio-temporal reproduction machines and practices, including moving pictures. From the inventor's side, we have Edison's celebrated claim in 1888 that his new instrument would "do for the eye what the Phonograph has done for the ear"—a phrase at once typically self-promoting and visionary.[1] But equally important for future developments was the growth of a *business* of promoting and selling sound recording equipment that effectively started in that same year. For it was in 1888 that Edison launched the third version of his original apparatus, now known as the Perfected Phonograph, and in competition with the Bell-Tainter "Graphophone," developed in Washington by the Volta Laboratory, which had been set up by Alexander Graham Bell with prize money awarded to him by the French government in 1880. Shortly after the agents of Edison and Volta set about publicizing their rival machines, a first generation of entrepreneurs started exploiting them. One of these, no doubt typical of many, was the future distributor and producer Charles Urban, who records in his memoirs how, around 1893, he "booked vocal and Instrumental Concerts via Schools and private Parties at $10 per evening."[2] Other pioneers of this new business worked the fairs, charging an audience to listen to this latest technological marvel: one such fairground exhibitor was Charles Pathé, soon to launch the first vertically integrated international film company. There must have been many more who also made the transition into moving pictures, albeit less successfully.[3] For, as we know from Charles Musser and Carol Nelson's invaluable work on one traveling showman, Lyman Howe, there were others who combined sound and picture presentation, through at least the first decade of the century.[4]

Yet if it is readily conceded that the phonograph business provided a useful advance model for the moving picture business, a still more fundamental group of questions remain: What was the attraction of recording sound? What kinds of uses were envisaged and essayed, once the technology existed? One of the earliest and most persistent ideas was undoubtedly the "talking book," which we find at the end of the seventeenth century in Cyrano de Bergerac's satirical account of a visit to the moon.[5] This gained a new impetus with the development of modern mercantile culture in the early nineteenth century, which also prompted Isaac Pitman to develop his shorthand system in 1837, based on the principle of notating sound rather than orthography. Soon after came the telegraph, the first versions of the telephone (from 1860), and the phonograph—a closely linked sequence of inventions that established Edison's reputation.[6]

One of the first domestic uses proposed for the phonograph was in fact to record telephone callers' messages, widely considered intrusive due to their unpredictability. Carolyn Marvin quotes a contribution to an 1893 Ideal Home competition in *Answers,* which foresaw "phonographs for communicated messages fixed to front and back door."[7] Earlier, in 1886, the Nadars, father and son, undertook a pioneering photo-interview with the hundred-year-old chemist Michel Chevreul.[8] Nadar *père* had in fact proposed a "Daguerrotype accoustique" as early as 1856. Now his son Paul took a hundred photographs at 1/333 second, and claimed that he had wanted to record Chevreul's answers to his father's questions on a phonograph, but could not obtain one.[9]

Around this time, Henry Edmunds, a young English engineer who would later introduce Charles Rolls to Frederick Royce and so help create Rolls Royce, had become the English agent for the American Graphophone Company (AGC) and was busy promoting his new product. In late 1888, he filed a patent application for the use of the Graphophone to be attached to a telephone "to allow fleeting words to be recorded for future reference."[10] In a lecture to the British Association for the Advancement of Science in the same year he outlined what was by now the standard "business agenda": "business men may carry on negotiations, recording each word spoken, preventing misunderstandings as to what was said . . . the stenographer may read his notes to it, leaving it to dictate to others to write them out."[11] And in another lecture at the Royal Society of Arts three months later, he expanded on this, as well as giving a plug for his new patent:

> I have been much interested to note the enormous diversity of uses that have been suggested. Physicians ask for it in order that when returning home late at night they, without any fatigue, may simply speak into the machine as to the condition of the patient visited and suggest the necessary treatment. It also [is] suggested that residents in Bournemouth or Nice need not come to London to consult their medical men but can send samples of their cough by Graphophone, thus indicating the improvement or condition of their lungs. Blind people may also through the medium of their ears avail themselves of avenues of instruction and amusement to which their eyes have been so long closed. The small tradesman who cannot afford to have his own bookkeeper, and has not time during the press of business to put down the verbal orders he receives . . . can incidentally speak to this instrument . . . and leisurely take off the words thus spoken later in the day. . . . Connected to the telephone the other day, I was enabled to record the words spoken and to recall afterwards that which I had forgotten in the hurry of the moment, viz. whether I had made an appointment to meet a friend at London Bridge at six minutes past five or five past six.[12]

Alongside such uses, there is another less functional strand of hopes and plans that we might term *memorialization*—the desire to record for posterity famous voices—which is closely linked with fantasies about bringing the past to life. Marvin quotes the Washington correspondent of the *Saint Louis Globe-Democrat*, writing in 1888 (presumably linked with the AGC's promotion of their new machine): "Suppose we could have graphophone communication with the year in which Plato lived and philosophized, and we could listen to his voice and hear his discourse."[13] This journalist continues with fantasies about recording Shakespeare, Anthony and Cleopatra at the Pyramids, and ultimately the Garden of Eden—all of which tell us more about the cultural ambitions waiting to be met, but not by the gramophone. Meanwhile, a writer for the *Electrical Review* contemplated passing long summer evenings on the back stoop with recordings of "the lions in Daniel's den, the sound of Nero's fiddle and the clatter of the Roman Empire as she fell"—an agenda that moving pictures would go some way toward delivering fifteen years later.[14]

What was on offer to the early audiences for Phonograph and Graphophone demonstrations was a series of "audio autographs" of the still living or recently deceased. Alfred, Lord Tennyson, famously recorded for Edison's agent, Colonel Gouraud, in 1890, as did William Gladstone and Robert Browning. In fact, Browning was probably the first to undergo the "posthumous revival" process so widely discussed in early accounts of both the phonograph and moving pictures. A gathering held in London on the first anniversary of his death heard the phonograph record of his reading—complete with him forgetting a line and having to be prompted.[15]

The capacity of the new electro-photo-mechanical media to capture and preserve a life-like image was a fantasy fast becoming a reality, within a culture that was also fast developing an enhanced awareness of sound-image correspondence. Consider just two of many possible examples taken from late-nineteenth-century painting. Millet's *L'Angélus* of 1859 shows a peasant couple pausing in the fields as the Angelus bell sounds across the fields from the church spire seen in the distance behind the woman's bowed back. Much has been said about the social and religious significance of this widely exhibited painting, which criss-crossed the Atlantic between 1872 and 1890, but it can scarcely be denied that the whole composition is focused by an implied sound, that of the church bell, without which it would be open to quite different interpretations.[16]

Another example is Ferdinand Knopff's 1883 painting, *En écoutant du Schumann*, in which a woman is seated centrally, with her hand covering her face, as she listens intently to a piano only partly visible at the left of the picture. The specific reference to Schumann in the title is probably to indicate that this is serious, "deep" music (rather as Browning used to be considered so difficult that there were special societies that met and pondered his work). This seems to be a more developed instance of a painting that expects us to "hear" its sound in order to understand and empathize with its central image of intense listener-ship. By the mid-1880s, there is already an extensive culture of audio-visual representation in existence.

To trace the origins of this tradition of invention-cum-speculation it would be necessary to retrace the history of mechanized music making, including barrel organs, musical boxes, and various musical automata from the eighteenth century. This was still in full swing in 1870 when George Sand, the celebrated novelist and playwright, reported in a letter her visit to a M. Julien—*"inventeur marchand, physicien chimiste, truciste"*—who sold her a *Ludion* among other gadgets.[17] This, she reported to a theater colleague, "is worthy of your theatre, it can play serious or gay music, solemn airs, dance music, sad songs and human voices." It could play the overture for a serious play, she suggests, or stand in for a solo instrument: "the sounds are very beautiful, especially if the electric motor is dispensed with, since it stinks and makes a lot of noise."

Here is an apparatus that, to an experienced Parisian playwright, seems to offer the promise of automating at least parts of the theater performance: the idea seems at least as attractive as the—no doubt precarious—reality. However, the most developed of all fictional elaborations of the new technology is Villiers de L'Isle-Adam's novel *L'Eve future* [The Future Eve], published in book form in 1886.[18] This novel, notoriously, has a heavily mythologized Edison as one of its characters, a true modern magus as imagined by Villiers, far beyond even the self-promotion practiced by the Wizard of Menlo Park himself.[19]

Villiers' novel appears to have had several sources. One was his fascination with the progress of science, which he watched with a mixture of awe and horror, and frequently mocked. This ambivalence is reflected in a number of his stories, notably the 1874 "L'Appareil pour l'analyse chimique du dernier soupir" [Apparatus for the Chemical Analysis of the Last Breath]—in which a device is developed for preserving dying breaths to facilitate mourning—and a sketch of 1877, *Madame et son sosie* [Madame and Her Double], about the creation of a perfect automaton, both of which predate the Edison phonograph's first, sensational demonstration in Paris in March 1878.[20] Another source of interest for Villiers was the unsuccessful research of his friend, Charles Cros, directed toward the same goal as Edison. Cros's claims—or perhaps more precisely the claims of others on his behalf—that he in fact anticipated Edison are part of the partisan, chauvinistic chronicles of nineteenth-century invention.[21] What seems clear is that Cros at least tried to develop a system to record sound, probably based on the *phonoautograph*, which proposed tracing an analogue pattern of sound onto smoked glass by means of a stylus.[22] Cros may have experimented with this as early as 1860; at any rate he wrote some verses that express very well the romantic ambition of preserving the fleeting moment—a combination of the cult of the fragment and of intense emotion savored in recollection:[23]

J'ai voulu que les tons, la grâce,	*I wished that the sounds, the grace,*
Tout ce que reflète une glace,	*All that a mirror would reflect,*
L'ivresse d'un bal d'opéra,	*The intoxication of an opera ball,*
Les soirs de rubis, l'ombre verte	*The ruby nights, the green shadow*
Se fixent sur la plaque inerte.	*Would be fixed on an inert plate.*
Je l'ai voulu, cela sera.	*I wished it, and it will be.*
Comme les traits dans les camées	*Like the features in a cameo*
J'ai voulu que les voies aimées	*I wanted lively gestures*

Soient un bien, qu'on garde à jamais,	*To be a treasure, kept forever*
Et puissent répéter le rêve	*Able to repeat the dream*
Musical de l'heure trop brève;	*Music of the fleeting hour.*
LE TEMPS VEUT FUIR, JE LE SOUMETS.[24]	*TIME SEEKS TO FLEE, AND I SUBDUE IT.*

Cros also took an interest in color photography, apparently with as little practical success as his attempts at sound recording. But he may well have been the vital influence on Villiers's *L'Eve future*.[25] The theme of the novel, if not its text, is well known: Edison, the latter-day alchemist, offers to create a mechanical facsimile of his friend Lord Ewald's beloved, the singer Alicia Clary, so that Ewald will not be driven to despair by her. The resulting *andréide,* Hadaly, succeeds only too well in capturing Ewald's affections, with the aid of an elaborate phonographic apparatus that reproduces the real Alicia's voice. But Hadaly is not in fact wholly mechanical, since she depends for animation on a supernatural being, Sowana, whose influence is transmitted through a medium.

For Villiers, science alone cannot achieve the perfection of nature without a vital spark of humanity, or indeed divinity. And in the end, Edison's blasphemy —like that of Faust and Mary Shelley's Dr. Frankenstein—dooms him to damnation. Both Hadaly and her "original," Alicia, die in a storm; but in his last message to Edison (in Morse code), Ewald confesses that it is Hadaly he grieves for. For what he loved was an idealized "Alicia," symbolized by her singing voice; and this was what Edison had extracted and synthesized in Hadaly. Behind Villiers' intended attack on scientism and materialism, and indeed his misogyny, there is a fetishization of the *dis*-embodied female image. Edison explains to Ewald how the android suppresses passion and desire in the most ardent male; elsewhere he refers to her as an "angel," and angels are traditionally sexless.[26]

A similar theme appears in Jules Verne's rather untypical novel *Le château des Carpathes* [The Castle in the Carpathians] in 1892. Untypical, because it is a tale of romantic rather than scientific passion, closer than most of Verne's novels to the doom-laden atmosphere of E. T. A. Hoffmann's *Rath Krespel,* or indeed to *L'Eve future,* which some scholars believe directly influenced it.[27] In *Le château des Carpathes,* an opera singer dies during her farewell performance, leaving her fiancé heartbroken. Many years later, the still grieving fiancé happens to be traveling near a ruined castle in the Carpathians—which he finds after a highly significant transaction in which a peddler sells a telescope to a Transylvanian shepherd, which allows the latter to discover that the castle presumed empty is in fact inhabited. In another of those numerous *fin-de-siècle* tropes that anticipate cinema, assisted or mechanized vision reveals signs of life, but it turns out to be life held in suspension. The fiancé enters the castle, only to hear and apparently see his beloved performing once again. But when he rushes toward her, the image shatters: it turns out to have been a reflection of a lifelike painted portrait, accompanied by one of the recordings that a fanatical admirer—the mad count who lives in the castle—had made by means of concealed phonographs on stage.

There is a recurrent motif in this era of Symbolism of the Circe-like female hypnotizing the helpless male; but in Verne and Villiers she is made immortal by means of the new technology of representation, and the enduring image is thus of her disembodied voice. It appears that the supposedly hardheaded inventors of the age were equally susceptible to such associations. Emile Berliner, the pioneer of the gramophone, gave a speech to the American Institute of Electrical Engineers in 1890 in which he looked forward to the possibility of sound recordings cast in glass that would serve as dessert plates and then as after-dinner entertainment![28] What is telling here is the association between glass as a material and the spectral trace of the eminent dead, recordings of whom Berliner also thought might decorate the walls of future parlors and libraries.

The currency of such views, and their uncertain status between prediction and fantasy, may help to put in context the relatively familiar, but still curious, rhetoric that accompanied Edison's own venture into synesthesia, or as Noël Burch termed it, "Edison's lyrico-theatrical dream."[29] This was revealed publicly in the preface he contributed to the pamphlet written by William and Antonia Dickson in 1895 to promote his audiovisual inventions, which includes the following:

> I believe that in coming years by the work of Dickson, Muybridge and Marey and others who will doubtless enter the field that grand opera can be given at the Metropolitan Opera House at New York without any material change from the original, and with artists and musicians long since dead.[30]

The strangely morbid fantasy, seemingly untypical of Edison, effectively adopts Verne's scenario: the dead diva miraculously brought back to artificial life by means of recording. And it anticipates the similarly "resurrectionist" tone of the two famous press reports that appeared after the Lumières' first public show in Paris later in the same year:

> When apparatuses like this are available to the public, when everyone can photograph those who are dear to them, not only their posed forms but their movements, their actions, their familiar gestures, with words at the tip of their tongues, death will cease to be absolute. (*La Poste,* 30 December 1895)

> We already can collect and reproduce words; now we can collect and reproduce life. We might even, for instance, see our friends or family as if living again long after they will have disappeared. (*Le Radical,* 30 December 1895)[31]

The culture within which moving pictures began was obsessed by death and its rituals, an obsession reflected in the vast literature and iconography of Symbolism, stretching from Poe and Baudelaire to Maeterlinck and Yeats, and also embracing such popular figures as Kipling and J. M. Barrie; in painting, it includes Böcklin, Knopff, Whistler, Klimt, and the Russian symbolist painters. A theme of growing importance in this culture was communication between the living and the dead, reflected in the widespread interest in psychic phenomena, an interest by no means confined to the conventionally religious or the sentimental—

on the contrary, one very much the province of religious skeptics, scientists, and "seekers after the new."

It was for these that photography had provided both a metaphor and a quasi-technology for exploring "beyond death"; and so the phonograph offered an equivalent metaphor-cum-technology for the spectral or the "phantasmal," a term widely used by the scientific psychic researchers of the late nineteenth century in place of the vernacular "ghost" or "spirit."[32] Those gathered to hear Browning's recorded voice after his death could hardly fail to compare this experience with that of a séance; while during his last illness the Archbishop of Westminster, Cardinal Manning, actually recorded a phonographic message addressed to posterity.[33] Was it because of these funerary associations that recorded speech and music seemed to many at the turn of the century intrinsically melancholy? In his discussion of the phonograph, Marshall McLuhan writes of the "undercurrent of mechanical music" being "strangely sad," linking it with "the metaphysical melancholy latent in the great industrial world of the metropolis."[34] Music, or especially speech, without bodily presence; the moving likeness without sound (Gorky's "kingdom of the Shadows")—both of these spoke suggestively to a culture that was already accustomed to imagining life after death and to the denial of death's finality in many of its most highly acclaimed imaginative works.

In conclusion, it is worth noting that interest in the metaphysics of the phonograph did not end with the arrival of moving pictures. In 1919, the late symbolist poet Rainer Maria Rilke wrote a curious text, "Ur-Geräusch" [The primal scream], in which he drew a comparison between the zigzag line of the skull's coronal suture and the irregular groove of the phonograph. If the skull's line could be transferred onto a disc and "played," he speculated, might we not hear the "primal sound" and so get closer to the ultimate mystery of meaning and life?[35] A few years later, André Gide would suggest that the phonograph will "soon clear out of the novel all its reported dialogue," while the cinema will deal with exterior events and accidents, leaving the way clear for the *roman pur*.[36]

Notes

1. Edison's words appear in his caveat to the US Patent Office, October 1888.

2. Luke McKernan, ed., *A Yank in Britain: The Lost Memoirs of Charles Urban, Film Pioneer* (Hastings: Projection Box, 1999), 30.

3. Many of the early moving picture companies surveyed in John Barnes, *The Rise of the Cinema in England* (London: Bishopsgate Press, 1983) also dealt in phonographs.

4. Charles Musser and Carol Nelson, *High-Class Moving Pictures: Lymann H. Howe and the Forgotten Era of Traveling Exhibition, 1880–1920* (Princeton: Princeton University Press, 1991).

5. Cyrano de Bergerac, *L'Histoire comique des états et empires de la lune* (1665).

6. Edison's first success as an inventor was an improvement to the telegraph, followed by his development of the carbon microphone for the telephone, which led directly to the phonograph.

7. Carolyn Marvin, *When Old Technologies Were New* (Oxford: Oxford University Press, 1988), 79.

8. The Nadars photo-interview with Chevreul was published in *Le Journal illustré* 5 September 1886—described in Helmut Gernsheim, *History of Photography* (Oxford: Oxford University Press, 1955), 453.

9. Paul Nadar quoted in "Ignota, A Great Paris Photographer: M. Paul Nadar," *The Woman at Home,* October 1898, 151–156—cited in Gernsheim.

10. Paul Tritton, *The Lost Voice of Queen Victoria: The Search for the First Royal Recording* (London: Academy Books, 1991), 43.

11. Ibid.

12. Ibid., 45.

13. *Electrical Review*—quoted in Marvin, 203.

14. Ibid., 204.

15. *Chamber's Journal,* 28 February 1891, 142—quoted in Marvin, 204.

16. Painted in 1857–1859, Millet's *Angelus* was sold and resold repeatedly, moving from Paris to Belgium, then to the United States, before it returned to Paris and the Louvre in 1909 as one of the most famous and admired modern French paintings. Two further points are worth making. In a letter of 1873 that stresses the painting's "moralizing, educative role," Gambetta refers to "the bell having sounded the cease-fire of work," giving it a pivotal role in the picture's dramaturgy. A second point made by Herbert is that the subject was relatively common in England and France, but the figures were usually near, or in, a church. This suggests that Millet stretches his viewers' auditory imagination, by making the source of the Angelus bell so small and distant. See Robert Herbert, *Jean François-Millet* (London: Hayward Gallery/Arts Council of Great Britain, 1976), 87–89.

17. George Sand, *Correspondance* (Paris: Garnier, 1986), vol. 21, #14800, 3 February 1870, 810. The following description is from a second letter sent on the same day (#14802, 811–812).

18. Alan Raitt traces the origins of *L'Eve future* to Villiers's response to the first news of Edison's phonograph, but dates this to 1877, whereas reports of Edison's success did not reach Europe until early 1878. Whatever its initial inspiration, the first version of the novel, known as *L'Eve nouvelle,* began to appear as a serial in 1880. After two false starts, the final version appeared between 1885 and 1886, followed by book publication in the same year. See Raitt's "Préface" to the 1993 Gallimard edition, 7–8.

19. Edison was already established for the American, and increasingly world, public as "the Wizard of Menlo Park" when he succeeded in recording sound at the end of 1877, before moving his laboratory to larger premises in West Orange, N.J., at the end of the year and beginning work on the kinetoscope early in 1888, after a meeting with Eadweard Muybridge. He was already a master of public relations, regularly inspiring journalists to write admiring and credulous articles about his "latest" inventions. Villiers's opening chapter compares him to Gustave Doré, Archimedes, and Beethoven (the latter due to his partial deafness), but is in fact no more extravagant than Terry Ramsaye's mythological evocation in *A Million and One Nights* (New York: Simon and Schuster, 1926), 50–52.

20. Alan Raitt, *Villiers de l'Isle-Adam et le mouvement symboliste* (Paris: Corti, 1965), 177.

21. The false claim that Cros had succeeded in recording sound before Edison was apparently first suggested by an enthusiastic Paris newspaper article of 11 December 1877, then repeated by the humorist Alphonse Allais in an article of 17 February 1879,

which implied that he had done so while working at the Deaf-Mute Institute in the 1860s. (Contact with or personal experience of deafness was in fact a vital link between many of the sound pioneers of the nineteenth century, from Bell and Edison to Cros and Demenÿ). Cros had in fact proposed a recording technique to the Académie des Sciences in April 1877, three months before Edison's first patent, but did not succeed in realizing it practically. By the 1920s, his claim to precedence was widely accepted in France.

22. A printer, Léon Scott de Martainville, had suggested in 1857 this means of translating sound into graphic images, by connecting a stylus to a sensitive membrane. But there was no suggestion that this "Phonoautographe" would replay the sound.

23. The fragment, "complete and unfinished at once," was a key feature of Romantic art, explored in Charles Rosen and Henri Zerner, *Romanticism and Realism: The Mythology of Nineteenth Century Art* (London: Faber, 1984), 24–28. "Poetry," according to Wordsworth's famous dictum in the preface to the *Lyrical Ballads* (1802), "takes its origin from emotion recollected in tranquility."

24. Cros, inscription to *Le Collier de Griffes* (The Necklace of Claws), quoted in Louis Forestier, *Charles Cros: l'homme et l'oeuvre* (Paris: Université de Paris, 1963).

25. Cros was a friend of Villiers, and he published at least two pieces in 1874–1875 that deal with the mechanization of love, according to Felicia Miller-Frank in her valuable essay, "Edison's Recorded Angel," in *Jeering Dreamers: Essays on L'Eve Future*, ed. John Anzalone (Amsterdam and Atlanta: Editions Rodopi, 1996), 145.

26. This account of *L'Eve future* is indebted to Miller-Frank's highly suggestive reading.

27. Hoffmann's *Rath Krespel* provided the basis for Act II of Offenbach's *Tales of Hoffmann*, first performed in Paris in 1881, in which an opera singer dies after disobeying her father's order not to sing, while under the hypnotic influence of the sinister Dr. Miracle (borrowed from another of Hoffmann's stories, "Signor Formica"). Raitt, however, has no doubt that Verne was influenced by Villiers (and Leroux's *Phantom of the Opera*, of 1911, was no doubt at least partly inspired by Verne).

28. Berliner, "The Improved Gramophone," printed in *Western Electrician*, 3 January 1891, 5—quoted in Marvin, 80.

29. Noël Burch, *Life to Those Shadows*, ed. and trans. Ben Brewster (London: British Film Institute, 1990), 28.

30. W. K. L. Dickson and Antonia Dickson, *History of the Kinetograph, Kinetoscope and Kineto-Phonograph* (1895; reprint, New York: Arno, 1970).

31. "Lorsque ces appareils seront livrés au public, lorsque tous pourront photographier les êtres qui leur sont chers, non plus dans leurs formes immobiles, mais dans leur mouvements, dans leur actions, dans leur gestes familiers, avec la parole au bout des levres, la mort cessera d'être absolue" (*La Poste*, 30 December 1895).

"On receuillat déjà et l'on reproduisait la parole, on receuille maintenant et l'on reproduit la vie. On pourra, par example, revoir agir les seins longtemps après qu'on les aura perdus" (*Le Radical*, 30 December 1895).

Translations by Richard Abel.

32. Frederic W. H. Myers (1843–1901) was a classical scholar and cofounder in 1882 of the Society for Psychical Research, whose final testament was published posthumously in 1903.

33. Manning's recording, "Bequest to Humanity," was reported in a London journal, *Lightning*, in December 1896—quoted in Marvin, 205.

34. Marshall McLuhan, *Understanding Media: The Extensions of Man* (London: Routledge and Kegan Paul, 1964), 278.

35. Rainer Maria Rilke, *Ausgewalte Werke,* vol. 2 (Leipzig: Insel Verlag, 1948); English translation by G. Craig Houston in Rilke, *Selected Works,* vol. 1 (London: Hogarth Press, 1954) 53–54.

36. André Gide, *Les Faux-monnayeurs* (*The Counterfeiters*) (Paris: Gallimard, 1925), 78. My thanks to Dorota Ostrowska for this reference.

2   Doing for the Eye What the Phonograph Does for the Ear

Tom Gunning

I. The Systematic Splitting, Reproducing, and Derangement of the Senses

... when you fashion eyes in place of an eye and a hand in place of a hand, and a foot in place of a foot, and an image in place of an image then you shall enter the Kingdom of Heaven.

—The Gospel of Thomas

André Bazin in an essay review of the first two volumes of Georges Sadoul's *Histoire générale du cinéma* (those dealing with the invention and pioneers of early cinema) offered (in 1946!) a profoundly nonlinear reading of film history in which "every new development added to the cinema must, paradoxically, take it nearer and nearer to its origins. In short the cinema has not yet been invented!"[1] The basis of this temporal reversal lies in Bazin's radical interpretation of Sadoul's account of the first conceptions of cinema "as a total and complete representation of reality; they [the inventors] saw in a trice the complete reconstruction of the outside world, in sound, color and relief."[2] For Bazin's proclamation of a special ontology of film, a medium destined for the task of representing reality, the ambitions of cinema's inventors offered an Old Testament figuration of the new dispensation of the realist cinema of the post–World War II era. As Bazin claims, the actual invention of cinema was anticipated by the construction of its myth, fictional or speculative descriptions of an apparatus that could reproduce not only moving images in color and volume, but also sound. Bazin inaugurated the tradition of referring to perhaps the richest of these early fictional anticipations of cinema, now a *locus classicus* for discussions of cinema's origins, Villiers de L'Isle-Adam's *L' Eve future* (1880, 1886) in which a fictional Edison reveals a six-minute motion picture of a Spanish dancer accompanying herself with shouted *olés*, actually written several years before the real-life Edison announced his kinetoscope.[3] But what is striking is that while these "myths of total cinema" *do* precede the actual invention of the kinetoscope, they do so by just a few years. This close proximity of imagined inventions and their realization, rather than indicating the timeless desire for total representation Bazin describes, marks a historical moment, a peculiarly modern *topoi* that straddled the imaginations of poets and scientists.

The recording of sound and the recording of motion pictures therefore converged at the origins of cinema in numerous ways. If, following Laurent Mannoni, we view Georges Demenÿ as cinema's most direct father (his Phonoscope preceding Edison's kinetoscope as an invention designed to reproduce motion, an issue of only secondary importance to his mentor Marey), it is of more than incidental interest that this invention pairs sound and image in its name and was originally designed as a means of creating a record of the processes of speech for the training of the deaf. For Demenÿ, motion pictures began as an image of sound.[4]

Exploring the early imbrication of the reproduction and recording of sound and moving image in terms of their historical practices and receptions, rather than as an idealist merging of the original and the copy, we uncover a series of ontological insecurities. The myth of total cinema that Bazin discovers is not simply a desire to reproduce the "outside world," but more immediately to reproduce the human subject in its movements and to imitate its functions of perception and memory. The cinematic image, moving, in color, three-dimensional, and with sound, functions as much as mankind's technological double as a simulacrum of the "outside" world. In this respect, as Noël Burch had noted decades ago, the invention of cinema involved a "Frankensteinian" impulse to simultaneously create a perfect simulacrum of life and by doing so, to overcome death.[5] However, Burch entirely identifies this ambition to create a technological double with the desire to create "a 'perfect illusion' of the perceptual world."[6] Seeing both the perfection of illusionism and the overcoming of death as a bourgeois illusion, Burch contrasts it with the road to modernism exemplified for him by Baudelaire's scorn of photography as a mechanical art.[7] However, as Jonathan Crary's work has shown us, the attempt to seize the image in a photographic perfection of illusion (especially when the illusion of the third dimension in the stereoscope is considered) is not simply the fulfillment of one continuous tradition of "bourgeois perceptual realism" rooted in the primal sin of perspective and marching uninterruptedly toward cinema and the "perfect illusion" of the perceptual world.[8] The nineteenth-century attempt to capture a modern vision involves redefinitions of the act of seeing and of perception's relation to the outside world. Key among these, as Crary has shown, was the separation of the senses, the treatment of the human sensorium no longer as a single whole in which the various senses converged to produce a "true" representation of the outside world, but as a bundle of processes, each subject to different physical conditions and processes of stimulation. Ultimately this technological doubling of the human sensorium relates more directly to the fragmentation of artistic modernism than to idealist models of an ahistorical "realism." As Crary puts it, "Any effective account of modern culture must confront the ways in which modernism, rather than being a reaction against or transcendence of processes of scientific and economic rationalization, is inseparable from them."[9]

The technological double potentially calls into question the nature of human identity in a manner that parallels (and perhaps inspired) the initial development of an artistic Avant-Garde in the late nineteenth century, exemplified by

Rimbaud's artistic credo from 1871, "I am an other."[10] Far from expressing a disdain of new processes of reproduction, an attitude of symbolist disdain for the everyday world that Burch makes Baudelaire exemplify, I believe Rimbaud's statement provides a profound opening onto the world of the technological double. Certainly this was not Rimbaud's immediate reference in his "*lettre du voyant*" from which this statement derives. But, in fact, the burgeoning world of mechanical reproduction of sound and movement surrounded Rimbaud in a manner I find more than coincidental. The first and most powerful instance of Rimbaud's relation to the technological double comes through the fascinating and ambiguous figure of Charles Cros, an amateur scientist and inventor, symbolist poet and major figure in the turn-of-the-century Parisian bohemian cultural scene.[11] It was Cros who went with Paul Verlaine to pick up Rimbaud at the station on his arrival in Paris in 1871, and who primarily supported Rimbaud during his stay in Paris, in spite of his own modest circumstances.[12] A few months later Rimbaud, in one of his notorious displays of contempt for Verlaine's friends, apparently put sulfuric acid in Cros's drink.[13] Possibly in retaliation, it was Cros who showed Madame Verlaine Rimbaud's love letters to her husband.[14] And it is Cros that Roland Gelatt, author of the standard history of the phonograph, declares the first to conceive of a practical phonograph in April 1877, several months previous to Edison's invention, although, due to lack of funds, Cros did not produce a prototype.[15]

But this is not the only intersection between Rimbaud and the new culture of mechanical reproduction. In May of 1871, Rimbaud made his declaration "Je est un autre" ("I am an other" or "I am someone else"), a declaration against the classical conception of a unified self, in a now famous letter in which he set out the aspirations of an aesthetic Avant-Garde, involved in a dangerous and fundamental exploration of the limits of consciousness and experience. Now referred to as the "*lettre au voyant*," the letter of the visionary, this missive was sent by Rimbaud to his friend Paul Demenÿ, a minor symbolist poet. It is not known if Paul showed this letter to his brother Georges, but, as Laurent Mannoni has remarked, it was Georges Demenÿ who in some sense fulfilled Rimbaud's statement literally through his work in motion pictures.[16]

While this fraternal connection between technological reproduction and Rimbaud's Avant-Garde project may indicate nothing more than the contingent crisscrosses of history, the connection between Cros's poetry and his science seems to me quite significant for understanding the cultural roots of the fascination of modern technology. Although most descriptions of Cros as a "poetic" scientist simply refer to his lack of practicality in commercially exploiting his brilliant insights, I believe his nearly systematic engagement with the technology of reproduction derives from the symbolists' belief that they were creating a new art of the senses, what Rimbaud in his *lettre du voyant* describes as "the systematic derangement of the senses."[17] Cros not only discovered the principles of the phonograph ahead of Edison, he also described the basic technology of motion pictures as early as 1867 and labored for years perfecting a method of color photography, involving his friend Edouard Manet in the process.[18] The systematic derangement of the senses and their systematic reproduction, I maintain, went hand in hand. It is shortsighted to draw dichotomies between emerging modernism and this modern ambition of technological reproduction, which calls neither for condemnation as a naive "class fantasy" nor simple valorization as an anticipation of artistic modernism or an example of scientific "progress." Rather, like any product of modernity, it needs to be historically investigated and critiqued. To do this means venturing into the ambivalence of both its technical and commercial production and the range of imaginary scenarios that surrounded it, both inspired by and inspiring its own development. The nature of this doubling of the human senses should not be assumed, but uncovered and interrogated.

The manner in which motion photography and the phonograph implied each other is first evident in the process of invention itself. The invention of the phonograph by Thomas Edison in 1876 not only inspired Villiers's later prescient fantasy of sound motion pictures, but was the immediate inspiration for Edison's own, slightly later, work in motion pictures, exemplified by the almost mantra-like phrase that Edison used in his first motion picture caveat and intoned repetitively in later lawsuits: "I wanted to do for the eye what the phonograph does for the ear."[19] By this primordial intent and its later repetition, I believe that Edison indicated two things. First, that the phonograph was the original instrument of a new sort of reproduction, one that extended and transformed our conception of the human senses by recording them as they occurred in real time, and that could serve as a model for further similar experiments in recording and reproduction. Secondly, and implicitly, it indicates that the phonograph had in effect separated the human senses, divorcing ear from eye, and that Edison's original intention in pursuing motion pictures was to bring them back together. In other words, the relation between the phonograph and motion pictures shows both the process of the separation of the senses that Crary finds essential to nineteenth century investigations of perception[20] and an anxiety about this separation, a desire to heal the breach. In other words, Bazin's total cinema is a response to a previous sense of desperation and division.

The cultural history of the first reception of the phonograph demands the sort of careful research that has marked recent work on the invention of the cinema. However, in the absence of this research I want to make some provisional observations on its cultural reception. Edison's biographers agree that it was the invention of the phonograph that catapulted Edison to unprecedented celebrity and generated the legend of the "Wizard of Menlo Park."[21] This is somewhat surprising when one realizes the extremely modest commercial and even technological success of Edison's 1877 machine, which used tin foil as the recording medium. The sound reproduction ability of the tin foil was in fact minimal (enough to be recognizable and cause amazement, but difficult to understand in most circumstances). The tin foil apparatus demanded intricate handling and was rarely successful in the hands of anyone other than a trained expert. Its original purpose, as a sort of Dictaphone for business messages, proved totally impracticable. Its only success came as a scientific novelty, per-

2.1. Edison with the new improved commercial phonograph, 1888. Fred Ott seated left, William Kennedy Laurie Dickson standing behind him.

formed by experts for paying customers in theatrical situations, and, as with most such novelties, its appeal was short-lived. Within a year Edison had retired it, declaring it "a mere toy of no commercial value,"[22] and the company designed to exploit it became moribund. Only a decade later, under impetus from rival inventors associated with the Bell company, did Edison return to the phonograph and begin the work that made it commercially viable in the 1890s. This delay in the phonograph's development makes it, in its commercial form, less an ancestor of motion pictures than its only slightly older sibling. Edison was developing both of them in close proximity. The motion picture caveat of 1889 comes slightly over a year after Edison launched his technically perfected phonograph commercially. Many of the same characters clustered around the perfected phonograph and the kinetoscope; a photograph of the new phonograph shows Edison flanked by William Kennedy Laurie Dickson and Fred Ott, more familiar to historians of cinema for their work on the kinetoscope.

Although the original phonograph of the1870s generated very little income and exhibited such imperfections that Edison himself abandoned it for a decade, its original demonstration generated unparalleled media and public attention, resulting in a "phonographic craze." *Leslie's Weekly* declared the phonograph would "turn all the old grooves of the world topsy turvy and establish an order of things never dreamed of even in the vivid imagining of the Queen Scheherazade in 1001 Nights' Entertainment."[23] Edison's primitive recording device astonished scientific circles and journalists alike, and caused President Rutherford B. Hayes to rouse his wife in the middle of the night to come downstairs and listen to Edison's demonstrations in the White House parlor. If the phonograph was impractical and uncommercial, its initial novelty was electrifying.[24] Robert Conot in his biography of Edison repeats the claim, familiar from tales of the introduction of motion pictures, that at Edison's presentation of this early phonograph to the Academy of Sciences "two or three girls in the audience fainted."[25] What was it about this feeble noisemaker that seemed to have the potential to unhinge the cosmos?

This reproduced human voice opened a brave new world of technological reproduction while it seemed to simultaneously recall and abolish previous methods. As James Lastra in his forthcoming, extremely important work, *Sound Technology and the American Cinema: Perception, Representation and Modernity,* has shown, the prehistory of the phonograph can be traced from two aspects, inscription and simulation, corresponding somewhat to the complementary functions of recording and reproduction.[26] The recording of sound leads back to various methods of obtaining the inscription of sound, including various forms of phonetic alphabets (stenographers of the time were referred to as "phonographers)."[27] For instance, the father of Alexander Graham Bell, Edison's great rival in sound inventions, Melville Bell, had perfected a Universal Alphabet based on the positions of the vocal apparatus, which allowed anyone trained in his method (such as his young son, Alexander) to reproduce nearly any sound. The younger Bell described his service as a demonstrator of his father's system:

> [T]he members of the audience were invited to make any sorts of sound they desired, to be symbolized by my father. It was just as easy for him to spell the sound of a cough, or a sneeze, or a click to a horse as a sound that formed an element of human speech.
>
> Volunteers were called to the platform, where they uttered the most weird and uncanny noises, while my father studied their mouths and attempted to express in symbols the actions of the vocal organ he had observed.
>
> I was then called in and the symbols were presented to me to interpret; and I could read in each symbol a direction to do something with my mouth.[28]

While the inscription of sound relied on a sort of writing (phono-graphy), its reproduction here relied on a human agent, young Alexander, who could read the script. Alexander performed theatrically to demonstrate the full circuit of sound from recording to reproduction.

Early demonstrations of Edison's phonograph treated the apparatus *as though it was a human imitator,* a virtuoso performer who, like the young Bell, might be thrown off by the complexity of words or sounds or their speed. Bishop John Vincent, a founder of the Chautauqua Association, shouted into the phonograph a long string of formidable Old Testament names at a prodigious speed, and was satisfied at the machine's ability to reproduce them clearly.[29] Further, the phonograph could match and exceed Bell's most unusual mimetic powers, imitating barking dogs and cock's crows, sneezes (could they be Fred Ott's?) and coughs and musical instruments. A battle between the phonograph and cornetist Jules Levy was reported by one commentator: "Without loss of a note, the phonograph repeated it, and not only this, but even the peculiar expression imparted by the player."[30] In other words, the phonograph in performance was treated as a clever imitator, a human-like virtuoso with a genius for imitation, rather than simply a recording device. The fascination of the phonograph came from its separation of the sense of hearing and the reproduction of the voice from the human body, but the demonstrations and descriptions of the phonograph also resisted this separation by conceiving of the machine as somehow human-like.

Lastra also supplies a context for this humanization of the phonograph when he relates sound reproduction not only to the tradition of sound alphabets, such as Bell's, but to the tradition, deriving from the Enlightenment, of automatons, mechanical simulations of human figures able to speak and play musical instruments.[31] The automaton illustrates two assumptions: that a human being is basically a machine and can be mechanically reproduced, and that the best way to demonstrate this principle is through a simulacrum that not only acts but *looks* human, thereby maintaining the unity of the human subject, voice and body. The nineteenth century also saw a number of talking machines based on a careful scientific study of the larynx and other aspects of the human voice, including one made by the young Bell to the satisfaction of his father. The most successful of these, Farber's Talking Machine displayed at Barnum's Museum, which used a bellows and complex machinery to reproduce speech, still included a human head as a residual emblem of the earlier ambition to recreate the voice as part of the artificial creation of a total mechanical human being. Reportedly, Barnum challenged customers with a reward of ten thousand dollars if they could match the effects of Farber's device, a proclamation quickly removed when he heard rumors of Edison's phonograph.[32] The phonograph, however, limited its mimesis to the human voice; its apparatus had no visual resemblance to a human figure. But again this splitting of the human senses, the isolation of sound, seemed to strike some people as unnatural. In the popular imagination of the initial phonographic craze, devices of visual simulation were immediately suggested. Recordings of Henry Ward Beecher's greatest sermons could be placed within statues of the man.[33] Edison himself suggested that when the titanic statue of the "Goddess of Liberty" was erected in New York Harbor, a phonograph could be placed within to send out aural greetings.[34] Villiers's fictional Edison supplied his female automaton, Hadaly, with the power of speech from an interior phonograph, which would divert her lover with the best sayings of poets and philosophers, specially recorded.[35] The real Edison marketed talking dolls for a short while in the late 1880s, fulfilling a prediction he had made a decade before.[36]

While all of these simulations remained in the realm of fictional flights of fancy or toys intended for children, they reveal a popular reception of the phonograph as something on the order of an artificial human being and a desire to disavow its separation of voice from the total human being. The same playful personification of the machine operates in Edison's first public presentations of the machine. The editor of *Scientific American* reported that in Edison's presen-

2.2. Farber's talking machine as exhibited in Barnum's museum.

2.3. Edison's Talking Doll.

tation of the machine in the journal's office, he "turned a crank and the machine inquired as to our health, asked how we liked the phonograph, informed us that *it* was very well and bid us a cordial good night."[37] Likewise at its presentation to the American Academy of Sciences Edison cranked the machine, which proclaimed "the speaking phonograph has the honor of presenting itself before the American Academy of Sciences."[38] In these instances the phonograph in no way mimes the appearance of a human being, but its prerecorded speech mimes a human dialogue and subjectivity, as it addresses its audiences in a fictive first person. It calls on auditors to imagine a human being, or perhaps to notice with wonder the lack of a human body.

As playful as these instances are, they reveal a fundamental shift in human ontology, a shift that explains the sort of wondering acclamation the original phonograph received in spite of its impractical and uncommercial nature. While it certainly did not resemble a human being, the phonograph could seem to speak like a human subject. It undermined the most enduring mark of human individuality, authority, and, as Derrida has shown, presence, the voice itself, by separating it from an actually present speaker. The phonograph made manifest to the general public, with a tangible as well as entertaining object, the separation of the human senses that had been carried out on a theoretical level by scientists during the nineteenth century. But the phonograph could not entirely shake the effect of anxiety or uncanny wonder this demonstration occasioned. Voices that speak without a body are the traditional mark of divine inspiration, demonic possession, or madness. The then recent phenomenon of spiritualism, in which spirits of the dead spoke through trance-bound mediums, explains why for many occultists the phonograph seemed further proof of a new scientific revelation in which the material and the spirit world would be revealed as one. Madame Blavatsky, whose occult classic *Isis Unveiled* had appeared the year before Edison announced the first phonograph, enrolled Edison in her newly formed Theosophical Society and departed for India with one of the new inventions.[39] But if the phonograph could be seen as part of a new revelation, it could also be viewed with great anxiety for separating the voice from the human subject and depositing it into a machine. We can see it now as a harbinger of the modern redefinition of the human consciousness as a storage place of information for eventual retrieval, one exemplification of the grand archive that defines modernity, the outcome of the separation of the senses and the disciplining of the modern body that Crary describes.

II. Tales of the Technological Double

Tous avaient d'enivrants frissons
A l'écouter. Car dans ces sons
Vivaient la morte et ses chansons.
[All were given to shudders as they heard it. Because in its sounds the dead woman and her songs lived again.]

—Charles Cros, *L'Archet*

Edison's invention of the phonograph both inherited and transformed traditional ideas of sound inscription and of the creation of human simulacrum. Around the technological process of invention and, especially, the rather theatrical presentation of the phonograph cluster a series of scenarios that could be considered myths of modernity, toying with the ontological ambiguities of recorded sound, the separation of the senses and the desire to reunite them. These images and anecdotes receive fuller elaboration in works of speculative literature of the *fin de siècle*. Bazin, Michelson, Bellour, Grivel, and others have explored perhaps the richest of these, Villiers de L'Isle-Adam's *L'Eve future* from 1886.[40] Friedrich Kittler has shown the legacy of the technological reproduction implicit in Bram Stoker's *Dracula*, from 1897.[41] I will explore a more neglected work written between these two, Jules Verne's *Carpathian Castle* from 1892.[42]

But to indicate the way the technology of sound reproduction can rework older anxieties, I want to first compare Verne's novel to a gothic novel from a century earlier that deals with the uncertainty engendered by the separation of human voice from the human body, Charles Brockden Brown's *Wieland or the Transformation* from 1799.[43] Charles Brockden Brown is the first great American novelist, the inaugurator of the gothic tradition of dark allegories followed by Hawthorne, Melville, and Poe. *Wieland* is a tale of metaphysical uncertainty in which a series of uncanny happenings lead its narrator to the brink of madness and suicide, as he tries to determine if he is insane or the victim of a supernatural curse. A drama of consciousness that wrestles with the conflicting American legacy of Enlightenment rationality and Protestant belief in religious inspiration, *Wieland* stages a contest between reason and revelation in which one can no longer trust the evidence of the senses. The eponymous character in a fit of religious mania kills his wife and children, believing he is hearing the voice of God. However, his brother, the novel's narrator, discovers they have both been the victim of a profoundly ambiguous character, Carwin, the biloquist (an archaic word for a ventriloquist). The narrator discovers Carwin's trick, his ability, as he phrases it, "to speak where he is not,"[44] to separate voice from presence, and a repentant Carwin, who never intended the dire results of his tricks, informs Wieland that it was not God's voice he heard. However, Wieland realizes that if it was not the voice of God that ordered him to his deed, he is responsible for an unbearable crime, and kills himself. *Wieland* follows in the tradition of Anne Radcliffe's gothic novels by supplying a rational explanation for apparently supernatural events, and is thus an offspring of the Enlightenment. But here the rational explanation in fact undermines rational order, as the novel reveals the effect the fallible nature of the senses can have on a person's actions and motives. The possible errors in the interpretation of the evidence of the senses undermine certainty about either reason or revelation, leading to a world of murder, suicide, and infanticide. The separation of voice from the body, "speaking where one is not," becomes a dangerous tool that upsets the moral order of the universe.

I have maintained that Edison's desire to do for the eye what he had already done for the ear shows a desire to supplement the single strand of recording apparatus he had already invented, possibly to allay some of the anxieties this separation aroused. Likewise the apparent prophecies by Villiers and Verne of motion pictures *avant la lettre* (but after the phonograph) indicate a popular imagination that saw the phonograph as part of a larger project to reconstitute and record the whole human being. Thus Bazin's Myth of Total Cinema is partly a fetish designed to ward off the technological reduction of the human subject to a single strand of inscriptions of sound, the modern partitioning of the body as a technique of discipline and transformation. In opposition to this, in the popular imagination the voice demanded a body, as the ear desired an eye. As a fetish, however, this recaptured wholeness must also display in some way its artificial stopgap nature, its incomplete restoration of coherence. No act of the popular imagination could overturn the forces of modernization, and great works of speculative imagination understood this. Villiers makes clear the satirical nature of his artificial woman, Hadaly, and her recorded poetic speech as a fetishistic denial of reality. Villiers's Edison declares the artificial woman he invents offers "something better than a false, mediocre, and ever-changing Reality; what I bring is positive, enchanting, ever-faithful illusion."[45] Verne approaches the fetish more sentimentally than the ennui-ridden symbolist, but equally clearly, in *Carpathian Castle* as he presents this reconstituted illusion as an act of mourning for the dead, a desperate gesture against ultimate loss.

Carpathian Castle represents Verne's single foray into the realm of the gothic novel. Published five years earlier than Stoker's novel, it sets a complex tale of the uncanny aspects of modernity in the heart of Dracula country, in a manner that one suspects would set Kittler reeling. The novel revolves around the standard *topoi* of the gothic novel: a mysterious abandoned castle, high in the mountains, the subject of legends about family curses and more recent tales of the Gortz family conflicts that had led to its abandonment. When villagers see smoke coming from its chimneys, most are seized with superstitious fear, while some members of the village claim the smoke most likely has a natural explanation. As they gather at the inn to organize a party to investigate the castle, a mysterious voice suddenly proclaims that any visit to the castle will meet with misfortune. A young forester, Nic Deck, accompanied by the village doctor, a self-proclaimed rationalist who is actually a superstitious coward, arrive at the solitary castle at night. Suddenly they hear the clanging of the castle bell and a display of spectral figures in the sky over the castle, then a beam of supernaturally bright light that gives the two of them a cadaverous appearance. As Nic insists they go on, the doctor finds his feet are rooted to the spot on the drawbridge. Nic, grabbing hold of the drawbridge's hinges, receives a mighty blow from an invisible hand.

After the pair return to the village from their unsuccessful attempt to penetrate the mysteries of the castle, two travelers, Count Franz de Telek and his companion Rotzko, arrive and are fascinated by the stories they hear. The Count becomes even more intrigued when he learns the castle belongs to the Gortz family. Years before the young Count had become enamored of an Italian opera singer known as La Stilla. His obsession was shared by Baron Rodolphe de Gortz, who haunted her performances accompanied by his bizarre friend Orfanik, and whose sinister presence frightened La Stilla enough she considered retiring from the stage. Count de Telek offered to marry her, and she agreed. However, at her farewell performance she seemed terrified by the appearance of Rodolphe de Gortz and collapsed on stage in mid-song, dead. The Count sleeps that night at the inn, hearing once again the voice of his beloved singing, presumably in his dreams.

The next morning he decides to investigate the castle himself. As he arrives toward evening, the ruin appears uninhabited, but as darkness falls, the Count sees on the battlement the figure of his beloved La Stilla, a vision that fades as quickly as it appeared. Franz de Telek enters the castle and wanders through its labyrinthine donjons and passageways. He hears La Stilla's voice singing again, but she does not respond to his calls. Wandering apparently trapped in the crypt, he sees into the castle's chapel through a crack in the masonry and glimpses the Baron de Gortz and Orfanik laying electric wire. The wire explains the first mystery, the disembodied voice in the inn. Verne intervenes at this moment to reaffirm that this gothic novel takes place in the modern era:

At this period—it must be stressed that these events took place in the closing years of the nineteenth century—the use of electricity, which has justly been called "the soul of the universe," had been brought to its highest perfection. The illustrious Edison and his disciples had completed their work[46]

The sinister Orfanik is an inventor whose genius is matched by his hatred of mankind. The mysterious voice heard at the inn, as well as the knowledge the inhabitants of the castle gained of the villagers' plans, was carried by a form of improved telephone with no need of earphones. This device was undoubtedly inspired by Edison's combined aurophone and telescopophone, inventions he announced in 1878 as developments of the phonograph, designed to respectively broadcast his voice and pick up distant conversations. The telescopophone, he claimed, could hear a cow chewing grass two miles away. "Henceforth," he declared, "there can be no actual certainty of privacy in any conversation unless held in a desert." Combining the two, Edison bugged the lab above his office and shocked visitors by asking in his easily identifiable voice, "What do you think of the aurophone?" followed by a melodramatically blood-curdling laugh, as if aware of the sinister use to which Verne would put the innovation.[47]

Orfanik has converted the ancient castle into a technological marvel, aimed mainly at increasing the villagers' fear and guaranteeing its own isolation. The spectral visions Deck and the doctor had encountered were projections onto clouds from huge reflector lights; electromagnetism had immobilized the doctor's hobnailed boots, and a current of electricity had struck Deck like a mighty invisible hand, while the powerful pale light of an electrical arc lamp had illuminated the landscape. Also following the Radcliffe tradition, Verne offered rational explanations for the apparent supernatural, but in this case it is the novelty of electricity that produces the uncanny effects, expressing the aura of the magical that surrounds new technologies. Count de Telek overhears all of this, but he has not yet unraveled the mystery of the appearance and voice of his beloved La Stilla.

Franz creeps up to Rodolphe's bedroom, a dark room that contains a stage flooded with light. He is about to seize the seated Baron when La Stilla appears on the stage. She must see him, he reasons, but she does not return his gaze or acknowledge his presence. She begins to sing, and Franz is enraptured:

He was wrapped in the ardent contemplation of this woman whom he had thought he would never see again, and who was there, alive, as if some miracle had resuscitated her before his eyes![48]

As he moves forward to embrace La Stilla and carry her off, Rodolphe confronts him. Laughing at Franz's claim that La Stilla still lives, Rodolphe slashes at her with a knife. Her image dissolves into a shower of broken glass. Rodolphe seizes

2.4. Franz sees the vision of his "resurrected" beloved in Verne's *Carpathian Castle.*

a box containing a metal cylinder and cries out, "La Stilla is still escaping from Franz de Telek! But her voice—her voice shall stay with me." A bullet aimed by Franz's companion Rotzko at the Baron de Gortz shatters the box, and he collapses, crying, "Her voice—her voice! La Stilla's soul—it is gone—gone—gone!"[49] Rodolphe dies, and Franz goes mad.

This final mystery of the voice and figure of La Stilla, her apparent survival after death, likewise receives a rational technological explanation. The voice was captured by a phonograph, an instrument Orfanik had perfected. The apparatus of the visual illusion, which he describes as "a simple optical device," remains somewhat vague in Verne's description. Although to the modern reader it clearly anticipates motion pictures, Verne's explanation is more primitive, involving a portrait animated by powerful light and reflected onto glass (possibly inspired by the so-called Pepper's Ghost illusion).[50] Nonetheless, Verne's description of La Stilla's brilliantly illuminated living image shows again the desire to supplement the capturing of the voice with the capturing of the image, doing for the eye what the phonograph had done for the ear. For Rodolphe, this audiovisual apparatus kept alive the presence of his dead love, through a scene replayed nightly in his private theater. Rodolphe dies when his attempt to undo the effects of death is itself undone. However, Orfanik supplies other records of La Stilla's voice, which, when played for Franz de Telek, restore his sanity.

III. Conclusion: His Master's Voice

"Then there is no need to despair," says the Doctor. "Those are echoes, my
good fellow, those are not *Voices* you heard."

—Villiers de L'Isle Adam, "Doctor Tristan's Treatment"[51]

Verne not only rehearses the desire to join the recording of the human
voices with the recording of the moving visual image, but the desire, essential
to both phonograph and motion pictures, to preserve the human personality
after death, to create a technological double possessed of an *ersatz* immortality
through mechanical recording and reproduction, that class fantasy dismissed by
Burch. It was this desire that Thomas Edison had in mind when he proposed
the newly invented phonograph as "The Family Record—a registry of sayings,
reminiscences, etc., by members of a family in their own voices, and of the last
words of dying persons."[52] Likewise, Georges Demenÿ described his Phonoscope as a technological improvement on the family album's hedge against death
through the addition of motion, declaring, "How valuable it would be to illu-
minate the actual and varied expressions of these portraits which are too often
mummy-like, and to leave behind us documents of our existence which can be
made to live again like actual apparitions."[53] As an objective form of memory,
these recording techniques represented man's triumph over death, the ultimate
goal of reproduction. Yet, as Burch is unable to acknowledge, technological immortality is always a fetish, an acknowledgment of the lack through a never fully
successful attempt to deny it, like the image of La Stilla, endlessly replayed by
the Baron de Gortz and ultimately shattered by him.

The recording of sound and the recording of images share a similar ambivalence in the face of death. A consideration of the single most famous image of
the reproduction of sound, Francis Barraud's painting "His Master's Voice,"
highlights this ambivalence surrounding recorded sound. The dog, Nipper, sits
posed before human technology, his clearly readable physiognomy expressing
his recognition of "his master's voice" coming over this machine, and his confusion at this phenomenon. This visual image conveys an impression of sound.
Yet the dog's confusion comes from the lack of match between the recognizable
quality of the voice (his master's) and the visually unfamiliar machine, which
does not match his master's physical appearance (or, presumably, his scent).
Nipper therefore experiences the sense of disproportion that early audiences did
in experiencing sound reproduction without an attempt at visual simulation. As
much as an allegory of the faithful quality of the reproduction of sound (and
therefore seized upon by Edison's rival, the Gramophone Company, as its commercial trademark), the painting also stands as a wry imaging of the modern
separation of the senses and its inherent confusions.[54] But the separation of
sight and hearing in this image also relates to recording as a memorial trace.
According to Michael Taussig, Barraud intended his painting as a memorial im-

2.5. Francis Barraud with one copy of his painting *His Master's Voice.*

age. The master whose voice the dog recognizes was reportedly Barraud's dead brother, whose recorded voice had outlasted his earthly existence.[55] This presumably supplies another level to the dog's confusion, recognizing his master's call, which he can no longer heed beyond the limit of death. Separated from the body, the voices survives, but what are the delights of this immortality, of speaking where one is not?

My argument about the relation between the recording of sound and the creation of motion pictures at the turn of the century, then, has several claims. First, that Bazin is right: that we must view the invention of the motion picture in relation to a broader attempt to recreate and capture the sensual world in several dimensions, including, therefore, not only sound recording but also (as Burch also adds) stereoscopy, color photography, the panorama, and other devices. However, this series of interrelated methods of recording and reproduction do not simply add up to either Bazin's triumph of realism, a perfect copy of the outside world, or Burch's despised deception of bourgeois illusion. Instead, they indicate a fetish-like response in the face of a new threat of a loss of reality. This threat includes the project, as Crary demonstrates in his discussion of the growth of physiology and psychology during the nineteenth century, to take the human sensorium apart in order to examine and master each separate strand of the senses, for example, sight divorced from tactility, hearing divorced from sight. This dissolving of the human sensorium was exemplified by Edison's phonograph, which seemed to perfectly reproduce the human voice without a human body, separating aural simulation from visual, voice from physical embodiment.

In spite of its commercial failure, the phonograph grabbed the popular imagination, fascinating people with this technological capturing of one aspect of the human subject. However, the desire to supplement it with a visual counterpart quickly arose, both in the projects to embed the phonograph in an automaton-like body and in the almost immediately appearing fantasies of a parallel invention that could "do for the eye what the phonograph does for the ear." Edison himself was driven by this parallel. This desire to supplement the phonograph responds not simply to an idealist need for perfect representation or a bourgeois desire for coherence, but to a deep anxiety aware of the manner in which technology, while doubling the human, also seems to be splitting it up, transforming the nature of human subjectivity.

The belief that the technological double will provide a hedge against death, an obtainable ersatz immortality for the masses, reflects both the anxieties at issue here, the fear of the ultimate loss of the human subject and the admittedly inadequate nature of its technological solution. The recording of La Stilla's face and figure, the sound of the master's voice, remain on the level of a theatrical and technological trick, condemned to endless repetition rather than a glorious immortality. Motion pictures and the phonograph in their origin derive from peculiarly modern fantasies of control and equally modern experiences of limitation. While these moving phantoms and disembodied voices have become domesticated and are now familiar guests in our theaters, classrooms, and homes, I do not feel we have fully completed the investigation of our technological doubles or completely understood the degree to which, in our modern world of mechanically reproduced images and sounds, we are all, like Rimbaud, somehow another.

Notes

1. Andre Bazin, "The Myth of Total Cinema," in *What Is Cinema?* vol. 1, trans. and ed. Hugh Gray (Berkeley: University of California Press, 1967), 21.

2. Ibid., 20.

3. Villiers de L'Isle-Adam, *Tomorrow's Eve,* trans. Robert Martin Adams (Urbana: University of Illinois Press, 1982), 117–118.

4. Laurent Mannoni, *Georges Demenÿ, Pionnier du cinéma* (Douai: Editions Pagine, 1997).

5. Noël Burch, *Life to Those Shadows,* trans. Ben Brewster (Berkeley: University of California, 1990), 7.

6. Ibid., 6.

7. Ibid.

8. Jonathan Crary, *Techniques of the Observer: On Vision and Modernity in the Nineteenth Century* (Cambridge: MIT Press, 1990).

9. Ibid., 85.

10. This statement "*Je est un autre,*" appears in two letters by Rimbaud, May 15, 1871 to Paul Demenÿ (the famous *lettre du voyant*) and May 13, 1871 to Georges Izambard.

Rimbaud: Complete Works, Selected Letters, trans. Wallace Fowlie (Chicago: University of Chicago Press, 1966), 305.

11. For biographical information on Cros I have relied on the Chronology, Introduction, and Notes provided by Louis Forestiere and Pierre-Oliver Walzer, for Charles Cros, *Oeuvres complètes* (Paris: Gallimard, 1970).

12. Enid Starkie, *Arthur Rimbaud* (New York: New Directions Book, 1961), 142–148.

13. Forestiere and Walzer, 8.

14. Ibid.

15. Roland Gelatt, *The Fabulous Phonograph: From Tin Foil to High Fidelity* (Philadelphia: J. P. Lippincott Co., 1955), 23–24. Cros's own descriptions of his phonograph can be found in *Oeuvres complètes,* 580–582; and in Charles Cros, *Inédits et documents,* ed. Pierre E. Richard (Paris: Éditions Jacques Brémond, 1992), 195–209.

16. Mannoni, 12.

17. Rimbaud, 307.

18. See "Procédé d'enregistrement et de reproduction des couleurs, des formes et des mouvements," in *Oeuvres complètes,* pp. 493–498. Cros's discussions of color photography in *Oeuvres complètes,* 498–510, and in Cros, *Inédits et documents,* 109–193.

19. Neil Baldwin, *Edison: Inventing the Century* (New York: Hyperion, 1995), 274.

20. Crary, 89–90

21. Baldwin, 87–92; Robert Conot, *Thomas A. Edison: A Streak of Luck* (New York: Da Capo Press, 1979), 106–109; and Matthew Josephson, *Edison: A Biography* (New York: John Wiley and Sons, 1992), 164–172.

22. Josephson, 173–174.

23. Quoted in Josephson, 164–165.

24. Baldwin, 98.

25. Conot, 109.

26. James Lastra, *Sound Technology and the American Cinema: Perception, Representation and Modernity* (New York: Columbia University Press, forthcoming).

27. Conot, 98.

28. Quoted in Douglas Kahn, "Death in Light of the Phonograph: Raymond Roussel's *Locus Solus,*" in *Wireless Imagination Sound, Radio and the Avant-Garde,* ed. Douglas Kahn and Gregory Whitehead (Cambridge: MIT Press, 1992), 87.

29. Josephson, 168.

30. Gelatt, 28.

31. Lastra.

32. Philip B. Kunhardt Jr., Philip B. Kunhardt III, and Peter W. Kunhardt, *P. T. Barnum: America's Greatest Showman* (New York: Alfred A. Knopf, 1995), 63.

33. Josephson, 171.

34. Conot, 108.

35. Villiers, *Tomorrow's Eve,* 131.

36. Conot, 106.

37. Ibid., 107.

38. Josephson, 168.

39. Baldwin, 94–95.

40. The discussions of Villiers's novel in terms of pre-cinema are Bazin (briefly), "The Myth of Total Cinema"; Annette Michelson, "On the Eve of the Future: The Reasonable Facsimile and the Philosophical Toy," *October* 29 (Summer 1984), 3–23; Raymond Bellour, "Ideal Hadaly (on Villiers *Future Eve*)," *Camera Obscura* 15 (Fall

1986), 111–134; and Charles Grivel, "The Phonograph's Horned Mouth," in *Wireless Imagination*, 31–62.

41. Friedrich A. Kittler, "Dracula's Legacy," in *Literature Media Information Systems*, ed. John Johnson (Amsterdam: Overseas Publishers Association, 1997), 50–84.

42. Jules Verne, *Carpathian Castle* (London: Arco Publications, 1963).

43. Charles Brockton Brown, *Wieland or the Transformation* (New York: Harcourt, Brace and World, 1929).

44. Ibid., 245.

45. Villiers, *Tomorrow's Eve*, 164.

46. Ibid., 166.

47. Conot, 113.

48. Verne, 180.

49. Ibid., 182.

50. See the illustration of this illusion in Erik Barnouw, *The Magician and the Cinema*, (New York: Oxford University Press, 1981), 28.

51. Villiers de l'Isle-Adam, *Cruel Tales*, trans. Robert Baldick (Oxford: Oxford University Press, 1985), 227.

52. Quoted in Josephson, 172.

53. Quoted in Jacques Deslandes, *Histoire comparée du cinéma*, vol. 1, *De la cinématique au cinématographe 1826–1896* (Paris: Casterman, 1966), 168.

54. Gelatt describes the process by which Barraud's painting became the Gramophone trademark, 107–109.

55. Michael Taussig, *Mimesis and Alterity: A Particular History of the Senses* (New York: Routledge, 1993), 224.

3 Remarks on Writing and Technologies of Sound in Early Cinema

Mats Björkin

A short nonfiction film called "Tännforsen"[1] was inserted in a special performance at the Stockholm Opera on 9 February 1909 during the Nordic Games, an annual sport and culture event. The press paid attention to what was described as "magnificent" scenery, a white waterfall on a blue background.[2] One of the critics also commented on the sound, the "natural" sound of the waterfall.[3] The projected images seem to have been carefully placed within the opera set, behind stage trees, but the press did not treat this as anything more than just another opera effect. It may have been unusual to find film images at the Stockholm Opera at the time, but they nevertheless seem to have been familiar to the audience, and attractive, since they applauded loudly. This is not surprising: opera is, after all, a very technological art form. The inclusion of film images in the opera is not out of sync with the Wagnerian dream. As Avital Ronell points out:

> A totality without contamination is the Wagnerian dream. But something had to
> be sacrificed to the dream of transparency, something had to go the way of repres
> sion. Surprisingly, the orchestra itself became the excluded negativity—the scrip
> tural space that converts the score into sound was driven underground. The site of
> technicity, where music and instrument coincide, slipped into darkness. Stuff the
> orchestra in a darkened pit, Wagner said, under the stage, suffocate it the way you
> drive out the index of otherness. Collapse one of opera's lungs. The otherness of
> the orchestra to the living operatic body is something Wagner made explicit for us.[4]

Of course, cinema was not yet "a totality without contamination," if it ever has become that; rather, the "contamination" seems to have been present wherever a film was shown. The brief remark on the realistic noise of the cinematic waterfall at the opera, a sound effect made behind the scene, is the starting point for this essay's short remarks on the issue of "contamination" of and by media in the early twentieth century. Much has been said about different sound technologies in early cinema, so I will instead go the other way around, beginning with some literary treatments of sound.

Swedish author August Strindberg is particularly interesting in relation to media technologies. He frequently used telephones in his plays, and in some novels and short stories telephones, phonographs, and other machines were important narrative devices. In the written descriptions of his scientific experiments we can find many uses of contemporary media technologies. Just as interesting is the role of technology, especially sound technology, in his spiritual writing, where his "wickerwork" of nerves was straightened out when he no longer was aware of other people's presence, when he no longer heard the noise of the other, when listening no longer was separated from his other senses. In this essay I want to examine some of Strindberg's many descriptions of his battles with demons from the 1890s because they can tell us something about the perception of the separation of the senses, when telephony, phonography, and cinema had begun to have an impact on the human senses.

In *Inferno*, written in May and June 1897, one of the most debated and discussed Swedish literary works, August Strindberg presents a mind tortured by demons, evil spirits, and a multitude of incomprehensible phenomena. It is a description of paranoia, or maybe rather, as Christoph Asendorf calls it, of electro-hysteria.[5] It is also a description of an experience of the technologization (or technicization) of modern perception and presence, as if the modern subject was constantly overheard and recorded, re-presented. One night in his hotel room in Paris Strindberg became curious about his neighbor:

> This unknown man never uttered a word; he seemed to be occupied in writing something behind the wooden partition that separated us. All the same, it was odd that he should push back his chair every time I moved mine. He repeated my every movement in a way that suggested that he wanted to annoy me by imitating me.
>
> This went on for three days. On the fourth I made the following observation. When I went to bed the man in the room next to my desk went to bed too, but in the room on the other side, next to my bed. As I lay in my bed I could hear him getting into his on the other side of the wall; I could hear him lying there, stretched out parallel to me. I could hear him turning the pages of a book, putting out the lamp, breathing deeply, turning over and falling asleep.
>
> Complete silence then reigned in the room adjacent to my writing desk. This would only mean that he was occupying both rooms. How unpleasant to be besieged on both sides at once![6]

The sounds of the other man made Strindberg aware of his own actions. The walls of his room became a sound machine that reproduced his own sounds and sent them back to him. The problem was this other man, the medium that produced the sounds. The presence of someone's hostile mind became a perceptual noise, "contaminating" his relation to other people.[7] This noise, however, was not necessarily different from the noise created by a telephone or a phonograph recording. In a phonographic recording of this neighbor of his (or if the neighbor was heard over the phone), the sound of him would have been contaminated by a lot of noise. Even if we accepted Strindberg's description as if it were our own experience, the difference would still be constituted by this contamination: a contamination of sense perception, as well as a contamination of the real, as the real is perceived through the media. When we distinguish between "pure" and "contaminated" sounds, the difference is impossible to think about without a medium through which this distinction can be made; it could be writing; it could be phonography. Could it also be another person?

German philosopher and media theorist Friedrich Kittler may not be a media historian, but some of his thoughts can be useful for an understanding of early cinema, even if they often are too generalizing. Kittler argues that modern man is created by a technological division between matter and information.[8] This division, however, is perhaps not only a technical one. If the technical differentiation made modern man possible, could the modern man himself be a medium (not only in a spiritualistic sense)? Is the neighbor in *Inferno* a media man-machine, or just a creation of a psychotic mind? In *Inferno* the mysterious sounds continue to haunt Strindberg. A problem worse than the unseen but overheard neighbor is the sound of seemingly absent persons:

> [E]very time I sat down at my desk and took up my pen, Hell was let loose. They had hit upon a new device for driving me mad. As soon as I had settled in a hotel an uproar would break out, very like that in the Rue de la Grande Chaumière in Paris. People walked about, dragging their feet and moving furniture. I changed my room, changed my hotel; the noise was always there, just above my head. I visited restaurants, but hardly had I chosen a seat in the dining-room before the row would begin. And, please note, I always asked the other people present if they could hear the same noise that I did, and they always answered "Yes," and their impression of it always tallied with mine.[9]

So, the sounds are "real," that is, his perception has been analyzed (by himself) and verified by others. Could it be a conspiracy? A ghostly, devilish plot against him:

> "So," said I to myself, "this is not an aural delusion but a carefully planned widespread intrigue." But one day, when I entered a shoe-shop quite by chance, the noise instantly began there too. So it was not a well-planned intrigue, it was the Devil himself. Hunted from hotel to hotel, beset wherever I went by electric wires that passed along the very edge of my bed, attacked by those currents of electricity that lifted me off chairs and out of beds, I prepared to commit suicide in due form.[10]

Was the devil electrified, or was electricity a tool in the hands of the devil? In any case, Strindberg seems to argue that the electrified world is filled with both technological and spiritualistic media, imbricated but distinguishable:

> The weather outside was horrible, and I dispelled my misery by carousing with my friends. One day, after such a bacchanal, I had just finished breakfasting in my room. The tray of china and cutlery was still on the table and I had my back turned to it. A dull thud attracted my attention and I saw that a knife had fallen to the floor. I picked it up and put it back carefully, so that the same thing should not happen again. It was lifted up of itself and fell.
>   So, it was electricity.

That same morning I was writing to my mother-in-law, complaining to her about the bad weather and life in general. Imagine my surprise when, just as I had finished writing the words "the earth is dirty, the sea is dirty, and the heavens rain slush," I saw a drop of crystal-clear water fall on to the paper.

Not electricity this time. A miracle![11]

Not electricity, maybe the devil, but probably not the alcohol, can be seen as a reasonable explanation here. The sounds of the neighbor in the next room, the sounds in the restaurant (and in the shoe-shop), the electrical currents, the falling knife, and the drop of water are, by Strindberg, analyzed as if they carried a particular meaning—a plot against him. The sounds differ from the other phenomena because they manifest a separation of the senses. Something is wrong when the eyes cannot verify the sounds.

When Strindberg separates hearing from seeing, it also affects the text *qua* text. The technological (re)production of sound, well known to Strindberg, is within the text separated from other senses. The sounds, mediated by the neighbor, are given a position outside the realistic narrative. Strindberg knew that the reader could imagine what is described in the text, images as well as sounds, but *Inferno* puts the strange sounds beyond realism by making them plausible. For the seemingly psychotic mind behind the story, everything becomes realistic. As long as we regard this mind to be psychotic, we will only read this text as either a fictive story or a description of mental illness. What happens, then, if we read this text as a story of involuntary techno-addiction, of a mind that does not know how to deal with a mediated world, or how to deal with the separation of physiology from information technology? Strindberg was addicted to this form of perception, and he could not, and did not want to, be cured of it. The problem with contamination was in this particular case not the separation between noise and pure sound, but the lack of control over his perception. Losing control of hearing is more complicated than losing control of vision, because sound normally has to be verified by vision—at least so long as recording can be mixed with "real" sound in such a way that the contamination is not yet discernible. Yet the quality of recordings at this time should have emphasized the contamination enough for anyone to separate a recording from reality. The reason why the contamination still was a problem for Strindberg was, on the one hand, that real sounds also are contaminated by other sounds, by walls or doors and the like. This was the major difference between sound and images, or hearing and seeing, at the time (and still is). On the other hand, he (or anyone else) could not shut his ears as he could shut his eyes. Neither alchemy nor Swedenborg could have silenced the sounds. Perhaps he needed a phone call?

We have a problem not only in defining different media and different perceptions of media historically. These (new) media also are intertwined in a "wickerwork" of media practices and media effects, contaminating each other and our perception of the real. The question is neither whether a specific form of media represents the real in a correct, uncontaminated way, nor whether a network of media (such as different sound and early film practices) is synchronized or not. It is a problem only if we consider this contamination of the real as an advantage or a deficiency of a specific medium. Should a recorded sound represent a sound as we are used to perceiving it in films today, or as heard through a loud audience? The difference between the written or spoken language and the phonograph in regard to their ability to record sound is this: what is added and what is excluded in and by the recording, and how do we relate to these added and excluded sounds? Obviously, media have contributed to a contamination of the real by emphasizing sounds (or noises) we have never perceived before. The phonograph made people listen to new sounds, new noises, and the phonograph separated noise from other sounds in a new way. How would the opera audience have perceived a phonograph recording of the waterfall? Would they have perceived it differently than a cinema audience would?

According to Kittler, literacy was supposed to supplement optical and acoustical information, so that when writing became silent (and painless), reading had to become silent. Educated people understood sights and sounds through letters, and through face-to-face communication—presence and simultancity became the only supplement to reading. When sounds and images could be stored through any medium, the memories of these sounds and images no longer were necessary; their "liberation" became their end.[12] The monopoly of writing before modern media had, according to Kittler, made the words tremble with sensuality and memory:

> All the passion of reading consisted of hallucinating a meaning between letters and lines: the visible or audible world of romantic poetry. And all the passion of writing was (according to E. T. A. Hoffmann) the poet's wish "to pronounce the inner being" of these hallucinations "in all its glowing colors, shadows, and lights" in order to "hit the favorable reader as if with an electric shock."[13]

Electricity brought Hoffmann's, but not Strindberg's, electric shocks to an end. When memories and dreams as well as the dead and even specters became technically reproducible, the hallucinatory power of reading (and writing) had become obsolete. The realm of the dead was no longer to be found in books, but in photographs.[14] In, for example, spirit photography, as Tom Gunning has showed, we find an overcoming of death through the technical device of mechanical reproduction:

> As visual spectacles and entertainment, such manifestations opened the way for the enjoyment of appearances whose very fascination came from their apparent impossibility, their apparent severance from the laws of nature. Instead of a discourse of visuality that underwrites a new worldview of material certainty with apodictic clarity, we uncover a proliferating spiral of exchanges and productions of images, founded in a process of reproduction for which no original may ever be produced.[15]

Indeed, the specters of images and last words of the dying (to speak with Edison), or even the dead, haunted the discourses on communication technologies at the end of nineteenth century. The experience of anonymity by means of mass transportation and the homogeneity of (even foreign) individuals who only see each other without speaking (the railway), which Georg Simmel describes, indicate the anonymity of silence in face-to-face interactions, the difficulty of communicating in the modern public sphere.[16] The problem here, of course, is that storage and communication as well as presence and simultaneity are difficult to separate, or rather that different media such as writing, photography, telephony, phonography, or cinema create different relations to and between presence and simultaneity. For example, after the phonograph writing no longer was the only means of representing sound, whether live or recorded.

If the phonograph overcomes death, that is, time, the telegraph and especially the telephone were thought of as technologies of overcoming distance, with the possibility of overcoming cultural differences as well as communicating with anyone anywhere. But, as Carolyn Marvin has pointed out, the idea of cross-cultural contacts following the invention of the telephone did not include mutual recognition, so it became a technology potentially in the service of colonialism. One could not talk to (and of course never talk with) a culture that did not know how to talk properly.[17] The same can be said for any electronically reproduced sound: it is only when it is done "properly" that the contamination will be merged with the real sound, and we will treat it as a "correct" representation.

More than ten years elapsed between *Inferno* and the special gala performance at the Stockholm Opera, ten years of cinema, phonographs, and telephones, but this does not mean that we cannot join them together. Strindberg's problem of identifying the cause of the noise (electricity or the Devil) can be seen as a question of how to "talk properly." In 1909, cinematic images were a "proper" way of representing a waterfall, anywhere. One of the reviewers of the opera performance called the film images "illusionary." This does not mean that they were unrealistic, but that they had become part of the world of opera. Illusion was a proper mode of representation. Sounds created in the same way as other sound effects were also proper, at the opera. But this is common knowledge in film studies. A recording of an opera singer is more "contaminated" at the opera than in a cinema.

My point is rather that the dreams of totality and transparency come close to the perception of conspiracies, "sensual conspiracies." Strindberg may have been an extreme case, but perhaps it is in literature that we can find the best understanding of early sound films. In literature we confront a problematization of the separation of noise and pure sounds; the contamination is still repressed, and the noise is "stuffed" under stage. The different perception of images and sound is still a problem, not in the cinema, but in contexts with higher cultural status. Again, that is an issue of contamination. Sound technologies add new noises to perception, while visual technologies add only old ones, aberrations the audience already was aware of through photography. Or with August Strindberg's words:

Spirits have become positivists, in harmony with the times, and are therefore no longer content to manifest themselves only in visions.[18]

Notes

1. "Tännforsen" is a waterfall in northern Sweden, a major landmark for the northern Swedish landscape at the turn-of-the-century.

2. *Dagens Nyheter,* 10 February 1909; *Nya Dagligt Allehanda,* 10 February 1909; *Stockholms Dagblad,* 10 February 1909; *Svenska Dagbladet,* 10 February 1909.

3. *Stockholms-Tidningen,* 10 February 1909.

4. Avital Ronell, "Finitude's Score," *Finitude's Score: Essays for the End of the Millennium* (Lincoln: University of Nebraska Press, 1994), 22.

5. Christoph Asendorf, *Batteries of Life: On the History of Things and Their Perception in Modernity* [1984], trans. Don Reneau (Berkeley: University of California Press, 1993), 174.

6. August Strindberg, *Inferno* [1897], in *Inferno/From an Occult Diary,* trans. Mary Sandbach (London: Penguin, 1979), 172–173.

7. My use of the concept of contamination is influenced by Avital Ronell's chapter "The Worst Neighborhoods of the Real: Philosophy—Telephone—Contamination," in *Finitude's Score,* 219–235. The concept of contamination refers both to the discourses on the danger of modern media, especially cinema, at the turn of the century, and to the infiltrating and disseminating character of media practices. It is therefore not media specific and can thereby refer to both the media and the real.

8. Friedrich A. Kittler, "Gramophone, Film, Typewriter," in *Literature, Media, Information Systems,* ed. and intro. John Johnston (Amsterdam: G+B Arts, 1997), 46. [Originally as Introduction to *Grammophon Film Typewriter* (Berlin: Brinkmann and Bose, 1985).]

9. Strindberg, 250.

10. Ibid., 250–251.

11. Ibid., 251.

12. Ibid., 39ff.

13. Quoted in Kittler, 40. [E. T. A. Hoffmann, *Der Sandmann* (1816), *Späte Werke,* ed. Walter Müller-Seidel (Munich: 1960), 343.]

14. Kittler, 41.

15. Tom Gunning, "Phantom Images and Modern Manifestations: Spirit Photography, Magic Theater, Trick Films, and Photography's Uncanny," in *Fugitive Images: From Photography to Video,* ed. Patrice Petro (Bloomington: Indiana University Press, 1995), 68.

16. Asendorf, 175.

17. Carolyn Marvin, *When Old Technologies Were New: Thinking about Electric Communication in the Late Nineteenth Century* (New York: Oxford University Press, 1988), 198.

18. Strindberg, 146–147.

4   "Next Slide Please": The Lantern Lecture in Britain, 1890–1910

Richard Crangle

For a variety of reasons, many of which are valid, scholars of the early moving picture have tended to take for granted its formal and practical relationships with the magic lantern. The two media used superficially similar machinery to project a picture onto a screen for a multiple audience; both provided a mixture of factual views and narrative texts, sometimes with propagandist messages riding alongside those with entertainment value; and both, at least some of the time, used a lecturer or commentator to provide an element of the overall text that was perceived to augment or explain the projected image. This essay offers an initial step toward a wider understanding of the latter of these relationships.

To British observers around the turn of the twentieth century, the presence of a lecturer—almost invariably a man in evening dress wielding a stick to point out elements of the picture—was one feature whose continuity between the magic lantern and the moving picture was self-evident. Contemporary representations (Figures 4.1 and 4.2) show few differences between the lantern lecturer and the moving picture commentator. As Stephen Bottomore has noted,[1] this often included a misinterpretation of the nature of the moving picture, showing the then familiar lantern "disk" rather than the rectangular window on the world to which moving picture consumers have always been more accustomed. However, before making further assumptions about the interrelation of these two media, we have to note that the formal lecture was only one of a number of popular genres of magic lantern practice, and most of the other genres involved a verbal element of one form or another that was less like moving picture commentary. We have to be aware also that the lantern lecture did not relate very closely to the moving picture in either its textual content or its apparent audience.

* * *

In the last twenty years of the nineteenth century, and particularly in the early and mid-1890s, the lantern trade in Britain was at its most commercially developed, with successful enterprises covering most sectors of the market for supply of lanterns and slides. In particular, there was a tendency to segment the trade and to specialize: at a manufacturing level, some companies would produce lanterns and ancillary equipment, while others produced slides and accompanying written texts; at a trading level there were a few large concerns

4.1. Comic postcard: "I don't wish to lecture you . . . " Edinburgh and London: W. and A. M. Johnston, circa 1903. Collection: Bill Douglas Centre, University of Exeter.

trading mainly as wholesalers or hirers of slides and equipment, and a network of retail outlets mainly based in related trades such as photographic suppliers, opticians, and chemists. There were overlaps between these generalized functions, and there is some evidence of a complex set of trading partnerships (for example, lanterns or slides clearly produced by one of the large manufacturers, but labeled or packaged as the product of the wholesale house, who then sold them on), but there was little or none of the "vertical integration" that would dominate the later cinema industries.

In the context of wider research into late-nineteenth- and early-twentieth-century magic lantern texts and practices, the main sources for the present study have been the 1908 catalogue[2] of the British slide manufacturers and hirers, Riley Brothers of Bradford, and the large collection of copies of lantern lecture and narrative texts in the Magic Lantern Society Slide Readings Library.[3] Riley Brothers was one of the most successful slide suppliers in Britain between the late 1880s and the First World War. An offshoot of a family textile business, the company rapidly built up a considerable stock of slide sets bought from the major manufacturers (and produced some slides of its own, mainly religious subjects), which it then hired to lecturers, clergymen, educational users, and other entertainers. The company also supplied lanterns and equipment, and in the later 1890s ventured temporarily into supplying cinematograph equipment such as the Riley Kineoptoscope. The 1908 Riley slide catalogue lists 1,480 sets of slides[4] by a wide range of British manufacturers, representing the stock accumulated over twenty years since its lantern and slide hire business began

4.2. Comic postcard: "London, after dark: The Bioscope." London: publisher unknown, circa 1905. Collection: Bill Douglas Centre, University of Exeter.

around 1887. While it gives only a selection of the output of the slide manufacturing trade as a whole, and certainly shows some subject biases in the direction of religious instruction, correlation of the Riley catalogue with other dealers' catalogues of the period shows that it does indeed offer a representative general picture of the subjects judged to be most commercially attractive over the great years of the magic lantern as an organized trade. The catalogue is arranged chronologically, with each year's new sets added in numbered sequence, slide sets are categorized by subject, and the slide manufacturers are credited. It can therefore be used to derive statistical information on a whole range of trends within the trade.

"Lectures and Other General Subjects," to use Riley's category title, made up approximately 29 percent of its stock of 1,480 sets on offer in 1908. Subjects of these lectures ranged widely, but principally covered British history, biological and physical sciences, and views of the world both as travelogues and as political or social geography. Typical titles included *The Glorious Reign of Queen Victoria, Microscopic Gems from the Three Kingdoms of Nature, Liverpool to Chicago by the Pennsylvania Railroad,* and (a personal favorite, at least in its title) *Worms and Their Work.* The other categories in Riley's catalogue were "Life Model and Other Stories, Poems, etc." (about 27 percent of the total number of slide sets), "Scriptural and Religious Subjects" (9 percent), "Illustrated Hymns" (4 percent), "Illustrated Songs" (13 percent), and "Comic Slides" (18 percent).[5] The quantity of slides varied from genre to genre—on the whole, lecture sets contained the largest numbers of images, followed by Life Model stories.

Analysis of the catalogue suggests that the popularity (or the perceived commercial value) of lecture sets declined over the twenty-year period, as did that of most other categories in terms of the number of new subjects added to stock each year: in 1894 Riley added twenty-five new lecture sets to its stock, in 1906 only six. A detailed consideration of that decline is beyond the scope of the present study, but would tell us more about the complexities of the relationship between the magic lantern and the moving picture. In the changing entertainment climate of the British 1890s and 1900s, the rise in popularity of the moving picture must have played some part in most trends that can be identified.

The requirements of the various slide genres for accompanying narration or interpretation were very different. A fictional narrative or factual lecture was generally supplied with a "reading" pamphlet providing a full script for a lecturer or narrator to read aloud to the audience; a variant of this was the "service of song," a narrated story with intervening hymns, which were sung by a choir or the congregation in the context of a religious service. An illustrated song would often show lyrics on the slides to allow audience participation. Comic slides sometimes were supplied with readings, sometimes relied on captions on the slides, and sometimes were solely visual or relied on a narrator's improvisation for their comedy. There was, therefore, quite a range of different requirements for verbal intervention by a lecturer or commentator, varying considerably according to the nature of the text and context. Clearly a full investigation of all the sound practices (including incidental music and nonverbal effects) of the magic lantern show and their comparative relations to those of the moving picture, if achievable at all, would be a long and complex piece of work.

The remainder of this essay will focus on the factual lecture, which in general offered an authoritative description of an aspect of the world at large, with accompanying slides that were usually photographic in origin. The slides of a lantern lecture typically showed topographical or other "documentary" views, varying in accordance with the subject at hand, and possibly also included photographs of maps, diagrams, and formal portraits of relevant personalities. They were less likely to include "action" scenes (views of historical events in progress, for example) and more likely to feature posed or composed general views—a nontopical, but therefore nonperishable, treatment of the world similar to that of the early moving picture.

It is difficult to judge whether the contemporary audience regarded one element of a lantern lecture as the primary attraction of the text—that is, the slides "illustrated" the lecture, or the lecture "explained" the slides—or whether, as we would perhaps tend to do today, they saw the whole as a single text with distinguishable but indivisible portions. It is also important to note that a typical magic lantern show of the period was quite likely to include texts of several genres assembled as a kind of variety bill, though the limited contemporary evidence of handbills, firsthand accounts, and occasional press reviews tends to suggest that the serious factual lecture was less likely to vary its content with comic or song sets than were some of the other genres.

The lecture sets listed in Riley's catalogue consist on average of forty-five slides (compared to averages of nineteen slides for fictional narratives and poems, eight for illustrated songs, and ten for comic subjects). A verbal description of one or two paragraphs, about 150–200 words, usually accompanied each view on the screen, indicating a slide change every one or two minutes. In conjunction with a study of lecture reading pamphlets, this gives a very rough calculation of average lecture length, which would be about an hour, assuming that all went smoothly and both lecturer and lanternist were reasonably competent.

Publication of lecture texts appears to have been most commercially viable in the 1880s and 1890s. It seems quite common for readings from this period to have run into several editions, and printers' marks on the covers of some suggest print runs of five hundred to one thousand copies; clearly this was a professional operation. In the twentieth century, in parallel with the decreasing number of factual lectures in overall slide production, commercial production of lecture readings appears to have declined, and it was certainly effectively over by the time of the First World War. Thereafter, duplicated typescript or manuscript seems to have been the norm for lecture text dissemination; in any case, the public lecture had by that time largely vanished as a trade practice.

The lantern trade as a whole appears to have been in decline from around the turn of the century. To judge from the readings in the Magic Lantern Society Library (admittedly a random selection, and often difficult to date with any precision) and from slide manufacturers' catalogues, this decline accelerated in the later 1900s. This must have had some relation to the rising popularity of the moving picture, but there was no overnight "death of the lantern" and no connection as obvious as a smoking gun in the hands of the cinematograph operator. Some slide distributors, such as Newton and Company of London, continued to publish texts for Sunday School and other religious subjects until at least the 1930s, but in general new slide readings seem to have been very scarce after around 1910. The Riley Brothers hire business, according to William Riley's own recollections in his autobiography,[6] declined catastrophically as the rush of younger people to volunteer for the First World War claimed both the company's staff and the audiences of the religious lecture circuit, which was by then the major component of its business. A younger brother attempted to restart the business, publishing Sunday School lectures in duplicated typescript, but with little success.

In the present comparative context, it is crucial to attempt some understanding of the audiences and exhibition contexts of the lantern lecture. These were not the same as those of the early moving picture, certainly in Britain and quite probably in other national contexts as well. Clearly this has an effect on the apparent relationship between the functions of the lantern lecturer and the moving picture commentator, both as we see them now and as they were seen by their contemporary audiences. While the moving picture found its success predominantly as a variety act and a fairground attraction,[7] the magic lantern show, and especially the lantern lecture, was never established in either of these contexts.

More or less by definition, the lecture placed its emphasis on instruction or education, in a broad sense. This was unlike the early moving picture, which, while its subjects may have been largely documentary in nature, was more clearly conceived as a popular entertainment medium. That does not mean, though, that the lantern lecture was not also seen as an entertainment. A rare contemporary account by an audience member, in the 1893 diary of an undertaker's laborer from Bristol, gives an insight into the interest that could be generated by a lantern lecture, especially a supposedly firsthand account of exotic experiences. The lecturer here was Frederic Villiers, then a war correspondent with the *Graphic* and later an early moving picture camera operator:[8]

> I went over to the Merchant Venturers Hall, in Unity Street, paid 1d, and got a good seat. The place soon fills up, with a good many standing. A big sheet was up on the platform, the gas was turned out, and Mr. Villiers came forward. He was in campaign dress, Norway jacket, havresack and knife, then the lantern goes to work, with views. [Several descriptions of military scenes in Africa follow.] All the time, Mr. Villiers explained his thrilling doings and adventures in the campaigns he showed. I wish I was able to take his words in, as twould have interested me indeed, but I could not unfortunately.[9]

As that account begins to suggest, the quality of delivery of a lantern lecture could be variable. By the nature of their business, the British slide companies dealt with enthusiastic amateurs as well as the relatively small group of people like Villiers who could make at least part of a living by lecturing. York and Son of London, one of the largest slide manufacturing and publishing companies of the time, offered "Hints to Amateur Lecturers" at the front of their reading pamphlets, which indicate a few of the technical problems they expected clients to run into:

> It is recommended to amateurs to carefully study the reading in private before attempting to render it in public. This will make the public reading more easy, and enable the reader—by familiarity with the emphasis and leading points—to deliver the reading with much greater effect. [. . .]
> It is further recommended to amateurs by the author of this reading not to adopt the too common mode of signalling to the operator by at one time rapping with the pointer, at another giving directions with the voice. The customary "*rap-tap-tap*" alternating with "*Now, then, if you please, the next picture*," has a grotesque effect on the audience, and is not infrequently perplexing to the operator himself.[10]

The lecture texts themselves were usually written as fully formed presentations, with introductory remarks and a style allowing discussion of the subject as though with familiarity and personal knowledge. York and Son, who seem to have not entirely trusted their customers not to botch presentations of their slides, inserted marks in the text for a signal to the lanternist to change the slide, "to admit of the reading on to the next view being proceeded with, without the awkward pause that so often spoils the smoothness of the whole entertainment."[11] The authority of pronouncement that an 1890s instructional approach demanded was, it appears, closely related to smooth continuity of presentation of both the verbal and visual texts.

*   *   *

The present discussion consciously offers an outline of only one side of the comparison between lantern and moving picture practices, and its assumptions about commentaries accompanying the moving picture in Britain are, to say the least, open to debate. But it will be useful in conclusion to summarize the relevance of study of the lantern lecture for examination of the moving picture, always subject to revision in the light of a better understanding of the role of the moving picture commentator. In general, there appear to have been four areas of broad similarity, and four areas of clear difference. The similarities are:

1. Both gave a verbal explication or elaboration of a visual scene, usually to locate the scene in a wider context and especially in a narrative or informative sequence.
2. Both included an element of individual performance, that is to say, an ephemeral element.
3. They had similar technical characteristics, in terms of equipment and personnel required.
4. Overall, both were "hybrid texts," consisting of a number of elements dependant on each other—the verbal element could not logically function without the visual element, and the visual element was perceived to be not fully delivered without some form of additional explication.

And the differences are:

1. The lantern lecture presented a series of single pictures, often not individually similar to each other, whose sequential logic was defined by the verbal text; the moving picture presented continuing pictures whose sequential logic, although clarified and enhanced, did not *necessarily* depend on the accompanying commentary.

2. The lantern lecture was generally pre-scripted, sometimes with a definitive published text tied to a particular set of images, but the moving picture commentary, in Britain at least, does not seem to have used a published script apart from synopses in producers' catalogues, and was more of an improvised or individuated presentation.

3. Treatment of subject matter was different—although both offered a "view of the world" or a "view of contemporary life," the lantern lecture attempted to give an educative explanation of that view, while the moving picture presented it as a spectacle whose movement provided a large proportion of its attraction.

4. Most importantly, presentation contexts and hence audiences were quite different—the lantern lecture was presented in the church hall, mechanic's institute, museum, or other public meeting room, while the moving picture was predominantly in the variety theater and fairground until fixed-site projection venues began to be commercially established in the later 1900s.

In general, then, it would appear that there are or were demonstrable connections between early moving picture commentary and the lantern lecture, and possibly also between the moving picture and the other lantern genres. The temptation has been to see the practice of moving picture narration as a formal "evolution" of lantern practice, a growth of an existing practice in response to new (and therefore superior) technological conditions in parallel with the technological evolution represented by the undeniable relationship between the magic lantern and the cinematograph projector. This, though, is one Darwinism too many: as this essay has tried to show, the practice of lantern lecturing was sufficiently specialized, and in spite of some similarities, sufficiently *un*like moving picture practice, to raise more questions than it answers about comparative views of the two media.

A more successful working model for beginning to understand these connections would be not a formal evolution, but a bricolage. It was not the case that one practice gradually changed into another, nor that a new practice superseded an old one instantaneously; it was more that a new textual practice borrowed features of a pre-existing practice and used them alongside features borrowed from a range of other practices. This is very much in tune with the entire nature of the early moving picture: as Michael Chanan has suggested,[12] until its own textual and technical norms became more clearly defined in the later 1900s, moving picture development proceeded as a bricolage of narrative, technical, economic, presentational, and audience practices taken from here, there, and everywhere, as indeed were the worldview subjects that fed its audience's appetite for attractions. The presence of a lecturer was one aspect among several that it borrowed from the magic lantern trades, but as is always the case in bricolage, in the process of borrowing, the practice itself became something different.

Notes

1. Stephen Bottomore, *I Want to See This Annie Mattygraph: A Cartoon History of the Coming of the Movies* (Pordenone: Le Giornate del Cinema Muto, 1995), 44.

2. *Catalogue of Optical Lantern Slides Published by Riley Bros. Ltd.* (Bradford: Riley Brothers, [1908]). I am indebted to John Finney for generously allowing me access to a copy of this catalogue.

3. This collection of photocopies of slide reading texts, copied from originals in the private collections of members of the Magic Lantern Society, currently totals approximately 1,400 titles covering a wide variety of slide manufacturers and subject genres. As such it is probably the largest research collection of this type of material in the world and continues to expand. Further information may be found at http://www.magiclantern.org.uk

4. 1,480 sets of slides are listed in the catalogue, although the serial numbers of the sets reach 1606. The discrepancy is accounted for by discontinued sets, particularly from the earlier years—these sets were presumably damaged or lost in the hire trade, or deleted from stock because a later set superseded them (in a few cases this is noted in the catalogue). It seems unlikely that these missing sets would change the overall conclusions about the nature of Riley's stock.

5. The exact figures are: "Lecture and Other General Subjects": 427 sets (28.85% of total stock); "Life Model and Other Stories, Poems etc.": 398 sets (26.89%); "Scriptural and Religious Subjects": 136 sets (9.19%); "Illustrated Hymns": 63 sets (4.25%); "Illustrated Songs": 193 sets (13.04%); "Comic Slides": 265 sets (17.90%); subject unidentified: 1 set.

6. William Riley, *Sunset Reflections* (London: Herbert Jenkins, 1957). After the demise of his lantern business, Riley pursued a successful career as a popular novelist. His autobiography contains little direct or reliable factual information on the Riley Brothers lantern business, but is nonetheless a useful source for a contextual understanding of some aspects of the 1890s and 1900s British lantern trade.

7. See Vanessa Toulmin, "Telling the Tale: the Story of the Fairground Bioscope Shows and the Showmen Who Operated Them," *Film History* 6, no. 2 (Summer 1994), 219–237, and Vanessa Toulmin, "The Fairground Bioscope," in Colin Harding and Simon Popple, *In the Kingdom of Shadows: A Companion to Early Cinema* (London: Cygnus Arts, 1996), 191–206, for excellent introductory accounts of the importance of fairground exhibition in the early British moving picture trade.

8. See Stephen Bottomore, "Frederic Villiers: War Correspondent," *Sight and Sound* 53, no. 4 (Autumn 1980), 250–255, for more on Villiers's cinematographic activities.

9. W. H. Bow, *The Diary of a Bristolian 1893* (Bristol: Engart Press, 1986), 153–155. Spellings and grammar reproduced verbatim from the original text.

10. "Preliminary Hints to Amateur Lecturers," in *The Human Body, or the House We Live In* (London: York and Son, [circa 1890]), flyleaf. Identical text appeared in the front matter of most of York's published slide readings from the 1890s.

11. "Preliminary Hints to Amateur Lecturers."

12. See Michael Chanan, *The Dream That Kicks: The Prehistory and Early Years of the Cinema in Britain* (London: Routledge and Kegan Paul, 1980), 51–53.

5   The Voices of Silence
François Jost

As I was perusing the French press of 1908, I gradually became convinced that the multiplicity of sound contexts then in existence in the cinema, which Rick Altman has nicely brought to light, was not simply a profusion randomly expanding along available facilities or material contingencies. It also had a logic of its own, which depended on the status of the films screened, and the *film d'art* played a crucial part in the formation of this paradigm of sound within cinema.

The relationship between sound and image in the early years of the century could be described along very different theoretical (semantic or syntactic) modes. I will here hypothesize that this relationship heavily depended on the artistic value vested in these projected images. In support of my claim, I will focus on the period in film history where silence became an aesthetic stake: the launch of the *film d'art*.

In spite of standard terminology, sounds are never produced by images. Hence, an obstacle that cinema as a whole has tried to smooth away: how could a sound be anchored in an image? The operation requires that three conditions be met:

- Iconicity: the sound produced must resemble the object it represents enough for spectators to identify it, and a know-how of sound effects is necessary;
- Redundancy: for the visual anchor to work, spectators need to find in the image semes it shares with the sound sign;
- The temporal coincidence of the sound with a visual movement (gesture or movement of the lips) will fix this relationship.

Backstage sounds gird the first two dimensions, but not necessarily, as has often been stated, with the only objective of heightening realism. Do we truly recognize thunder in these jalousie-like devices "whose held-back wood strips are brusquely let back down"? This is hardly relevant since, as a *Ciné-Journal* writer suggested, these sounds have as their main function to impress.[1] We would have to hear the sudden, explosive irruption of thunder in Handel's *Amadigi di Gaula* along with the proper musical context to imagine the startled reaction of an audience absorbed in the image and expelled from their inner silence by the racket produced by a "device made of alternated barrel staves and metal sheets slipped onto a rope" and let loose from the top of the flies. Iconicity is less a matter of resemblance between sounds than it is between the frights effected by the surge of some unexpected noise.

As to the criterion of synchronism, the survey of the sounds to which audiences were exposed in certain film theaters showed that they were continuous, horizontal rather than punctual, as well as spread over time. To phrase this in a more current language, they created what we call *atmosphere*, that is to say, they were sound masses whose particularity was their lack of orientation and the fact that they were not anchored in any specific point of the image.

Whereas imitation in the theatrical model depended on the skillfulness of a man and consequently widely varied from one sound effect performer to another, the "portative piece of furniture for backstage sounds" marked a break in the history of cinema. First of all, it made it possible to replicate identical sounds ("In the past, as in fact still today, we produced these sounds backstage according to the system and traditions of theater."). The shores of performance grew more and more distant, as did the strong autographic component of cinema. Like intertitles, which guaranteed an absolute iterability of the verbal narrative (as opposed to the lecturer), the portative device, available for rental and therefore transportable, assured a continuity of the show independently of the performer or place.

The other important shift concerned the nature of sounds and the manner in which they could be reproduced: "the falling stone makes a noise as it drops, the child who rings a bell is heard." To the atmosphere based on sound durations was added the possibility of easily producing *effects*, punctually and in synchrony with some visual aspects: "out of movement comes noise, as is the case in life." Cinema was moving from accompaniment to an extraction of visual details through sound.

In this varied, vibrant context, what was the place for silence? This is the issue that concerns us here. One thing we can be sure of: silence was often emphasized by film theorists. It should however be mentioned that in cinema, silence does not consist of the absence of all sound. Rather, it results from an action of one of the sound sources over others, an action whose success ends in the reduction to silence.

In the first place, it is likely that silence accompanied the screening of didactic films. If any proof were needed, the complaints in *Fascinateur* of professionals such as M. Louis Fabry, the president of the Projectionists' Association in Marseilles, about the problems posed to his profession by "mis-wound film reels," would serve as evidence:

> Assistants to the lecturer then place the print inside-out, what should appear to
> the left appears on the right, the lecturer has to interrupt himself to insert the film
> correctly; or, when he remains silent, the spectators who know *the landscapes think
> aloud,* which distracts the rest of the audience and lessens the potential benefits of
> the lecture.[2]

Evidently, genres call for different attitudes, and the most didactic of them require the public's silence.

However, in order to examine the importance of silence or to truly understand what may have appeared at a certain period as "the sound of silence," it is fruitful to pay heed to the initial screening of the *films d'art* and more particularly to *L'Assassinat du duc de Guise* (The Assassination of the Duke of Guise). In keeping with my hypothesis that genres, far from being self-evident categories, are rather loci of encounter, and sometimes of conflict, for the various forces of cinematographic communication, I will examine the role of silence in, respectively, the reception and the writing of works.

Let us first turn our attention to criticism. Georges Dureau's article, dated November 19, 1908 and titled "Visions of Art," is all the more interesting because the author did not attend the November 17 screening in the Charras theater, and it may be assumed that he is reporting on the Parisian buzz in the wake of the event.

At once, *L'Assassinat du duc de Guise* is introduced as a "silent play," by contrast with the term *pellicule* (film) whose pejorative connotation is mentioned by the director of *Ciné-Journal*. This expression captures the artistic paradox of what are also called "visions of art," which derive their value from both their theatricality and their silence—a silence perceived less as an impediment than as an artistic choice. In this respect, it does not bring upon itself the reproaches then commonly addressed to the cinematograph, namely of being a "spectacle for the deaf."[3]

If we are to believe Dureau, the players mime "the death of the poor Duke of Guise," and this miming goes against the expression of thought: "What is to be left of M. Lavedan's ideas as a playwright, as the absence of verbal expression makes them hardly perceptible?" While asking the question in itself presupposes a mistrust of the end product (which again, the critic had not seen), the fact that it cropped up both on the occasion of this film and in *Ciné-Journal* nevertheless suggests that in a context where silent films are accepted as a given, the silence in *L'Assassinat du duc de Guise* is more noticeable than in other films.

Why would the silence in question have appeared so threatening? Probably because in the first place, in Victorin Jasset's words, "Well-known artists acted without running around; they achieved an increasing intensity of effect."[4] The absence of movement was then emphasized *a contrario* by the absence of sound (whose presence was tied to movement, as we have already seen). But most of all, this threat arose because the film also appeared as part of the emergence of representations of psychology in cinema—and Dureau could hardly conceive of these representations as compatible with silence. "What will have become of the gestures of M. Albert Lambert, the magnificence of Mrs. Robinne, as both are reduced to the gesticulations of their *passions bereft of words*?"

What is striking at this point of his article is that Dureau sees a solution to the problem posed (one which, he adds, the film's producers were also aware of) in the music by Saint-Saëns used for the film: "the promoters of these works cannot imagine them without the help of a *powerful music* which from the point of view of the audience will replace the *human voice* in the minute details of its expressivity." Through this text we can see the emergence of a use of music at odds with those that had been traditionally mobilized by the cinematographic spectacle. Minor genres usually featured a musical accompaniment often foregrounded in the architecture of the theater. In the case of *L'Assassinat du duc de Guise,* however, "there is the great display, the whole kit and caboodle of *invisible* yet *present* music, the mystery appropriate for cinematographic evocations." This present invisibility sharply contrasts with another type of show, where spectators are welcomed with the sound of an orchestra, which could also introduce and conclude the program (that was the case at the Hippodrome movie theater, for instance). Indeed, it seems that, from then on, these two uses of music co-existed: on the one hand, accompaniment—with its share of stereotypes and clichés—aided the understanding of the meaning of actions, while stage music had other functions, which I will shortly specify.

Yet, before I proceed, I should still insist on the central role of silence in the aesthetic revolution played by the *film d'art.* According to Adolphe Brisson's famous article (Brisson had visited the Pathé factory in Vincennes), sets were small theaters opening onto "a mute world where everything was accomplished in silence."[5] There, a "new form of theater" came into existence, the "cinematographic play" whose "aesthetics" Lavedan and Le Bargy had "codified," endowing silence with a particular meaning strongly contrasting with the production of staples.[6]

If I was able earlier to put forward the idea that music was the continuation of silence by other means, I owe it to the fact that, for the people who codified the *film d'art,* silence was in paradigmatic opposition only to speech. While the latter supports thinking processes and abstraction, with silence "we are within the domain of concrete objects." To some extent, Brisson's definition of the constraints of silent cinema is reminiscent of the first rule of the Cartesian method. From Descartes, "The first was never to accept anything as true that I did not know evidently to be so; that is, carefully to avoid precipitous judgment and prejudice; and to include nothing more in my judgments than what presented itself to my mind with such clarity and distinctness that I would have no occasion to put it in doubt."[7] By comparison Brisson writes that "characters must act and must do so *clearly* and not *confusedly,* and each of their movements must be *expressive* as well as produced with an overall coherence through a constant relation of cause and effect." Brisson's "reasons," in this case, are more artistic than scientific, although style is thought of as a simplification of nature, just as was reasoning for the philosopher.[8] To this almost rational emphasis on silence, he adds an argument inspired by a quasi-Rousseauian conception of communication, namely that the transparency of souls could be achieved only as long as human beings could communicate without resorting to language. "In spoken theater, the detail of the dialogue, the wide range of intonations substitute to some extent for the precision of gestures. Here gestures, because they are laid bare, have to be *truthful.*"

That this art "from which words are absent" might be beyond language would seemingly find confirmation in the fact that Brisson opposed it to pantomime, with "its language, its own grammar, its immutable signs whose meaning never changes," while "cinema abstains from resorting to its alphabet; its ambition is life."

To this almost heuristic value of a silence that helps the understanding of the action, to the authenticity it brings with it, Brisson added what might be called its communicational force and its strong effect on spectators: "This visual narrative pieced together by Lavedan with painstaking and passionate dedication makes its mark on the mind in unforgettable ways." He then concluded that "vision cannot be matched in its teachings." Thus silence was to free the eye from the confusion in which verbal narratives had put it.

In order to grasp the discourse that surrounded the screening of *L'Assassinat du duc de Guise,* we should take it for what it is, not so much a faithful account of the actual practice of a period as a defense of a poetics of silence whose existence may have had no reality other than discursive—a prescriptive rather than a descriptive discourse.

Indeed, although the specialized press stated that the authors of the first *film d'art* claimed the label of "silent play," a close look at the script shows that at the writing stage, speech held an important role, as this excerpt demonstrates:

> The Cardinal of Guise half rose, a frightened look on his face, as if to get to his brother. Yet his brother stops him with his hand and makes him sit down again. The Cardinal falls back in terror. Everyone is looking at him. He is also looking at others, with a brave, enigmatic, derisive air . . . *as if to ask them "Where am I going? What is to become of me? I have an idea. So do you. And yet I am going. And we will see."*

The film itself confirms the omnipresence of dialogue since, far from contenting themselves with miming as Dureau suggested, actors speak continuously. This concurs with Isabelle Raynauld's insistence on the sounds presupposed by the film.[9] Where, then, does the impression come from that these films seem silent? Where does the illusion of those who focus on the visual narrative originate?

First and foremost from the fact that the numerous lines that crowd the screenplay are less intended for the characters' utterance than they are comments that spectators could make to themselves:

> The cardinal quickly tells him a few words in a low voice, words *which we assume* express anxiety, give advice or else "be careful, watch out." Guise answers with an evasive smile and shrugs. [. . .] He seems to be telling them: Where am I going? What is to become of me? I have an idea. So do you. And yet I am going. And we will see.

In other words, the letter matters less than the spirit. If spectators don't know the exact words uttered by the actors, they have to reconstitute their meaning through the situation set up by the screenplay as a whole or through the actors' gestures. Thus, after the death of the Duke of Guise, they might infer that the following exchanges are taking place:

All parted to let him see the body from afar: "As you can see, Sire, it has been done." The King, still holding his little dog, slowly came forward. . . . After a couple of steps, he stopped and timidly asked: "Are you sure that . . . —Oh yes, quite sure," a few people replied.

What also makes *L'Assassinat du duc de Guise* a visual narrative is the fact that intertitles, admittedly rare in the film, transcribe almost none of these lines reconstructed through spectatorial identification with the conspirators. In this respect, two remarks come to mind:

- First of all, the director abandoned the idea of visually representing the lines as had been planned during the writing stage. Thus, about Pétremol's request to the king in favor of the poor Scottish soldiers who had been waiting for their pay for six months, the script mentioned: "Words appear on the screen as Pétremol pronounces them." This idea to visualize what is said is all the more noteworthy given that at this stage of the writing process no intertitle had been planned.
- Secondly, none of the aforementioned critics actually referred to the existence of any intertitles, and accordingly to the role of a visualized verbal narrative.

This probably made less of an impression during the Charras screening than did the absence of any lecturer or speaker: "Will you believe it? After an hour and a half into the show [. . .] we felt a strong need to hear a human voice." Whatever the written commentary included in the projected film, the presence of the music and the absence of a speaker in the theater probably put the audience in a situation of silent reading and drew their attention away from seeing the sound that the film still involved. In a way, the impression of silence, the illusion perhaps, first and foremost results from an increase in the spectator's visual activity, itself a byproduct of the conjunction between words and music.

At the time when *L'Assassinat du duc de Guise* was big news in Paris, *Ciné-Journal* printed two articles from the *Revue internationale de photographie*, possibly for their relevance in the context of the aesthetic break heralded by the *film d'art* and given the interest for the phenomenon shown by *Ciné-Journal*.

The first argues in favor of "programmatic music, that is, music whose character is purely instrumental and has as its origin a clearly defined literary or artistic theme." Contrary to accompaniment music, which, as its name indicates, goes with the image, programmatic music "does not only move us through sounds, but also awakens other feelings in us, through the spontaneous conjuring-up of images, of scenes involving well-defined mood and actions." When characterizing this music capable of creating images in the spectators' mind, the author, who received pictorial training, curiously uses the same word as the *film d'art* poet-theorist: "musical composition is not necessarily *abstract*, it can conjure up landscapes or themes so that the listener attentive enough, even without musical knowledge, eventually discovers the scenes it contains."[10] From there it is a short step to the notion that this virtual synesthesia in music may support silent comprehension (without the lecturer bringing linear order to images, that is)—and why not? Synchronism may indeed be taken from its linguistic applications and applied to the relations between music and images. Rather than mobilizing it in the service of realism, it would henceforth facilitate spectatorial intelligibility:[11]

> Music helps the understanding of the cinematograph. M. Camille de Saint-Saëns wrote the score to *L'Assassinat du duc de Guise* in front of the screen as the film was being projected. The music must accentuate, accompany, add precision to the gestures. Musical phrases should coincide perfectly with the action.

In more semiological terms, one might say that two missions which had been the lecturer's now fell to the music—to punctuate movements and gestures, and to constitute syntagmatic units and mark them off from each other.

The author of the piece then reveals to his readership that, in order to ensure synchronism at the time of the shooting, M. Lavedan appointed two assistants to the set supervisor—a musical director and a conductor. Using a method close to our modern lip-synching, "the artist models his/her gestures on the music which was composed at the same time as the scenario. S/he practices with a phonograph."

The advent of film music as such reverses the logic of musical accompaniment. While the latter followed the filmed performance of actors, film music, on the contrary, shapes their gestures and facial expressions, dictating its rhythm. Accordingly, the reversal of the speech-sound hierarchy appears quite manifest, since actors have to conform to musical time. One may wonder whether this articulation between image and music is responsible for the impression of rapidity that appears slightly odd to us today: "its images succeed one another, sometimes a little too fast and feverishly, other times too compactly, yet strangely enough, always suggestively."[12]

In parallel to the concern for a syntactic articulation between the audio and the visual, *Ciné-Journal* underlined the visual composition, as an article simply titled "De la composition" ("On Composition") attests. The piece points out that the course followed by the spectators' eyes in the image may be monitored by the organization of the scene: "It is undeniable that the eye may be led to choose, in a landscape, certain parts which, laid out in one manner or another, will obey the laws that underpin properly conceived art" (predominance, balance, and repetition).[13]

What was the impact of such theories on the work of Lavedan, Calmettes, and Le Bargy? It is difficult to say at this point. What we know of their musical aesthetic permits us to think that it is not unlikely that they were aware of these theories or even that they cared to conform their work to them. Whatever the answer, the silent screening of *L'Assassinat du duc de Guise* (that is, once again, without any linear ordering by the lecturer but with the musical linearization) not only must have intensified the activity of the eye but also must have increased the spectators' awareness that they were facing a screen. As living speech deserted the movie theater, the eye was driven by the movements of characters across the screen and the ocular fixedness imposed by reading.[14] As an example as well as a conclusion, let us observe the movement of the eye as an intertitle comes to interrupt visual action.

The first note, which warns the Marchioness of Noirmoutiers against what might happen to the Duke of Guise, divides the action of reading into two parts. Yet the end of the message, determined by the Western reading mode (from left to right), leads spectators toward the right edge of the screen, where the reader is located. Consequently, the entrance through the left edge marks a perceptive break that sets it apart de facto. The same lateral composition occurs when the Duke of Guise, after reading the note and adding that "he wouldn't dare," stands up and exits the room. Thus, it is possible that the absence of sound and "the invisible presence of the music" give a particular importance to the movement of the eyes and the composition of the image.

It is difficult to go any further in this direction for the time being. I will only point out, by way of conclusion, that the presence of music has two main consequences: one cognitive, the other emotional. From the perspective of cognition, as we have just seen, music paradoxically reinforces the activity of the eye. From the point of view of emotion, music does not just emphasize or illustrate feelings, it gives the film a tragic dimension. Isn't there, indeed, something necessarily tragic in its characters, who silently move about while music carries us with its own movement and logic in a world of which they are oblivious but which encompasses them all the same?

Translated by Franck Le Gac and Wendy Schubring

Notes

1. "At a time when Directors of theatres and film theatres concern themselves with the accompaniment of moving images by the various sounds they involve in order to make an impression on the public, we think it fit to mention here a few of the backstage devices most commonly used." *Ciné-Journal,* 1 September 1908.

2. *Ciné-Journal,* 10 April 1909.

3. "Visions d'art," *Ciné-Journal,* 19 November 1908.

4. "Etude sur la mise-en-scène en cinématographie," *Ciné-Journal,* 21 October 1911, translated in Richard Abel, *French Film Theory and Criticism, 1907–1939: A History/Anthology,* vol. 1 (Princeton: Princeton University Press), 56.

5. "Chronique théâtrale," *Le Temps,* 22 November 1908.

6. Delluc actually noted that it "is difficult to mime without speaking when you did not receive training as a cinema actor" and regretted that "actors with no experience in film acting speak as they are filmed, and since the dialogue they use is completely left to them, you can imagine which style this resulted in." Delluc added an anecdote: "Recently, I was present on the set of a film about fashionable society in which a couple of aristocrats quarreled with high-flown expressions on their faces. The husband exclaimed, 'Bitch! . . . Louse! Whore!' and so on . . . " *Le Cinéma des cinéastes* (Paris: Cinémathèque française, 1985), 59.

7. René Descartes, *Discourse on Method* and *Meditations on First Philosophy* [1637],

trans. Donald A. Cress, 3rd ed. (Indianapolis/Cambridge: Hackett Publishing Company, 1993), 11. [translator's note]

8. "Dès que la nature est simplifiée par l'effort du cerveau humain, le style apparaît." ("As soon as nature is simplified through the effort of the human brain, style appears.") Brisson.

9. See Isabelle Raynauld's essay elsewhere in this volume.

10. *Ciné-Journal,* 3 December 1908.

11. See Rick Altman on the use of microphones at the outset of sound cinema and the similar conclusions he draws about them in "Technologie et représentation: l'espace sonore," in *Histoire du cinéma. Nouvelles approches,* ed. Jacques Aumont, André Gaudreault, and Michel Marie (Paris: Publications de la Sorbonne, 1989), 121–130.

12. Brisson.

13. *Ciné-Journal,* 16 August 1909. (Signed L. F. and reprinted in the *Revue internationale de photo*).

14. This impression can be experienced on viewing the sound version of *L'Assassinat de Duc de Guise* restored by the Archives du Film of the Centre National de la Cinématographie Française.

6   The Event and the Series: The Decline of *Cafés-Concerts,* the Failure of Gaumont's Chronophone, and the Birth of Cinema as an Art

Edouard Arnoldy

Ça fait rire les enfants,
ça dure jamais longtemps . . .

—For Alex, Nathalie, and the already present future

History(-ies) of Cinema and *Series* (*of Series*)

Thinking the history of (sound) cinema? We might as well put a stop to it and affirm once and for all, as Paul Veyne did, that *there is no such thing as a history of (sound) cinema.* It might prove more fruitful to borrow from Michel de Certeau and propose that "the history of (sound) cinema verges on the unthinkable." These two (or three) witticisms have no other purpose but to point to the *guiding spirit* of my article. The initial question aims to emphasize the fact that the following pages will probably not completely satisfy readers avid for a new history of (sound) cinema, one which would restore unknown films to favor, bring hitherto unpublished documents to light, pile up discoveries, or provide a list of significant historical facts and events to connect the dots in a global, comprehensive, and *definitive* history of (sound) cinema. That history, in effect, does not exist. Or rather, it is *endless* since, not truly aware of what it is looking for, it denies its own partiality, its distinctively fragmented dimension. *Let us not confuse an effect with a cause.* In no way will I consider unveiling the hypothetical origin of the "sound revolution" or giving a particular value only to the (allegedly) significant facts in the history of (sound) cinema. A passage in Lucien Febvre's *Combats pour l'histoire* captures what might constitute the agenda of a history of (sound) cinema only hinted at here: "writing, not an automatic, but a problematic History."[1]

Too often, the history of (sound) cinema is considered separately from its roots or artificially circumscribed to a period of transition, *to the change from one type of cinema to another,* or inordinately thought of in terms of progress or revolution. In these pages, this history will instead be seen in terms of intersections and intertwinings and, to quote Gilles Deleuze on Michel Foucault, will "never be content."[2] Viewed from that angle, the history of sound cinema will have as its permanent concern the refusal to found its discourse on a birth date (as it happens, the release of *The Jazz Singer* on October 6, 1927), a (happy) event that turns all others into trivial facts. From this perspective, *The Jazz Singer* will not invariably be the starting point (or the end point) of the history in question, but indeed an element in a series (of series).

The term *series* is an *operating concept* around which the history of (sound) cinema may be, advantageously in my opinion, organized. The recurrent concern in the adoption of series would be, as André Gaudreault has suggested, "to work on a problem rather than on a period or, rather, to work on a period only if it originates from a *problematized periodization*."[3] As they encompass the history of (sound) cinema, series (of series) could dialogue with each other, reveal more of their specificity, and fit together like the tiles of a roof. An unfurling of the multiple times first envisioned by Fernand Braudel, the *history in series* is, first and foremost, a radical refutation of the illusory claims of a total history (of sound cinema). To postulate *the analysis of series,* then, does in no way consist in segmenting history in ever smaller units under cover of a fallacious precision on the part of the historian. Nor does it amount, accordingly, to the constitution of finer and finer slices of history (as when we talk of "slices of life") impervious to related series. In the 1970s, François Furet expressed this very clearly:

> Serial history ... [...] describes continuities in the discontinuous mode ... [...] Since, by its very nature, it distinguishes the different levels of historical reality, it must by definition destroy any pre-established conception of a "global" history: for it questions the very postulate of a supposedly homogeneous and identical evolution of all the elements within a society. [...] the result is also an atomization of historical reality into such distinct fragments that the classical claim of history to be able to grasp reality in a global way has been called into question. [...] That is not to say that it should limit itself to the microscopic analysis of one single chronological series; it can bring several such series together and at that point offer interpretations of a system, or a sub-system.[4]

Thinking the history of cinema and its series involves, following Michel Foucault, a refusal of the "total description [that] draws all phenomena around a single center."[5] Ultimately, this implies that a breach is made in the history of twentieth-century arts where cinema, established arts, entertainment, *technique, art,* and *(popular) cultural practices* should all have their place since, as Paul Veyne has vigorously pointed out, "it is impossible to decide that one fact is historic and that another is an anecdote deserving to be forgotten, because every fact belongs to a series and has relative importance only within its series."[6]

As a plural discipline, the history of cinema calls for *series (of series)*. In this sense, André Gaudreault's premise of a history of cinema that would (also) be *the history of cultural series* seems wise. By focusing on the close ties that firmly bind together the "singing and talking pictures" of the 1910s to *café-concert* shows in France, I want to avoid the strict causality between the (relative) failure of the former and the (partial) decline of the latter. I also want to avoid, in Marc Bloch's words, "confusing ancestry with explanation," to instead look at the history of "talking screenings" in the silent era in a new light.[7] Accordingly, my attention here will essentially concentrate on the almost unfailing ties linking these two elements of a cultural series: the Gaumont phono-scenes and the (song-based) shows of Parisian *cafés-concerts*.

The Decline of *Cafés-Concerts* and the (Relative) Failure of Gaumont's Phono-Scenes: The Event and the Series

At the dawn of the 1910s, cinema seemed to be shaken by a seismic upheaval without an epicenter. Film, both as an art and as an industry, was torn in every aspect and affected by deep movements, although no major event seemed to be at the origin of these shifts. There were multiple tremors, which varied in their amplitude and consequences. The first corporate periodicals appeared (*Phono-Ciné-Gazette, La Revue du Phonographe et du Cinématographe,* then *Ciné-Journal*), the *film d'art* seemed to have a bright future, the film industry was being structured and gradually moved away from the popular venues that had accommodated screenings in their programs since 1903. In 1908, in the middle of the turmoil, Gaumont published a catalog almost entirely devoted to its "films for talking shows" and to the Chronophone, the synchronization system (for sound and image) it had developed in its laboratories. Journalists, scientists, or exhibitors agreed on the extreme technical perfection of the process. Given this reception, the enigma posed by the (relative) failure of the Chronophone seems to have much to do with the larger troubled context of the years 1905–1910. By contrast to a company such as Pathé and its "phonocinematographic scenes," Gaumont did not randomly scatter its "singing and speaking" pictures through catalogs devoted to its silent production. This privileged treatment reveals the high importance then attached by Léon Gaumont to phono-scenes.

In the Gaumont catalogs, one finds representative scenes from theater, popular song, and opera classics next to each other without any apparent hierarchy, as noble and less noble genres were featured on the list of phono-scenes for sale. By juxtaposing opera excerpts and popular tunes, Gaumont apparently performed an audacious balancing act between high-flown bombast and naughty remarks. This disparate, composite nature of the catalogs directly came down from the sometimes mixed programs of *cafés-concerts*, which brought to the same stage completely different genres and a variety of shows. Although Gaumont would have it differently, the Chronophone thus came into direct competition with the *cafés-concerts,* the very places that had boosted the development of the cinematograph.[8] Tapping directly into the *café-concert* repertoire, Gaumont (which was, literally, *stealing the show from them*) seemed assured of the success of its "singing and speaking pictures" in 1908. Despite the fact that the company announced "additions of ever more artistic topics to the catalogue," it probably disregarded the debates that spread across entire pages of newspapers at the time. Coming from the most ardent advocates of theater and cinema as an art, these journalistic denunciations targeted the *café-concert* spectacles from which the phono-scenes evidently drew their inspiration.

From January 1907 on, *Phono-Ciné-Gazette* (founded in 1905 by Edmond Benoît-Lévy) echoed the statements made in *L'Intransigeant* or *La Patrie.* Following the "changing tastes of the audience," concerned about keeping fares low, cinema had by then become a formidable competitor for theater as well as *cafés-concerts.* In mid-January, Fernand Divoire noted in *Phono-Ciné-Gazette* that "theaters are preoccupied by the competition of the cinematograph, just as they were by the development of *cafés-concerts,* without being able to act on it."[9] Still, in a particularly unfavorable context, a somewhat paradoxical alliance was sealed between theaters and the cinematograph despite the fact that they were then avowed enemies. Without any formal understanding between theater directors and film exhibitors, the former applauded the fatal blow that the development of the cinematograph might strike to the *cafés-concerts.*[10] The success of the cinematograph benefited theater directors at least on this account: *cafés-concerts,* whose expansion they had never been able to prevent ever since their appearance in the first half of the nineteenth century, now had a rival by no means insignificant.[11] Theater or cinematograph owners, whether fierce advocates of the *authentic* repertoire or of young cinema, all concurred in welcoming such competition. This compelled *cafés-concerts* to offer a more "high-brow" type of entertainment, such as operettas, a (popular) genre socially more acceptable than the traditional potpourris commonly associated with fairgrounds. From then on, the *cafés-concerts* looking for respectability excluded coarseness and biting taunts, which were too often directed at the Church and at the homeland. Instead, they partook in the larger circulation of serious plays *for the people.* Established newspapers, in a particularly condescending and elitist manner, occasionally praised the concern on the part of some great artists to share their (noble) art with the people. Around 1908, *Le Temps, Le Figaro,* and *Comoedia,* until then the eulogists of a culture for the elite, joined in the chorus in stating the benefits of a popularization of the classics.[12]

The newly formed contacts between a so-called popular theater and a repentant *café-concert* were reviled by filmgoers. On September 1, 1908, *Ciné-Journal* attached great importance to the stir caused among cinematograph owners by a decree promulgated on August 10. The newspaper mentioned a passage in the official text which stated that "establishments have been categorized along different lines than those in the 1898 ordinance, which divided them between theaters and *cafés-concerts.*" Henceforth, they would be distinguished "based on the dangers which installations and stage facilities could present."[13] For the journalists of *Ciné-Journal,* the ordinance stated in black and white that theater and the *café-concert* were equals. For the advocates of the cinematograph, the confusion between theater and *café-théâtre,* which was already perceptible in the programs offered by the establishments in question, had been made effective with the promulgation of the August 10 ordinance. Georges Dureau could then take a malicious pleasure in writing that "theater and *café-concert* are one and the same thing."[14] He then denounced the hypocrisy of the not-so-subtle opponents of cinematograph who dared question its morality while they themselves assiduously attended ghastly locales. In a June 11, 1909, *Ciné-Journal* editorial, Georges Dureau drew a clear boundary between cinema and theater. In his manifesto, the breakup was complete:

> The daily press, as the righter of wrongs that it is, does not fail to periodically rise up against what it pompously calls the immorality of the cinematograph. [...] Since [proper publications] are entrusted with the preservation of French taste, they lament the fact that the public stray away from theaters and instead go see a few films in the land of silence, in the delight of expressive gestures and suggestive landscapes. [...] This last Sunday, as a good Frenchman who knows what he is worth, I went to the *café-concert.* The theater—one of the finest in its category— was full of people who had come for some entertainment and were sucking cherries "after grinding" all week. There was no film screening. On the other hand, the comic of the house gave as his reference the most remarkable Parisian brand of smut. The more the singers and storytellers stressed how filthy their tirades were, the happier ladies and girls (this was a family outing) seemed. There was no embarrassment felt whatsoever in this sickening atmosphere. Here was our pleasant bourgeoisie in their Sunday best, elegantly dressed, comfortably moving about in this rottenness. [...] But lo and behold! Of this phenomenal stupidity, of this pornography with which any spirituality is incompatible, no mention is made in the great, educational press. It draws revenue from the press releases of these greasy spoons, it has easy access to them, which exempts it from hailing them as immoral. To this press, all bells are made of silver, and they ring alike to its ears; the *café-concert* and theater are but one and the same—great—art. [...] And as a means of diversion, [the newspapers] turn against cinema. [...] The inevitable neutrality [of the screenplays] removes every element that could make film pernicious and necessarily opposes it to the pornography which thrives in *cafés-concerts.* Moreover, art cinematograph is in the air, and success will go more and more to subtle comedy, sober, well-acted drama, travelogues and reports on great events. If the smut of a few greasy spoons suffers from this . . . all the better![15]

In the Land of Silence and Cinematographic Art

The "Sensational Premiere of *L'Assassinat du Duc de Guise*" marked, for the editorial staffs at the *Phono-Ciné-Gazette* and *Ciné-Journal,* the birth of a "new cinematographic art" and an "artistic cinema." In December 1908, Edmond Benoît-Lévy greeted the return "of these spectators who had not been to the cinematograph since the first shows at the Café de la Paix and could not imagine what progress had been made in the past few years."[16] In September 1908, *Ciné-*

Journal founder Georges Dureau had already pointed in that direction when he gave a first review of the short history of the cinematograph. In his opinion, up to that point, spectators had been under the almost hypnotic spell of the invention of moving pictures and could satisfy themselves with "the pranks of a *Toto Gâte-Sauce*, the frantic chases popularized by the Pathé company, dramas galore, various, more or less colored extravaganzas, comedies and spectaculars, travelogues and news."[17] This, he thought, was no longer the case. Two months before the release of *L'Assassinat du Duc de Guise*, Georges Dureau did not deny his liking for "on-location pictures," but could not but

> praise the relations between Cinema and real Theater because, by getting closer to drama and art, screenplays as well as the artists who perform them will necessarily be ennobled. There Cinema, once confined to mediocre aspirations, will gain a new dignity.[18]

On-location pictures, subtle, well-acted comedies, news, meticulous set design and scripts, there was the land of cinematographic silence dreamt of—in these very terms—by the director of *L'Organe hebdomadaire de l'industrie cinématographique*. Without denigrating "sensational melodramas, blood-and-thunder-type pieces, pleasant vaudevilles or the detective story now brilliantly entering cinema with the adventures of *Nick Carter*, the best private investigator around," Georges Dureau admitted to little affection for cheap comedic effects, wild chases or extravaganzas, in short "cinematography tailor-made to suit the latest fads, not unlike what music-hall revue artists do, inspired by the fleeting trends of Parisian life whose swift, similarly short-lived manifestation it gradually comes to be."[19] Georges Dureau could tolerate certain deviations but refused in a quite radical manner all the films that retained any ties with the world of spectacle and *cafés-concerts*. To this "tailor-made cinematography," to these attractions and films that remained too close to Parisian fairgrounds and cabarets, he now preferred the *Cinema*.[20] Having for some time striven to convince "*people one can associate with*" to become "*ordinary filmgoers*," he "congratulated filmmakers for outdoing one another in artistic endeavor" in early 1910.[21] In the spring of 1911, however, Georges Dureau admitted with a certain disappointment that "people with a somewhat elaborate culture still do not attend our screens very assiduously."[22] "The wave of Cinematographic Art" that he had announced in June 1909 was no longer so high and mighty. In such a climate *in the land of cinematographic silence*, films that were too close to "the smut of greasy spoons" (as were the phono-scenes sold in the 1908 Gaumont catalog) could hardly escape the sarcasm of the advocates of cinematographic art, let alone expect a mild treatment from them.

In 1908, Émile Maugras (a lawyer, associate director at Omnia-Pathé, and president of the Pathé Board for Cinema-Theater) and M. Guégan (doctor of law and director of the national cinema branch of Pathé) wrote a 140-page document tersely titled *The Cinematograph and the Law*. In it, they dealt with a variety of topics, including the necessity to protect the "genius" of the author as well as copyrights, to defend the interests of film producers and stand in the way of counterfeiters and their activities. In order to secure a permanent place for the cinematograph among the fine arts, the emerging cinematographic art (from the point of view of our two lawyers) had to seize every opportunity to radically distance itself from some shows whose reputation was sometimes quite bad. This was, in their opinion, a condition for its survival. Acknowledging the popular roots of the cinematograph (its cheapness, its penchant for simple stories with a swift resolution, etc.), Maugras and Guégan nevertheless saw in it (in contrast to theater and literature) the benefit of an *added moral value:*

> Cinematography has so far been as moral as it gets, never will you find improper scenes and dubious situations in it. It seems as though this art, in the midst of the ever-increasing immorality surrounding theater, had sought to free itself from the depraved tastes and dangerous ideas of modern literature. Cinematographic scenes are pantomimes, but short ones, admirably performed, always honestly executed, often fine in spirit. [. . .] In these conditions, it seems even easier for us to count among the arts these cinematographic films whose triumph owes as much to the perfection of their scenes or landscapes as it does to the morality of the shows.[23]

In 1908 (yet again), when the respective interests of Pathé and Gaumont seemed to lead the two powerful companies on the way to an art cinema, an Italian poet much admired by Guillaume Apollinaire wrote a highly lyrical text—Ricciotto Canudo urged *the cinematograph to triumph.* The poet had firm hopes, but then went on to write that "the cinematograph is not art yet, as it lacks the elements of typical choice, of plastic *interpretation* as opposed to the *copy* of a subject. *Cinematograph is therefore not an art, as it stands today.*"[24] When he predicted the triumph of the cinematograph, Ricciotto Canudo confirmed the divorce between a cinematographic art and a cinematographic attraction, between an art cinematograph and variety shows. Incidentally contemplating the seventh art as part of a series (of series), the poet's article finalized the division whose seeds were already contained in the editorials of *Ciné-Photo-Gazette* or *Ciné-Journal*—on the one hand, a plastic Art in movement, cinema; on the other hand, filmed theater, or the word:

> And this expression of art will conciliate the Rhythms of Space (plastic Arts) and the Rhythms of Time (Music and Poetry). Theater has until now enacted this conciliation; yet it was ephemeral because the plastics of Theater is closely tied to that of actors, and is accordingly always very diverse. The new expression of art should be precisely quite the contrary—*a Painting and a sculpture developing over time,* just as Music and Poetry coming to life, imparting their rhythm to the air during the time of their performance. The Cinematograph (whose name it is pointless to change, although it is not a nice one) shows the way. A genius could create a tremendous wave of new aesthetic emotions with a *plastic Art in movement.*[25]

In 1908, Ricciotto Canudo invented silent cinema.

TRANSLATED BY FRANCK LE GAC AND WENDY SCHUBRING

Notes

1. Lucien Febvre, *Combats pour l'histoire* [1952] (Paris: Armand Colin, 1992), 42.

2. Gilles Deleuze, *Foucault* (London: Athlone Press, 1988).

3. "Travailler sur une problématique plutôt que sur une période ou, plutôt, ne travailler sur une période que si elle provient d'une *périodisation problématisée*." André Gaudreault, "Les *Vues cinématographiques* selon Georges Méliès, ou: comment Mitry et Sadoul avaient peut-être raison d'avoir tort (même si c'est surtout Deslandes qu'il faut lire et relire) . . . ," in *Georges Méliès, l'illusionniste fin de siècle?* ed. Jacques Malthête and Michel Marie (Paris: La Sorbonne Nouvelle/Colloque de Cerisy-la-Salle, 1997), 117. Gaudreault's piece in its entirety revolves around the question that opens this article: *Thinking the history of cinema?* Moreover, Rick Altman himself has already proposed that we think of film history in different terms in "Penser l'histoire du cinéma autrement: un modèle de crise," in *Vingtième siècle* 46 (1995), 65–74. *Thinking history*: admittedly, the issue has been preying on the "New History" for almost half a century now.

4. François Furet, "Quantitative Methods in History," in *Constructing the Past: Essays in Historical Methodology,* ed. Jacques Le Goff and Pierre Nora (Cambridge: Cambridge University Press and Éditions de la Maison des Sciences de l'Homme, 1985), 21–22. This term of "series" here is not without correspondence with the (precise) meaning Foucault gives it in *The Archaeology of Knowledge* and *The Order of Things.*

5. Michel Foucault, *The Archaeology of Knowledge,* trans. A. M. Sheridan Smith (London: Tavistock, 1972), 10.

6. Paul Veyne, *Writing History,* trans. Mina Moore-Rinvolucria (Middletown, Conn.: Wesleyan University Press, 1984), 22.

7. Marc Bloch, *The Historian's Craft* (New York: Vintage Books, 1953), 32.

8. I went into more detail about the correlations between phono-scenes and the staging of the shows in *cafés-concerts* in an article for the Spanish periodical *Archivos.* Choosing three phono-scenes from the Gaumont catalogs (*Le Frotteur de la Colonelle* [Polin, n° 134, cat. 1908], *Questions indiscrètes* [Mayol, n° 154, cat. 1908], and *Le Vrai jiu-jitsu* [Dranem, n° 167, cat. 1908]), I analyzed, among other things, a common concern to "include" spectators in the show.

9. Fernand Divoire, "Cinéma et théâtre," *Phono-Ciné-Gazette,* 15 January 1907, 32.

10. Given the prominence of songs and music in the programs of Parisian *cafés-concerts* (whose expansion took place in the first half of the nineteenth century), along with the use of a platform, the *cafés-chantants* were renamed *cafés-concerts* around 1860. From then on, the *customers* of the *cafés-chantants* became the *spectators* of the *cafés-concerts.* On the history of the *café-concert,* there is a reference that in my opinion cannot be ignored: André Chadourne's *Les Cafés-Concerts* (Paris: Ed. Dentu, 1889). Almost 400 pages long, André Chadourne's work broaches the phenomenon of the *café-concert* from a variety of angles. It provides a historical account, while paying as much attention to clauses in artists' contracts and to their salary as it does to the works and their direction or to copyright and censorship. More recently, Lionel Richard published a booklet on the different types of cabarets in Europe: *Cabarets, cabaret* (Paris: Plon, 1991). Also see Georges d'Avenel, *Le Mécanisme de la vie moderne* (1902); Edmond and Jules de Goncourt, *Idées et sensations* (1893); Alfred Delvau, *Les Plaisirs de Paris (Guide Pratique)* (1867); Jules Lemaître, *Impressions de théâtre* (1900); as well as articles in *Comoedia, Le Figaro, Le Temps, Phono-Ciné-Gazette* and *Ciné-Journal* (published roughly between 1890 and 1915). Moreover, Jacques Deslandes and Jacques Richard's *Histoire comparée du*

cinéma, 2 vols. (Tournai: Casterman, 1966–68), and Jean-Jacques Meusy's *Paris-Palaces* (Paris: Éditions du CNRS, 1995) deal with the cinematograph as a feature of the Parisian *café-concert* programs.

11. See for example François Vallery, "La fin du beuglant," *Phono-Ciné-Gazette*, 1 July 1908, 644.

12. For more information on the programs of the theaters between 1906 and 1910, see *Le Temps, Le Figaro,* or *Comoedia.* See also articles published in *Le Figaro* on 8 January 1908, as well as Adrien Bernheim, "Trente ans de theater," 5 June 1907, 6.

13. All these quotations are drawn from the same article, which appeared in *Ciné-Journal:* "Le Nouveau régime des Théâtres et Cinématographes," 1 September 1908, 4–5 (unsigned).

14. Georges Dureau, "Littérature de Bouis-Bouis et cinématographe," *Ciné-Journal,* 5 June 1909, 1–2. See also Georges Dureau, "Le Cinéma et le théâtre," *Ciné-Journal,* 15 September 1908, 1–2.

15. Dureau, "Littérature de Bouis-Bouis et cinématographe," 1–2.

16. Calling *Le Temps, Gil-Blas, Le Matin, Comoedia,* and *Le Gaulois* as witnesses, Edmond Benoît-Lévy opened the columns of his newspaper to editorialists traditionally hostile to the cinematograph, Jules Clarétie and Adolphe Brisson among others. Bringing a dissonant note in an apparent unanimity, Victor Jasset would not say in 1911 that the *Film d'Art* was the historical landmark or turning point in "the early 1910s." See Edmond Benoît-Lévy, "Une première sensationnelle," *Photo-Ciné-Gazette,* 1 December 1908, 804–806; "M. Clarétie et le cinématographe," *Ciné-Journal,* 26 November 1908, 5–7; "Ce que M. Brisson pense du Film d'art," *Ciné-Journal,* 10 December 1908, 7–9; Victor Jasset, "Etude sur la mise en scène," *Ciné-Journal,* 21 October–25 November 1911, reprinted in Richard Abel, *French Film Theory and Criticism, 1907–1939: A History/ Anthology,* vol. 1 (Princeton: Princeton University Press, 1988), 55–58.

17. Georges Dureau, "Le Cinéma et le théâtre," 1–2.

18. Ibid., 2.

19. Ibid., 1–2.

20. In this respect, the trouble with an *artisan* such as Georges Méliès in the eyes of the devotees of cinematographic art was probably the fact that he primarily presented himself as an unparalleled *cameraman.* Approaching Méliès's few texts and filmed work from that angle would probably provide additional insights into them. See for instance Georges Méliès, "Les vues cinématographiques," *Annuaire général et international de photographie* (Paris: Librairie Plon, 1907), 363–392. This text is translated in Abel, *French Film Theory and Criticism,* 35–47.

21. Georges Dureau, "Soignons le public," *Ciné-Journal,* 16 January 1910, 1–2.

22. Georges Dureau, "Le Cinématographe, Théâtre du peuple," *Ciné-Journal,* 20 May 1911, 1–4.

23. Émile Maugras and M. Guégan, *Le Cinématographe devant le droit* (Paris: V. Giard and E. Brière, 1908). Many thanks to André Gaudreault, who loaned me a copy of this book.

24. Ricciotto Canudo, "Lettere d'arte. Trionfo del cinematografo," *Il Nuovo giornale* (Firenze), 25 November 1908; reprinted in Ricciotto Canudo, *L'Usine aux images* (Paris: Séguier/Arte éditions, 1995), 27.

25. Canudo, 24–25.

Part Two: *Sound Practices in Production*

7   Dialogues in Early
Silent Sound Screenplays:
What Actors Really Said

Isabelle Raynauld

Commonly described as being "before the talkies," the films produced between 1895 and 1929 have long been considered silent or without sound. If there is some truth to this statement, if only from a purely technical vantage point, it is nonetheless false from the vantage point of narrative. In fact, this essay will demonstrate that, even if films were projected without integrated synchronous sound,[1] the presumed silent stories told were actually happening in a sound world and not in a "deaf world." In other words, silent stories took place, intra- and extra-diegetically, in a hearing world. The films not only represented sound, the act of hearing and of listening in many inventive ways, but also showed silence, as well as noisy and talky situations.[2] It can be said with certainty that the writers and directors of early cinema used the dramatic potential of sound to create complex stories.

Certain myths, assumptions, and preconceived ideas about silence, improvisation, deafness, hearing, and, more specifically, dialogue in silent films, therefore, demand interrogation. Why choose to have characters speak, if the spectators cannot hear them? What exactly are they saying? Why is it still so often repeated in film histories that actors discussed unrelated topics while filming, that they improvised everything, talked about what they would eat after the shoot, or commented on an actress's looks while filming a death scene? How were spectators led to believe that what was said in a silent film was not important, that the spoken word was of no value? If indeed this had been the case, why wouldn't the screenwriters, directors, and actors have done away with dialogue altogether?

Much of my previous research on early screenplays has focused on texts for which the films have been lost. Over the past three years, however, I have been able to do a comprehensive study of original screenplays and films written and shot in France between 1895 and 1915. In searching for sound references, I have identified more than 3,616 different sound occurrences in a total of 4,934 Pathé and 414 Méliès synopses and screenplays examined.[3] It is important to note that out of the 5,348 titles inventoried, 1,588 had no script or synopsis attached to them because the subjects were *actualités,* sports and travel. It also means that out of the remaining 3,346 Pathé scripted titles and stories, I found as many as

1,925 to be in fact what I will term "early sound screenplays." Also, the Méliès database revealed that out of 414 titles, 217 were narratively speaking sound-dominated screenplays. This means that on average, 57 percent of these texts contained explicit references to numerous sound events, many of which used sound as a crucial dramatic element to tell the story. In addition, I was able to systematically pair several screenplays and films, and submit them to a comparative analysis. This confirmed that the dialogues in silent screenplays were not just calligraphic entertainment for the reader's eye but were indeed lines intended to be performed by the actors. As a matter of fact, describing filmmaking in 1907, Gene Gauntier wrote: "If the director wished certain words to register, they were enunciated slowly and distinctly, leaving no doubt of what they were in the spectator's mind."[4]

The results of this research reveal a paradox: early film characters were neither deaf nor mute: they spoke, but even more importantly, they could hear. The fact that the vast majority of popular silent photoplay characters were not deaf and that the mise-en-scène often relied on sound information as a motivation for action opens up a whole new way of perceiving the so-called silent cinema.[5] Moreover, this may explain why a majority of adaptations originated from the repertoire of the stage,[6] despite the belief, in France as well as in the U.S.A., that "stage is all talk, screen is all images." As Rick Altman also has pointed out: "The term silent drama, stressing the contrast between dialogue-rich theater and dialogue-poor cinema appears in virtually all the professional publications of the period as well as in popular discourse."[7] What becomes clear is that the relationship between words and images is very different in early cinema mise-en-scène: sound is not only present, it is *represented* in novel and unique ways. Instead of doing away with sound entirely, the early cinema writers and filmmakers found a chorus of strategies to make sound be *heard inside* the story and be seen on the screen.

Essentially, the verbal and auditory context of the drama, its aural potential, is and always has been prominent in cinema ever since Méliès.

Here are two short (!) examples taken respectively from Méliès' Star Film and Pathé screenplays:

> The cook who hears his boss's footsteps approaching because he heard the sound of broken dishes hides in the pantry.[8]

Now the Pathé:

> He goes to listen through his door and hears with fear a series of gun shots.[9]

From a dramaturgical point of view, what we see in early "silent" stories is that if a character can hear, he can usually also react, on screen, to a sound happening off-screen.[10] More importantly, because he/she can hear, the character becomes the spectator's delegate in the story: by his posture and gestures, he/she signifies to the spectator that he/she has heard something. This also serves to explain why more than half of the early screenplays submitted to analysis tell stories that revolve around "sound events" in the diegesis. By "sound event" I mean: an action or event that provides narrative information and/or changes the situation and the course of the action by moving the story forward. According to the statistics generated by my still growing database, at least 2,142 screenplays, dated between 1896 and 1915, explicitly refer to essential intra-diegetic sound events and information, on and off screen.[11] As many as 3,616 sound occurrences have been inventoried. For the purpose of this study, these sound occurrences have been divided into fourteen categories, beginning with *noise, screams, silence, hearing, listening, singing, music,* and *dance.* In the dialogue section, several different speaking postures were identified, namely: *to announce, to ask, to call, to command, to laugh,* and, of course, *to speak.* It is important to note that, as the inventory of screenplays continues, these numbers keep growing. Also, what still needs to be done is a narrative hierarchy of the sound occurrences: it would be very interesting, for instance, to differentiate the minor sound occurrences in the storytelling from the crucial narrative sound events in all the screenplays.[12]

At the time of the release of these films, many spectators complained that what was said by the actors should have been heard (i.e., understood).[13] Writers also were quick to conclude that if dialogue couldn't be heard, it meant that "silent" cinema was deficient and lacking. This perception is still prevalent today. However, as the remainder of this study will show, this notion of early cinema as "deficient" is far removed from its fundamental narrative and dramatic modus operandi. It is as much a misconception to consider "silent" cinema as lacking sound as it is to believe, for example, that deaf people are mentally deficient.

The following anecdote may shed a light on the origin of our belief that early actors said inconsequential things on screen. In my family, the majority of my aunts, uncles, and cousins were born deaf. We have grown up together communicating with whatever we had—arms, hands, lips, ears, bodies—that made sense to the other. When we were little, my cousins tried to read my lips, while I watched their hands gesture and listened to their fragmented sounds. As we looked at each other intensely, in my head I struggled to construct words, sentences, and intentions while they tried to figure out my emotions and imagine my voice by touching my throat with their hands. It is what Oliver Sacks has aptly and beautifully called the process of *seeing voices.*[14] I was curious to learn about their "silent" world because I wanted to play and interact with them, whereas they had to learn to lip read and to speak out loud in order to function in the hearing world. To this day our New Year's Eve parties are extremely lively but quite silent! All that you hear when you arrive at a party where the majority speaks in sign language are occasional screams and exclamations and the sounds that hands and arms make, while signing emphatically on well-ironed shirts and dresses. All that you see is a crowd of people who tap on each other's shoulder or leg all the time to keep the contact going, while looking at each other intensely, because, as the saying goes "what a deaf person doesn't see he doesn't get."

Interestingly enough, it is the deaf spectators of early cinema who apparently signaled certain discrepancies between words and images to the exhibitors when, for instance, they broke out in laughter on occasions in the middle of dramatic scenes. Because they could lip read, they apparently saw actors crack lines like "Ed, your hat's on crooked" or "Watch out! you're backing up into the goldfish!"[15] However comical, this anecdote has been remembered, amplified, and repeated as if it applied to all the films of the silent era. Needless to say, such an anecdote has proved to be quite detrimental to our perception of the early fiction films.[16]

Whether or not this ad-libbing anecdote reported by deaf spectators was an isolated event or a common practice is unclear. Still, if in fact this was the case, the actors quickly stopped talking nonsense and learned their lines. As professional stage actors rapidly replaced the amateurs and the "unknowns," the professionals requested "roles" instead of being cast only as "types." This shift from an amateur to a professional approach to making movies corresponds to the extremely rapid standardization of the industry in the late 1900s and early 1910s. As the practice of writing scripts rapidly expanded, so did the writing of *dialogue*. Not only were lines pre-scripted for intertitles, but the lines to be spoken by the actors became an important part of the standard screenplay. Of filming in Ireland during the summer of 1911, Gene Gauntier says:

> We always used a brogue in our dialogue, and one who has not had the experience cannot know how it helped us to acquire the true Irish gestures and characteristics. All actors are very susceptible to environment and unconsciously take on the "feel" of their surroundings. Living out here among the peasants, far from any town or modern conditions, seeing and hearing none but these isolated folks of the Gap region [County Kerry], we were all near to becoming Irish ourselves.[17]

As is still a common practice today, depending on the desired length of the scene, the director would ask the actors either to expand on the dialogue or to keep it short, using as few words as possible. This is not to say that they *improvised* lines. In fact, most screenplays contain detailed lines and most often look like this sample Pathé example:

> He puts a knee down on the ground: "I love you!" "No sir, we don't come in like that in a young woman's home." [. . .] But Jean pushes her back: "Unfortunately you brought me to this. Go away, you misguided me!" [. . .] She lifts herself a little and says: "Forgive me, my John, I never loved anyone but you.[18]

Indeed, early screenwriting manuals, in both France and the U.S.A.,[19] actually insist on the importance of not writing *too much* dialogue, as it was said to slow down the action. For early screenwriting manuals do not proscribe dialogue altogether—which may seem surprising, as writers were dealing with a supposedly nonspeaking medium. Instead, the manuals and specialized articles only stress the importance of "limiting" the use of words.

While the French insist on creating "strong characters," the Americans encourage showing emotion through action. They explain how to visualize a situation but insist that the story be believable, natural, and realistic.[20] Naturalness, being and looking natural, comes from motion. To permit the spectators to "see voices," the actors were thus required to move their lips: in short, they had to speak. The spectators were then free to imagine phantasmagorical voices and make the characters say what they felt was appropriate in the context of the scene. The deaf call this "eye-music."[21]

This may help explain why the first talking movies, after the novelty had worn off, proved to be somewhat of a turn-off for a large segment of the audience. After having fantasized for years about hearing actors speak, they heard voices that did not seem to "stick" to the actors. Hence all the savory anecdotes relating the spectators' horror upon hearing that their favorite leading man's voice had none of the virility of his (silent) screen persona, or had a strange, unattractive accent. The actors' voices were rarely as seductive as the imaginary voices—what Sacks[22] calls "phantasmal voices"—each spectator had formed in his/her mind. The "real" dialogues were most often found to be drier than what had been imagined. The other disappointment was born out of the lack of sound perspective: a character far away in the background seemed to be speaking in the spectator's ear—that is, too close to him/her. The discrepancy between the "phantasmal" and the "real" was such that spectators were led to believe that the sound dialogues they now could hear came from "talkie screenplays." Therefore, if these false-sounding lines came from writers, if the actors now had to submit themselves to playing a text, they concluded that they had been much better off before the talkies, when there were no scripts (they thought), no actual dialogues, just "improvisation."

Out of this traumatic shift from "seeing voices" to hearing dialogues emerged two of the most persistent, ill-conceived, and damaging prejudices about screenwriting, dialogue, and action: the first being that screenplays did not exist before the talkies; the second being that even though the actors seemed to be talking on the screen, all they were doing was improvising lines as they went along so as to always be seen "in motion," and that what they were saying wasn't important. In short, the assumption was that improvisation was the golden (and only) rule by which filmmakers swore, and that ultimately improvisation was best.[23]

Verifying these assumptions proved essential if my research was to progress beyond mere hearsay. To this end, I extended my sample of texts and asked a deaf person and professional lip reader to screen more than twenty-five Gaumont films for which the corresponding screenplays were available. The texts were not shown to the subject before the screenings. He was asked to watch the films and to read the actors' lips. Without much surprise, he confirmed what I had long suspected: the characters say the lines that are written in the script. While they often expand upon them, they nonetheless *always* stay in the context of the action, respect the unfolding of the story, and refrain from going into unrelated nondiegetic topics such as the ones mentioned above.

To give an example, the subject viewed *Bébé fait visiter Marseille à son cousin Toto* (Gaumont, 1913). The screenplay comes from the Bibliothèque des Arts du Spectacle (Pavillon de l'Arsenal, Paris) and the film from the Gaumont archives (Paris). This film was chosen for two specific reasons: (1) because of the frontal position of the characters, and (2) because the actors are children. The assumption was that it would be more probable for a child actor to deviate from his lines, if he could, than for an adult. This proved to be incorrect: the child actors of the film say their lines and stay in the context of the action. In short, they act their parts.

The detailed reading of the screenplays revealed that not only are dialogues an essential element of the storytelling practice, but the film subjects themselves very often revolve around sound and speech. Common filmed situations are *trials* (is there anything more talky than a court trial?); *burglaries* during which the sound made by the robbers either scares the family or gets the bad guys caught; stories about *drunks* whose nocturnal noise and delirium wake up a whole house; and *plots based on overhearing* crucial conversations leading to blackmail, listening through closed doors, or eavesdropping from an open window (very common in the silent era screenplays). For example:

> The next day, the Indian, walking about in the woods, overhears the conversation between two robbers discussing how to divide the goods.[24]

Also from the Pathé collection:

> He starts to fall asleep when he suddenly hears, next door, his host and his wife speaking in covered voices and, through an opening in the wooden door he sees the man [. . .] with a big knife shining between his teeth.[25]

Even more striking are the scripts in which off-screen sounds and conversations are the reason for a character to "move" from one shot or scene to the next, the storytellers using this off-screen sound event to change locations and the course of the action. Here are a few examples:

> At the sound of her master's scream the old servant runs in, followed by the terrorists.[26]
> But when the car leaves, the concierge, woken up by the sound, leaves her apartment and catches the robber.[27]
> [H]e lays out on the table the results of his previous robberies (a gold watch and money) when a small noise at his door makes him go into hiding suddenly. [. . .] During that time the tenant comes in, finds his room devastated, the bed in a mess . . . he calls out to the rest of the house's occupants [. . .] policemen arrive.[28]

And one last example:

> When he suddenly hears the voice of his young mistress, he runs in the direction of the voice.[29]

This comparative analysis of screenplays and films, as well as the lip-reading experiment, reveals not only that early cinema characters dialogued but that they also spoke their lines for a number of plausible reasons: (1) early cinema practitioners wanted to rejoin senses from which they had been separated, as Gunning[30] has pointed out (they probably also wanted to perform according to the laws of drama and acting as they knew them); (2) spectators understood even if they could not hear the dialogue, because of the actors' body movements and the spectator's ability to "hear the mind"; (3) the plot often was available to the spectators beforehand (it was common practice to post a synopsis outside the theater[31]); and (4) the emerging art of cinema was coming out of a sound world, not a mute, silent, or deaf one either.

For instance, when the deaf interpreter watched the film *Drames du Pôle* (Gaumont, 1913), a few plot-related elements eluded him; as soon as he read the accompanying booklet, however, all became clear. If seeing a silent movie was perhaps less frustrating an experience for the interpreter than seeing a sound film in which the off-screen sound is not visually signified (for example, if a character does not visually react to off-screen sound), he felt that films produced before the talkies were nonetheless made for and by the hearing world. For this deaf interpreter, the only element the dialogue added was "naturalness" to the situation; the actors articulate well enough to be understood, but more importantly, they move their lips to show they are *talking*. The characters' universe is not a silent world, they do not use sign language, they do not have to look at each other to show that they understand; they look at us, they speak to us eye to eye. It is we, hearing spectators, who temporarily lose our ability to hear. We are the ones suddenly "lacking" a sense, we are struck by deafness as we try to read lips and experience the silent drama. In brief, when we watch a film from the retrospectively called silent era, we are asked *to look at sound and to see voices.*

In conclusion, I wish to point out how much the deaf members of my family have unconsciously brought me to research early cinema and in turn given me the sense to see, read, and apprehend it in a new light. Amusingly, as is so often the case with coincidences and paradoxes, it is because of deaf spectators' reactions to certain badly acted scenes in early cinema that film history needed to be revisited. It is their lip reading ability and people's tendency to generalize a practice from one isolated event that must have mistakenly transformed a viewing anecdote into a film history "certainty." It is also lip reading today that brings me back to a simple yet essential understanding of early cinema screenwriting and acting practices. Sound was an integral part of early cinema's storytelling practice: the "silent era" actor not only had to memorize his pre-scripted lines, but he had to speak his part for the hearing world, *keep his mouth in motion for the spectators to see,* whether they could hear him or not! As for the blind, well . . . I will keep that for a future research topic!

Notes

1. Despite and with all my respect to the important contributions to the field made by Richard Abel, Rick Altman, Martin Marks, Eileen Bowser, and others (see bibliography).

2. On the specific subject of sound occurrences in screenplays written before the talkies, see also Raynauld, "Le son dans les scénarios et les films de Georges Méliès,"

in *Georges Méliès et le deuxième siècle du cinéma* (Paris: La Sorbonne Nouvelle/Colloque de Cerisy-La-Salle, 1997), 201–217; Raynauld, "Lecture des scénarios français et américains avant 1914: rôle du spectateur et du son dans les scénarios 'dits' muets," in *Le cinéma au tournant du siècle* (Cinema at the Turn of the Century), ed. Claire Dupré-La Tour, André Gaudreault, and Roberta Pearson (Québec/Lausanne: Éditions Nota bene/ Payot Lausanne, 1998), 291–302; and Raynauld "Importance, présence et représentation du son dans les scénarios et les films Pathé," in *La firme Pathé Frères, 1896–1914,* ed. Michel Marie and Thierry Lefebvre (Paris: L'Association française de recherche en histoire de cinéma, forthcoming).

3. A computerized database was created, which made it possible to trace the frequent and multiple sound references in the screenplays. The database was compiled by Patricia Blais, Pierre Sidaoui, and Christophe Gauthier at the Université de Montréal. This research was funded by the FCAR (1995–1998) and the CRSH (1998–2001), respectively, of Québec and Canada.

4. My warm thanks go to friend and colleague Herbert Reynolds for this quote. *Blazing the Trail,* typescript, 16; Film Study Center Special Collections, Museum of Modern Art. The published version can be found in "Blazing the Trail," *Woman's Home Companion,* October 1928, 182.

5. This article focuses primarily on dialogues because it is in direct continuation with my previous work that first paid attention to sound occurrences. See endnote 2.

6. Richard Abel, *The Ciné Goes to Town: French Cinema, 1896–1914* (Berkeley: University of California, 1994).

7. Rick Altman, "The Silence of the Silents," *Musical Quarterly* 80, no. 4 (Winter 1996), 669.

8. "Le cuisinier qui entend les pas du patron attiré par le bruit de la vaisselle cassée va se cacher dans le buffet." (Georges Méliès, *La vengeance du gâte-sauce,* in *Catalogue français de la Star film,* 84).

9. "Il va écouter à sa porte et entend avec frayeur une slave de coups de revolver." *Rigadin, garçon de banque,* janvier 1912, in Bousquet, *Catalogue Pathé des années 1896 à 1914 (1912–1913–1914)* (Paris: Éd. Bousquet, 1995), 514.

10. Richard Abel describes and analyzes the use of off-screen sound cues in early Pathé films such as *La Revanche de l'enfant* (1906), *Le Braconnier* (1906), *Un Drame à Venise* (1906), and *Le Petit Ramoneur* (1908)—see Abel, *Ciné Goes to Town,* 131, 147, 185.

11. This database has proved to be of immense value in confirming Tom Gunning's recent statement that silent cinema is without doubt a retrospective concept in film history.

12. When a sound event is a plot point in the screenplay. I wish to thank Henry Jenkins and his Master's students for inviting me to their Media in Transition seminar, discussing this *hierarchical* aspect with me, and offering other inspiring questions and suggestions about the uses of the silent screenplays sound database. Winter 2000, Comparative Media Studies Department, MIT, Boston.

13. As reported by Jacques de Baroncelli in "Pantomime, musique, cinéma," *Ciné-Journal,* 4 December 1915, reprinted in English translation in Richard Abel, *French Film Theory and Criticism, 1907–1929 : A History/Anthology* (Princeton: Princeton University Press, 1988), 125.

14. Oliver Sacks, *Seeing Voices* (New York: Harper Collins, 1990).

15. Croy Homer, *How Motion Pictures Are Made* (New York: Arno Press, 1979; New York: Harper and Brothers, 1918), 144.

16. James P. Kraft—in *Stage to Studio. Musicians and the Sound Revolution, 1890–1950* (Baltimore: Johns Hopkins University Press, 1996)—reminds us of the fact that often small orchestras played mood music during shooting to inspire the actors; in such a context, it is difficult to imagine the actors saying anything *but* their lines.

17. Gene Gauntier, typescript, 118–119. These pages were omitted from the version published in *Woman's Home Companion*. Thanks again to Herbert Reynolds.

18. Pathé, *De l'amour à la mort* (Paris: n.d.), 3 pages. I wish to thank Richard Abel for sending me photocopies of this as well as the following wonderful Pathé screenplays.

19. As a sample of the works consulted in the course of this research, beyond those listed in the bibliography, see Eugène Kress, "Le Scénario," *Cinéma-Revue*, October–December 1913; Americus; "La Technique du scénario," *Le courrier cinématographique*, 10 January–21 February 1914; "Technique du scénario (suite), le fond et la forme," *Le courrier cinématographique*, 17 January 1914; E. J. Muddle, ed., *Picture Plays and How to Write Them* (London: Picture Play Agency, 1911); J. Arthur Nelson, *The Photo-Play, How to Write, How to Sell, Being a Practical and Complete Treatise upon the Form, Structure and Technique of the Modern Motion Picture Play, Together with an Analytical Comparison of Contra-Literary Forms and Structures, an Investigation of Themes and Their Sources. Suggestions Covering How to Sell to the Best Advantage* (Los Angeles: Photoplay Publishing Company, 1913).

20. In *Writing the Photoplay* (1911), E. W. Sargent writes that "a story should unfold naturally."

21. Sacks, 5.

22. Ibid.

23. Among the statements made by earlier film historians about film at the turn of the century, see Lewis Jacobs: "Making movies was not yet an extensive business. A business office, a camera, and enough money to pay for the film and to cover the cameraman's modest salary were the only necessaries." Lewis Jacobs, *The Rise of the American Film* (New York: Teachers College Press, 1978), 9. Such statements often have persisted and long have been used to characterize the entire silent era.

24. "Le lendemain, l'Indien, errant dans les bois, surprend la conversation des deux voleurs qui se disputent leur butin . . . ," *Fierté indienne,* February 1912, in Bousquet, *(1912–1913–1914),* 523.

25. "Il commence à s'assoupir quand il entend, à côté, l'hôte et sa femme chuchoter à voix basse et, par les fentes de la porte, il aperçoit l'homme [. . .] un grand couteau luisant entre les dents." *Histoire de brigands,* February–March 1907, in Bousquet, *Catalogue Pathé des années 1896 à 1914 (1907–1908–1909)* (Paris: Éd. Bousquet, 1993), 8.

26. "Au cri poussé par son maître, la vieille servante accourt, suivie des terroristes." *Charlotte Corday,* Pathé manuscript (Paris: n.d.), 3 pages.

27. "Mais lorsque la voiture s'en va, la concierge, éveillée par le bruit, sort de sa loge et prend le rapin au collet." *Déménagement à la cloche de bois,* Pathé manuscript (Paris: n.d.), 3 pages.

28. Pathé, *À voleur, voleur et demi,* July 1907, in Bousquet, *(1907–1908–1909),* 32.

29. "Lorsque tout à coup il entend la voix de sa petite maîtresse . . . il s'élance du côté de la voix." *Deux bons amis* (3rd version); Pathé manuscript (Paris: n.d.), 3 pages.

30. Gunning, "Doing for the Eye What the Phonograph Does for the Ear," which appears earlier in this volume.

31. I wish to thank Eileen Bowser for this information during the discussion following my presentation at the 1998 Domitor conference.

Bibliography

Abel, Richard. *The Ciné Goes to Town: French Cinema, 1896–1914.* Berkeley: University of California Press, 1994.

Altman, Rick. *Sound Theory / Sound Practice.* New York: Routledge, 1992.

———. "The Silence of the Silents." *Musical Quarterly* 80, no. 4 (Winter 1996), 648–718.

Ball, Eustace Hale. *The Art of the Photoplay.* New York: Veritas Publishing, 1913.

Bousquet, Henri. *Catalogue Pathé des années 1896 à 1914 (1907–1908–1909).* Paris: Éd. Bousquet, 1993.

———. *Catalogue Pathé des années 1896 à 1914 (1912–1913–1914).* Paris: Éd. Bousquet, 1995.

Bowser, Eileen. *The Transformation of the Cinema, 1907–1915.* New York: Scribner's, 1991.

Dench, Ernest A. *Playwriting for the Cinema: Dealing with the Writing and Marketing of Scenarios.* London: Adam and Charles Black, 1914.

Harrison, Louis Reeves. *Screencraft.* New York: Chalmers Publishing, 1916.

Homer, Croy. *How Motion Pictures Are Made.* New York: Arno Press, 1979; New York: Harper and Brothers, 1918.

Jacobs, Lewis. *The Rise of the American Film.* New York: Teachers College Press, 1978.

Kraft, James P. *Stage to Studio. Musicians and the Sound Revolution, 1890–1950.* Baltimore: Johns Hopkins University Press, 1996.

Lore, Colden. *The Modern Photoplay and Its Construction.* London: Chapman and Dodd, 1921.

Lytton, Grace. *Scenario Writing Today.* Boston: Houghton Mifflin, 1921.

Marks, Martin Miller. *Music and the Silent Film / Contexts and Case Studies, 1895–1924.* New York: Oxford University Press, 1997.

O'Dell, Scott. *Representative Photoplays Analyzed.* Los Angeles: Palmer Institute of Authorship, 1924.

Patterson, Frances Taylor. *Scenario and Screen.* New York: Harcourt, Brace, 1928.

Sacks, Oliver. *Seeing Voices.* New York: Harper Collins, 1990.

Sargent, Epes Winthrop. *The Techniques of the Photoplay.* 2nd ed. New York: Chalmers Publishers, 1913.

Weis, Elizabeth, and John Belton, eds. *Film Sound: Theory and Practice.* New York: Columbia University Press, 1985.

8   The First *Transi-Sounds*
of Parallel Editing
Bernard Perron

This essay is the outcome more of a theoretical reflection on early cinema than of historical research. It is meant to expand on the text I wrote for the 1996 Domitor conference about the Pathé Frères company.[1] On that occasion, I gave a comparative analysis of *The Physician of the Castle* (*Le Médecin du château*), a 1908 Pathé production, and *The Lonely Villa* (directed by Griffith in 1909), two films that rely on the farcical, yet terrifying, plot of the family threatened by thieves who have lured the father away from the house beforehand. Taking *The Physician of the Castle* as a paradigm of the state of film narrative at the be-ginning of the system of narrative integration (1908–1915),[2] I have attempted to account for one of the phases in the process of systematization of parallel editing. However, as Richard Abel pointed out in a later discussion, I neglected an essential element, intradiegetic sound. I intend here, therefore, to answer this omission in my analysis of the Pathé film and to consider some more general theoretical propositions.

Referring to Figure 8.1, I will first give a summary of my conclusions on *The Physician of the Castle*. The mode of representation and the articulation of shots in the Pathé film are the product of a theatrical conception. Long shots are ex-plicitly modeled on a proscenium-style theater, and the cuts are largely moti-vated by the entrance or exit of characters. When these entrances or exits occur in depth, they conform to the theatrical convention in which a character leav-ing on the right should also reenter on the right, which prevents the creation of a simple and coherent line of action (from left to right as in Griffith's *The Lonely Villa*, for example). These entrances and exits are punctuated with empty frames creating some distance between the locations of the diegesis. In this re-spect, *The Physician of the Castle* is unable to establish the contiguity of the two rooms of the physician's house it presents to us, namely the living room and the office (see Fig. 8.2). It doesn't connect these two rooms; it juxtaposes them. It is not even able to articulate proximal disjunctions between on-screen (*here*) and off-screen (*there*) spaces in order to, retrospectively, create a parallelism within the same place (of the A1–A2 type) (see Fig. 8.1). Off-screen space remains a vacillating metonymic region that neither surrounds on-screen space nor exerts a continuous pressure on it. Rather, each shot is considered as an autonomous unit, a setting for an event to take place, in short, a scene. The expanse off-screen is not so much spatial (the *there* of a *here*) as narrative. What I call the "off-

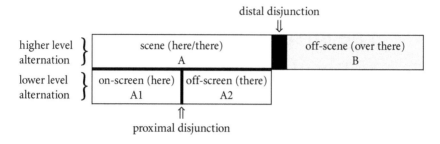

Figure 8.1

screen scene" is this portion of diegetic space that is nonvisible as well as non-contiguous to the setting (*over there*), yet connected to it through the narrative's development.

Because there is always a gap between diegetic spaces, *The Physician of the Castle* articulates distal disjunctions only between a scene (*here-there*) and an off-screen scene (*over there*). Clearly marking, with a car ride and a title ("Arriving at the Castle"), the distance separating the HOUSE from the CASTLE where the physician is lured, the film, in this instance, effortlessly takes advantage of an alternation at a higher level between these two narrative segments (of the A–B type) (see Fig. 8.1). In fact, this alternation is made up of three series:

A) the physician at the CASTLE
B) the wife and the son in the office at the HOUSE; and
C*) the two criminals in the living room at the HOUSE.

If a proximal disjunction had been established, the series A–C* would then have been considered an A1–A2-type alternation. This conception of the scene/*off-scene* correlation could have come about only in light of the knowledge that parallel editing was referred to as "parallel scenes" in 1908 parlance. This does not, however, prevent the Pathé film from situating the locations of the drama and connecting them to one another. Once the terms are set down, the alternation unfolds as follows:

Title: "Arriving at the Castle."
A) CASTLE: gate—The physician's car pulls in (shot 13).
living room—The physician meets with the family; everyone turns out to be in good health (shot 14).
B) HOUSE: office—The physician's wife and his son enter on the right and barricade the door. Staying close to the door, they are all ears (shot 15).
C*) HOUSE: living room—The two criminals enter the living room and prick up their ears in order to locate the office. They exit in the background to the right (shot 16).

8.2a-c. Three frame enlargements from *The Physician of the
Castle* (Pathé, 1908).

B) HOUSE: office—The wife stops listening, but the son stays on his
guard next to the office door. The wife finds the castle's phone
number and calls there (shot 17).
A) CASTLE: living room—The physician is still with the family. A servant
informs him that his wife has called (shot 18).

B) HOUSE: office—The physician's wife on the phone (close shot 19).
A) CASTLE: living room—The physician on the phone (close shot 20).
            living room—The physician leaves the family (shot 21).
            gate—The physician's car pulls away (shot 22).

Regarding Méliès's films and scenarios and the Pathé films before 1914, Isabelle Raynauld has noted that "sound is an integral part of the mise-en-scène and influences the way the story is being told. It is an essential dramatic element of the film narrative in this [silent] period."[3] *The Physician of the Castle* supports this observation. Within the parallel construction just described, we find two major intradiegetic sound events, that is to say, two actions directly related to sound which bring narrative information and change the course of the narrative situation.[4]

The first is undoubtedly the more interesting. It involves the listening done by characters in the HOUSE, which is explicitly visualized in shots 15, 16, and 17 (Fig. 8.2). Among the three authors (Abel,[5] Gunning,[6] and Salt[7]) who have devoted enough attention to *The Physician of the Castle* to be able to describe its action, none has noted this explicit listening despite the fact that it constitutes the cornerstone of this initial larger-scale parallel construction (living room/office). Like the characters' entrances and exits, the visualization of sound permits the gradual investing of the invisible field, as it decenters the image. From this perspective, and to use a Deleuzian expression that Livio Belloï employed in his "Poétique du hors-champ,"[8] while there is no thread uniting on-screen and off-screen spaces yet, there certainly is a "wave" that starts from the scene and connects it to the off-screen scene. The articulation of proximal disjunctions and clear, compact spatio-temporal transitions within the same place may not have been possible yet, as they were difficult for spectators to understand. On the other hand, what I call transi-sounds[9] were quite conceivable (see Fig. 8.3)

The so-called silent cinema—this is a basic fact that needs to be stressed— may not truly appeal to hearing, but it appeals nevertheless to understanding.[10] *The Physician of the Castle* relies on the expectations of an audience versed in theater as well as everyday, ordinary perception of sound. Just as in theater, where an intradiegetic sound process would mark the resonance of hidden rooms, the mise-en-scène in the Pathé film points to the reality unfolding outside the spectators' field of vision and turns the *off-stage* into the *off-scene*.[11] The

TRANSI-SON

higher level ⎫ alternation ⎭	scene (here/there) A	→	off-scene (over there) B

Figure 8.3

sound belongs as much to the here as it does to the there or to the over there. Characters listen to noises produced beyond the stage. The audible, as Mikel Dufresne wrote in his *L'Oeil et l'oreille*, holds two co-present dimensions:

> sound simultaneously invests me from everywhere, surrounds me, incorporates me, and is situated in a given direction which gives some indication as to its source.[12]

Through its spatial range, which exceeds visible information, and the attention given to the localization of its source, sound makes it possible to bridge the gaps separating diegetic spaces. Most of all, it permits the realization of intelligible transitions between these spaces (hence the arrow in Fig. 8.3). In this way, the supposed proximity of the scenes inside the physician's HOUSE (the living room and the office) is established through the actions of the characters as they prick up their ears toward an off-scene source. The sound event sets up the terms of the parallelism. This is a clue given to the audience so that they can understand the film and fill in the gaps between shots or scenes. In *The Physician of the Castle*, the action of listening literally serves as a point of *transi-sound* (hence the gray dot, which both exceeds and incorporates on-screen space in Fig. 8.3).

The term *transi-sound* permits one to emphasize both the idea of passage and the importance of sound. In my opinion, this casts a new light on Eileen Bowser's reflection on the systematization of parallel editing in cinema:

> It seems significant to me that the early examples of parallel editing deal with adjacent spaces and not distant ones. This is evidently the first step in the development of the concept.[13]

Elsewhere, she notes that several of these early examples "might be interpreted as the need to show visual equivalents of sounds, sounds to which the characters react."[14] The parallel scenes in *The Mill Girl*, the 1907 Vitagraph film which Bowser studied in detail and from which she drew her conclusions, are eloquent. The action takes place near a window inside and outside a house. Unable to articulate proximal disjunctions, Vitagraph was careful to leave the window of the house outside the field of vision of the audience, as Bowser noted. Like the criminals in *The Physician of the Castle*, the main protagonist of the film moves his hand near his ear in order to listen to outside noises and locate the assailants in the off-scene. As for the assailants, they make noise as they place a ladder against the wall, which earns them a rebuke from their leader who orders silence through gesticulations. The intradiegetic sound encroachment plays an important role here. Again, the parallel structure rests on transi-sounds. This is also the case in another canonical example mentioned by Bowser, Edison's 1907 *The Trainer's Daughter; or, A Race for Love*. Here, the shot of a man who calls jockeys by blowing into a cornet is inserted in a scene at the stable, where said daughter must prepare for the race. In this case, the comprehension of the link between spaces much farther apart from each other is made possible by the reach of the cornet. This type of amplified sound communication[15] leads me to a quick discussion of the second sound event in the parallel structure I have described above.

The second larger-scale parallel structure in *The Physician of the Castle* (HOUSE/CASTLE) stages a suspenseful phone call. This instance also involves another sound device that several other contemporary films have used. It is probably understood at this point that the use of an instrument that makes it possible to transmit sounds from a distance and connect spaces remote from each other perfectly illustrates my point. Accordingly, I will not expand on the representation of phone calls, but I will still segue from Bowser[16] and Gunning[17] to note that the introduction of this new technology allowed for a naturalization of cinema's power to move through time and space. Curiously, it is at this time that Pathé opts for a shift in the space of the scene of *The Physician of the Castle* in order to provide us with two exceptional close shots of the physician and his wife on the phone. The visualization of the act of listening produces a strong dramatic effect. Yet, if all phone conversations were reproduced through parallel editing after 1908, it is well-known that they were initially the product of a theatrical conception. Filmmakers re-created phone calls in long shots by using divided sets or screens, which directly juxtaposed scene and off-scene. In order to express simultaneity, filmmakers did not resort to spatio-temporal transitions between distally disjunct shots but instead used transi-sounds between distinct areas of action. Porter's famous *College Chums* (1907) remarkably exemplifies such a practice. Inside irises positioned at the extremities of the frame and placed above the image of a city, a couple is seen conversing on the telephone. To express their exchange, Porter animates letters, which seem to drift in the air toward the man and the woman, creating a wave connecting the interlocutors. This is a lovely example of a literal transi-sound!

The neologism I have just introduced and the conception I have laid out allow for a better terminology and definition of one of the processes used in early spatio-temporal articulations. Of course, transi-sounds were not the only way to effect passages between two diegetic spaces (some "mute" transitions existed[18]). They were not limited to either parallel editing or early cinema, since they took on more and more importance in cinema as it underwent institutionalization, as well as in sound cinema. Yet we have to reckon that, from 1907–1908 on, the visualization of sound and listening played an important part in the suturing of space (particularly within the same place) and the systematization of parallel editing. In order to see it, one simply had to lend it an ear.

TRANSLATED BY FRANCK LE GAC AND WENDY SCHUBRING

Notes

1. This text was written within the framework of GRAFICS (Groupe de Recherche sur l'Avènement et la Formation des Institutions Cinématographique et Scénique; Research Group on the Creation and Formation of Cinematographic and Theatrical Institutions) at the Université de Montréal, supported by the Conseil de recherches en sci-

ences humaines du Canada (Canadian Council on Research in Human Sciences) and the FCAR fund (Quebec).

2. *The Physician of the Castle* (1908) stands at the cusp of two modes of filming practice: the system of monstrative attractions (1895–1908) and that of narrative integration (1908–1915). See André Gaudreault and Tom Gunning, "Le Cinéma des premiers temps: un défi à l'histoire du cinéma?" in *Histoire du cinema: Nouvelles approches*, ed. Jacques Aumont, André Gaudreault, and Michel Marie (Paris: Publications de la Sorbonne, 1989), 49–63.

3. "Importance, présence et représentation du son dans les scénarios et les films Pathé dits muets," in *La Firme Pathé Frères, 1896–1914*, ed. Michel Marie and Thierry Lefebvre (Paris: L'Association française de recherche en histoire de cinéma, forthcoming).

4. See Isabelle Raynauld, "Présence, fonction et représentation du son dans les scénarios et les films de Georges Méliès (1896–1912)," in *Georges Méliès, l'illusionniste fin de siècle?*, ed. Jacques Malthête and Michel Marie (Paris: La Sorbonne Nouvelle/Colloque de Cerisy, 1997).

5. In *The Ciné Goes to Town: French Cinema, 1896–1914* (Berkeley: University of California Press, 1994), 285. Since he put me on the track of sound by pointing out the listening by the gangsters, it is curious that Abel would not note the importance of sound in this Pathé film, whereas in other instances he makes sure to mention certain "sound cues" (pp. 131, 135, and 147). In any case, he told me after my talk that he had paid more attention to the close shots in the film than to the mise-en-scène of sound.

6. In *D. W. Griffith and the Origins of American Narrative Film* (Urbana: University of Illinois Press, 1991), 190. Although Tom Gunning explained to me at the conference that his analysis concerned the articulation of the shots in *The Physician of the Castle* and not its sound, it is worth noting that when he described the shots in Griffith's 1909 *The Lonely Villa*, Gunning mentioned the sounds heard (p. 198). This is, in my opinion, revealing in terms of the status of the two films and the additional attention received by Griffith's film compared with Pathé's. On this topic, see the introduction to my analysis of *The Physician of the Castle*: "L'alternance du *Médecin du Château* (1908): scène/hors-scène," in *La Firme Pathé Frères*.

7. "The Physician of the Castle," *Sight and Sound* 54 (Winter 1985–86), 284–285.

8. In *Revue belge du cinéma* 31 (1992).

9. I am aware that the translation of my neologism in English does not work as it does in French (where only an "i" is missing in the passage from *transition* to *transi-sons*, while in English "sound" and "-tion" are pronounced quite differently). I still think that the term *transi-sound* expresses the idea that I want to emphasize just as well as, if not better than, does *sound link* or *sound bridge*. The latter terms, whether translated or used in French, emphasize only what serves as a link, not the notion of transition.

10. Translator's note: the French term used in the original text is *"entendement,"* which means "understanding," but is derived from the same root as the verb *"entendre"* (to hear).

11. Patrice Pavis, *Dictionary of the Theatre: Terms, Concepts, and Analysis* (Toronto: University of Toronto Press, 1998).

12. Mikel Dufresne, *L'Oeil et l'oreille* (Paris: Jean-Michel Place, 1991), 86.

13. Eileen Bowser, "Towards Narrative, 1907: *The Mill Girl*," in *Film before Griffith*, ed. J. L. Fell (Berkeley: University of California Press, 1983), 338.

14. Eileen Bowser, "Griffith's Film Career before *The Adventures of Dollie*," in *Film before Griffith*, 370.

15. "We have a *proximal* disjunction any time the audience may assume, from the spatial information provided by the film, a possibility for non-amplified sound or visual communication (the telescope, for instance, is a means of visual amplification while the telephone would constitute a means of sound amplification) between two non-contiguous spaces brought together by editing." In André Gaudreault and François Jost, *Le Récit cinématographique* (Paris: Nathan, 1990), 95.

16. Eileen Bowser, "Le coup de téléphone dans les films des premiers temps," in *Les Premiers ans du cinéma français,* ed. Pierre Guibert (Perpignan: Institut Vigo, 1985), 218–224.

17. Tom Gunning, "Heard over the Phone: *The Lonely Villa* and the de Lorde Tradition of the Terrors of Technology," *Screen* 32, no. 2 (1991), 184–186.

18. In fact, right before the excerpt to *The Physician of the Castle* that I have described, there are direct, "mute" spatio-temporal transitions between the HOUSE and the CASTLE. However, these are two spaces between which the distance has been clearly established.

9 Sound, the Jump Cut, and "Trickality" in Early Danish Comedies

John Fullerton

Consider two brief extracts, the first from *Ingmarssönerna* (*The Ingmarssons*), which premiered in Sweden in 1919, the second from *Tryllekunstneren* (*The Conjurer*), a Danish comedy, which premiered in 1909. Both demonstrate a concern for the ways in which sound may interrelate with editing. In the case of the Swedish film, the extract is taken from the shot series in which the Ingmarssons begin to search for Brita. The action opens as Mistress Märta comes out of a farmhouse. Two servant-girls run into the frame as two farm workers also leave the farmhouse. As Mistress Märta begins to speak to them, the film cuts to a long shot of Lill Ingmar. He is looking toward foreground right, but soon turns to look foreground left as, raising his head, he calls out Brita's name in alarm. The film cuts to an extreme long shot of an empty landscape with trees and hayracks silhouetted on the skyline, then cuts back to Lill Ingmar who, looking agitatedly about, turns and sprints through the gap between two farmyard buildings. Although the shot of the landscape, exposed to produce a silhouette effect, heightens dramatic tension, it also strikingly demonstrates the way in which character subjectivity could be figured by an implied aural cue while being displaced onto the shot of the surrounding landscape. In this process, editing is an important mechanism for securing rhetorical affect through a filmic trope.

In *The Conjurer*, a jump cut, used for comic effect, is retrospectively motivated by an implied aural cue. A landlady is showing the conjurer, standing to the right of her, the apartment that she is trying to interest him in renting. As they talk, she points toward the living room ceiling, whereupon a jump cut "magically" transposes the conjurer to the left of the landlady (Fig. 9.1). She looks about her, turns to the right in a state of confusion, moves to the right, and then turns to face left as, raising her hands in surprise, she discovers the conjurer standing opposite her at left, mid-field center. The landlady clasps her hands together as she registers relief at finding him still in the room. The conjurer leans forward and points to his right ear (Fig. 9.2) to indicate that his sudden transposition in space was motivated by the fact that he is (supposedly) hard of hearing in his right ear. The cut, in this instance, is motivated, with comic effect, by a character drawing attention to the "absence" of sound.

9.1 and 9.2. Frame enlargements, *Tryllekunstneren,* Nordisk Films Kompagni (photographer: Axel Sørensen), 1909.

Both extracts exemplify the way in which a cut may be motivated by sound or its perceived absence. In this essay, I will examine the ways in which implied sound in the diegesis motivates the device of the jump cut for trick effect. Limiting myself to a consideration of surviving Danish comedies in the period up to 1910, I will examine the ways in which sound may be related to what André Gaudreault has termed "trickality," an effect that, achieved through cutting, produces a sudden or unexpected transformation in the diegesis.[1] Since, with one exception, all the surviving films produced by Nordisk Films Kompagni are known to have been photographed by Axel Sørensen (also known as Axel Graatkjær), and are known, in many cases, to have been directed by Viggo Larsen, this group of films more properly represents a subset of a genre whose pertinent characteristic may be defined by the fact that their running time rarely exceeds five minutes. Excluding comedies that may be held outside the Danish archive and the National Film and Television Archive in London, I have viewed 35mm prints of seven surviving films: *Den anarkistens svigermor* (*The Anarchist's Mother-in-Law,* 1906), *Tryllesækken* (*The Magic Sack,* 1907), *Motorcyklisten* (*The Non-stop Motorcycle,* 1908), *Heksen og cyklisten* (*The Witch and the Cy-*

clist, 1909), *Tryllekunstneren* (*The Conjurer,* 1909), *Fabian på rottejagt* (*Fabian Goes Rat-Hunting,* 1910), and *Den nye huslærer* (*The New Teacher,* 1910). My concerns are three in number. The first relates to the way in which sound may have been used in the exhibition context. The second relates to the way in which the jump cut may be motivated by action and gesture, and thus used to imply sound in the diegesis. The third relates to the way in which sound could also be figured in the diegesis through a cut. I will argue that jump cuts and other filmic devices were often motivated by implied sound cues, and that other forms of "trickality" could, on occasion, figure sound.

Sound, the Jump Cut, and the Exhibition Context

The Magic Sack is a comedy that developed from a circus clown routine. The first section consists primarily of an acrobatic routine; the second, inaugurated by a jump cut, introduces the theme of assault on the clowns' bodies. Without a cut, this theme is developed in the third section of the film when one of the clowns hides in a sack. Although this section elaborates the theme of bodily assault, once the clown in checkered costume has stood up the sack containing the other clown, action and jump cut are closely related. As the clown, with outstretched arms, approaches the sack toward foreground right and attempts to embrace it, a jump cut transposes the sack to mid-field left (Fig. 9.3). The clown looks down to register surprise at the disappearance of the sack, then goes over to mid-field right, where he scratches his head, baffled by the apparent ability of the sack to move by itself. The clown turns and, seeing the sack again, points toward it. He crosses over to the sack and, as he is about to embrace it, a further jump cut transposes the sack, still containing the other clown, to mid-field right. The clown momentarily exits frame left then reappears at frame left. Turning and gesturing toward the viewer, he goes over to the jumping sack and as he grabs hold of it, a further jump cut effects the escape of the clown inside the sack, so leaving the sack hanging limply in his hands. As the clown flings the sack across the set, one more jump cut reanimates the sack, now containing the other clown once more. A further series of jump cuts involving both clowns as they console one another brings the film to conclusion.

Two points may be made. First, we can be certain that the series of jump cuts identified in this extract, and indeed in all the Danish films discussed in this essay, are original since, in all instances, the trace of the original splice—a thin white line—can be identified in the upper part of the frame, parallel to the top frame-line. We may observe, therefore, that the process of splicing had been largely standardized not only in those films Larsen directed for Nordisk, but in the group of films as a whole since each cut is consistently spliced. Second, we may propose, on intermedial grounds, that falls and bodily assault would not only have been accompanied by sound effects familiar from circus routines, but that they would probably have been employed, as in circus performances, with near-synchronized precision. Depending on the exhibition venue, therefore,

9.3. Frame enlargement, *Tryllesækken,* Nordisk Films Kompagni (director: Viggo Larsen), 1907.

"trickality" would likely have been accompanied by sound effects similar to those viewers would have encountered at the circus. In this respect, sound and the jump cut would have stimulated a multimedial response in the historical spectator, bringing some of the aural events associated with live circus performance to the experience of viewing the film.

"Trickality" and Action

The second way in which sound was associated with jump cuts involves the use of bodily gesture to represent what, in human interaction, would normally be communicated aurally. In this context, verbal response to a given narrative situation (often involving excitement, fear, frustration or anger) is figured through gesture. What is important here, as distinct from the more general issue of acting in early film, is that such processes, typically, are highly demonstrative. Not only do they respond to sudden changes in narrative situation effected by a jump cut, but they may also arise in response to other forms of filmic manipulation, particularly reverse-action footage. In this context, many examples may be cited from surviving films where action takes on exaggerated charge as a result of narrative mishap or misfortune. Examples include *The Witch and the*

Cyclist, The Conjurer, Fabian Goes Rat-Hunting, and *The New Teacher.* I will examine the opening of *The Witch and the Cyclist.*

The film opens with a man cycling down a country lane at the edge of a wood. Pausing to take a rest, the cyclist settles down on the verge and falls asleep. Suddenly, accompanied by a jump cut, a witch appears, which development marks the transition to what we, retrospectively, understand to be a dream. The witch is standing toward foreground right looking away from the camera in the direction of the approaching cyclist. She holds out her hand to beg from him, but the cyclist, as he approaches, waves his left hand to get her to move out of the way. As he cycles past, the witch tries to grab hold of the cyclist's left hand, but he repels her. The witch raises her right hand to curse him. The cyclist looks back, waves his left arm at her again, then exits foreground left as the witch, waving her stick several times, casts a spell on the cyclist. The film cuts to two reverse-action shots of the cyclist cycling backward, away from the camera in shot 3 and toward the camera in shot 4. There now follows a series of shots in which the cyclist vents his anger at the witch, who casts a further series of spells, all accompanied by jump cuts. In shot 5, the cyclist, now cycling (in reverse motion) backward, enters the shot from foreground left. As he approaches the witch, a jump cut effects the transition to the following shot, in which the cyclist dismounts. He goes over to the verge and lets his bicycle fall to the ground. He turns toward her, then raises and lowers his right arm quickly as he begins to remonstrate with her. After a series of verbal altercations, which become increasingly vehement, the witch, shouting at the cyclist and raising her right arm, casts a spell, whereupon a jump cut, motivated by her speech and action, effects the transition to shot 7 (Fig. 9.4). The cyclist's clothes have been transformed: his leather boots have been replaced by shoes, his Norfolk jacket and trousers have been replaced by an open shirt, a waistcoat, and a pair of patched trousers, and his tweed cap has been replaced by a soft cap. Four more jump cuts occur, in rapid succession, during which the bicycle is transposed from the verge to a tree, the witch "magically" changes her clothes, and the cycle is transposed to the witch, who now mounts it and exits foreground left before the cyclist, standing at foreground left, awakens from his dream as we discover him, after one further jump cut, sleeping on the verge as at the opening of the shot series.

In this extract, jump cuts are used not only to effect sudden transformations in pro-filmic space, an aspect that Gaudeault's study of "trickality" draws to our attention, but are motivated by implied sound cues as the sound of the witch's voice is displaced onto bodily gesture. In this respect, the jump cut, motivated by an implied aural cue, not only effects sudden transformation in the diegesis, but may, on occasion, also effect a development in the filmic discourse, as when reverse-action footage is introduced in the exchange between the cyclist and the witch. We may observe, therefore, that in the context of early Danish comedies, implied aural cues were used not only to motivate transformations in the diegesis through the device of the jump cut, but also to motivate transitions in filmic discourse.

9.4. Frame enlargement, *Heksen og cyklisten,* Nordisk Films Kompagni (director: Viggo Larsen), 1909.

"Trickality" and Sound

Nowhere is the close relation between sound, action, and filmic manipulation more evident than in the closing stages of *The Anarchist's Mother-in-Law,* in the scene where the anarchist, who has been caught flirting with the maid by his mother-in-law and wife, takes his revenge on the mother-in-law. After pursuing the man around the house and down into the street outside, the mother-in-law reenters the living room and, after further misadventure, ends up on the floor propped against a table lying on its side. The son-in-law reenters the living room and, at frame left, waves his left hand forefinger in the air as he decides upon a course of action. He exits frame left and shortly reenters carrying a large box marked "Dynamit" (Dynamite). He puts the box down at foreground left, then moves the box over to foreground right and takes out a canister with a makeshift wick. He places the canister behind the mother-in-law, who, unconscious, is still leaning against the table. Taking out a box of matches, the son-in-law bends down to light the fuse (a small jump in the print indicates that some footage is missing). He backs away from the bomb, steps gingerly in front of the box, and exits frame left. Shortly, the film cuts to two frames that have been treated chemically to denote the initial explosion of the bomb. The first frame, with original splice mark visible toward the top of the frame and

9.5. Frame enlargement, *Den anarkistens svigermor*, Nordisk Films Kompagni (director: Viggo Larsen), 1906.

parallel to the top frame-line (Fig. 9.5), represents the initial burst, and has been treated chemically so that the emulsion is scratched with a 'star burst' effect. The following frame (without a splice) has been similarly treated, after which, a second (original) splice returns us to the living room, where the "remains" of the mother-in-law fall into the room from above the frame-line. Whether intended to represent the sound or flash or, in a process of synesthesia, the sound and flash of the explosion, chemical treatment of the film emulsion bears testimony to the way in which sound could be represented visually on the film strip.

The three processes of filmic manipulation discussed here (the jump cut, reverse-action footage, and chemical treatment of the film emulsion) arise from a desire to imply or figure sound in the diegesis. Argued here is that these processes not only were used to effect transformations in the narrative but, in the case of the jump cut and reverse-action footage, occasioned the displacement of the human voice onto gesture. I have also argued that in the context of film exhibition, projection may have been accompanied by near-synchronous sound effects typical of the circus to promote a multimedial experience of film viewing for the historical spectator. Finally, I have argued that in treating the film emulsion, "trickality" could also, on occasion, figure sound by way of the film discourse itself. While the element of display locates these films firmly within the conventions of the cinema of attractions, in figuring sound through editing,

The Anarchist's Mother-in-Law also exhibits a feature more typical of the later classical cinema. In this respect, the film exhibits hybrid tendencies.

Notes

1. André Gaudreault, "Theatricality, Narrativity, and Trickality: Reevaluating the Cinema of Georges Méliès," *Journal of Popular Film and Television* 15 (Fall 1987), 110–119.

10 Setting the Pace of a Heartbeat: The Use of Sound Elements in European Melodramas before 1915

Dominique Nasta

To date, theoretical surveys of sound elements in silents made before 1915 seem to have been largely conditioned by historical criteria (most of which had purely statistical aims) or by technical parameters related to the synchronizing of real dialogue, prerecorded noises, or quotational and originally composed music. The time has obviously come for a "dynamic, multilevel analysis"—in Rick Altman's terms—of the diegetic and pragmatic aspects triggered by the extremely diversified use of auditive elements in one-reel fiction films, as well as in more complex multiple-diegesis films shot between 1912 and 1915.[1] The tentative analytical strategy I would like to develop in this essay has been limited to a European corpus of melodramas because I gradually realized the particular impact of the European style on the elaboration of complex aural representational worlds. The different series of discussions held during the Fifth Domitor Congress in Washington revealed new insights on the similarities and differences between American and European uses of auditive parameters, be they extra-filmic (accompaniment by noise or music-making, by original music identified and analyzed, or by cue-sheets for illustrated songs) or intra-filmic (markers in the visualized discourse without an aural actualization). Moreover, the debate on the uses of music for accompanying what is commonly coined in the USA as "action melodrama"—referring in particular to Porter's *Great Train Robbery* and to several Griffith productions—has confirmed the gap between this American concept of melodrama and its European counterpart.[2]

It appears that American film melodramas before 1915 were much closer to the theatrical and operatic models inherited from the nineteenth century, where music and sounds were used to serve as a constant emotional background to the action or to herald effective action pauses or extra-filmic interludes. In Nicholas Vardac's terms, not only is the "stock-melodrama pattern" or situational scheme from the theater transposed to early films, but so are countless stylistic devices related to excessive noise-simulation and to the overuse of music and dance occurrences.[3] The European concept of filmic melodrama only partially relies on its theatrical and operatic antecedents; paradoxically, its reliance is not so much content-conditioned as it is stylistically related to its genre ancestors. We do find—and some of the Gaumont productions analyzed in what follows will demonstrate this—a series of action melodramas in which visualized sound serves as a vehicle for the ongoing action and underlines its emotional impact on the audience. However, in most European melodramas the situational often leaves room for the symbolic: shouts as well as ringing bells, and later on music or dance occurrences, reveal melodrama's penchant for excess, but also, in some cases, its original treatment of what Peter Brooks has called "the moral occult."[4] Thus, sounds are visualized so as to ensure that they are somehow associated with the act of real hearing or listening, but the very act of hearing or listening frequently allows both the protagonists and the audience to consider sound as the key to transcendence, to mental subjectivity or to character psychology. In her essay "French Melodrama: Theory of a Specific History," Maureen Turim has demonstrated to what degree film melodrama from the early years is much closer to an experimental style that encourages creative tropes than to the wide range of later, commercially produced "bourgeois melodramas." For Turim, aesthetic exploration often occurs within ordinary plots and distinguishes itself not only through the use of sophisticated visual effects but also by a strong emphasis on sensory elements.[5]

As presented on the occasion of the Fourth Domitor Congress (Paris, 1996), my rhetorical survey of some early Pathé melodramas already made brief references to figures of excess that relied on sound, both as narrative vector and as emotional catalyst.[6] At that time, however, I had not realized to what extent sound elements could create an authentic double discourse. What my recent research has made salient is a complex entity, inside which auditive perception sometimes proves more active than visual perception, even if we are dealing with silent films (or, in some exceptional cases, with original scores added to films). I will therefore focus largely on the phenomenon psychologists have called *subception*, or "subliminal auditive perception." When voices or music are only simulated visually, one has to find a justification for the inaudible sound. *Subception* presupposes an indirect identification with such stimuli and a partial recording of visual information. When the viewer partially perceives and identifies an image, some information is already there, previously recorded.[7]

In most silents of the early teens *subception* is doubly articulated:

1) *Internally,* by means of very diversified auditive stimuli that either facilitate narrative progression or suspend the diegesis to focus on purely emotional states. The examples that follow are chosen to emphasize the fact that, on many occasions, simulating the act of hearing or listening to something in particular provides the key to further visualized events. Elsewhere, the visualization of characters dancing, singing, or playing a particular instrument within the limits of carefully designed deep staging eventually proves to be a very effective emotional catalyst.

2) *Externally,* by inducing a particular type of audience participation that is both active and empathic. This amounts to saying that, in most cases, audiences—past or present—do not need a materialized sound counterpart in order to have access to the visualized discourse. Such an assertion is best

validated when we are able to compare a totally silent picture, or in Michel Chion's more appropriate terms, a "deaf" picture, with its original music. Such an experience might be extremely rewarding, but it can also prove very frustrating.[8]

Religious as well as fable-like early melodramas offer a fertile ground for this double articulation. The thematic redundancy of subjects related to an easily recognizable Christian pattern results in countless representations of angels, priests, feminine equivalents of the Virgin, masculine devil-impersonators, and the like. The viewer is faced with extraordinary situations, abrupt reversals due to confrontations with characters transcending the real world, and, eventually, moral resolutions that often call for an "immaterial" empathy. As one example among many, the 1908 Gaumont catalogue features a considerable number of films from the above-mentioned category. We find titles such as: *Le Noël de Monsieur le Curé, Le Noël de la fille perdue, Le Noël du pauvre hère,* whose synopses deal with miracles that help overcome poverty, death, suicidal attempts, and other kinds of moral dilemmas.

A closer look at several French melodramas from the Alan Roberts collection at the Belgian Film Archive raises an important question: did the authors of these films intend to render their stories more accessible, more realistic, by overusing sound elements, or rather did they complicate their legible diegeses with hyperbolic aural figures that would attract the viewer's attention in a different, more challenging way? Both hypotheses prove valid. In fables imbued with religiousness such as *La légende du vieux sonneur* (Camille de Morlhon, Pathé, 1911) or *Le fil de la vierge* (attributed to Louis Feuillade, 1910), church bells or improvised gate bells are there to ensure the filmic verisimilitude of events and to challenge the viewer's narrative inventiveness.

In the first example, which may serve as a paradigm for *subception* occurrences, the hyperbolic nature of the bell-ringer's various auditive reactions increases the melodramatic potential of an otherwise simplistic intrigue.

An old bell-ringer is about to ring his church bells, when suddenly the Devil makes a brief appearance at his side, scares him and eventually immobilizes his bells (Fig. 10.1). The old man rejects the satanic vision and runs out of the church. In what follows, the bell-ringer explains the vision to his page and, on arriving home, receives a letter from the bailiff threatening to "burn him as an heretic if his bells do not ring the Angelus" (Fig. 10.2). In the meantime, an angel makes her appearance in front of the church and further turns into a beggar trembling with cold: on seeing her, the bell-ringer is touched by her poor condition and brings her back home. Once inside the room, some other devil substitute presents the bell ringer with a fake letter and subsequently re-appears as Satan himself, surrounded by his customary paraphernalia (clouds of orange smoke) and happy to fool the old man who cries over his fate. The beggar proves more than a simple visual witness to the bell-ringer's annoyances (she has witnessed the whole scene from behind a curtain): she leaves the room without being seen by the old man and rings the bells for him, only to become an angel again after having annihilated the satanic figure. Thanks to a well-orchestrated alternating pattern, the old man reacts in the most

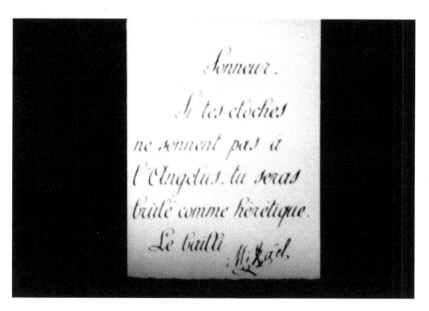

10.1 and 10.2. Frame enlargements, Camille de Morlhon, *La Légende du vieux sonneur* (Pathé 1911).

10.3 and 10.4. Frame enlargements, Camille de Morlhon, *La Légende du vieux sonneur* (Pathé 1911).

10.5. Frame enlargement, Louis Feuillade, *Le Fil de la vierge* (Gaumont 1910).

excessive and persuasive way: on hearing the bells from his room, he cannot "believe his ears" and rushes to stop the deafening noise (Fig. 10.3). Once at the church, the bell-ringer sees the angel ringing the bells: she now stops, indicating that she will ascend, and he thankfully joins his hands in prayer (Fig. 10.4). While the church bells are immobilized by the devil's visually spectacular "Méliès-like" appearance, what clearly motivates the story's continuity and suspense are the sound elements related to the act of ringing.[9]

The fable's metaphysical closure fits into the pattern of a distinct category of early European melodramas, which often transcend the antithetic duality between good (the kind-hearted bell-ringer) and evil (Satan and his variants) by means of a supernatural intercession. While this metaphysical aspect is translated in a rather naïve manner, it is counterbalanced by a high degree of realistic motivation supplied by the wide range of aural effects. These effects are almost exclusively "hearing-dependent," hence they presuppose a high degree of *subception* on the part of both the main protagonist and the audience.

In the second example there is only one important sound effect based on *subception,* but its suppression would obviously diminish the story's "dosage" of realism, as well as the particular impact of its conclusion. *Le fil de la vierge* is the story of two abandoned orphans, wandering desperately in an unknown forest: their supernatural reunification with their dead mother is enabled by a piece of wool presented in that same forest by an angel, the Virgin's messenger. The orphaned children not only follow the Virgin's barely visible thread (Fig. 10.5), they also use the thread to "ring the gate bell" of a mysterious house (Fig. 10.6). Only after this auditive event is successfully performed do "the gates of Para-

10.6 and 10.7. Frame enlargements, Louis Feuillade, *Le Fil de la vierge* (Gaumont 1910).

dise" open to welcome them at their dead mother's side (Fig. 10.7). Compared to de Morlhon's moralizing fable, Feuillade's story appeals to the viewer's emotions in a different way: the death of a mother is a stronger vehicle for empathy than the fact of having some church-bells immobilized. Consequently, the sound effect derived from the act of ringing the "gate-bells of paradise" can be related to a figure I have identified, using Peter Brooks's terminology, as the equivalent of a filmic oxymoron. The oxymoron is a literary figure in which two contradictory concepts are associated in a meaningful way (for instance, "eloquent silence"). In our case, such a figure could be presented in the following way: though the mother is dead, the children still can be reunited with her through the act of following the thread and ringing the "gate bells of paradise."[10]

Several action melodramas from the key year 1913, belonging to the realistic line of Gaumont films, offer striking examples of the way sound simulation under all its forms (exclamatory titles, visualized shouts, knocks on the door, eavesdropping, etc.) serves to diversify empathic devices. However, the emotional impact of scenes using sound effects is different from that produced by fairy-like stories such as the ones analyzed above. Here, occurrences based on subliminal auditive perception have more immediacy, one could even say more brutality; they obviously increase the dramatic tension present within several stories and position melodramatic excess as a bi-polar entity, both visual and aural. Henri Fescourt's *Jeux d'enfants* (1913) is a typical action-melodrama, almost exclusively performed by children. Young Delphine is getting bored at home: she decides to take her cousins to play at the deserted factory her parents own. She gets stuck in a hydraulic lift, and a last-minute rescue seals her friendship with Mathieu, a valiant lower-class boy. As Richard Abel has noted in his analysis of this film, its originality lies not in the type of intrigue, highly common for that period, but rather in the extremely dynamic intercutting of inside and outside spaces.[11] What I would like to add to his comprehensive analysis is that sound elements are important emotion catalysts because of their diversified capacity to suggest both the visual source of actual sounds and the way characters aurally react to them. The film's first climactic scene is a relevant case in point: Delphine has mistakenly turned on a hydraulic lift, which will descend on her in eight minutes unless she is rescued in time. Half-hidden by obscurity, she cries out her mother's name, while her shouting is visualized through exclamatory titles (see Fig. 10.8). In the meantime, a friend of hers brings along the maid Marie, who, on hearing Delphine, shouts back and vainly tries to open the blocked entrance door. After a second series of desperate cries, the maid and the other little girl rush off to seek help (Fig. 10.9). The visualization of such a diversified range of sound elements—intensive shouting, repeated exclamatory titles, variations on the act of hearing and/or of listening behind closed doors, simulating the fear caused by the noise of the hydraulic lift, and so on—implies that *subception* is at the core of the film's narrative enterprise. As in *La légende du vieux sonneur,* sound effects are used in a hyperbolic way: their repetitive, ex-

10.8 and 10.9. Frame enlargements, Henri Fescourt, *Jeux
d'enfants* (Gaumont 1913).

— Maman! Maman!

— A l'aide! A l'aide!
Il n'y a donc personne ici!

aggerated nature asks for an immediate identification on the part of the viewer, whose strongest impressions are auditive rather than visual.

Similarly, in *L'Enfant de Paris* (Gaumont, 1913) a European parallel to Griffith's epics, Léonce Perret uses sound elements to diversify the narrative, while considerably increasing the degree of audience participation. As indicated in the title, *L'Enfant de Paris* is another child-based narrative, telling the story of the kidnapping and the liberation of Marie-Laure, the young daughter of a widowed military officer. Marie-Laure runs away from her boarding-school and is seized by a blackmailing villain and sequestered in some fashionable hotel of the French Riviera, before being rescued by a valiant orphan boy. Most film historians fit Perret's masterpiece into the category of "European pictorialist melodramas" because of the visual virtuosity at work (expressive location filming, extensive use of backlighting, dramatic situations deployed in depth). In *Theater to Cinema*, Lea Jacobs and Ben Brewster emphasize the film's pictorial organization of several scenes, stressing its similarity with theatrical "tableau" techniques, meant to maintain the high points of situations in a single scene.[12] Nonetheless, as far as the use of auditive parameters is concerned, the approach I would suggest is closer to the one developed by Richard Abel, who refers to an "unusually supple syntax," which exploits countless representational strategies.[13] Thus, the sequence relating the failed attempt of the police to reunite the father with his kidnapped daughter reveals the way aural titles based on *subception* serve as "fiction tie-ins."[14] An initial shot shows us the arrival of the police; the second is a title that justifies the previous shot and anticipates the following one: "*On hearing the noise* signaling the arrival of the police, Le Bachelier (the villain) had run away, taking Marie-Laure along" (Fig. 10.10); in the third shot we see the kidnapping—this scene visually confirms what has been announced by the title, but remains very expressive stylistically. The next frame still (Fig. 10.11) illustrates the way the little girl, asleep in the room where she has been locked, is called upon by her rescuer. Here, Perret is using a European frame-dissection principle, typical of theater staging. What strikes one is that the link between the room where Marie-Laure is peacefully sleeping and the adjacent space, from where le Bosco is trying to break open the door, proves emotionally relevant only when, in the next shot (a closer midshot), Marie-Laure signals the viewer that she *has heard* the noise: she wakes up and realizes that there is somebody calling behind the door. Once more, the part played by *subception* in the unfolding of the scene cannot be underestimated. The importance of aural effects for the cinematic structuring of this scene is also confirmed by the original screenplay, conserved at the BIFI, in Paris. It reads as follows: "He arrives in front of a closed door and calls Marie-Laure's name. The child is obviously there ("est bien là")." This last sentence clearly implies that a signaling other than visual has helped identify her presence.[15]

I would also like to concentrate on the complex aural—mainly musical—dimension of a distinct type of European melodrama, where psychology prevails over action, and where children are replaced by adult female protagonists.

10.10. Frame enlargements,
Léonce Perret, *L'Enfant de Paris*
(Gaumont 1913).

Several film theorists, the most persuasive of all being Eric de Kuyper, have argued that the aesthetic parameters of the teens are extremely difficult to define. For de Kuyper, the "backwardness" pointed out by film historians (in cutting, camera angle, acting technique) when comparing the teens to the glorious twenties is clearly an *"idée fausse."* Many of these films seem stylistically retarded only because they follow rather atypical continuity rules: some scenes last too long, others unfold too quickly, there are lots of unmotivated repeated shots, titles sometimes do not supply immediate information about the ongoing story.[16] In my view, what accounts for their complexity is their intrinsic lyrical, hence often musical, dimension. Contrary to what happens in the twenties, when the interest shifts to sophisticated scores written *for* the films, in the early teens the dominant trend is not to pursue the synchronizing practices developed by the Gaumont Chronophone, but to visualize significant pieces of music *in* films. Recent work has shown that the visualization of musical occurrences did not always ask for a performed counterpart. In his controversial essay "The Silence of the Silents," Rick Altman shows that early cinema was characterized by diverse sound practices, some of which did not require "live accompaniment" and were shown under the label of "silent drama." Music was used intermittently during film projections, often in the form of independent musical numbers. The audience, argues Altman, was not bothered by silence, having been trained to accept various categories of sound effects.[17] In some cases, the entire narrative structure of a film is conditioned by the use of some musical dimen-

10.11 Frame enlargement, Léonce Perret, *L'Enfant de Paris* (Gaumont 1913).

sion, which can be either abundantly visualized or simply mentioned in a crucial scene.

There is a German film from the early teens that could serve as a serious contender to Gance's more famous *La dixième symphonie* (1918). I'm referring to Franz Hofer's *Kammermusik* (1914), where aural memories unleash a multiple diegesis: An old woman recalling her life of sacrifice (she married a sick musician) is literally inhabited by past and present music.[18] The "fiction tie-ins" appearing in the titles are often related to the act of hearing or listening to music: "While I was sleeping, I *heard* wonderful sounds from the other room." The visualization of musical performances (her future husband, her father, and later on her son, are seen playing different instruments) frequently stands for unspoken dialogue lines, so that *subception* is both internally (character reactions) and externally (audience participation) motivated. At the end of the picture, highlights of the heroine's sacrificial existence are exclusively associated with music, through a kind of metonymical transfer.[19]

Other melodramas produced approximately at the same time introduce musical occurrences at precise psychological keypoints, so as to increase the visuals' emotional impact. In Evgeni Bauer's *Child of the Big City* (1914), the final tango routine that Yuri Tsivian finds "too laborious" creates a *contrasting* counterpoint entirely based on external *subception*. While the betrayed lover waits outside for an answer to his letter before deciding to commit suicide, Bauer's mise-en-scène demands that the perverted mistress go on dancing for quite a while with her guest, using exacerbated, hyperbolic movements. The audience *must* perceive aurally the tango's sensuous rhythmics in order to fully experience the shock of the victim's subsequent suicide.[20]

A final comment on an apparently less sophisticated dance occurrence, this time from Gustavo Serena's realistic melodrama, *Assunta Spina* (1915).[21] A few moments before the film's "inciting incident" (the scene of physical aggression on behalf of which Michele, Assunta's fiancé, will unjustly be sent to prison), there is the celebration of Assunta's birthday. As in any melodrama respectful of its genre's narrative codes, a joyful celebration is counterbalanced by a conflicting event: while everybody is dancing in the foreground, Assunta's other suitor, Raffaele, calls her from the background of the real location scene. The dancing imperturbably goes on in the next shot, masking almost entirely the background flirtation, nonetheless still visible. Later on, a medium shot taken from a totally different perspective shows us the fiancé, Michele, gazing off screen and seeing Assunta: the answer to his looks is not a closer cut to Assunta and Raffaele, but the same deep staging showing the dancers in the foreground, with the illicit couple in the background. Assunta finally comes forward with Raffaele, and Michele joins them and starts an argument; the dancers stop and try in vain to persuade the couple to calm down. We, the audience, are on the side of the dancers, although no close camera angle identification occurs. We have been visually entertained by this music, we have felt like dancing, but now the show is over, disrupted. Thanks to a wonderful combination of cutting and deep staging, the film sets subliminal auditive perception at the core of its narrative comprehension: if we eliminate the aural effect produced by the dancing and isolate its protagonists, its empathic potential will clearly be reduced.

The examples analyzed here should serve as starting points for further investigation. There is much work left in the field of early aural narrativity as well as in that of sound pragmatics. Numerous questions ask for answers. Relating occurrences to narrative genre conventions is one possibility among many, obviously facilitated by the tight bonds existing between the realm of sounds and that of emotions. Still, following the Virgin's thread may prove easier than hearing the gate bells of paradise . . .

Notes

I wish to thank my doctoral assistant, Muriel Andrin, for her constant help, Clémentine Deblieck and Alison McMahan for their assistance while I was doing research on this essay, and Gabrielle Claes, Curator of the Belgian Film Archive, for graciously allowing me to show the print of *La légende du vieux sonneur* on the occasion of the Washington Congress (June 1998). I would also like to express my gratitude to Richard Abel, whose suggested revisions contributed positively to the final form of this article.

1. Rick Altman, "Dickens, Griffith and Film Theory Today," in *Silent Film*, ed. Richard Abel (New Brunswick: Rutgers University Press, 1996), 145.

2. See David Mayer and Helen Day-Mayer, "A 'Secondary Action' or Musical Highlight? Melodic Interludes in Early Film Melodrama Reconsidered," which appears later in this volume.

3. Nicholas Vardac, *Stage to Screen: Theatrical Method from Garrick to Griffith* (Cambridge: Harvard University Press, 1949), 244.

4. Peter Brooks, *The Melodramatic Imagination: Balzac, James, Melodrama and the Mode of Excess* (New Haven: Yale University Press, 1976), 20–21.

5. Maureen Turim, "French Melodrama: Theory of a Specific History," *Theatre Journal* 39, no. 3 (October 1987), 317–318.

6. Dominique Nasta, "Ne pleure pas maman, c'est ta fête aujourd'hui: Figures de l'excès dans les mélodrames Pathé d'avant 1915" (paper presented at the Fourth Domitor Congress, Paris, Cinémathèque Française, December 1996).

7. For more details on the phenomenon of *subception,* see Dominique Nasta, *Meaning in Film: Relevant Structures in Soundtrack and Narrative* (Bern: Peter Lang, 1991), 93–99.

8. A relevant case in point, to my mind, is the score Pietro Mascagni composed for Nino Oxilia's *Rapsodia Satanica* in 1914. A couple of years ago, Italian television showed the newly restored version with its original musical accompaniment: the viewer-listener is so absorbed by the overwhelming, highly redundant score that one is led to passively accept both the intricate narrative and its sophisticated visual style.

9. In her essay on sound elements in Méliès' films, "Présence, fonction et représentation du son dans les scénarios et les films de Méliès: Mise en scène du son," Isabelle Raynauld mentions a quite similar example, though belonging to a different genre. In *Le Diable au couvent* (Méliès, 1899), the devil unexpectedly rings the bells, and this "aural event" prompts the nuns to rush for the mass. See *Georges Méliès, l'illusioniste fin de siècle?,* ed. Jacques Malthête and Michel Marie (Paris: La Sorbonne Nouvelle/Colloque de Cerisy-la-Salle, 1997), 201–217.

10. Brooks, 57–80.

11. Cf. Richard Abel, *The Ciné Goes to Town: French Cinema 1896–1914* (Berkeley: University of California Press, 1994), 342–343.

12. Ben Brewster and Lea Jacobs, *Theatre to Cinema, Stage Pictorialism and the Early Feature Film* (New York: Oxford University Press, 1997), 195–197.

13. See Abel, *Ciné Goes to Town,* 381–382.

14. The term belongs to Ben Singer. See "Fiction Tie-ins and Narrative Intelligibility 1911–1918," *Film History* 5 (1993), 489–504.

15. See *L'Enfant de Paris,* in Archives scénaristiques du Fonds Léonce Perret [9 pages], BIFI, Paris.

16. Eric de Kuyper, "Le cinéma de la seconde époque: Le muet des années 10" (essay in two parts), *Cinémathèque* 2–3 (1992), 29–35, 32–66.

17. Rick Altman, "The Silence of the Silents," *Musical Quarterly* 80, no. 2 (1997), 669–706.

18. See also Elena Dagrada's interesting essay, "The Voyeur at Wilhelm's Court: Franz Hofer," in *A Second Life: German Cinema's First Decades,* ed. Thomas Elsaesser (Amsterdam: Amsterdam University Press, 1996), 277–285.

19. Two years later, in 1916, Hofer directed the famous *Heidenröslein,* directly inspired by a Schubert lied (text by Goethe). The director even suggested a live accompaniment for crucial scenes, but the result was inferior to what he had expected. In terms of *subception,* nonetheless, the film manages to convey the feeling of a coherent aural entity, with effects ranging from ringing bells to violin and piano playing in on-screen occurrences.

20. See Yuri Tsivian, "Russia, 1913: Cinema in the Cultural Landscape," *Griffithiana* 50 (1994), 139.

21. Several interesting essays have focused on *Assunta Spina*. See for example: Ettore Massarese, "La memoria di Assunta Spina," *Cinegrafie* 6 (November 1993), 109–113; and Claudio Camerini, "Les formes italiennes du divisme: Les années du muet," in *Le cinéma italien,* ed. Aldo Bernardini and Jean A. Gili (Paris: Centre Georges Pompidou, 1986), 66–68.

11 Talking Movie or Silent Theater? Creative Experiments by Vasily Goncharov

Rashit M. Yangirov

Early Russian cinema is traditionally considered an artistic phenomenon closely linked to the national theater culture as well as greatly inspired by achievements of contemporary stage productions. Generally this is true, but recently scholars have reexamined the historical evidence and demonstrated that the relationship between early cinema and theater in Russia was reciprocal. Indeed, some early Russian film experiments are of special interest since they had a serious impact on both the country's film and its theater.

One of the most interesting of these experiments was introduced by Vasily Goncharov (1861–1915), who is recognized as a pioneer of Russian film and co-author of the country's first feature film *Stenka Razin* (*Brigands from the Lower Reaches*), released in October 1908. In the past, I myself have made brief general biographical references to Goncharov,[1] but new archival evidence demonstrates that modern discussions of his role in early Russian film completely ignore or misinterpret his creative originality. The aim of the present essay is to correct this misunderstanding.

Goncharov served for many years as a railroad officer in the far southern provinces of Russia, but he had ambitions to be a playwright. In the late 1880s and early 1890s, he began to work as an amateur actor and playwright, writing several dramatic and comedy pieces, which, although passed by theater censors, had little stage success.[2] Nevertheless, thanks to his ambition Goncharov managed to become a member of the Russian Society of Dramatists and Opera Composers as well as the Society of Russian Writers and Scientists, which gave him a degree of personal pride as well as some literary authority. After moving to Moscow in 1905, Goncharov became seriously interested in film. It was about that time that he traveled to Paris, where he acquired a basic knowledge of cinematography, which was to inspire several subsequent radical experiments.

His first attempt to introduce film into a stage performance came in late autumn 1906, in a satirical farce of manners entitled *City Council Session*.[3] Despite the play's simple plot and the author's relatively poor knowledge of dramatic rules and language, its extraordinary effects were nevertheless absolutely new to the contemporary Russian stage. The play presented a group of honored citizens in a small provincial town who proudly are discussing the social and cultural achievements of their local community. As often happens in an official meeting of a close circle of gentlemen, discussion turns to female beauties and the men's personal experiences in love affairs. Curiously, most of the discussion focuses on French-style entertainments like the *café chantant,* on romances with dancers or grisettes in Paris. Suddenly, however, the clever talk is interrupted as the stage setting changes and they watch with horror as the devil himself appears on a background film screen and flies over the town to greet them. The town council members are deeply shocked at his appearance, fearing that the apocalypse has arrived on Earth. But shortly they hear a heavy blow behind the curtains. The film projection stops, and the devil appears to them on stage. Despite the general commotion, he is very friendly and quiets the audience by introducing himself as a special agent of Satan sent to check on the life of mortal beings. The devil then gives a very personal, revealing account of the state of local life. Referring to the private lives of the council members, he reminds them of their immoral behavior, and then goes further to demonstrate the immorality of their wives as well. The film projection begins again, and the council members are forced to watch their wives' infidelities with young lovers while the husbands are busy with their so-called public duties.

The surviving playscript describes the appearance of the film-within-the-play quite thoroughly. The back scenery comes up in total darkness and opens to reveal the film screen, on which are shown the moving pictures of adultery. Some of these could be considered quite risqué from the censors' point of view. Both film excerpts were silent, but according to Goncharov's script, the stage characters commented on them during the projection. Ultimately, the members of the town council are more shocked by the film show than by the devil's appearance. His work accomplished, he suddenly disappears from the stage and waves goodbye from the film screen, within the same setting as in the first film excerpt.

Clearly Goncharov's first film experiment was an extraordinary one for contemporary Russian drama, and for cinema as well. The influence of Georges Méliès's "devil" films on the play is perhaps obvious, but Russian cameramen of the time were by no means capable of making the inset films, either artistically or technically. There is no evidence that Goncharov ever managed to have his creative project of 1906 performed, but one can be sure that it had a serious impact on another stage play, *999 Cuckolds,* which was written and staged two years later by the popular Russian farce collaborator Simon Saburov. This new farce used the same trick of filming unfaithful couples and projecting it before the main characters, a farce that, by the way, was very well received by Moscow theater audiences.[4]

Despite the failure of this initial project, Goncharov was not discouraged, and continued searching for new subjects for his stage and film experiments. Having been deeply impressed by the historical paintings of the famous Russian artist Vasily Surikov,[5] one day the playwright realized that his fame as a widely recognized author would come in the historical genre as popular entertainment. Accordingly, Goncharov's next project, later to be recognized as one of his most

11.1. Vasily Surikov. *Stenka Razin,* 1903–1910. Oil on canvas. State Russian Museum, St. Petersburg.

important contributions to Russian film history, was about the legendary figure of Stenka Razin. If one studies Goncharov's original version, it becomes obvious that modern film historians have not interpreted the work correctly: they see it as a "pure film" and miss its artistic peculiarities. Originally it was a stage drama, and the author called it *Brigands from the Lower Reaches,* characterizing it as a "Popular tale with singing, choirs and dancing."[6]

According to the original manuscript, the work was designed for a theater stage supplied with a screen projection and enriched with sound effects. The performance opens with a film excerpt, described in the script. The film screen was a part of the scenery, and it was located center stage, decoratively framed by a painted river and a forest. Further, according to the manuscript, the moving pictures shown were exactly the same as what would become the first shots of the later film, *Stenka Razin:*

> The cinematograph shows the Volga River, where one can easily watch the boats. The first boat contains Stenka Razin, the Persian Princess and rower. Others contain brigands. Behind the curtains a folk song is sung softly. [. . . .] As the boats approach the viewers, the singing becomes louder. The cinematograph projection stops.[7]

After that, the drama's plot depicts the same events as we know from the later film. The characters even perform actions that coincide with the film's intertitles, which turn out to be descriptive comments except for the text of the false letter from the Persian princess. Finally, the play ends with a second screen projection:

> The cinematograph picture is the same as the first. A song again is heard softly behind the curtains. Razin raises the princess up high with both arms. His voice declaims behind the curtains [by the way, the film's last intertitle reproduces his speech nearly word for word]. He throws her in the water. One can hear the

princess's scream and fall in the water, and after that brigands shouting: "Long live our ataman! Hurrah!" The song fades away.[8]

A general comparison of the playscript with the filmscript shows that the latter closely coincides with the former in its beginning and ending shots; moreover, the earlier script clarifies the meaning of the film's central section, introducing some key psychological motives that technically could not be represented.

No doubt the playwright spent a lot of time trying to interest various theaters in this play and looking for a technician who could assist him in filming. By the summer of 1908, he finally managed to make a deal with Shuvalov, who directed a popular Moscow theater called the Aquarium, and with Alexander Drankov in St. Petersburg, who himself was trying to improve his cinema career, after the failure of an attempt to screen Pushkin's drama *Boris Godunov*. Theater rehearsals went on in Moscow while Drankov shot the film sections in the environs of the Russian capital, but Goncharov was not involved in directing either of these enterprises.[9] Apparently, during filming, the adventurous and wily Drankov convinced the naive and ambitious playwright to adapt the central part of the drama for film as well, in order to arrange multiple showings and thereby to make the work more profitable.

When the play was ready to be premiered, Drankov for the first time introduced the practice of "jumping the gun," which would become his trademark in later years. Under the same title as the play, the film was screened in the St. Petersburg theater, Coliseum, on 15 October 1908, one day before the theater premiere in Moscow, where the Aquarium had exclusive rights to Goncharov's drama.[10] Theater owner Putintsev[11] and later the playwright himself protested Drankov's piracy to the Union of Dramatic and Musical Writers. According to the published records, its chairman received

> the statement from Mr. Goncharov [. . .] about what he has written and reproduced on cinematography film. He asked [. . .] to have his authorial rights protected in all cinematograph theaters. However, the Union has turned down Mr. Goncharov's request on the grounds that his work is mechanical and does not fit the definition of a work of literature and that the development of cinematograph theaters in general is detrimental to the development of "genuine theatrical enterprises." [12]

Nevertheless, Goncharov's drama was staged throughout the country. Yevgenii Petrov-Kraevsky, for instance, who acted as the protagonist in Drankov's film, took the same role in the play when it was staged in the Siberian town of Omsk in 1907–1909. At the same time there was another production performed by an unknown theater company in Goncharov's native Don region.

The story of *Stenka Razin* ended to the advantage of Drankov, establishing him as the "First Russian filmmaker," with no credit granted to Goncharov. However, Goncharov continued his creative activities, turning again to his favorite theme. His next play was another historical drama of the sixteenth century, *Yermak Timofeevich—Conqueror of Siberia*.[13] It was written right after *Brigands* (and dated November 1907). The new project seems to have been the

11.2. Yevgenii Petrov-Kraevsky acted the role of Stenka Razin on stage and in film. Kiev. ca. 1900. Postcard from the author's collection.

most ambitious work of the dramatist, building on his previous stage and film experiences. At the same time, it reveals that Goncharov was composing a musical score as one of its key artistic features. First of all, the script was supplied with special references demonstrating the author's thorough knowledge of historical details. Another reference is of special interest, and needs to be quoted:

> In both capital cities, the staging will be directed by me personally. All the film excerpts will be filmed in the Moscow environs by the French company of Gaumont, under my personal direction and that of the historical painter Surikov. The Moscow branch of Gaumont will produce all the gramophone records designed for the staging [. . .] using the Elgephone "singing machines." The film production budget will come to about 15,000 rubles.[14]

According to the manuscript, ten moving picture excerpts were worked into the drama as narrational *son-et-lumière* introductions to the various acts, all differing in their setting and chronology. Goncharov showed himself to be a much more skilled artist than before; he was now competent in the technology of filmmaking. All of the film excerpts were marked off as special intervals from two to five minutes each and were designed to occur when the curtains were down and the scenery was being changed; in a few cases the screen was even designed to be closed by a painted backdrop that reproduced the landscape of the film. All of the film excerpts represented outdoor settings somewhere in Siberia or in an ancient Moscow street, with only one exception (excerpt number eight), which presented the interior of the Kremlin palace. All of them also were accompanied by singing by means of the Elgephone. For example, the prologue pictured an old Russian folk singer somewhere in Siberia, who sang a folk song about Yermak, evoking his legendary spirit. Excerpt number five was designed to reproduce the famous painting by Surikov, *Yermak Conquers Siberia,* representing a battle between Russians and Tartars on the Irtysh River. The final film excerpt, which closed the stage show, depicted the heroic death of Yermak in his last battle with the Tartars.

Goncharov's new play was announced shortly after *Brigands* by the same theater,[15] but the project's extraordinarily high budget for its time forced the Moscow branch of Gaumont to turn it down, and the script was left unperformed for a while. On his side, the playwright quickly found the new sound technology was far from satisfactory, so he had to abandon that innovation. But Goncharov was devoted to this work, so two years later he adapted the work purely for the stage and had it produced by the theater company of the St. Petersburg People's House named after Nicholas II.[16] This version was different from the original—a few of its film scenes were completely excluded from the show, while others were converted into stage pantomimes. The theatrical production was well received in the Russian capital, but Goncharov was persistent and, soon after joining the staff of Khanzhonkov's company, convinced the owner of the extraordinary artistic value of the stage work and his personal ability to turn it into a film. In 1909, he directed the first screen version of *Yermak,* which was released in February 1910. To judge from the surviving film print, it repeated all the scenes of the original script of 1907. At the same time, Goncharov managed to direct the screen version of another historical drama, called *A Song about Merchant Kalashnikov,* which he adapted from the poem by Lermontov.[17]

Meanwhile, Goncharov was still dreaming of a full production of *Yermak* and returned to it in 1911 in what could be considered the best art work of his life, which he managed with thoroughness and full creative scope. The filming took over three years and employed the entire staff of the company at one time or another. A completely new musical score was written by Mikhail Ippolitov-Ivanov.[18] Goncharov even tried to adapt Khanzhonkov's ambitious project of constructing a chain of cinemas to his own needs, getting a new film theater called Pegasus built, specially designed for stage dramas with screen projection.[19] The premiere of *Yermak* finally took place at Pegasus in November 1914, accompanied by a reciter, a symphony orchestra conducted by the composer, and a choir; moreover, it appeared simultaneously with the special publication of the film script (the first one in Russian cinema history).[20] Although the film was warmly received by audiences and the press, unfortunately it has not been preserved in film archives, so its artistic originality is impossible to evaluate.

Goncharov's experiments in combining drama and film, sound and image, on stage were of great importance for the time, even if they were rarely completed as he envisioned them. His creative works had a considerable impact on Russian theater and film, especially in the development of the historical genre.

Its distant echo reverberated much later—modernized by such avant-garde masters as Sergei Eisenstein, Vsevolod Meyerhold, and others. Today Vasily Goncharov's creative heritage deserves to be reconsidered as making a unique contribution to Russian artistic culture as well as to general cinema history.

Notes

My research could not have been completed without the friendly advice of Ellen Zbinovsky (Moscow) and Andrew Braddel (London). I am also greatly indebted to my editor and cheerful host, Tamara Dikhanoff (Bethesda, Maryland). The original Russian titles that follow have been translated into English by the author.

1. *Silent Witnesses: Russian Films 1908–1919* (London-Pordenone: BFI—Edizioni Biblioteca dell'Immmagine, 1989), 554–560. See also the same essay, in Russian, in *Odyssey of Alexander Drankov* (Moscow: Cinema Art, 1995), 1.

2. *In Modern Manner or Murders Out of Law:* a tragedy in five acts (1884); *Mad Day or A New Morals:* a drama in four acts (1886); *One Can Lay Hands On:* a comedy in one act (1893); *New Year's or The 200,000 Ruble Prize:* a comedy in one act (1893).

3. *Town Council Session:* a fantasy in one act (1906). Accepted by the St. Petersburg Board of Theater Censorship on 28 February 1907.

4. This farce was staged in Moscow. See "Hermitage," *Theater Weekly Gazette,* 19 October 1908, 3. A synopsis of the play can be found on pages 21–22.

5. Vasily Surikov introduced his painting of Stenka Razin in the course of the thirty-fifth exhibition of Russian Itinerant Artists, which was held in St. Petersburg. See E. Arnoldi, "On the 50th Anniversary of the First Russian Feature Film," *Neva* 12 (1958), 198. In fact, there is nothing in common between Surikov's art work and Goncharov's drama, except the fact that the painting presumably awakened Goncharov's creative imagination.

One should avoid thinking that the "aggressively nationalist" spirit of Surikov's historical canvas and his "glorification of military exploits and territorial expansion" are the essence of the artist's creative activities—as in E. Valkener, *Russian Realist Art, The State and Society: The Peredvizhniki and Their Tradition* (Ann Arbor: University of Michigan Press, 1972), 86, 177. In the case of Goncharov, Surikov was no more than an attractive source for his imagination and an impressive reproducer of national popular mythology.

6. *Brigands from the Lower Reaches:* a historical drama in one act. Accepted by St. Petersburg Board of Theater Censorship on 22 March 1907. In fact, Goncharov was not alone in his interest in this popular character of Russian folklore in the native dramatic tradition. Bibliography data show that his play was at least the sixth depicting Razin since the 1870s. There also were four more dramas by other authors after 1907.

7. Ibid., 1. In fact, according to Goncharov's script, not only the folk song, "From the Island to the Deep Stream," but an original score by the composer Vladimir Benevsky should have accompanied the opening scene. Mikhail Ippolitov-Ivanov composed the final music score.

8. Ibid., 10.

9. Goncharov is, however, present in a shot of the brigands' revelry.

10. *Stage: A Weekly Publication of the "Coliseum" Electro-Theatre* (1908), 59. Its owner Lebedev advertised his enterprise as specially designed for screenings of "electric opera, electric drama and electric ballet." By the way, exclusive screenings of Drankov's

film in that theater were followed by Film d'Art's *L'Assasinat du duc de Guise,* which took place only five days after its Paris premiere, as well as by SCAGL's *L'Arlèsienne.*

On the theater premiere, see *Theater,* 18 October 1908, 2; and 21 October 1908, 6. Synopses of Goncharov's drama can be found in: *Theater,* 19 October 1908, 25; *Theater Season News,* 16 October 1908, 3; and *Theater Season News,* 18 October 1908, 16.

11. *Theater Season News,* 24 October 1908, 4.

12. *Cine-Fono* 19 (1907/1908), 8.

13. *Yermak Timofeevich—Conqueror of Siberia:* historical drama in five acts and ten scenes with a prologue. Accepted by St. Petersburg State Board of Theater Censorship on 22 February 1908. Its music score again was to be composed by Benevsky. According to censorship files, Goncharov's play was the twelfth about Yermak in the list of operas, tragedies, and dramas on the Russian stage dating from the early nineteenth century.

14. Ibid.

15. *Stage,* 19 October 1908, 9.

16. *Yermak Timofeevich—Conqueror of Siberia:* historical drama in five acts and seven scenes with a prologue written by Vasily Mikhailovich Goncharov and with a music score by Mikhail Ippolitov-Ivanov. Accepted by St. Petersburg State Board of Theater Censorship on 30 September 1909 (Moscow: Simon Razsokhin Theater Publishers, 1909).

17. *A Song about Merchant Kalashnikov:* from a poem by Mikhail Yuryevich Lermontov, in two acts and two scenes. Original text by Lermontov and partly by Vasily Goncharov adapted for the stage. Music score by Mikhail Ippolitov-Ivanov. Accepted by St. Petersburg Board of Theater Censorship on 27 November 1909 (Moscow: Simon Razsokhin Theater Publishers, n.d.).

18. The music score, bound in a special cover decorated with Khanzhonkov's company logo, is in the composer's files preserved in the Manuscript Department of the Russian National Library (St. Petersburg): 1/188.

19. *Ciné-Journal,* 1913, 15, 46–47. The new film theater was designed for 1,500 spectators.

20. *Volga and Siberia. Yermak Timofeevich—Conqueror of Siberia:* historical drama by V. M. Goncharov. Adapted for the Cinematograph (Moscow, n.d.).

Part Three:

Sound Practices
in Exhibition

12 Sleighbells and Moving Pictures: On the Trail of D. W. Robertson
Gregory Waller

Mapping the history of American entertainment in the late nineteenth and early twentieth century depends, in part, on following the itineraries of professional performers. That is, tracking how their travels linked venues, audiences, and localities across the United States; describing the particular shows they offered and the more inclusive programs in which they often participated; and speculating about how they, perhaps unknowingly, undertook the daily business, to borrow Lawrence W. Levine's phrase, of "defining and redefining the contours of culture."[1]

To begin one such investigation, here are three rave notices for a turn-of-the-century entertainer who specialized in—among other things—a quite specific sort of musical performance:

(a) *Pontiac (Illinois) Daily Leader* (1902): he "gave several selections on his musical sleigh bells which were fine. These bells are arranged in strands according to pitch and in giving each a slight shake he was able to produce the sweetest music, giving many old favorite pieces."[2]

(b) *Marinette (Wisconsin) Daily Eagle* (1901): he "possesses rare talent for bell playing and his apparatus is of the best. These bells have a singular sweetness and mellowness which surpasses the majority of instruments of this kind."[3]

(c) *Ottawa (Kansas) Evening Herald* (1898): he "shook more music out of a set of sleigh bells than we ever heard before."[4]

Brief as they are, these comments have an interesting resonance. For one thing, they cast into relief certain aspects of what we might call the aesthetics of turn-of-the-century popular entertainment.[5] Here the quality of the directly visible "apparatus" and the virtuosity of the musician are much prized. So, too, is the novelty of the performance, though these reviews clearly suggest that this performer is not the only bell shaker around.[6] And both virtuosity and novelty are very much in the service of the familiar and the traditional, meaning in this case the replaying of "old favorite pieces"—sweet music somehow rendered sweeter when shaken forth in this novel fashion. In fact, the production of "sweetness" itself becomes a prime attraction.

Here, then, is an intriguing example of crowd-pleasing entertainment during the pre-nickelodeon period, linking sites in Illinois, Wisconsin, and Kansas between 1898 and 1902. For the purposes of film history, what makes this performance of artfully shaken sleighbells even more notable is that the bell ringer in question was D. W. Robertson, one of the most prominent first-generation traveling moving picture exhibitors in the United States. The comments quoted above are taken from local newspaper accounts of Robertson's appearances at independent chautauqua assemblies, those midsummer gatherings that attracted large crowds of farmers, small-town citizens, and even urban folk principally in the midwestern United States. Clearly this sleighbell performance more than fit the bill for such assemblies, and that is what interests me in this essay, although Robertson's offering could also likely have found a place in a lyceum series or at a church fair, in a musical recital or perhaps even on a small-time vaudeville stage.[7]

Charles Musser and Carol Nelson's work on Lyman H. Howe and other traveling exhibitors provides an excellent starting point for tracking Robertson's career, supplemented by the coverage offered in *Talent*, the monthly trade magazine for agents, teachers, and performers who worked the chautauqua and lyceum circuits.[8] Robertson began his professional career in 1878 as a musician with the Spanish Students Concert Company in Brooklyn, then formed the New York and Brooklyn Entertainment Bureau, which provided talent for church groups and small opera houses.[9] Through the 1880s and into the 1890s, he continued both to perform and to serve as a booking agent. For example, a full page ad in the May 1892 issue of *Talent* touted the "most wholesome entertainment" of the "YMCA Entertainers," a trio managed by Robertson, who was described as being "the only acknowledged artistic performer on his novel musical instruments"—including what was called the "Tumbleronicon." The YMCA Entertainers also featured Marion Short, with a full repertoire of humorous dialect bits and bird imitations, and Elmer Ransom, praised for carefully arranging his "program of prestidigitation so that the Christian people can enjoy and be highly entertained."[10] In the early and mid-1890s, Robertson managed and sometimes performed with a range of other talent that all look to be quite typical of a certain church-friendly sector of commercial entertainment: glee clubs and vocal quartets, the Alabama Jubilee Singers, and a lecturer who offered "illuminated recitals on the Hawaiian Islands."[11] Robertson had particular success between 1894 and 1897 at chautauqua assemblies when teamed with Ransom, the magician, for "two hours of conjuring, mystery and music."[12]

Given his particular understanding of "entertainment" and his target audience, it is not surprising that Robertson was one of the first purchasers of an Edison projecting kinetoscope in 1897, beginning what would turn out to be a quite successful career as a traveling exhibitor.[13] By September 1900, he could boast in his advertising that he had filled 259 engagements during the preceding season,[14] and a columnist in the August 1901 issue of *Talent* declared that "the chief drawing card and money-maker for western [chautauqua] assemblies this year, as heretofore, is 'D. W. Robertson's Projectoscope,' moving pictures and concert program. This attraction made money for and actually pulled some committees out of the 'hole of deficit.'"[15] Robertson's ads came to feature testimonials from big-name orators like Colonel George Bain and the evangelist Sam Jones, who deemed the show "a splendid, clean, uplifting, interesting entertainment from start to finish."[16] By the 1905–1906 season Robertson had five moving picture companies on the road, still catering specifically to what was then called the "platform" circuit.[17]

Elsewhere I have discussed the range of visual attractions—moving pictures, illustrated lectures, slide shows, fireworks displays, magic acts—that were frequently booked both at the original or "mother" Chautauqua, which began in 1874 on the shores of Lake Chautauqua in upstate New York, and at independent chautauqua assemblies founded in the 1880s and 1890s at a host of sites across the United States, but concentrated principally in Ohio, Indiana, Illinois, Iowa, and Kansas.[18] (Independent chautauquas, in turn, are not to be confused with "circuit" chautauquas, the seven- or ten-day tent show tours that became immensely popular across the United States and Canada in the 1910s.) Independent assemblies were nonprofit gatherings held at tent-filled, gate-enclosed enclaves, usually located at an isolated glade, large park, lakeside development, or some other "natural" site within proximity by railroad of small towns or larger cities. Broadly nonsectarian Protestant in their orientation, these assemblies offered educational course work, Temperance Day celebrations, political speeches, outdoor recreation, daily lectures, religious services, and a host of public performances that fell under the category of "entertainment." In this essay, I will focus more directly on the uses of sound entertainment by the D. W. Robertson Company and offer some preliminary speculations about the independent chautauqua assembly as an example of what Rick Altman calls a "culturally important musical event."[19]

For a more concrete sense of this particular type of venue, consider one such independent assembly, the Northern Chautauqua, organized in 1897. This assembly was held yearly for two weeks in midsummer on a fifty-acre wooded site bordering Lake Michigan, approximately midway between Marinette, Wisconsin, and Menominee, Michigan. Covered "with a beautiful growth of evergreen, maple and hardwood," the grounds were perfect for camping, and quite handily fulfilled what the first manager of this assembly deemed a primary "requisite of a high class Chautauqua, not only that the assembly grounds be attractive and spacious, but that they be located away from the noise and confusion of the town. At the same time they must be easily and quickly accessible, and a well-equipped street car or railway line connecting them with the city is of the first importance."[20] By 1904, the Northern Chautauqua could promise visitors the best of both worlds: "delicious air and pure artesian water," as well as "graded streets, water works, electric lights, fire protection, [and] police control."[21]

Initially, a two-thousand-seat tent served as the Northern Chautauqua's auditorium, which contained a stage decorated with palms, ferns, bunting, and a banner that expressed one of chautauqua's guiding principles: "We Live to Learn." Over the entrance to the grounds, "chautauqua" was spelled out in colored incandescent lights. From the outset, local merchants and civic boosters supported the Northern Chautauqua, which, as the *Marinette Daily Eagle* wrote in an 1897 editorial, "serves a useful purpose of advertising our city far and wide as the home of people of taste and refinement."[22] Still, the assembly almost always ran in the red, forcing certain generous citizens to cover the losses. For example, in 1900, the talent for twelve days cost $3,500, and with other expenses the total outlay was over $6000, about $1000 more than was received from selling tickets and renting concessions.

Who bought these tickets? Who made up the audience at an independent assembly? The camping space and, later, the cottages on the grounds were rented by individual families from the surrounding area, and in the first years, at least, there were large tents occupied by the local YMCA, the Epworth League, and Baptist, Swedish Methodist, and Swedish Lutheran churches. Local chautauqua organizers referred to themselves as "college bred and highly educated" men.[23] On one occasion the Marinette newspaper noted that wood and paper mills on the lake gave employees an afternoon off with pay to attend the chautauqua. Whatever the actual demographics, the audiences at the Northern Chautauqua —like so many other audiences during this period—were enlisted as symbols of a heterogeneous and egalitarian public sphere: at this assembly, wrote a reporter in 1897, "every type of city life, the poor man and the rich man, employee and employer sat down together and were happy."[24] Happy and friendly, precisely as an audience.

Evenings were the prime time for entertainment at the Northern Chautauqua, beginning with a daily concert usually featuring a large military-style band. This particular assembly also regularly scheduled lectures in the evening: inspirational speakers, commentators on current political events, travelers and guides to distant locales (India, Norway, the Grand Canyon). The Northern Chautauqua also set aside one or two nights each session for choral recitals and stage plays that relied in part on local performers. It is within this loosely defined category of "entertainment" that we find the D. W. Robertson troupe, which quite often served as a headline attraction, booked for the first two days of the Northern Chautauqua and other independent assemblies.[25]

Even when he billed his four-member troupe as the Edison Projectoscope Company or later as D. W. Robertson's Famous Moving Picture Company and touted his new "views," Robertson always paired his moving pictures with various sound entertainments, creating a show that combined or alternated different media and different pleasures. In 1899, for instance, his opening night performance at various chautauqua assemblies began with a piano solo, followed by two ballads illustrated with slides ("Mid the Green Fields of Virginia" and "The Girl I Love in Sunny Tennessee"), both sung by M. J. Colgan. Colgan also presented a "monologue," entitled "A Happy Pair," which was "illustrated throughout by the projectoscope." (It is unclear whether the illustrations were moving pictures or, more likely, slides.) The evening's entertainment concluded with a series of moving pictures, including *Cinderella,* several war pictures, and what was billed as *The Man in the Moon at Close Range.*[26] For the second evening's show, Robertson offered a two-part program with more stereopticon views and moving pictures (including a few repeated by request); his own sleighbell performance divided the evening in half. Some variation was possible from booking to booking. For instance, at the Ottawa, Kansas chautauqua, Robertson was co-billed with a lecturer, so the sleighbell performance preceded a lecture on the French Revolution, after which the projectoscope "delighted the audience" with "chaste, interesting and instructive" pictures.[27]

When Robertson returned to the Northern Chautauqua for the 1901 season, the company had replaced its male singer with Helen Darlington (described as a "prima donna soprano"). She opened the evening's show, followed by Robertson on sleighbells, and then forty-five minutes of moving pictures interspersed with three illustrated songs by Darlington, including "New Born King" and "My Own Wild Western Rose."[28] By 1903 Robertson—who still performed his sleighbell solo—had replaced Darlington with Harry Williard, a singer who doubled on banjo, mandolin, and violin. The following season, a columnist for *Talent* testified to this company's pre-eminence among moving picture exhibitors on the platform circuit, noting that while Robertson does offer the "newest pictures shown in the best style," he "doesn't surfeit me with pictures, but introduces musical novelties of one kind or another. I sometimes laugh at Mr. Robertson's pronunciation of idea, Des Moines and other words that New Yorkers will get wrong, but I go to see his entertainment whenever I get an opportunity."[29] Note that part of the pleasing novelty here is Robertson's own New York accent, which might very well have suggested to Wisconsin or Iowa audiences the geographical and cultural source of his entertainment in the eastern metropolis.

At this point in my research I cannot say with absolute certainty precisely when Robertson began to base his entertainment more exclusively on moving pictures. His ads in *Talent* in 1906 and the *Moving Picture World* in 1907 make no mention of sleighbells or mandolins. Yet he continues to promise a "whole show" with "descriptive musical accompaniment,"[30] which perhaps indicates a shift in how sound—now referred to as "descriptive music"—was integrated into a moving picture program, rather than playing a central role in a larger, more inclusive and varied evening's worth of entertainment.

Quite clearly, D. W. Robertson's moving picture company was in the business of performing music as well as projecting films, and in so doing it was for a decade at least extremely successful on the chautauqua circuit. Unlike other popular chautauqua standbys like the inspirational lecture or the stereopticon-illustrated travelogue, Robertson filled his prime-time slot with a series of distinct attractions: vocal and instrumental music, slides and moving pictures, monologues and mandolins, the novel and the familiar, the sweet and the stirring. In its modular format, his show had certain affinities with vaudeville, though it was probably much more akin to the performance of another platform favorite, the musical quartet, which frequently offered sentimental readings and humorous novelty turns along with singing (both solo and ensemble) and sometimes instrumental virtuosity as well.

Even this admittedly sketchy look at the career of D. W. Robertson helps to fill in or at least draw attention to certain aspects of the history of traveling moving picture exhibition, particularly how these exhibitors organized and delivered what Robertson in his advertising called the "whole show," which in his case made much use of sound—singing, piano playing, spoken words, novelty instruments.[31] Perhaps more important, Robertson's traveling leads us directly to what I would argue is a crucial—and much overlooked—site for entertainment at the turn-of-the-century: the platform or chautauqua circuit, where both visual attractions and sound performances occupied a central place.

Consider, by way of conclusion, the Northern Chautauqua as a musical—or, more broadly, sound—event. In addition to Robertson's illustrated songs and sweet sleighbell solos, during any given year this assembly would also offer daily concerts by a twenty-six-piece semi-professional brass band, a large-scale choral performance enlisting amateur talent, a multi-purpose vocal quartet booked for several days, and an illustrated travel lecture or two. Then there were the professional readers. In 1897, for instance, the featured reader, Isabel Gargahill, gave five performances, including presentations of Dickens' *Christmas Carol* and the chariot race in *Ben Hur,* a story in black southern dialect, and an imitation of a country fiddler. In 1901, another female reader "assumed with rare ability" both male and female roles as she enacted the high points of *Cyrano de Bergerac,* and a clergyman gave "very dramatic and thrilling" recitations from *The Merchant of Venice* and *Julius Caesar,* pausing after each reading to explain the moral lesson therein.[32] In 1904, Elma Smith specialized in bird calls and humorous anecdotes presented in child dialect, while Ellsworth Plumstead in 1906 gave what were called "impersonations in costume" including selections from African-American author Paul Laurence Dunbar.[33]

Throw in other independent assemblies, and the list of performers—readers, monologists, impersonators, lecturers, musicians, magicians, moving picture exhibitors—goes on and on, enough to fill the nine hundred or so entries in *Talent*'s 1906 directory, *Who's Who in the Lyceum.* This is not to suggest that chautauqua allowed on its platform all the varieties of American "entertainment" available in this historical period. Nor is it to assume that the entertainments it did entertain were somehow untouched by or antithetical to chautauqua's deep commitment to cultural uplift, civic responsibility, and nondenominational Christianity. But as a sound event and a performance site, the platform circuit welcomed moving pictures, illustrated songs, and sleighbell melodies, as well as female Cyranos, white impersonators of African-American poets, and reverends reciting Shakespeare. Understanding this sort of heterogeneity and mixture is the necessary first step toward writing chautauqua into the cultural history of entertainment in early-twentieth-century America, along with amusement parks, vaudeville, tent shows, and nickelodeons.

Notes

1. Lawrence W. Levine, *Highbrow/Lowbrow: The Emergence of Cultural Hierarchy in America* (Cambridge: Harvard University Press, 1988), 256.

2. *Pontiac* (Illinois) *Daily Leader,* 5 August 1902, 2.

3. *Marinette* (Wisconsin) *Daily Eagle,* 2 August 1901, 1.

4. *Ottawa* (Kansas) *Evening Herald,* 16 June 1898, 3.

5. What clearly merits more attention here is how this type of "attraction" differs considerably from those pleasures and displays that Tom Gunning, Miriam Hansen, and others associate with the cinema of attractions. See, in particular, Hansen's notion of the "excess of appeals" in *Babel and Babylon: Spectatorship in American Silent Film* (Cambridge: Harvard University Press, 1991), 23–42.

6. See, for instance, the advertisement for J. C. Deagan, Chicago manufacturer of "Musical Specialty Instruments, Bells and Novelties as used by the leading artists over the world," in *Talent* 15, no. 6 (December 1904), 98.

7. Richard Abel notes that Robertson's troupe performed at the Schubert Theatre in Des Moines in 1906; see *The Red Rooster Scare: Making Cinema American, 1900–1910* (Berkeley: University of California Press, 1999), 192, n. 15.

8. At this time the lyceum program was typically a series of lectures and entertainments offered in a public or church hall during the fall and winter. It offered many of the same performers and attractions as the chautauqua circuit.

9. *Talent* 15, no. 1 (July 1904), 23; Charles Musser with Carol Nelson, *High-Class Moving Pictures: Lyman H. Howe and the Forgotten Era of Traveling Exhibition, 1880–1920* (Princeton: Princeton University Press, 1991), 77; and Charles Musser, *The Emergence of Cinema: The American Screen to 1907* (New York: Scribner's 1990), 166.

10. *Talent* 2, no. 11 (May 1892), 9.

11. *Talent* 3, no. 6 (December 1892), back cover; *Talent* 2, no. 12 (June 1893), 16. Robertson was apparently willing to stretch the boundaries of what might be taken as "wholesome" entertainment: the Brooklyn press criticized him in 1893 for booking certain "skirt dancers." *Talent* 4, no. 4 (October 1893), 2.

12. *Talent* 5, no. 12 (June 1895), 7.

13. Musser, *Emergence of Cinema,* 166, 303. Although Robertson is not mentioned by name, it is likely that it was his company that appeared as the Edison Projectoscope Company at several locations in 1898, including the Midland Chautauqua in Des Moines, Iowa. The local newspaper described this particular show as opening with a "a patriotic selection given by one of the company by means of a series of bells. It delighted the immense crowd of boys on the front seats"—see *Des Moines Leader,* 17 July 1898, 8.

14. *Talent* 11, no. 3 (September 1900), 10.

15. *Talent* 12, no. 2 (August 1901), 7.

16. *Talent* 14, no. 2 (January 1904), 15.

17. It is not clear at this point in my research precisely how and when Robertson expanded to five touring companies. Musser indicates that even after the nickelodeon era was well under way, Robertson's traveling shows continued to find success with programs designed for "church-affiliated groups and cultural conservatives." Eventually, however, Robertson's business for church groups "shifted away from motion picture exhibitions," though his American Entertainment Bureau remained in business "throughout the 1920s and 1930s"—*High-Class Moving Pictures,* 180, 273.

18. See *Main Street Amusements: Movies and Commercial Entertainment in a Southern City, 1896–1930* (Washington: Smithsonian Institution Press, 1995), 56–60; "Motion Pictures and Other Entertainment at Chautauqua," in *Cinema at the Turn of the Century,* ed. Claire Dupré la Tour, André Gaudreault, and Roberta Pearson (Quebec: Editions Nota Bene, 1998), 71–79; and "Film Exhibition at Independent Chautauqua Assemblies" (paper delivered at the 1997 Society for Cinema Studies conference).

19. Rick Altman, "The Silence of the Silents," *Musical Quarterly* 80, no. 4 (Winter 1996), 655. It is also worth noting, in the context of continuing debates over the makeup

of the audiences for early film, that independent chautauquas at the turn-of-the-century constituted a major exhibition site for many of these assembly-goers.

20. *Marinette Daily Eagle,* 24 July 1903, 1; 20 July 1897, 3.

21. *Marinette Daily Eagle,* 28 June 1904, 2.

22. *Marinette Daily Eagle,* 7 August 1897, 2.

23. *Marinette Daily Eagle,* 2 June 1897, 1.

24. *Marinette Daily Eagle,* 3 August 1897, 1. In his advertising Robertson boasted of "fitting the bill" for "the popular audience—for men and women, for children and adults, for people in every walk and station." *Talent* 17, no. 3 (September 1906), 85.

25. Robertson's large ad in *Talent* 17, no. 3 (September 1906), 85, lists a host of satisfied repeat customers, including the Northern Chautauqua and some 35 other assemblies.

26. *Des Moines Leader,* 14 July 1899, 2. *The Man in the Moon at Close Range* probably was an early trick film by Georges Méliès—see the Vitagraph ad in the *New York Clipper,* 13 May 1899, 217; and the Lubin ad in the *New York Clipper,* 10 June 1899, 300. Méliès made a version of *Cinderella* in the fall of 1899, but it was not shown in the USA until January 1900.

27. *Ottawa Evening Herald,* 16 June 1898, 3.

28. *Marinette Daily Eagle,* 31 July 1901, 3.

29. *Talent* 15, no. 1 (July 1904), 23.

30. *Talent* 17, no. 3 (September 1906), 85.

31. For a look at these issues from the perspective of the small-scale itinerant exhibitor, see Kathryn H. Fuller, *At the Picture Show: Small-Town Audiences and the Creation of Movie Fan Culture* (Washington: Smithsonian Institution Press, 1996), 1–27.

32. *Marinette Daily Eagle,* 10 August 1901, 2.

33. *Marinette Daily Eagle-Star,* 30 July 1906, 1.

13   The Story of Percy Peashaker: Debates about Sound Effects in the Early Cinema

Stephen Bottomore

It has become a nostrum of modern silent film aficionados that "silent films were never silent." While this is not strictly true,[1] it is certainly the case that the majority of film shows in the silent (and probably even in the early) period had some kind of sound accompaniment. The theory and practice of accompanying early films both with music and with the voice of a lecturer (*bonimenteur, erklärer*, etc.) have been quite well aired in recent scholarship. But the sound element that has been least covered in such discussions has been the use of sound effects, despite the fact that this was apparently quite a common practice.[2]

From the early years of the century, screenings of films, certainly in Europe and America, were often accompanied by effects, produced by individual "traps," and later using special sound effects machines, such as the Ciné Multiphone Rousselot and the Allefex, which incorporated a wide array of possible noises. Many commentators and audiences appreciated the addition of these sound effects to film shows, but a growing antagonism also developed to the practice: some people simply criticized the inappropriateness of some of the effects and the lack of skill of the operators, while others suggested that sound effects had no place at all in accompanying films. In the opinion of one sober writer of the time the question of whether or not to use effects "is undoubtedly a vexed one."[3] It seems likely that the widespread use of effects lasted less than half a dozen years, and the high-water mark may well have passed by the coming of the Great War. Live sound effects were certainly used throughout the twenties and beyond, but it seems not to the same extent as earlier. And perhaps one reason for this was the heated criticism that had been directed at effects in the early period.

When the earliest films were presented in the 1890s, they often took place either in silence or with only music or a lecturer to accompany them, but a number of the more enterprising showmen soon provided effects accompaniment. In the period after about 1906, as a wave of story films came onto the market, the number of film venues increased rapidly in Europe and America, and the use of sound effects was increasingly recommended to improve these shows. In 1907 the British *Kinematograph Weekly* was calling for the use of well-rehearsed effects for film shows, and suggesting that some firm could do good business if it put appropriate noisemaking devices—"living picture properties," as it called them—on the market.[4] A similar line was taken by the American trade press in the early years of the nickelodeon boom. Sound effects were seen as an additional attraction at film shows, and *Views and Film Index* suggested that patrons would really miss effects in some films, for example in a film that showed objects being smashed. *Views* added that well thought out effects might even help to clarify a film's plot.[5]

By 1909 the *Bioscope* was talking of the unnaturalness of seeing events such as explosions, typhoons, and battles without their accompanying sounds, and of the need to break this "silence of death" in films.[6] The journal proclaimed that such effects gave

> a swing and "go" to the general effect which cannot be surpassed by any other means. It should be as indispensable to the pictures as the wig is to the actor; and the reward comes with the delighted comments of the audience, and the increased cash takings.[7]

But within a few years a heated debate developed about the use of sound effects. William Selig, on a trip to London in the summer of 1909, told his interviewer that effects "are overdone, and the tendency is to spoil the pictures."[8] Over the next few years the trade press of Britain and America was full of comments critical of sound effects. The complaints were on several different grounds. For a start, there were objections that effects were out of sync with the picture. Thus the *Kine Weekly* in 1910 complained of a "misuse of effects," noting:

> The sound of musketry firing, before the emission of the smoke is also ludicrous, and the toot-toot of the horn of a motor car after the vehicle has been brought to a standstill is far removed from reality.[9]

Then there was the question of whether the *created* sound effect was a true representation of the sound that one would expect from the *real* scene. The *Moving Picture World*, in a 1909 editorial entitled "Sound Effects: Good, Bad and Indifferent," suggested that inaccuracy was the major problem with effects for films:

> The imitations should be fairly accurate or they shouldn't be attempted. Inaccuracy is worse than nothing. It creates wrong impressions and often it wrongly interprets the pictures. They must correspond or else they should be let alone.[10]

Sometimes the inaccuracy was merely annoying: for example, a heavy chain was used to supply sounds to accompany images of a troop of cavalry in *The Charge of the Light Brigade*.[11] But sometimes the effect could be quite ludicrously inappropriate: one critic complained of the "continuous use of a motor horn" in a screening of *The Last Days of Pompeii*.[12]

The sound of horses' hooves (often produced using coconut shells) was the cause of several complaints. The objection was that the "quick, sharp ring" that was made for the hooves was the same whether the horse shown on screen was seen running over soft earth, over hard earth, or on a road. In the real situation,

13.1. "Our Village Cinema,"
Punch, 19 February 1913.

OUR VILLAGE CINEMA.

Showman. " 'Ere, I say, it be 'orses' 'oovs, not 'orns or 'ail-storms.' "

critics pointed out, the sounds would be quite different depending on the nature of surface the horse was running over.[13]

Similarly, both cars and trains were often given exactly the same sound effect of a motor running. Yet, as a *Moving Picture World* editorial stated: "everybody knows they are different and the imitation should be different to correspond or else be omitted."[14] The sound used for cars was itself often very inaccurate. One writer suggested that the "throb" effect generated in many cinemas during car scenes was "little short of a libel on the modern automobile," being more like the sound of cars of ten or a dozen years before.[15] Another objection to effects was that they were too loud. From its premiere in Melbourne in December 1906, *The Story of the Kelly Gang* was accompanied by extensive sound effects, but this was not to everyone's taste, one journalist complaining:

> [T]here is a deal too much racket in connection with the show—sometimes you can't see the picture for the noise of horses, trains, gunshots and wild cries, but all the same it is the sort of bellowdrama that the lower disorders crave.[16]

During the summer of 1908, at a screening in New York of Edison's *Crossing the Plains in '49,* the effects apparently antagonized the entire audience, and led to vocal protests:

[T]he din and racket intended to represent rifle shots was strongly objected to by the audience, and cries of "cut it out," "stop the noise," and "keep still" were shouted from different parts of the house.[17]

Sometimes this excessive volume was due to the effects man's sounds failing to reflect the scale of the images on screen. So *Kine Weekly* noted in 1909:

The view appears somewhat in the distance, yet we often hear the sounds apparently in our midst. The "sound effect man" cannot well judge of this, and should receive his instructions as to volume of tone from someone situated in the middle of the hall during the time that the set of films are first run through.[18]

But whether or not lack of rehearsal was the cause, the excessive sound levels continued. In 1911 a spectator in Oregon objected to a screening of *The Three Musketeers* due to the outrageous level of the effects: "During the battle I thought I was in a cafeteria, being treated to a free lunch. That's the kind of effects we get to represent the dignity of the sword."[19] Not only was this kind of thing annoying to the audience, it might also adversely affect the pianist: "What good musician would play with a horrible banging to distract his attention," asked *The Cinema* in 1913.[20]

In the same year one writer in the *Kine Weekly* was so annoyed at this kind of accompaniment to films that he described the sounds as "perverted effects" and "cacaphonic embroidery." He suggested that this had reached its nadir in slapstick comedies, where sometimes the sound man

turns all the loudest handles within reach and an appalling crash follows which suggests the simultaneous collapse of Westminster Abbey and the Houses of Parliament. Later, perhaps, we have a heavier smash in the film—the odds are that our friend, having reached the maximum of din, turns again to his "thwack" handle. So the evening wears merrily away—resounding thuds and smacks where no blows are passed, enthusiastic effects of a motor engine when the car is seen to have broken down, "cavalry" effects when a tired horse ambles gently over grass, and so on, while those with a sense of humor in the audience grin ever broader and broader and the others seriously discuss the advisability of cotton wool.[21]

This writer was also indicating another problem with the practice of effects. It was not only that effects were inaccurate and excessively loud, it was also a more general problem: that effects were being used in an unthinking and crude manner, being added willy-nilly to anything in the image. Critic Louis Reeves Harrison also noted this wild and unthinking use of effects: the tendency to make a noise for anything, no matter how unimportant it was within the scene, while failing to take a cue from the *mood* of the scene. He coined the contemptuous name "Percy Peashaker" for drummers who worked in this way:

When there is water in the picture it goes to Percy's cerebrum. If there is a lake shown on the screen, no matter if it is a mile away, calm or stormy, he shakes his box of peas so that we may know that it is principally made of water. Realism becomes intense when a vessel appears and Percy blows a whistle "Oo-Oo" to enforce the fact that it is a steamer and not a full-rigged ship. "Bow-wow" indicates that we are looking at a dog and not a door-mat.[22]

The point was that the effects men were taking a far too literal approach to their job of reflecting in sound what was on screen. H. F. Hoffman had made a similar point the previous year, attacking the "irritating men" making loud and irrelevant sounds for films. For example, in a love scene that happened to have a horse in the background, every hoof beat was caught "with a keenness that soon attracts the attention of the audience to the horses' feet and away from the actors." Hoffman visited one theater with an especially diligent sound man where a film was shown that included a scene of the painful parting of two lovers:

> All at once a bird began to sing with great violence. I looked at the piano player in wonderment and found him looking the same at me. "What's that for," he asked. "You've got me," I replied, "I'll go and see." I found my friend with his cheeks and his eyes bulging out, blowing for his very life. "What's the trouble?" says I. "The bird! The bird!" says he, without removing the whistle. "Where?" says I. "There!" says he, pointing triumphantly with a stick to a diminutive canary in a tiny wooden cage on a top shelf at the far corner of the room. "Good boy!" I cried, giving him a wallop on the back that made him almost swallow his blooming whistle.[23]

Clearly the immediate culprits for this aesthetic quagmire were the operators of the effects devices. These were frequently unskilled youths—"effects boys"— who could be employed for very low wages. "Many proprietors imagine," noted the *Kine Weekly* in 1912, that effects can be worked "by any irresponsible or unimaginative youngster." But the result, it argued, was frequently "overdone or misapplied" effects.[24] The *Kine* the previous year suggested:

> It is often the case that a youth with no imagination, and with very limited brain power, combined with a spirit of mischief, "lets himself go," when presiding over the sound machine, the consequence being that dramatic pictures are made farcical by incongruous noises, and humorous pictures are accompanied by a "babel of sounds" that gets on the nerves.[25]

In the smaller cinemas in Paris, effects were also treated in this cavalier fashion, and often left to unskilled employees, especially youths.[26] British showman Waller Jeffs employed one man and half-a-dozen boys to "sound" his film shows, but noted that "sometimes the lads, with a heaven-sent opportunity to be noisy without the usual consequences of being naughty . . . greatly exceeded their duties."[27] And yet one could not blame the boys alone. Sometimes the manager himself demanded a regime of constant effects. Former effects boy H. H. Fullilove recalled that his boss hated any silence during the screening of films, and effects or music were demanded throughout the show. So for example, "Bird whistles were expected in country scenes whether birds were to be seen or not" and the effects were generally "very noisy."[28]

The taste of such managers sometimes went counter to the instinct of the

13.2. An overenthusiastic "noise expert," using an Allefex machine. *Johannesburg Sunday Times*, 25 December 1910.

operators of the effects. One theater in America was showing a film with a scene of a man dying of TB, in which his wife kisses the dying man. At this point the manager asked the drummer to imitate the sound of the kiss. The drummer wrote to a trade paper to complain: "Of course the people laughed—they always laughed when a kiss is imitated—and I think it spoiled the picture, because the scene was a sad one."[29] Sounds for kissing scenes became quite an issue. Apparently some effects men would "imitate" the kissing sound by "whacking the top of a barrel with a board,"[30] while in some theaters the rowdier element would imitate the effect themselves with a chorus of lip-smacks.[31]

Young Fullilove was allowed to do much the same: "I would also kiss the back of my hand to represent screen kisses, and in extreme cases pull a cork from an empty bottle!" Indeed he often made effects specifically to get laughs, and he liked

> to give my own interpretation of appropriate sounds. An example of this was in a comedy where if a character knocked on a door, I would ring a bell and vice versa, which seemed to have been much appreciated by the audience.[32]

It was said by the Yerkes company in America in 1910 that effects were especially effective in comedies, and could make audiences laugh "to the splitting point."[33]

This intentionally comic use of sound was made rather easy to do with some of the comic effects on sale or incorporated in effect machines. One of these was a baby cry, apparently used by some drummers when they saw a baby in a scene, provoking a big laugh from the audience.[34] Another effect "trap," recommended by one writer, was even more hilarious: costing a mere ten cents, the "Nose-Blo" was

> a ridiculously true-to-life imitation of a man blowing his nose. . . . There are many places where you can use it in the picture, and it is a pleasing change from the siren whistle and rattle and it will cause a gale of merriment to flow over the audience when used.[35]

Many believed that this kind of effects working was getting out of hand, and some thought that effects should be dispensed with altogether. "Why," asked the *Photo-Play* of Sydney in 1912, "are the beauties of modern films spoilt by the hideous clamor that is usually put up from behind the scenes?" The journal added that these effects were sometimes so annoying that it made one want to shout "Shut up, while I look at the pictures":

> I think as matters are at present in this line, if votes were taken by the audiences to abolish the effects' man, and his appliances, the proposition would be carried unanimously.[36]

In September 1911, a writer in the *Moving Picture World* also suggested that theaters organize votes to determine whether patrons wanted effects in addition to music or not: the writer himself was very anti-effects. Interestingly, though, the article was published back-to-back with one by a drummer that (unsurprisingly) was very much in favor of effects.[37] There were clearly strong views on both sides in the American film industry.

But some writers took a more neutral approach to the subject, being neither entirely pro nor entirely con, suggesting that one should have effects, but more *subtle* effects. In Britain, Frederick Talbot believed effects were a good idea for the cinema, as in the theater, "provided they are judiciously managed."[38] In France a similar line was being taken. G.-M. Coissac said sound effects could be very successful, "but they must be done with much circumspection."[39] One French effects man (*bruiteur*), Barat, told his new assistant that this should be artistic work: the eyes of the audience were being filled with images from the screen, and the sound men had similarly to please their ears![40] In America the critic Stephen Bush as usual had interesting things to say. As early as 1908, he recommended: "Attempt no effects that have not been thoroughly rehearsed," and added: "All effects that work well and are skillfully prepared will delight, all others will disgust."[41] Three years later Bush reiterated that effects could help a film, but only if rehearsed and performed carefully. He also addressed the effects-with-everything issue, stating that: "Each picture must be studied by itself and only such effects introduced as have a psychological bearing on the situation as depicted on the screen."[42]

This idea of a *psychological bearing* was an important one. The problem, as we've seen, was that sound men were taking their job too literally, and simply supplying sounds for anything that they saw on screen. But if one used the Bush approach, this might mean varying this practice in two ways: firstly, making sounds for some things that were not necessarily visible in the picture, and secondly, not making sounds for some things that *were* in the image.

A nice example of the former came in 1911. The *Film Index*'s music critic described the process of working out the effects on a short Pathé subject, *Butter Making in Normandy*:

> It is a short subject but, a very pretty picture and when the cows were shown on the screen I told the effect man to use a cow bell. He waited for a cow to appear with a cow bell hanging on it. But there was no cow bell shown in the picture. After the first show was over I asked him why he did not use a cowbell in the scene and he told me there was none in the picture, and I told him to use the effect [in] the next show regardless of the fact that there was none shown in the picture. The next show he used the bells and that night the manager remarked about the number of comments he had received on that short picture, that might otherwise have gone unnoticed. I have found that in many pictures you can draw a little on your imagination in working effects and get very good results.[43]

The corollary of this approach of imaginatively *adding* effects was whether to *reduce* the number of sounds. In other words, should one supply sounds for *everything* in the image or just some *particular* sounds? When in 1911 a reader wrote in asking how to make the sound of a car engine, *Kine Weekly*'s expert suggested using two cycle pumps, but added:

> [R]eally, the public is by this time quite educated to doing without the engine sounds in moving picture motor chases. Only don't forget to honk a motor horn occasionally.[44]

In other words, the advice was to selectively *indicate* the car through a horn, not to *imitate* it with an engine sound. On the other hand, the *Bioscope*'s Paris correspondent criticized a show for taking exactly this approach: in a film of a fire brigade in action the sound of engine horns was added in one show, but no sound was supplied for the horses' hooves or the bells on the horses. The writer thought that *all* of these sounds should have been added.[45]

One of the most interesting contributions to this "some or all" discussion of effects came from the *Bioscope*'s music columnist in 1913. He suggested:

> Effect-working to cinematograph pictures must necessarily be a very incomplete art, because the sounds which it is possible to imitate can, at the best, be only about a quarter of those actually suggested by the film. And it is very essential, therefore, to select for imitation only those sounds which would be unusually prominent and important in actuality.[46]

He made the point that in many domestic dramas there was actually little going on in the image that would generate any sound (and the human voice was out-

13.3. A rare moment of silence from an effects set-up and the pianist too. From "Jackass Music," *Moving Picture World*, 21 January 1911.

side the realm of effects, he thought), so to provide the few effects that suggested themselves in such films was surely inappropriate, for

> to maintain silence throughout the main portion of a long film and then to cut in suddenly for about two seconds with the absolutely unimportant sound of a motor-car or a horse galloping, is simply to draw attention to the limited nature of your effects.

The most suitable films in which effects should be used, he thought, were those in which the effects could be continued through much of the film: such as railway journeys, travel films, industrial and topical films. As for dramas, only a few, such as those with battle scenes, called for effects.[47]

Emmett Campbell Hall in the *Moving Picture World* moved the discussion on to suggest that if one omits *some* sounds, one might eliminate them all: "[W]e are treated to a merry honk-honk when an automobile comes down a crowded city street, while cars, trucks and horses flit noiselessly by like visions in a fevered brain." Similarly a huge battle scene was accompanied by "a futile little popping," and a powerful express train by a mere "toot-toot." This was, he thundered, "sound-effect vandalism":

> To make this *occasional-sound* [my italics] business approach intelligent [*sic*], it would be necessary to presuppose a condition of hearing somewhat corresponding

to color blindness, only infinitely greater in effect; the ability to hear sounds only of a peculiar and determined nature."

And to do the job properly, "the sound artist would have to have as many hands as a centipede has legs, and about a carload of effects to 'sound' an average picture."[48] Hall's radical suggestion, therefore, was that effects should be abolished entirely. But if sound effects were banished, what sound accompaniment to films would take their place? Some theorists suggested that the piano alone was sufficient accompaniment for films. In an article entitled "Coconuts or Ivories?" Bert Vipond argued that

> the use of even the most perfectly constructed mechanical effects is unnecessary and artistically wrong, because there is something which can produce every conceivable effect, *including* the human voice, in a way that is not mechanical. This instrument is, of course, the piano.

With an intelligent performer, the piano could replace mechanical effects with what he called "musical effects" (he mentions one pianist who even managed to play "a clever musical representation of a sneeze").[49] Emmett Hall also suggested that music was sufficient accompaniment to films, as it "does not attract the conscious attention."

Another theorist, Clarence Sinn, in late 1910 expanded on this idea of music as effect, and provided a useful dichotomy of two types of music: "The instruments in a picture show orchestra are used for twofold purposes, viz., to provide music and furnish sound effects." The musical side was "descriptive, and is merely accessory to the picture," while the sound effect side was "part of the picture." That is to say, the former was effectively "mood music," while in the latter case, the musicians were imitating something within the scene. Included in this "effects" role of music was that of accompanying scenes in which characters played instruments. Sinn suggested that: "The difference between the 'accessory' and the 'sound effect' can be made apparent enough if the musician uses judgment."[50]

It is clear that this idea of "effect music" was quite important, and soon became a standard technique for musicians, especially in smaller theaters where the effects boys were already being given the sack. In one of the earliest published guide books for cinema musicians from 1913, the author, Eugene Aherne, devoted an entire section to this technique of "effect playing," that is, of imitating certain sounds using the piano's keys alone. He emphasized that such effects, especially comic ones, should not be overdone.[51]

> Many pianists of today who accompany silent films are effectively applying the same aesthetic: for example, when an on-screen character is playing a musical instrument, the theater pianist will try to imitate the style or even the tune. And when there is a crash in a comedy they might give an additional thump on the keys. It is worth adding that there was nothing new in this concept of music as effect, for it was even used in magic lantern shows in the nineteenth century: in *Jane Conquest,* for instance, "a cry of mortal fear" in the plot was to be indicated by "Music—a Weird Chord."[52]

13.4. Another overenthusiastic effects boy. *Kinematograph and Lantern Weekly,* 20 November 1913.

ᵖROGRAM Boʏ: " Wotcher get the sack for ? "
ᴇFFᴄᴛs Boʏ: " Why, one night I worked the bloomin' thunder so natural th⸱
turned the manager's beer sour. That done it ! "

It seems that with the passage of time, from the 1910s onward, effects were used less promiscuously in cinemas of all sizes. But they did not go away entirely. In later years sound effects were apparently most often used in certain genres that seemed to evoke loud noises, especially in military films: "a battle scene is so empty without these effects," said one writer in 1913.[53] Apparently during the First World War sound effects were often used when showing military films: in a screening of *The Battle of Jutland* in Harwich, thunder flashes were detonated, filling the cinema with smoke (and clearing the first three rows, it was said!).[54]

Effects were also sometimes used through the later teens and twenties, especially in larger theaters. In a theater with an orchestra, this might be the responsibility of a drummer (as in the teens), sometimes using the individual effect traps of former years.[55] Some cinema organs incorporated effects devices, which might be operated by the feet, to enable the organist to continue playing the music with his hands.[56] In non-Western countries there are anecdotes of live sound effects being introduced in screenings in later years: as late as 1942, in China, where footsteps and machine gun sounds were imitated for outdoor screenings.[57]

But the most interesting period for debate over effects was undoubtedly the early teens. And this debate should be seen within the context of a wider discussion about sound and film. During the early cinema period the use of all forms of sound accompaniment—lecturers, effects, dialogue, various forms of music, and experiments with sync sound—suggests that there was a feeling that the pictures alone lacked something, a feeling that was to be fully satisfied only with the "coming of sound" to the cinema in the late 1920s. The theoretical debate over sound effects—and especially about how, when, or whether to use them—not only was extremely interesting, but may well have laid the foundation for an aesthetic governing sound effects practice in later periods of cinema. When commercial sync sound arrived in the late twenties there was already a tradition of both theory and practice to build on in working out how to make sound, and sound effects, mesh with the pictures. Perhaps this is one reason why the practice of incorporating effects along with other sound elements was so swiftly mastered in the 1930s. But that is another story.

Notes

1. See Rick Altman's important essay, "The Silence of the Silents," *Musical Quarterly* 80, no. 4 (Winter 1996), 648–718.

2. An earlier section of this essay, which covers many other aspects of effects (including their use in pre-cinema and in the first film shows, and the various effects traps and machines, especially the Allefex), appears as "An International Survey of Sound Effects in Early Cinema," *Film History* 11, no. 4 (1999), 485–498.

3. Colin N. Bennett, *The Handbook of Kinematography*, 2nd ed. (London: Kinematograph and Lantern Weekly, 1913), 280.

4. *Kinematograph and Lantern Weekly*, 5 September 1907, 258; 12 September 1907, 274–275.

5. *Views and Film Index*, 13 October 1906, 3.

6. *Bioscope*, 7 October 1909, 5.

7. "Effect Machines," *Bioscope*, 8 November 1909, 4. Effects were also praised as improving the films in *Kinematograph and Lantern Weekly*, 17 June 1909, 285.

8. *Kinematograph and Lantern Weekly*, 19 August 1909, 709.

9. *Kinematograph and Lantern Weekly*, 18 August 1910, 925.

10. *Moving Picture World*, 2 October 1909, 441—reprinted in *Bioscope*, 14 October 1909, 29.

11. *Kinematograph and Lantern Weekly*, 7 November 1912, 200.

12. *Kinematograph and Lantern Weekly*, 13 November 1913, 3.

13. *Moving Picture World*, 2 October 1909. On hoof sounds see also *Picture Theatre News*, 9 August 1911, 7.

14. *Moving Picture World*, 2 October 1909.

15. *Picture Theatre News*, 14 February 1912, 7.

16. *Sydney Bulletin*, 24 January 1907—quoted in Daniel Catrice, *Cinemas in Melbourne, 1896–1942* (master's thesis, Monash University, Monash, Australia, 1991), 16–17.

17. "Anti-Noise Movement," *New York Dramatic Mirror*, 1 August 1908, 7.

18. *Kinematograph and Lantern Weekly*, 27 May 1909, 145.

19. *Moving Picture World*, 21 October 1911, 189.

20. *The Cinema*, 27 August 1913, 69.

21. *Kinematograph and Lantern Weekly*, 20 March 1913, 2044–2045. See also P. Lindsay in "Picture Effects: Manipulating the 'Sound Makers,'" *Views and Film Index*, 18 January 1908, 11.

22. "Jackass Music," *Moving Picture World*, 21 January 1911, 124. At this time there was also rare praise for particular drummers: a correspondent to *Moving Picture World* praised a Bill Judd, who could play various instruments and sing, as well as make effects devices, including one to imitate the sound of a pump. *Moving Picture World*, 18 February 1911, 353.

23. "Drums and Traps," *Moving Picture World*, 23 July 1910, 184–185.

24. *Kinematograph and Lantern Weekly*, 14 November 1912, 331.

25. *Kinematograph and Lantern Weekly*, 4 May 1911, 1792.

26. See Jean-Jacques Meusy, *Paris Palaces, ou le Temps des Cinémas, 1894–1918* (Paris: AFRHC/CNRS Editions, 1995), 388–389.

27. John H. Bird, *Cinema Parade: Fifty Years of Film Shows* (Birmingham: Cornish Brothers, 1946), 30.

28. H. H. Fullilove, *Animated Pictures: The World before Your Eyes*, 3. Manuscript in BFI Special Collections.

29. *Moving Picture World*, 18 February 1911, 353.

30. *Film Index*, 21 November 1908, 11–12. The article notes that the same device was apparently used to generate many other sounds too.

31. One of the more annoying activities of the young men of Gopher Prairie (Sinclair Lewis's fictional Midwestern town) was their "smacking moist lips over every love-scene at the Rosebud Movie Palace." See Sinclair Lewis, *Main Street* (New York: Bantam Books, 1996 [1920]), 117.

32. Fullilove, 3–4.

33. "Yerkes Noise Makers on Tour," *Film Index*, 19 March 1910, 10.

34. "Our Music Page," *Moving Picture News*, 24 February 1912, 15. Such comic use of effects overturned a convention that sound effects in films are generally realistic (whereas when indicated in comic strips they are often exaggerated). See "Glop, pas glop . . . ," *Cinémaction* (Summer 1990), 48–51.

35. "Our Music Page," *Moving Picture News*, 24 February 1912, 15.

36. *Photo-Play*, 10 August 1912, 249—in a report from Brisbane. The following year the *Eclair Bulletin* in America made the same point, suggesting that managers whisper to their trap drummer, "Cut out all effects." *Eclair Bulletin* 36 (February 1913), 2.

37. Emmett Campbell Hall, "Those Sound Effects," and (pro) Clyde Martin, "Working the Sound Effects," *Moving Picture World*, 23 September 1911, 873–874.

38. Frederick A. Talbot, *Moving Pictures, How They Are Made and Worked* (London: William Heinemann, 1912), 139–140.

39. G. Michel Coissac, *Manuel Pratique du conférencier-projectionniste* (Paris: 1908), 202. Another French critic suggested that effects should be kept to a minimum "because the cinema is after all an art." *Ciné-Journal*, reported in *La Rivista Fono-Cinematografica*, 7 October 1911, 5. For effects practice in Italy, see *Immagine* 32 (1995), 20–25.

40. This was c.1907. See Meusy, 144.

41. "Hints to Exhibitors," *Moving Picture World*, 24 October 1908, 317. On care with effects and the need for rehearsal, see *Kinematograph and Lantern Weekly*, 20 February 1908, 253.

42. "When 'Effects' Are Unnecessary Noises," *Moving Picture World*, 9 September 1911, 690.

43. Clyde Martin, "Playing the Pictures," *Film Index*, 14 January 1911, 11. Martin notes that the sound effects man already had an attitude of working effects on "the principle features only."

44. *Kinematograph and Lantern Weekly,* 1 June 1911, 203.

45. *Bioscope,* 21 December 1911, 849.

46. *Bioscope,* 20 March 1913, 853. He also said that the chief requirement of an effects worker was "discretion . . . because effects rendered promiscuously and with no discrimination are very much worse than useless."

47. Another writer also advised that effects were best for "travels and industrials" or military scenes, but should not accompany "domestic plays." *The Cinema,* 12 March 1913, 40.

48. "With Accompanying Noises," *Moving Picture World,* 10 June 1911, 1296.

49. *Kinematograph and Lantern Weekly,* 2 March 1911, 1213.

50. Clarence Sinn in late 1910 in *Moving Picture World,* quoted in Altman. (Sinn also included the imitation of tom-toms to accompany Indian pictures as "effect" music.) *Moving Picture World*'s article was reprinted without attribution in "The Picture Musicians' Page," *The Cinema,* 12 March 1913, 37.

51. Eugene A. Aherne, *What and How to Play for Pictures* (Twin Falls: News Print, 1913), 53–55.

52. *Jane Conquest: An Illustrated Poem* (London: Warren, Hall and Lovitt, n.d.). The text is in the fabulous collection of David Francis, who brought this issue to my attention.

53. *The Cinema,* 9 April 1913, 37. Even military panoramas in the nineteenth century were presented with gunfire effects: see Herman Hecht, *Pre-Cinema History* (London: Bowker Saur, 1993), item 534B. Providing effects for military films could be done relatively simply, using a big drum to provide bangs coincident with explosions. See the letter from "Jim" in *Cambridge Daily News,* 2 September 1938, 6. (Courtesy Nick Hiley.)

54. Ad by Hawkes in *The Cinema,* 12 November 1914, 27; Chris Strachan, *The Harwich Electric Palace* (author, 1979), n.p. See also "Sunderland and Wearside Highlights," *Bioscope,* 1 October 1913, 43.

55. Albert A. Hopkins, "Noises for the Movies," *Scientific American,* January 1922, 30–31.

56. See the splendid illustration in *Illustrated London News,* 10 August 1929, 239. For a fine illustration of an American effects installation, see "Les Bruits du Cinéma," *La Nature* 47 (22 November 1919), 335–336. The North West Film Archive, Manchester, holds a transcript of an interview with Albert Jones, who made sound effects in British cinemas in the 1920s.

57. Jay Leyda, *Dianying* (Boston: MIT Press, 1972), 116. For Syria in the 1920s and 1930s, see Georges Sadoul, *Cinema in the Arab Countries* (Beirut: Interarab Centre of Cinema and Television, 1966), 100–101.

14 That Most American of Attractions, the Illustrated Song

Richard Abel

Several years ago, a local historian who knew I was researching early film exhibition in Des Moines gave me an article on the Radium Theater, which opened on May 30, 1907.[1] The article included a rare photograph of the Radium that day, and immediately I was struck by two things. One was the street corner entrance with its unusual "old English style" facade, described in the text as "half timbers finished in weathered oak and plaster." The other was the posters: one promoted a free Letter Carriers' Band concert that opening night; another listed the weekend program, with illustrated songs coming before the moving pictures. The singers were "well known," the text added: "Laurena L. Lewis [*sic*] and Floyd F. Garret [*sic*], formerly of the Chamberlain Quartet of Drake University."[2] Now that's odd, I thought: here's a nickelodeon that advertised itself as "the brightest spot in town," yet its main attractions were musical performances. But was it really so odd, I wondered? Given the heterogeneous "aesthetic of collective performance" that marked the nickelodeon,[3] could music have been an attraction equal to that of moving pictures, particularly when lantern slide images "illustrated" a song? That is the question I want to explore in this essay: first, by describing several moments in the brief history of illustrated songs, between 1904 and 1910, drawing on selected newspapers as well as the trade press for vaudeville and early cinema; then, by exploring several ideas about how illustrated songs functioned, what pleasures they elicited, in conjunction (or not) with moving pictures, especially in the context of the cinema's "Americanization" toward the end of this period.

The "song illustrator" (a vocalist, accompanied by a pianist and projected colored slides), let's not forget, was a common vaudeville act during the decade prior to the first nickelodeons.[4] This was especially true of "family" vaudeville, and Portland, Oregon (a city of about 150,000), provides a good record of that, from early 1904, when the first theater opened, to spring 1905, when five were competing for customers.[5] Some vocalists were local and regular performers at a particular theater: Kate Coyle at the Arcade or Edna Foley at the Bijou. Others had a regional reputation: there was the New York baritone, Raymond Baldwin, at the Lyric, or the "California favorite," Roscoe Arbuckle (later famous as Fatty), featured at the Star for two months in 1905. Family vaudeville programs ran anywhere from five to ten acts, and the illustrated songs and moving pictures usually came in tandem at the end, probably because they used the same

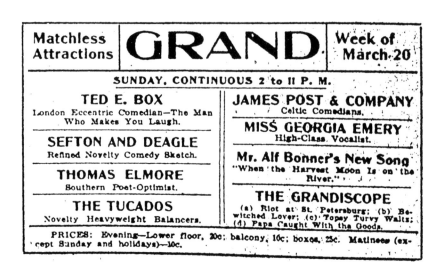

14.1. Grand Theater advertisement. *Portland Oregonian*, 19 March 1905.

projecting apparatus. When titles were listed, which was not infrequent, the songs were familiar: sentimental, nostalgic, patriotic—"In the Shade of the Old Apple Tree," "Only a Private, That's All," "Goodbye, Sis," "Your Dad Gave His Life for His Country."[6] Perhaps not unexpectedly, given the variety and varied pace of vaudeville programs, the songs often were set off from the moving pictures that followed. In late July 1904, for instance, at the Grand, Catherine Manning's rendition of "Way Down East" was juxtaposed to Edison's *The Great Train Robbery*. In January 1905, also at the Grand, Alf Bonner's "Down in the Vale of Shenandoah" contrasted with Pathé's *Life of Louis XIV*.[7] Two months later, at the same theater, Donner's version of that "great illustrated ballad," "When the Harvest Moon Is on the River," differed sharply in mood from two Pathé titles, *Riot in St. Petersburg* and *Bewitched Lover*.[8]

In a sense, the nickelodeons that emerged in 1905–1906 built their short programs around these popular tandem acts. Certainly, by then, the ads for popular songs and moving pictures were prominent in the vaudeville trade press. Music publishers sometimes flagged the manufacturers of their song slides, and Gus Edwards reproduced at least once the full set of slide images for his "cute and delicious song," "Two Dirty Little Hands."[9] The early trade press for moving pictures, of course, made film subjects the chief attraction of the nickelodeons, but illustrated songs were hardly ignored. Just three months after its founding in April 1906, for instance, *Views and Films Index* introduced a "new department" of the "latest song slides" available from two New York manufacturers: Elite Lantern and Harstn.[10] By January 1907, the list included two more firms in New York (DeWitt Wheeler and Scott & Van Altena) and two others in Chicago (Boswell and Chicago Transparency).[11] Moreover, as a sign of their importance, for several months the listing for song slides took up as much space as that for moving pictures. Similarly, in one of its first issues, in March 1907, *Mov-*

14.2. Song slide from "She Waits by the Deep Blue Sea" (Scott & Van Altena, 1906). Marnan Collection, Minneapolis, Minnesota.

ing Picture World published the names and addresses of a dozen New York music publishers that, having quickly recognized the nickelodeon's potential for advertising (however indirect), profitably sold or rented lantern slides to accompany their songs.[12] The following fall, in an oft-cited editorial noting "the tremendous demand for song slides," the *World* singled out three New York manufacturers for special praise: DeWitt Wheeler for the quantity of its offerings, Scott & Van Altena for the quality of its slides, and Henry Ingram for specializing in song slides for old ballads.[13] At the same time, in an interview given to *Show World*, shortly after he returned from a trip to Europe, Max Lewis, president of the Chicago Film Exchange (a major rental agency), noted the singularity of "the illustrated song and vocalist" in American nickelodeons: in most of the motion picture theaters he visited in France and Germany, Lewis claimed, "illustrated songs were absolutely unknown."[14]

If the trade press more than acknowledged the popular appeal of illustrated songs, what sense of that appeal do we get by looking at certain cities and towns in 1907? Here, the regular ads run by nickelodeons in the *Des Moines Register* suggest that the tandem act of pictures and songs was far from uniform in Iowa's largest city.[15] The Nickeldom (formerly the Bijou family vaudeville house) clearly stressed moving pictures from its debut in May 1906; this also was true of the Colonial, Jewel, and Dreamland (all three opened in the downtown shopping and entertainment district, between April and July 1907). Indeed, the Nickeldom and Colonial usually did not even mention songs in their ads, and Dreamland only once singled out a song, the "descriptive story ballad," She Waits by the Deep Blue Sea."[16] When it debuted in late May, therefore, the Radium was different. One of its initial ads placed the illustrated song, "Any Old Time," before its two pictures, *A Nervous Maid* and *Two Sisters*; another two months later featured that "peach" of a Harry von Tilzer hit, "Are You Coming Out Tonight, Mary Ann."[17] For several weeks in June, in both the *Register* and the *Mail and Times* (a women's club weekly), the Radium headlined tenor Lloyd Garrett and baritone Lawrence Lewis as the featured attraction on its

14.3. Radium Theater advertisement. *Des Moines Mail and Times*, 21 June 1907.

programs.[18] Moreover, in a directory of "Amusement Houses," the *Mail and Times* listed the Radium as the one theater featuring both "moving pictures and songs."[19] The Lyric, which opened in late July as a "combination house" (with vaudeville, moving pictures, and illustrated songs), also gave considerable attention to its singers, Miss Williams and baritone Harry Preston (from New York).[20] Except when it was showing Pathé's *Passion Play* as a two-week special that fall,[21] the Lyric continued to promote live performers over moving pictures. If the majority of nickelodeons in Des Moines featured moving pictures, two were distinctive in favoring songs and song slides.

A slightly different sense of how pictures and songs worked as a tandem act in 1907 comes from Ottumwa, in southeast Iowa, whose population of 20,000 was less than one-fourth that of Des Moines.[22] Opening almost simultaneously in June, the Nickelodeon and the Electric Theatre competed with regular ads in the *Ottumwa Courier*. The Electric's programs, comprising two songs and anywhere from three to six films, lasted an hour. The Nickelodeon, by contrast, ran "continuous shows" of twenty minutes: one song alternated with one or two films. Both Ottumwa theaters, unlike those in Des Moines, consistently listed the titles of both pictures and songs but never named the singers (they used either local amateurs or, less likely, phonograph records); an exception was Professor Hawley's Colored Quartette featured one week night at the Electric. What is intriguing about these programs is how frequently the pictures and songs explicitly complement or "counterpoint" one another. One weekend in late August, for instance, the Nickelodeon showed Edison's version of the Irish melodrama *Kathleen Mavourneen* together with the nostalgic ballad "Farewell My Annabelle." By contrast, in early October, the Nickelodeon juxtaposed Pathé's historical drama *A Venetian Tragedy* (a husband kills his wife's lover) with "Hattie Williams' big song hit" from New York, "My Irish Rosie."[23] Finally,

146 *Richard Abel*

and most blatantly, in early November, the theater combined Pathé's *A Slave's Love* (two lovers commit suicide in ancient Greece) and *Pay Day* (a drunken worker unsuccessfully tries to negotiate the streets of Paris) with what was heralded as the "greatest patriotic song ever written," "The Good Old USA"—with the "most wonderful slides" by Scott & Van Altena.[24]

Before turning more fully to those promised pleasures, let me touch on one last moment in 1909, when *Moving Picture World* and the *New York Dramatic Mirror* already were claiming that illustrated songs were "degraded" and their popularity was on the wane.[25] Whether or not this was the case in New York, the center of both trade weeklies' attention, it seems not to have been true in St. Louis (then the sixth-largest city in the country).[26] Just look at the ads in the *St. Louis Times,* an evening paper, during the weeks before and after Christmas, 1909–1910.[27] Of the nearly thirty theaters represented, varying widely in location, size, and kind of performance, more than half included illustrated songs on their programs. A half dozen did no more than mention them, but the rest signaled the attraction of the singers or songs. The Grand Central (one of the more prestigious theaters in the city) featured "vocal selections by Myron J. Wilkoff" (among them, "Come to Me in Dreamtime"), while the Bell Theater hailed Jack Houren as "St. Louis' most popular baritone." The Hippodrome had Signor Bandiera Giovanni ("formerly of the Merry Widow Company") performing in both English and Italian. The Histograph featured "illustrated songs by Charles Voerg" as well as "contralto soloist Cherry Boyd"; the Surprise Theater, "illustrated songs by Chas. Fawcett" or "Mrs. J. T. Renick." At the Orpheum (opened Christmas Day), Mr. Wells was singing popular tunes such as "Beautiful Eyes," while at the Casino (another major downtown theater) Frank Witt was doing the "latest hits" of Harry von Tilzer, the well-known New York music composer and publisher, "with great success." As the very last ad on this page reveals, most of the slides for these illustrated songs probably came from St. Louis Calcium Light, the "oldest song slide exchange" in the country and the source of the largest archive of song slide material still extant, the John Ripley collection, now part of the Marnan Collection in Minneapolis.[28]

As this brief survey suggests, the tandem act of illustrated songs and moving pictures flourished at a particular historical moment in early cinema's emergence. Together, songs and pictures made of the nickelodeon a unique mix of national mass culture and local popular culture. Both were cultural commodities that could circulate throughout the country, almost simultaneously; yet both became "finished products" only in performance.[29] Specifically, the illustrated song depended on an already centralized industry of production: New York's Tin Pan Alley of music publishers and New York or Chicago song slide manufacturers. For its part, the industry sometimes even hired out its own singers or "pluggers" as a means of generating more sales of sheet music.[30] The illustrated song was no less dependent, however, on a decentralized component of local performers: a pool of vocalists, pianists, or even small orchestras, and audiences willing to engage in sing-alongs (the chorus of a song usually was printed on the last slide of a set). That many of these performers were young

14.4. Song sheet cover for "Beautiful Eyes" (1909). Marnan Collection, Minneapolis, Minnesota.

women is now well documented, whether they "tickled the ivory," "warbled" the latest song lyric up front, or simply joined in singing the chorus. On the one hand, illustrated songs offered an acceptable means of employment for young women who were then entering the work force in record numbers. In 1908, for instance, in Grand Rapids, Michigan, singers earned ten to eighteen dollars a week and pianists, five to twelve dollars; one theater owner even made their work less grueling by hiring two shifts a day.[31] On the other hand, the songs and sing-alongs also helped establish nickelodeons as reputable places especially for women to gather, whether for "drop-in" visits after work or on lunch breaks, while shopping in the afternoon, or for evening family outings.[32] Moreover, from St. Louis to Ottumwa, the singers and song slides linked "provincial" capitals and small towns more closely to the country's centers of culture.[33] As Jack Sands, from Roseville, Ohio, put it in the last lines of a bit of doggerel,

> Don't you know that song is a New York "Hit"?
> And the moving pictures are really IT.[34]

Within a metropolitan center like New York City, illustrated songs probably functioned differently from one district or neighborhood to another, but one in particular stands out when compared to what they meant at some venues in Des Moines or even St. Louis. As a number of historians (myself included) have argued, in certain areas of New York (as well as other urban centers), nickelodeons served as a significant venue of assimilation for the masses of new immigrants from eastern and southern Europe.[35] From travelogues to dramatic and comic stories, American moving pictures offered immigrants models of behavior and personal appearance to imitate or at least to accept as standard and superior to that of their country of origin. In parallel fashion, the illustrated songs, much as television does today, helped the immigrants learn the common language of their adopted country. Here, for instance, is Mrs. Joe Fleischer recalling her early movie-going on the Lower East Side: "After we heard a song several times, with the pictures, and joined in the singing, most of us could understand what the song was about. That's how we learned to speak English."[36] Yet in other areas of high immigration, nickelodeons seem to have served, at least for a time, as "community centers" for maintaining ties to the "old country." One telling example was Barberton, Ohio, on the outskirts of Akron, fast becoming the new center of the rubber industry, especially for automobiles: there, at least one theater claimed that "all of its songs" were sung "in the Slavish language" of its many recent immigrants.[37]

In Des Moines, by contrast, nickelodeons could be aligned with the city's middle-class pretensions to high culture. Such pretensions were characteristic of the Midwest at the turn of the last century, according to Jon Teaford, and depended on the strong musical tradition of the great numbers of German immigrants who earlier had settled there.[38] Theaters like the Radium and the Lyric, therefore, could exploit illustrated songs as a form of cultural capital. Implicitly endorsed by the local women's club, through the *Mail and Times,* and linked at least once to Drake University's Conservatory of Music, the singers and songs gave these two theaters a measure of distinction, a special aura of legitimacy.[39] At the same time, of course, this aura served to uplift and legitimate the new "cheap amusements" as a whole. That Des Moines was far from being an anomaly for this kind of uplift is clear from the similar practice of promoting illustrated songs and singers even at a later date, and in a larger city such as St. Louis (whose population also included many former German immi-grants). In their initial ads in the *Times,* during the late summer of 1909, certain theaters there clearly exploited their singers and songs as a mark of distinction.[40] The Savoy, for instance, put its "musical artist," Harry Mayer, at the top of its first ads; the Bell and the Liberty were quite specific about the singers they fea-tured each week but little more than generic about the "latest moving pictures" shown; the Grand Central and the Hippodrome may have listed film titles on their daily programs, but they gave more attention to their singers' names as well as the popular songs they performed.[41] By the end of the year, as noted ear-lier, these and other theaters regularly were featuring the attraction of local and touring vocalists well known as "high culture" performers. At least in St. Louis, this kind of advertising assumed that "legitimate" singers doing popular songs lent a greater sense of respectability to moving picture theaters than did a simple listing of film titles (even if identified by their manufacturer's trade-mark).[42]

Let me conclude with one further point of difference. Although pictures and songs worked in tandem on nickelodeon programs, they ultimately sharp-ened and enforced a significant national cultural difference. The nickelodeon emerged and flourished, after all, partly because of the quantity and quality of French films supplied with regularity by Pathé-Frères.[43] Well into 1908, often a majority of the moving pictures shown in nickelodeons were "foreign" (most of them from Pathé). By contrast, illustrated songs were expressly, blatantly "American." If by 1908, as I have argued elsewhere, American films tended to be characterized in the trade press as "upbeat" in comparison to French films, whose stories increasingly were denounced as "depressing" or "in bad taste," the distinction was equally if not more valid for illustrated songs.[44] Evidence of that was apparent even in Ottumwa, as shown earlier in the contrast between "The Good Old USA" and *A Slave's Love* and the drunken comedy of *Pay Day.* But the "upbeat" quality of these song slides also is plain to see in surviving series such as "Only a Message from Home Sweet Home" (1905), "Sunbonnet Sue" (1906), and "Here Comes the Whippoorwill" (1908), reproduced from the Mar-nan Collection in performances of The Living Nickelodeon.[45] No less plain to see is how strikingly similar are the white middle-class figures (often depicted as romantic couples) inhabiting the colorful "dream world" of the song slides to the "Anglo-Saxon models" of youth (both men and women) then populating the ads and covers of the new mass magazine such as *Ladies Home Journal* and *Saturday Evening Post.* The latter, as T. J. Jackson Lears describes them, were the "smoother, cleaner, more activist and athletic" figures, who—to quote a Gil-lette ad in the *Saturday Evening Post*—had "the country's future . . . written in [their] faces."[46] In short, that future was one that moviegoers of all kinds, almost everywhere, also were being invited to share or at least aspire to.

Once the cinema's emergence in the United States is framed as a struggle for dominance between "American" and "foreign" (that is, French) interests, as it was by 1908,[47] then even all those popular songs—however romantic, sentimen-

14.5. Nickelodeon advertisement, *Ottumwa Courier,* 8 November 1907.

tal, or nostalgic—and often gorgeously colored slides on nickelodeon programs take on a seriously combative role. For their very presence, hailing an audience into vocal response, helped to secure the nickelodeon as an American institution, celebrating an "American way of life," especially if the moving pictures shown in tandem were indelibly marked as French or "foreign."[48] In a sense, then, illustrated songs assured a firm base from which, as film manufacturers from "the good old USA" finally began to displace Pathé and other European competitors, the cinema itself could become more truly American.

Notes

In revising this essay, I am grateful to Margaret and Nancy Bergh for letting me research the song slides, sheet music, and other material in the Marnan Collection, Minneapolis, Minnesota. Thanks also to Rick Altman for helping to arrange this research and for his comments on the original text.

1. "The Radium," *Midwestern,* July 1907, 59–60. See, also, the initial ad for the Radium, in *Des Moines Register and Leader,* 26 May 1907, 3, 2.

2. See also the Radium ad in *Des Moines Mail and Times,* 21 June 1907, 8.

3. I borrow this term from Tim Anderson, "Reforming 'Jackass Music': The Problematic Aesthetics of Early American Film Music Accompaniment," *Cinema Journal* 37, no. 1 (Fall 1997), 5. Rick Altman offers a thorough survey of the heterogeneity of sound in the nickelodeon (although one can question his emphases) in "The Silence of the Silents," *Musical Quarterly* 80, no. 4 (Winter 1996), 648–718.

4. See, for instance, "Song Slide Department: Beginning of Illustrated Songs," *Film Index,* 18 December 1909, 18. Also see the Jos. W. Stern ad in the *New York Clipper,* 27 May 1899, 258; and the M. Witmark ad in the *New York Clipper,* 17 June 1899, 318–319.

5. The following information comes from consecutive issues of the *Sunday Oregonian,* published in Portland, between 17 April 1904 and 7 May 1905. The population of Portland more than doubled from 90,000 in 1900 to 207,000 in 1910—see *Thirteenth Census of the United States* (Washington, D.C.: GPO, 1913), 64.

6. The first three songs, respectively, are promoted in the following ads: Jerome H.

Remick, *New York Clipper,* 25 February 1905, 18; Miles Bros., *New York Clipper,* 25 February 1905, 19; and F. B. Haviland, *New York Clipper,* 4 March 1905, 40. Haviland was still advertising its song slides for "Goodbye, Sis," done by DeWitt C. Wheeler, in *New York Clipper,* 28 July 1906, 617.

7. See the DeWitt C. Wheeler ad (for the slides), *New York Clipper,* 3 September 1904, 640; and the Chas. K. Harris ad (for the song), *New York Clipper,* 3 September 1904, 641.

8. See the Jos. W. Stern ad (for the song as well as the DeWitt Wheeler slides), *New York Clipper,* 5 November 1904, 871; and the Miles Bros. ad, *New York Clipper,* 25 February 1905, 19.

9. See the Gus Edwards ad, *New York Clipper,* 14 April 1906, 216; and the M. Witmark and Sons ad for "The Stars and the Stripes and You," *New York Clipper,* 30 June 1906, 523.

10. "New Department: Latest Song Slides," *Views and Films Index,* 21 July 1906, 3.

11. "Illustrated Songs" and "Popular Films," *Views and Films Index,* 12 January 1907, n.p. See, also, the "Comprehensive List of Electric Theatres and Nickelodeons for the Use of [among others] . . . Music Publishers," in *Billboard,* 15 December 1906, 32–33.

12. "Music Publishers Who Issue Song Slides," *Moving Picture World,* 30 March 1907, 62.

13. "Editorial: The Tremendous Demand for Song Slides," *Moving Picture World,* 28 September 1907, 467–468. The quality of the Scott & Van Altena slides—in terms of color and design—is evident in the surviving slide sets in the Marnan Collection.

14. "Talking Moving Pictures Latest European Invention," *Show World,* 7 September 1907, 9. Illustrated songs did show up on music hall programs in England, if only briefly and infrequently, and oddly all were American—see, for instance, "Notes on Current Topics," *Kinematograph and Lantern Weekly,* 1 August 1907, 179. Harstn was perhaps the only American manufacturer of song slides to advertise in the British trade press, but by early 1909 Walter Tyler was distributing its slides (and free music)—see the Walter Tyler ad in *Kinematograph and Lantern Weekly,* 18 March 1909, 1279. For a very different perspective on Germany, see note 48.

15. The following information comes from ads and articles in the *Des Moines Register and Leader,* between May 1906 and October 1907, and in the *Des Moines Mail and Times,* between June and November 1907. The population of Des Moines rose from more than 60,000 in 1900 to nearly 90,000 in 1910—*Thirteenth Census of the United States,* 63.

16. See the Dreamland ad in *Des Moines Register and Leader,* 15 August 1907, 6. The song and slides (by Scott & Van Altena) were one of F. B. Haviland's "eight . . . biggest successes"—see the company's ads in *New York Clipper,* 4 March 1905, 40, and 28 July 1906, 617.

17. See the Radium ads in *Des Moines Register and Leader,* 29 May 1907, 6, and 1 August 1907, 6. Harry von Tilzer began advertising the second song in *New York Clipper,* 8 December 1906, 1126.

18. See, for instance, the Radium ads in *Des Moines Register and Leader,* 16 June 1907, 6, and in *Des Moines Mail and Times,* 21 June 1907, 8.

19. The Radium also was the only Des Moines nickelodeon to advertise in *Midwestern,* June 1907, 82.

20. See the Lyric ad in *Des Moines Register and Leader,* 21 July 1907, 3, 7.

21. See the Lyric ads in *Des Moines Mail and Times,* 27 September 1907, 10, and 4 October 1907, 8, and in *Des Moines Register and Leader,* 29 September 1907, 3, 7.

22. The following information comes from the *Ottumwa Courier,* between June and

December 1907. The population of Ottumwa rose from 18,000 in 1900 to 22,000 in 1910—*Thirteenth Census of the United States,* 68.

23. See the Francis, Day, and Hunter ad for "My Irish Rosie" in *New York Clipper,* 8 December 1906, 1115.

24. Another of F. B. Haviland's "biggest successes," repeatedly featured in the company's ads in *New York Clipper,* 5 May 1906, 303; 7 July 1906, 543; 28 July 1906, 617; 22 September 1906, 828; and 13 October 1906, 896.

25. See, for instance, the range of articles from "The Picture Show Singer," *Moving Picture World,* 12 December 1908, 475, to "'Spectator's' Comments," *New York Dramatic Mirror,* 5 February 1910, 16, and H. F. Hoffman, "The Singer and the Song," *Moving Picture World,* 4 June 1910, 935. Altman reproduces several cartoons from *Moving Picture World* during this period in "The Silence of the Silents," 668, 684. By contrast, in late 1909, *Film Index* began to take an active role in promoting illustrated songs, with a full page devoted to new song slides and advertisements, as well as occasional articles.

26. The population of St. Louis rose from 575,000 in 1900 to 687,000 in 1910—*Thirteenth Census of the United States,* 62.

27. The following information comes from the *St. Louis Times,* between the middle of December 1909 and early January 1910. One page from the *St. Louis Times,* during the week before Christmas, was reproduced, as a model of advertising, in *Film Index,* 15 January 1910, 19.

28. John Ripley, "Romance and Joy, Tears and Heartache, and All for a Nickel," *Smithsonian* 12, no.12 (March 1982), 77.

29. Charles Musser makes this point especially clear in reference to moving pictures in "Pre-Classical American Cinema: Its Changing Modes of Film Production," *Persistence of Vision* 9 (1991)—reprinted in Richard Abel, ed., *Silent Film* (New Brunswick: Rutgers University Press, 1996), 85–108.

30. See, for instance, "Timely Tattle," *American Musicians and Art Journal* 22, no. 8 (24 April 1906), 14; and "Publishers' Gossip," *American Musicians and Art Journal* 22, no. 11 (12 June 1906), 28. I thank Margaret and Nancy Bergh for sharing their notes on this little-known trade journal.

31. "The Nickelodeon as a Business Proposition," *Moving Picture World,* 25 July 1908, 61.

32. John Collier was one of the first to take notice of audiences singing and to link that to the moving picture show's "elevation," in "Cheap Amusements," *Charities and the Commons,* 11 April 1908, 75.

33. All this, of course, is in sharp contrast to the way blues and jazz performers transformed black moving picture shows in Chicago, during the 1910s and 1920s, into lively "counterculture" spaces—see Mary Carbine, "'The Finest Outside the Loop': Motion Picture Exhibition in Chicago's Black Metropolis, 1905–1928," *camera obscura* 23 (May 1990)—reprinted in Abel, 234–262.

34. Jack Sands, "Meet Me Down at the Picture Show," *Moving Picture World,* 11 April 1908, 320.

35. One of the first essays to make a persuasive argument for this, especially for women, was Judith Mayne's "Immigrants and spectators," *Wide Angle* 5, no. 2 (1982), 32–41. I myself make this argument for early "Indian and Wild West Subjects" in "'Our Country,' Whose Country?: The Americanization Project of Early Westerns," in *Back in the Saddle Again: New Writings on the Western,* ed. Ed Buscombe and Roberta Pearson (London: British Film Institute, 1998), 77–95.

36. Quoted in Ripley, 82.

37. See "Trade Notes," *Moving Picture World,* 20 July 1907, 312. That, in some nick-elodeons, song slides were accompanied by singing in languages other than English demands further research on where, when, and how often it may have occurred.

38. Jon C. Teaford, *Cities of the Heartland: The Rise and Fall of the Industrial Midwest* (Bloomington: Indiana University Press, 1993), 59–60, 85–89.

39. There is evidence that some theaters in the New York area also exploited the "le-gitimacy" of their singers—see, for instance, Hans Leigh, "How the Vogue of the Motion Picture Show May be Preserved," *Moving Picture World,* 8 August 1908, 101.

40. Selected moving picture theaters in St. Louis began printing their ads daily and en bloc as a special column in the "Want Ads" section of the *Times* during the first week of August 1909. These ads are a little known yet valuable source of information on exhibition practices and the circulation of films and songs in a major city in the United States during the late nickelodeon period. Earlier that year, when an effort was made "to organize the numerous nickelodeons and moving picture shows throughout St. Louis," it was discovered that "more musicians [were] employed in these places than there were at the theaters"—see "Musicians in Nickelodeons," *Nickelodeon* 1, no. 2 (February 1909), 48.

41. An intriguing example at the Grand Central is Joe Herzog singing "I Am Going to Do What I Please," whose slides (by Scott & Van Altena) tell the story of a woman who refuses to marry until she has made money of her own. See "Moving Pictures and Vaudeville," *St. Louis Times,* 22 September 1909, 11.

42. The business of making slides and music for illustrated songs also provided work to a good number of people who later became important in the cinema industry, from Roscoe Arbuckle and Abe Balaban (singers) and Sam Katz (pianist) to Norma Talmadge, Anita Stewart, Alice Joyce, and Florence Turner (models for song slides): see "Appendix A: Samuel Katz," in Joseph Kennedy, *The Story of the Film* (Chicago: A. W. Shaw, 1927), 350–351; Carrie Balaban, *Continuous Performance: The Story of A. J. Balaban* (New York: A. J. Balaban Foundation, 1964), 24, 26; and Anthony Slide, *Early American Cinema,* rev. ed. (Metuchen, N.J.: Scarecrow, 1994), 137–138.

43. I first developed this argument in "Pathé Goes to Town: French Films Create a Market for the Nickelodeon," *Cinema Journal* 35, no. 1 (Fall 1995), 3–26.

44. I develop this argument in "A Crisis in Crossing Borders, or How to Account for French 'Bad Taste,'" in *Images across Borders, 1896–1918,* ed. Roland Cosandey and François Albera (Lausanne: Payot, 1995), 299–313; and in "The Perils of Pathé: The Americanization of Early American Cinema," in *Cinema and the Invention of Modern Life,* ed. Leo Charney and Vanessa Schwartz (Berkeley: University of California Press, 1995), 183–223.

45. See Rick Altman, "The Living Nickelodeon" printed later in this volume.

46. See T. J. Jackson Lears, "American Advertising and the Reconstruction of the Body, 1880–1930," in *Fitness in American Culture: Images of Health, Sport, and the Body, 1830–1940,* ed. Kathryn Grover (Amherst: University of Massachusetts Press, 1989), 47–66. The Gillette ad appeared in *Saturday Evening Post,* 18 June 1910, 41. For an extended analysis of turn-of-the-century advertising and its celebration of a new "American way of life," see Richard Ohmann, *Selling Culture: Magazines, Markets, and Class at the Turn of the Century* (London: Verso, 1996).

47. I develop this argument most fully in *The Red Rooster Scare, or Making Cinema American* (Berkeley: University of California Press, 1999).

48. During one of the discussion sessions at the Domitor conference, Karel Dibbets

(University of Amsterdam) made the provocative point that, at this time and even later, the German *tonbilder* may have had a function similar to that of the American illustrated songs: these short sync-sound representations of German performers singing German songs also fostered a sense of national identity in cinemas and other venues where French (usually from Pathé) and Italian films tended to dominate.

15 "The Sensational Acme of Realism": "Talker" Pictures as Early Cinema Sound Practice
Jeffrey Klenotic

The following item appeared in a February 1908 issue of *Moving Picture World:*

> AUDIENCE APPLAUDS HIS SHRIEKS OF AGONY
> Burlington, N.J., February 13—Reaching into the sheet-iron cage that covered a moving-picture machine with which he was giving an exhibition, John Riker seized a bare electric wire instead of the switch. He was held fast while a current of 1,000 volts went through his body.
> He shrieked for help. His cries, coming through the narrow aperture of the booth, sounded to the audience like a phonographic accompaniment to the blood and thunder drama that was being portrayed in the moving pictures. The audience, not suspecting the dangerous plight of the man, applauded.
> Andrew Harris, the piano player, saw that something was wrong and broke into the cage. He shut off the current. Riker's hand still gripped the wire and had to be pried off. His hand was almost roasted by the strength of the current.[1]

In a bracketed comment appended to the end of the story, the *World*'s editor admonished movie operators for their stubborn ignorance (asking, "When will operators learn?"), and spelled out the obvious lesson to be drawn from John Riker's shocking tale: never use uninsulated electrical wire. For their part, movie exhibitors—though no doubt sensitive to the dangers of projection and more or less sympathetic to the plight of the nearly roasted Riker—may have discerned three quite different truths in this incident: first, sensational vocal effects make for a crowd-pleasing show; second, when hidden from view, a human "talker" can be taken by the audience as phonographic accompaniment, thereby providing a lower-cost substitute for mechanized talking pictures; and third, never underestimate the value of a good piano player to the success of any last-minute rescue.

Ninety years later, the account of this event remains instructive, especially for its suggestiveness concerning the complexities involved in the American movie-going experience of 1908, a year of proliferation in the use of mechanized and non-mechanized synchronized sound systems. In particular, the story prompts questions about the function of sound in constructing a separated but overlapping relationship between film space and theater space. On one hand, the story implies the audience was cued to locate the shrieks in a source outside the image, emanating rather suddenly from a spatial position in the rear of the theater. This source was wrongly identified as mechanical, apparently because the projector booth's narrow portal produced an aural effect akin to a phonographic horn. Riker's cries for help—no doubt bloodcurdling in their intensity—were perhaps distorted and amplified in a manner consistent with the audience's prior experience of phonographic vocal performance. Yet even as the off-screen, non-diegetic "shrieks of agony" cued the audience to a space outside the film, they simultaneously achieved temporal and emotional synchronicity with the "blood-and-thunder" drama unfolding on screen. In doing so, the operator's cries cued the audience to superimpose sound and image, bringing theater space and film space, exhibitor space and producer space, into an overlapped relation. This overlap would seem to have aided in heightening the sensational effect experienced by the audience in their enjoyment of a climactic scene.[2]

Assuming this configuration of film and theater space adequately describes the experience of these moviegoers, we might wonder whether their spontaneous applause was doubly motivated: a response to a spectacular operator sound effect—a vocal display that appealed to the audience, and was judged by them, on its own terms as a type of exhibitor attraction[3]—as well as a response triggered by the experience of intensified realism at a key dramatic moment. We might wonder, even, if the applause was a blend of both responses: an expression of appreciation for the "behind the scene" house operator's ability to "pull off" or "present" a voice/image combination that provided a relatively powerful illusion of heightened realism as a sensational attraction in its own right—as a perceptual trick.[4]

To explore these matters further, I want to share some limited and preliminary research on the synchronized sound system John Riker unintentionally performed back in 1908. Contrary to what the audience may have inferred, I suggest the operator's cries for help were closer in spirit to human "talker pictures" than to mechanically produced "talking pictures."[5] As suggested by my title, "'The Sensational Acme of Realism,'"[6] I am particularly interested in the notion of film "talk" as an early sound practice through which differing aesthetic traditions could be mediated: on one hand, the stage director's tradition of well-rehearsed and absorbing theatrical realism; on the other, the showman's tradition of sensational attractions, magical illusions, confounding "tricks," and amusing improvisations.

As a non-mechanical attempt to synchronize voice and image, "talker" films relied on the efforts of live performers rendering character dialogue (and sometimes sound effects) from a station behind the projection drop. Known by the names of the companies that produced and/or performed the "talk"—Humanovo, Actologue, and Dramagraph, to name a few—this practice seems to have emerged in a meaningful way in late 1907 and reached its widest application and audience appeal the following year.[7] As Sydney Wire observed in August 1908, the Humanovo's "phenomenal success from the start" soon inspired imitation, with "at least a dozen different concerns [now] engaged in the promotion of moving talking pictures."[8] National Film Company of Detroit appears to have been one of the more successful concerns, as their number of tour-ing Actologues—performer troupes comprising three to six talkers contracted out for two-reel, week-long theater engagements at houses in the upper Mid-west—increased from ten to fifteen between July and September 1908. And with more Actologues being readied to meet the continuing demand, the company's rehearsal hall in Detroit's Telegraph Building was "alive and active twelve hours a day" preparing "a repertoire of nearly one hundred playlets" now owned by the company.[9]

Though film "talk" received less notice in the trade press after 1908, the practice appears to have carried on with some success through 1909 and into 1910. On May 29, 1909, for example, *Moving Picture World*'s Our Own Critic reported an enjoyable visit to the Bronx Theater, where a "fresh and absorb-ing" Humanoscope presentation of Selig's *Rip Van Winkle* was on the bill.[10] In Springfield, Massachusetts, where the Nelson Theater was alone in presenting talking pictures of any kind, the Dramagraph remained a constant feature on the bill from December 21, 1908 to May 28, 1910. During this seventeen-month engagement, Dramagraph films were the primary novelty on a regular program that included silent films and illustrated songs. The Nelson offered two different "talker" films per week, with changes on Monday and Wednesday through Oc-tober 1909, and changes on Monday and Thursday thereafter. When Drama-graph's run at the theater finally ended, its slot was taken up by a variety of singing vaudeville acts.[11]

Like the revival of the film lecturer around the same time, the use of film "talkers" was an occasionally heralded if temporary response to several pressing exhibitor needs: the need to differentiate product, the need to clarify increas-ingly ambitious film narratives, and the need to promote cinema as an instru-ment of cultural uplift without losing the interest of a core working-class audi-ence. Left unattended, these problems could introduce a fair degree of volatility into the exhibitor's enterprise. In Springfield, for instance, three of the city's six movie theaters went out of business or dropped movies from their programs over the summer of 1908 alone. As reported in the *Springfield Homestead*, "Until something really new is evolved in the motion picture shows it is a foregone conclusion that the limit of popularity for this type of amusement has gone its limit. . . . [T]he familiar picture show will need something new and original as an adjunct if it is to prove more than a passing fancy."[12]

Film "talkers" hidden behind the screen provided one such adjunct. Pro-moted to local audiences as "talking pictures" or "talking machines,"[13] such oral performances enabled exhibitors to claim the latest technological advance in the quest for perfectly realistic illusion. That there was nothing really new nor me-chanical involved in the "talker" system was likely beside the point. This was especially true for operators approaching the novelty from within the "trick" tradition, where the effectiveness of the trick hinged on "behind the scene" ma-nipulation.[14] To reveal the specific basis of the trick would undermine the plea-sure of the audience, not only in terms of enjoying the illusion and pondering how it was accomplished, but also in terms of the very anticipation of being tricked. Masking "talker" troupes as "talking machines" or "talking pictures" simply provided a starting point for raising the level of confusion, wonder, and expectation about the nature of the trick.

Newspaper publicity for the Nickel Theater in Manchester, New Hampshire, for example, introduced the "Humanovo" this way: "The Humanovo is a process that renders it possible that vaudeville sketches can be put on the stage, whereby comedy of a refined character can be performed. The details of the plan will not be presented here, as the management is desirous that the public tell for itself how the thing is done."[15] The wording of the first sentence obfuscates the actual effect to be achieved, but it does offer the veiled promise of a difficult trick. That the trick will attempt an illusion of high order is communicated to the Nickel's skeptical, knowing audience by way of reference to a broader code of cultural distinction—vaudeville sketches will be magically transformed by the Humanovo into refined comedy.[16] Reminiscent of both magician and circus barker traditions, the theater's publicity obscures the mechanics of the trick and raises a curiosity—what is this? is it a put on?—that could be satisfied only by a visit to see and hear the illusion. Or as the theater's advertising put it: "see the great Humanovo"; "come and see for yourself" the "show that talks."[17] Exhibitors no doubt hoped moviegoers, after witnessing the illusion, exited asking a related question: it wasn't real, but how'd they do that?

In wrapping a cloak of ambiguity around "talkers," some exhibitors were simply passing on to the audience their own experience of being tricked. Indeed, in May 1908, *Moving Picture World* reported apparently widespread exhibitor misunderstanding about the new "talking pictures." Theater managers "in all parts of the country" were said to be "under the impression that the simultaneous reproduction of voices and pictures which has been in the course of experiment so long, can now be had at 'popular prices.'" The *World* was quick to point out that the only "talking pictures" most exhibitors would be able to afford were "like the famous old sacred white elephant of the circus. They are only pictures retouched, as it were, . . . relying upon . . . the liberal use of 'props,' and men and women behind the sheet [to] add realism to the productions with their voices."[18] Of course, for many exhibitors, such clarity on the link between "talker pictures" and "white elephants" would only sharpen interest in the novelty, as they would know exactly how to proceed in successfully presenting it to their audiences.

The experience of being tricked, however, could be more or less pleasurable, depending upon the quality of the illusion and the performance of the "talkers" relative to the moviegoer's horizon of cultural, aesthetic, and technological expectations. Exhibitors of "talker" pictures surely hoped auditors who "heard through the illusion" would nonetheless enjoy the satisfaction of uncovering the ruse and pondering its power over others. But a negative reaction was always possible. For instance, in a report describing the experience of their "informant" at the Manhattan Theater, *Moving Picture World* observed that "many people in this city are being fooled into believing they are viewing the new invention of 'talking pictures' when they are only listening to a very bad vocal operator hid-

15.1. "The Nickel—See the Great Humanovo." *Manchester Daily Mirror and American,* 13 July 1908, p. 7.

den behind the screen." Though the informant entered the theater expecting a Cameraphone presentation,

> what he heard convinced him that it was not an automatic machine that was doing the talking, but a man, and a poor talker at that. The pronunciation was incorrect and in the bad, slangy dialect of the illerate [sic] hanger-on about the theater stage. "Dis" and "dat" and "dem," were the methods of pronunciation used. . . . Yet [the informant] believed that he had seen the wonderful talking pictures, but marveled greatly that such a sorry representation should be given with French subjects. . . . [However,] he is now convinced that the talking in Manhattan was the work of a stage hand and not of the instrument. He says that if it was the work of a cameraphone he would advise the owners to remove the instrument or send someone there to operate it who will not make a burlesque of it.[19]

Even in this presumably informed attempt to distance legitimate "talking pictures" from "burlesque" imitations, however, the exhibitors' power to conceal the basis of their particular "talking picture" trick plants a seed of doubt that is not easily overcome. Thus, the informant's conclusion waffles: this was cer-

160 *Jeffrey Klenotic*

15.2. "The Nickel—There's No ? About It." *Manchester Daily Mirror and American,* 23 July 1908, p. 7.

tainly the work of a stagehand but, if it was not, here is what I advise be done to correct the problem.

Promoted by exhibitors as the latest novelty attraction, "talker" films added value to a program by differentiating it within the local market. But "talkers" also gave exhibitors another practical benefit, in that films shown at the theater as "ordinary pictures" months before could occasionally be repeated without necessarily losing their drawing power.[20] In Springfield, for instance, the Nelson used its publicity to periodically alert audiences when a film was to be repeated, as occurred when *Mabel, the Factory Girl* and *The Yellow Jacket* returned to the bill: "The two talking pictures of the week have been selected because when shown some months ago as ordinary motion pictures each was received with marked evidences of favor, and with the benefit of the spoken dialog should prove more enjoyable now."[21]

It is here that the issue of film "talkers" as a particular kind of solution to the exhibitor's need for an external means of clarifying film narrative is broached. This problem was given blunt voice in August 1908 by W. Stephen Bush, who in making the case for film lecturers as the remedy of choice, asked: "Why do so many people remain in the moving picture theater and look at the same picture two and even three times? Simply because they do not understand it the first time; and this is by no means in every case a reflection on their intelligence."[22] At a time when the film industry was working toward an internal system of narration that could effectively address this problem, lecturers and "talkers" became increasingly attractive to exhibitors as adjunct methods for heightening the comprehensibility and realism of film narratives.[23]

Determining precisely how—and how well—film "talkers" served this function is difficult. This is partly because much film "talk" was performed in an improvisational mode, leaving no written record of such "talker" dialogue to speak of. Even when film "talk" was not improvised—as when the complete text of a play was spoken[24] or when a troupe carried a prepared original "script" into its performance—it remains impossible to know how the live rendering of the dialogue actually corresponded with, or was specifically adapted to, the visual narrative of a given film. These problems notwithstanding, however, it is possible to use the trade press to form a tentative impression of how the more sophisticated "talker" picture concerns approached the dual tasks of aiding narrative clarity and heightening realistic illusion.

At the pre-performance stage of "talker" production, the primary interpretive agent was the dialogue writer.[25] The process of dialogue creation began with the writer screening the selected picture several times to gain clarity on its subject and narrative logic. The picture was then viewed several times more, with the writer now speaking out "impromptu dialogue" to be recorded in shorthand by a stenographer. In the development of "impromptu dialogue," attention appears to have been paid not only to fleshing out character psychology and vocal mannerisms, but also to directing the viewer's eye toward that part of the frame where significant narrative information was being presented. As Sydney Wire pointed out in *Moving Picture World,* the effectiveness of the author's role hinged on his or her being "quick of eye, as the overlooking of some small situation is sometimes apt to spoil the entire story."[26] To further insure the narrational primacy of dialogue over film, "talker" picture companies found it advisable to cut their films such that "all letters and titles before scenes . . . be taken out, so that the story will not be told before the actors and actresses have read their lines, as this will have a tendency to kill the dramatic climax."[27]

After finalizing the "impromptu dialogue" and eliminating titles, actors and actresses were cast, rehearsed, and sent on the road. Though performers were selected, in part, for their ability to study a script quickly and vocalize it with "good grammar and proper pronunciation,"[28] they were also expected to be "capable of extemporizing when occasion demands."[29] To increase realism, actors and actresses were advised to deliver lines from a position directly behind the character they were "impersonating" and to "act out the character thoroughly, as if . . . appearing on the stage without being hidden by the drop." Performers were also instructed to keep their eyes on the screen at every moment to avoid "talking when characters are not seen before their entrance or after exit," which would break the illusion.[30] If the task wasn't complicated enough, "talkers" were also trained to perform mechanical sound effects, not only because they knew the film subject best and could thus produce more realistic effects, but also because this produced "better results than by relying upon the different house employes [sic], who are often neglectful and careless, and are often absent when the cue for effects arrives."[31] One area where house employees did serve a crucial role, however, was projection. As James Clancy advised in the *World,* an effective "talker" picture required an operator who had been "drilled carefully and thoroughly in regard to the running speed of films, of struggles, horses galloping, battle scenes, which must be run very fast, while scenes in offices and homes must be run at a certain speed to bring out the desired effect of the character, and to give the necessary illusion."[32]

It would be wrong to suggest the mode of production for "talker pictures" described above constituted the prototypical definition of "talk" as a form of performance. Rather, it seems likely there were degrees of professionalization, ranging from fully organized, stage-directed, third-party companies such as Humanovo, Actologue, and Dramagraph, to performances put forward on a less formal (and less expensive) basis by any given exhibitor using house employees or other local talent behind the screen. Thus, the practice might vary considerably from theater to theater, even when the same film was being "talked," gravitating in any particular case toward the more standardized performative norms of the theatrical stage director or the more aleatory norms of the local exhibitor and house audience.

In the latter instance, film "talkers" might even work *against* dramatic realism, as Kathryn Fuller has observed, by displaying a "tendency, like roguish musical accompanists, to spoil dramatic film scenes with continual and misplaced jokes and satire."[33] Because such irruptions affirmed the primacy of theater space over film space and obtrusively asserted the narrational agency of the "talkers" over the film, they no doubt did "spoil" the dramatic illusion for some patrons. At the same time, the very fact that contrapuntal "talker" commentary was in keeping with roguish musical traditions may have made it quite welcome to others in the audience, increasing their delight in the film.[34] Indeed, at some houses, the practice of film "talk" may have been more easily adapted to the showman's aesthetic of attractions than to the stage director's aesthetic of realistic illusion. As Carl Herbert observed in *Moving Picture World*, "It is too great a tax on our imagination to watch a figure whose lips do not even move and believe him to be uttering the more or less ungrammatical, colloquial speeches coming from behind the sheet. A clever speaker, resourceful in gags, humor and disguises of voice can, however, infuse much interest and add greatly to the enjoyment of the average film in this way."[35] Given his role as general manager of Cameraphone, Herbert's negative assessment of film "talk" as an adjunct to screen realism should be taken with a hefty grain of salt. Nonetheless, his comments do suggest how film "talkers" might have drawn, however successfully in the eyes and ears of audiences, from differing aesthetic traditions and modes of address.

Ultimately, it may have been the uncontrolled aspect of "talkers" that posed the greatest problem to their long-term survival. Like the film lecture, the practice of film "talk" was caught in what Miriam Hansen describes as a larger "struggle for control over the film's reception between national production and distribution companies on the one hand and local exhibitors on the other."[36] Whether produced and performed by professional third-party concerns, or carried out on an informal, aleatory basis by exhibitors, film "talk" brought the sound of autonomous and unpredictable voices into an overlapped relation with the increasingly standardized image of the film industry. No matter how tightly this overlap might have been made to fit, there would always be a gap—a buffer that would allow film titles to be cut or mocking commentary inserted.

In closing, I return to John Riker, who ninety years ago narrowed the gap between film and theater space when he accidentally grabbed a bare projector wire and shrieked in agony. His cries for help shot through the aperture of the booth, hoping to find a responsive ear as they made their way to rendezvous with the blood-and-thunder drama on screen. And find an ear they did. The audience applauded, apparently mistaking Riker's voice for an aesthetic performance—and a good one at that. While this story prompts reflection on the multiple aesthetic traditions within which the audience's response might have made sense, it also serves as a reminder of just how unshocking it could be for the human voice to register a presence within the unsettled silent cinema of 1908–1910.

Notes

1. *Moving Picture World,* 22 February 1908, 138.

2. I presume the switch Riker reached for was one to shut down the machine at film's end. Thus my use of the term "climactic" to describe this moment in the film.

3. It has been a useful (if grim) heuristic to think of the operator's "cries for help" and "shrieks of agony" as an unintentional sonic version of the sort of visual "temporal irruption" or "sudden burst of presence" that Tom Gunning describes as part of the aesthetic of "attractions." Gunning's notion that "films that precede the classical paradigm are complex texts which occasionally interrelate attractions with narrative projects" (p. 4) has been helpful to me in trying to think through the aesthetic logic of "talker" performance in relation to developing modes of narrative. Tom Gunning, " 'Now You See It, Now You Don't': The Temporality of the Cinema of Attractions," *Velvet Light Trap* 32 (Fall 1993), 3–12.

4. In discussing single-shot framing and editing in the "trick film," particularly as it pertains to the "strange intertwining of the traditions of realistic illusionism and the magic theater," Gunning asks us to consider "whether managing the illusion of reality does not fundamentally correspond with the trick." My use of the term "trick" here is an attempt to explore this possibility, but in the context of voice/image relations rather than image/image relations. Tom Gunning, " 'Primitive' Cinema—A Frame-up? or The Trick's on Us," *Cinema Journal* 28 (Winter 1989), 10.

5. I use the terms "talker" and "talker pictures" to distinguish this non-mechanical practice from other sync-sound practices. However, this practice was typically lumped under the term "talking pictures" in the trade press. On the local level, too, the practice was typically hyped as a "talking picture" or "talking machine" novelty, though on rare occasions newspaper summaries of theater programming would also refer to a picture being "talked." See, for instance, *Springfield Sunday Republican,* 21 November 1909, 22.

6. The phrase "Sensational Acme of Realism" was used by the Nelson Theater in Springfield, Massachusetts, to advertise the introduction of "Dramagraph Talking Pictures" to the local audience. *Springfield Sunday Republican,* 12 December 1908, 22.

7. This dating of the "talker" phenomenon comports with Charles Musser's discussion of the practice in *The Emergence of Cinema: The American Screen to 1907* (New York: Charles Scribner's Sons, 1990), 438–439; as well as Kathryn H. Fuller's discussion in *At the Picture Show* (Washington, D.C.: Smithsonian Institution Press, 1996), 72.

8. Sydney Wire, "How Talking Pictures Are Made: Scarcity of Picture Actors," *Moving Picture World,* 22 August 1908, 137.

9. *Moving Picture World,* 18 July 1908, 45; 8 August 1908, 103; 12 September 1908, 195.

10. Our Own Critic, "Weekly Comments on the Shows," *Moving Picture World,* 29 May 1909, 711.

11. "The Nelson," *Springfield Sunday Republican,* 19 June 1910, 23. In an excellent study of film "talk" in Quebec, Pierre Véronneau identifies 1908 as a key year in the development of this early sound practice and finds the practice being performed as late as 1913. See Pierre Véronneau, "An Intermedia Practice: 'Talking Pictures' in Montréal, 1908–1910," *Film History* 11, no. 4 (1999), 426–432.

12. "Passing of Picture Shows," *Springfield Homestead,* 1 June 1908, 8.

13. See, for instance, Manchester *Daily Mirror and American,* 22 July 1908, 7; 23 July 1908, 7; 7 August 1908, 7; 17 August 1908, 7; 18 August 1908, 7.

14. Gunning, "'Primitive' Cinema," 10.

15. "The Nickel," *Manchester Daily Mirror and American,* 11 July 1908, 7.

16. My reference to a "skeptical, knowing audience" is intended to suggest the Nickel patron's familiarity with "cheap" vaudeville as a practice that would be hard to transform into "refined" comedy, thus straining credibility to a point sufficient to heighten curiosity in the proposed trick. Though not the focus here, it would be of interest to situate the meaning of this rhetorical appeal more thoroughly within the class context of the theater's audience, which does appear to have had a working-class orientation. For instance, *Moving Picture World* reprinted an editorial from the *Manchester Daily Mirror and American* in which the author notes that, upon attending the theater for the first time, "he found himself in a crowd the like of which he has not seen in a theater for a long, long time" (*Moving Picture World,* 26 October 1907, 541). Also, the *Daily Mirror and American* observed the Nickel's audience to include a "large number of patrons who stroll into the theatre after the manufactories are closed" (*Manchester Daily Mirror and American,* 26 August 1908, 7). Of course, the use of the Humanovo may have been intended precisely to attract middle-class patrons in larger numbers without losing the core working-class audience. Thus, the transformation of vaudeville into refined comedy may have been an equally incredulous proposition to this presumably more refined segment of the audience. For discussion of the "double audience of the nickelodeon—the actual one and the desired one," as it pertains to the practice of film lecturing, see Gunning, *D. W. Griffith and the Origins of American Narrative Film* (Urbana: University of Illinois Press, 1991), 92–93.

17. *Manchester Daily Mirror and American,* 13 July 1908, 7; 15 July 1908, 7.

18. "Talking Machines," *Moving Picture World,* 2 May 1908, 390.

19. *Moving Picture World,* 30 May 1908, 473.

20. I would not overstate the case on this point, for the extent to which "ordinary" films were repeated as "talkers" cannot be determined until more data is assembled.

21. "Nelson," *Springfield Sunday Republican,* 9 January 1910, 22.

22. W. Stephen Bush, *Moving Picture World,* 22 August 1908, 137.

23. Gunning, *D. W. Griffith,* 90.

24. For instance, at the Nelson, it was reported that the entire text of the play *East Lynne* would be read at a "talker" performance of the film *East Lynne. Springfield Sunday Republican,* 23 May 1909, 27.

25. Prior to dialogue creation, of course, there was picture selection. We need to learn more about the kinds of pictures most often selected for "talker" treatments and the rationale behind the selection process. As a start, I have compiled a title list, available to readers upon request, of every film "talked" at the Nickel and Nelson theaters between 1908 and 1910.

26. Wire, 137.

27. James Clancy, "The Human Voice as a Factor in the Moving Picture Show," *Moving Picture World*, 30 January 1909, 115.

28. Ibid.

29. Wire, 137.

30. Clancy, 115.

31. Wire, 137.

32. Clancy, 115.

33. Fuller, 72.

34. Misplaced jokes and satire may also have resonated with the audience's own performative tendencies (such as commenting actively during films) without necessarily having a silencing effect. Tendencies of audience performance are discussed in Jean Châteauvert and André Gaudreault, "Les bruits des spectateurs," appearing later in this volume.

35. Carl Herbert, "The Truth about Talking Pictures," *Moving Picture World*, 20 March 1909, 327.

36. Miriam Hansen, *Babel and Babylon: Spectatorship in American Silent Film* (Cambridge: Harvard University Press, 1991), 98.

16 "Bells and Whistles": The Sound of Meaning in Train Travel Film Rides

Lauren Rabinovitz

By paying attention to the undervalued, often ignored sounds of silent cinema, Domitor promises to redefine both the object and the institution of early cinema. This is true whether we are talking about sounds and silences that serve the movies—sound effects produced in the theater space, live musical accompaniment, early phonograph-projector synchronization—or the asynchronous programmatic relationships between sound and movies (e.g., music played in between movies, illustrated songs and sing-alongs, audience vocalizations of all other sorts, Graphophone and barker sounds emanating from the street entrance). Some of these were attempts to coordinate sound and image; others simply produced overlapping or conflicting cognitive cues. Whatever the case, we will necessarily have to think in new ways about early cinema and its exhibition within larger programs that involved different media. I would add that this will also necessitate our reconceptualization of the demands made on the spectator to make sense of this variety of sensory stimuli. In this essay, I aim to show that if sound contributed to a movie-going experience that always involved multiple senses, it grounded that experience in the audience's bodily awareness. From the outset then, movie-going produced an alternative kind of spectatorial pleasure to the monolithic, ahistorical model of "distracted" spectatorship that shapes our understanding of the history of cinema spectatorship.

In particular, illusion rides, or ride films, as we would call them today, represent more than a marginal practice in downtown storefront theaters and amusement parks because they attempted to coordinate visual imagery with sound and motion effects. *Hale's Tours and Scenes of the World* and its competitors from 1906 to 1909 were the culmination of a spectatorial experience of sensory fascination in early cinema: as travel films that offered a point of view from the front or rear of a moving vehicle inside a mock train, boat, or automobile that was outfitted for sound, motion, and atmospheric effects, these rides foregrounded the body itself as a site for sensory experience. They articulated a seemingly contradictory process for the spectator: they attempted to dematerialize the subject's body through its visual extension into the cinematic field while the kinesthetic effects of motion and wind repeatedly emphasized the corporeality of the body and the physical delirium of the senses. Sound cues bridged and smoothed over the gap between the in-the-body experience of motion and the out-of-the-body sense of panoptic projection. They carefully coordinated the spectator's physical and cognitive sensations, whereas one might argue that many other early cinema approaches involved substantial conflict between various cognitive cues. Thus my purpose here is threefold: (1) to describe the contribution of *Hale's Tours* and its competitors to a multiple sensory experience of cinema; (2) to argue for the defining role of sound in that experience; and (3) to conclude that these examples extended to audiences physical self-awareness of the pleasures of coordinated perceptions, thus promoting a cinema spectatorship of sensory fascination, a spectatorial knowledge grounded in the body and in conflict with traditional models.

Previous discussions of *Hale's Tours* have generally ignored or given only token mention to the varied sound components of such motion-simulation rides and to how those components contributed to the overall sense and meaning of the event.[1] *Hale's Tours* and other illusion rides routinely utilized a range of sound effects, including steam whistles tooting, train wheels clattering, paddle wheels churning water, automobile horns blowing, bells ringing, calliopes playing, and other effects associated with whatever activity was being depicted on-screen. This latter is especially important insofar as what was depicted on-screen could include anything from being robbed at gun point (e.g., *The Great Train Robbery* [Edison Manufacturing Company, 1903], *The Hold-Up of the Rocky Mountain Express* [American Mutoscope and Biograph, 1906]) to attempts to woo coy young ladies inside Pullman cars (e.g., *Grand Hotel to Big Indian* [American Mutoscope and Biograph, 1906], *What Happened in the Tunnel* [Edison Manufacturing Company, 1903]). *Hale's Tours* and its competitors were never purely visual travelogues addressing passive moviegoers but were fundamentally about the range of physical perceptions, social relations, and sensory excitement connected with the experience of travel. They suggest that what was fundamental to the illusion ride was not merely the sight of the travelers' "destination"—the picturesque, foreign, the exotic, the faraway—but the *experience* of being in that place, and that experience was dependent on the sound convincingly linking the motion and visual events of the ride. Illusion rides defined themselves as *fully a sound cinema* in the earliest years of movies, when sound practices were non-uniform, irregularly practiced, and unsystematic.

From their inception, movies played a key role in accustoming audiences to sensory-overloaded, hyper-real multimedia spectacles. Passion Plays, boxing films, Spanish-American War films contributed to theater programs different kinds of materials that produced great emotional affect and excitement. By the 1900 Paris Universal Exposition, cinema had been incorporated into multimedia spectacles on an extravagant scale, and, within a few short years, it served as one "prop" in the disaster shows (e.g., Trip to the Moon, Fighting the Flames) at Coney Island and other urban amusement parks.

Hale's Tours and Scenes of the World was first introduced by entrepreneur-promoter George Hale for the 1905 season at the Kansas City Electric Park.[2] *Hale's Tours* was composed of one, two, or three train cars that each seated 72 "passengers." The company advertised that an installation could "handle as many as 1250 persons per hour with ease."[3] Admission for a seven-to-ten-minute show was ten cents. Movies were shown at the front end of an otherwise closed car, creating the impression of a railway observation car. A show generally offered a filmed point of view from the front or rear of a moving train, producing the illusion of movement into or away from a scene. A mechanical apparatus and system of levers vibrated, rocked, oscillated, and tilted the car. Sound effects enhanced the sensation of travel: steam whistles tooted, an extra set of wheels revolved for the purpose of creating an illusion of movement and the "sound like the wheels of a car going over the rail-joints of a track."[4] Fans blew "blasts of air" at the travelers from the rear of the car.[5]

With his partner Fred Gifford, Hale took out two patents for his "illusion railroad ride," and they sold licenses and exclusive territorial rights for different regions of the United States for several years until it is likely that the increased systematization and consolidation of the movie industry forced them out of business sometime around 1909.[6] In 1906, Brady-Grossmann Co., the East Coast licensee, installed at least three *Hale's Tours* at Coney Island (at Dreamland, at Luna Park, and on Surf Avenue), one at Brighton Beach, one at Rockaway Beach, and one on Fourteenth Street. In addition, two variants of *Hale's Tours* simultaneously opened just outside Coney Island: *Hurst's Touring New York,* an illusion ride like *Hale's Tours* except it was set in an automobile (on Surf Avenue), and the touring-car illusion ride *New York to 'Frisco* (in the Bowery).[7]

In Chicago in the same year, *Hale's Tours* appeared on lower State Street and at the White City and Riverview amusement parks. Chicago's Sans Souci Park had *Palace Touring Cars,* an imitation of *Hale's Tours* railway illusion.[8] *Cessna's Sightseeing Auto Tours* was installed in a downtown storefront on Clark Street (129 S. Clark), two blocks from the *Hale's Tours* storefront installation.[9] Within a short period of time, there were more than five hundred *Hale's Tours* at amusement parks and storefront theaters at all major cities in the United States and Canada. This represents installations at approximately one-third of the estimated number of amusement parks in the United States in 1906 as well as in Mexico City, Havana, Melbourne, Paris, London, Berlin, Bremen, Hamburg, Hong Kong, and Johannesburg.[10] *Billboard* reported that both *Hale's Tours* and the *Trolley Tours* "raised the standard of attractions" at amusement parks and were enjoying "great popularity."[11] And as early as its initial 1906 season, *Hale's Tours* and its competitors became top-grossing, popular concessions across the United States.[12]

Other illusion rides quickly followed that imitated or varied the *Hale's Tours* cars and capitalized on their immediate success: for example, *Citron's Overland Flyer* and *Palace Touring Cars.*[13] *Citron's Overland Flyer* was a spring-supported railway car that could bounce or rock the passengers; it had revolving rollers underneath the car to create "a rumbling sound like the travel of wheels over a track," and it had draw-curtains at the side windows that could be opened and closed in synchronization with the beginning and end of the motion and sound

WILLIAM A. BRADY and EDWARD B. GROSSMANN

HAVING PURCHASED THE EXCLUSIVE PATENT RIGHTS

HALE'S TOURS AND
SCENES OF THE WORLD

Patent Insured and Protected by the Patent Title Guarantee Co., of New York.
for the Following Territory

New York, Pennsylvania, Maryland, Delaware, Vermont, Massachusetts, Connecticut, Rhode Island, New Hampshire, New Jersey, Maine and District Columbia

A 10 cent educational and amusement proposition.

The most realistic sensation ever accomplished in an amusement device.

The greatest money maker of all entertainment schemes ever known.

Greater than the Scenic Railway, the Chutes, or any of the famous successes in this line.

As Shown in Kansas City Park Last Summer

Protected by U. S. Patents Nos. 767281 and 800100 against infringement by

AUTO RIDES, CAR RIDES OR ANY OTHER VEHICLE RIDES

Operated in connection with Moving Pictures, thus producing
a dual effect.

As Being Exhibited now on State Street, Chicago.

FACTS

Now being operated on State Street, Chicago, in two expensively leased stores, with enormous profits. It is possible to take $2,500 a week with $50 a day running expenses, and your actual investment is comparatively small.

A wild scramble is going on at present between all amusement caterers in the world to secure the rights of this device, which has demonstrated itself as being the peer of all inventions for the amusement of our fun-loving public.

The company will install over 50 of these plants in our territory, but is prepared to receive propositions for leased locations anywhere within its limits.

IT IS A REPEATER......   ......IT TEACHES AND PLEASES YOUNG AND OLD

It only takes 7 minutes to give a show. It can draw money on a thoroughfare or park. It is valuable summer or winter. It costs little to install and has wonderful earning capacity.

Beware of Fake Imitations.   **We Are Fighters, and Will Defend Our Rights**

FOR FULL PARTICULARS ADDRESS

THE BRADY-GROSSMANN CO.
New York Theatre Building, NEW YORK.

WM. A. BRADY, President.   EDWARD B. GROSSMANN, Vice-President.

16.1. Hale's Tours and Scenes of the World advertisement, *Billboard,* 10 February 1906, p. 22.

effects.[14] *Trolley Car Tours* opened during the 1906 season at storefront theaters and amusement parks. The company relied chiefly on product differentiation to sell itself: "Our car is the latest and best in a car device for travels and tours—the most natural way to the masses. Few ride in Pullmans; everybody hits the trolley."[15] *Auto Tours of the World and Sightseeing in the Principal Cities* likewise improved upon the *Hale's Tours* phenomenon of showing point-of-view moving pictures out a front window by adding painted moving panoramas to the sides of the open car and by combining the show with an electric theater screening as well.[16]

White and Langever's Steamboat Tours of the World applied the *Hale's Tour* concept to water travel, beginning in the 1907 season. They employed an actual ferry to transport the patrons to the "marine-illusion boat," where moving pictures were projected in the front of a stationary mock boat that seated up to two hundred people. A mechanical apparatus rocked and oscillated the mock boat, rotating paddle-wheels arranged beneath the deck "simulat[ed] the sound of paddle-wheels employed for propulsion,"[17] and fans blew breezes in the face of the audience to "give the impression that they are traveling."[18] The illusion boat included a steam calliope as well.

Hruby and Plummer's Tours and Scenes of the World appropriated all these concepts but made them more generic for traveling carnivals rather than dependent on a permanent installation. They advertised:

> A moving picture show in a knock-down portable canvas car, boat, vehicle or ordinary tent that can be easily set up, quickly pulled down, readily transported, yet mechanically arranged that the bell, the whistle, and the swing of a moving train, boat or vehicle is produced. Trips or views can be constantly changed to suit your fancy, scenes of any railroad vehicle or boat ride, on land or water, produced with full sensation of the ride, together with "Sightseers" sightseeing side trips covering Principal Cities of the world.[19]

It was outfitted with Edison films and projector, a motion-simulation apparatus, a portable structure for housing the entirety, an advertising front, and portable generator for powering the exhibition.[20]

A Trip to California over Land and Sea, however, may have been the most ingenious of the imitators. It combined railway and marine illusion travel, offering first the fantasy of a rail journey across the United States to California and then the sensation of dropping the car into the water to turn the vehicle into a boat for travel down the coast of California, "the car being instantaneously transformed into a beautiful vessel which gives you a boat ride along the coast, the performance ending with a sensational climax (a Naval Battle and Storm at Sea)."[21]

Advertisements to potential exhibitors for all these rides privileged the motion effects over the movies, and several noted the importance of fans blowing air on the audience for making realistic the physical sensation of travel. There is little detail about the kinds of bells, whistles, and calliopes being sold with these outfits, and there is even less information about how these sound-makers

SIGHTSEEING AUTOS!

Auto Tours of the World and Sightseeing in the Principal Cities

WE MAKE OUR OWN FILMS.   OTHER PEOPLE RENT THE ONES THEY SHOW.

ONE OF OUR FRONTS.

Our Moving Picture Shows Are Original, Instructive, Novel and Amusing.

ABOVE ALL, THE BIGGEST MONEY-MAKER OF ANY PICTURE SHOW IN THE UNITED STATES

Our pictures, which are taken from automobiles in the principal cities of the world, and along famous auto routes of both the old and the new worlds, are shown to the "Sightseers" from a Sightseeing Auto. The illusion of seeing the various countries and cities from an automobile is produced by a panorama of moving scenes attached to the wall beside the Sightseeing Auto upon which are seated the "Sightseers," and the throwing upon a screen in front of the Sightseeing Auto the moving pictures which were taken from a moving automobile, by this company, and which are the property of the Sightseeing Auto Co. By an original and clever idea the "Sightseers" are given a side trip which enables them to view a variety of moving pictures, thus taking away from the patrons of the Sightseeing Autos that "tired feeling" which is produced by a repetition of the same kind and character of moving pictures they would be forced to witness should they always remain on the auto. Our ideas concerning the manner in which the pictures are shown were thought of sufficient value by a leading firm of patent lawyers in Chicago that by their advice plans and specifications of same have been forwarded to Washington, and patents are now pending.

PARK MANAGERS WHO DESIRE THE "BIG THING" WRITE US.

Any person who can secure a concession for showing the Auto Tours of the World and Sightseeing in the Principal Cities, write for terms. You can do business with us, and we don't want it all, either. We will install and grant the license to operate for a percentage of the gross receipts: or we will install in parks and give a percentage of the gross for the privilege; or we will sell plans, giving right to operate, furnish fronts, and make you a proposition that will bring you a monthly rental of $150. This you will have every month in your pocket before you start business. We furnish the films at a weekly rental of $15. For full particulars address

CHAS. W. CESSNA,
Gen. Manager Sight Seeing Auto Co.,
DECATUR, ILLINOIS.

or **W. H. LABB CONSTRUCTION CO.,**
Gen. Agents for U. S.,
State Life Bldg., INDIANAPOLIS, IND.

16.2. Sightseeing Autos advertisement, *Billboard,* 27 January 1906, p. 23.

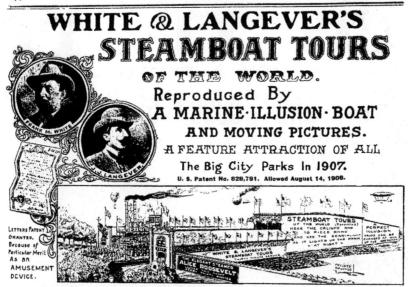

WHITE & LANGEVER'S
STEAMBOAT TOURS
OF THE WORLD.
Reproduced By
A MARINE·ILLUSION·BOAT
AND MOVING PICTURES.
A FEATURE ATTRACTION OF ALL
The Big City Parks In 1907.
U. S. Patent No. 828,791. Allowed August 14, 1906.

LETTERS PATENT GRANTED, Because of Particular Merit As an AMUSEMENT DEVICE.

An amusement device and illusion that brings expensive trips to your park patrons—a full size steamboat under full steam. Carries the patrons down a canal to the illusion boat, where life-motion pictures are produced in front of a rocking boat upon which the people are seated. Paddle-wheels agitate the waters about both boats, and mammoth fans blow a stiff breeze in the face of the audience, giving the impression that they are traveling. A steam calliope and searchlight are added features to the regular outfit on a river or lake steamer. Novel in its conception. **A Great Ballyhoo.** Unlimited in drawing power, with an earning capacity of $100 an hour, carrying 200 people on each trip.

═══════════════**WRITE US TO-DAY**═══════════════

WHITE & LANGEVER, Patentees; - - - **Room I, Langever Building, Fort Worth, Texas.**

NOTE—We are now selling exclusive rights to operate either for cash or on percentage or a partnership basis, whichever suits you.

16.3. White and Langever's Steamboat Tours of the World advertisement, *Billboard*, 22 September 1906, p. 44.

operated during a *Hale's Tours* or *Trip to California* show. Yet, the sound-makers were included among the advertised paraphernalia of the show, always there as if to serve some unspecified but integral function, and the patent applications always included a sound device for simulating the sound of forward movement.

The ambient sounds indicated—wheels clattering, paddle-wheels churning—punctuated by the announcements of whistles for braking and stopping, bells or horns that served "as fictional warnings" timed to coordinate with the visual appearances of pedestrians or animals on the street or tracks, provided a sound envelope that made the realism of the ride possible because it contributed to a cognitive convergence and blending of the discrete and somewhat disparate sensory information provided by motion and vision. If, as Barbara Maria Stafford has argued in her discussion of aesthetic illusion and multimedia, it is impossible for the brain to cognitively process simultaneously discrete sensory information and coherent thinking depends upon a synthetic convergence performed mentally, we may hypothesize it is the sound cues that hypostatized that union.[22] In this regard then, *Hale's Tours* and other illusion rides were the first

16.4. Hruby and Plummer's Tours and Scenes of the World advertisement, *Billboard*, 3 March 1906, p. 25.

virtual realities of the twentieth century, coherent representations that made it seem as if "you are really there" because they both combined and simultaneously coordinated many different sensory impressions: visual, kinesthetic, and aural. They offered virtual travel to scenic spots in the United States and Canada (including Niagara Falls, the Catskill Mountains, the Rocky Mountains, northern California, the Black Hills, and the Yukon), to foreign lands that were especially remote or pre-industrial (China, Ceylon, Japan, Samoa, the Fiji Islands), and even to urban centers via trolley, subway, or hot air balloon.

In general, *Hale's Tours* has been mentioned in film history only for its effort at achieving a proto-cinematic realism organized through two regimes of textual address—its visual form and conventions of narrative. First, visual cues emphasized fluid temporal movement into a deep field in which the features of the landscape seemed to fly toward the viewer. The films employed both editing and camera movements but usually only after presenting an extended shot (often one to two minutes or longer) organized by the locomotion of the camera. The camera was mounted at a slightly tipped angle in order to show the tracks in the foreground as parallel lines that converge at the horizon. Telephone poles, bridges, tunnels, and other environmental markers in the frame functioned as markers of flow. The repetition of all these elements contributed to an overall impression that the perceptual experience of the motion of the camera was a recreation of the flow of the environment.

The realism of this impression has been recounted many times, both during the 1900s and into the present. Early industry accounts reported rather apocryphal stories of the realistic effect produced. These stories are reminiscent of the reception of the earliest Lumière films: "The illusion was so good that when trolley rides through cities were shown, members of the audience frequently yelled at pedestrians to get out of the way or be run down."[23] It is noteworthy that in this report spectators do not jump out of the way (as they did in the reports about Lumière film showings) since they do not understand things coming at them inasmuch as they understand themselves moving forward. They instead yell out at pedestrians in the frame to get out of the way, further implying an acoustic space that defines their participation in the movie. Noël Burch summarized their position, "These spectators . . . were already in another world than those who, ten years earlier, had jumped up in terror at the filmed arrival of a train in a station: [they] . . . are masters of the situation, they are ready to *go through the peephole.*"[24] But Burch makes the mistake of thinking that it is purely the cinematic mode of address that accounts for this realism. For him, *Hale's Tours'* success depends entirely on its capacity to effect this visual, out-of-body projection into the diegesis. He, like others, fails to see that these illusion rides were always *more than* movies; they were about a physiological and psychological experience associated with travel.

Hale's Tours did not even maintain a strict cowcatcher visual point of view to get across its realism. The emphasis on flow and perspective of travel was frequently broken in order to display dramatic incidents and bits of social mingling between men and women, different classes, farmers and urbanites, train

employees and civilians, ordinary citizens and outlaws. Changes of locale occurred abruptly through editing, the camera position was moved, or the perspective from the front or rear of the train was abandoned altogether. When this
happened, the film usually expanded its travel format to offer up views of accompanying tourist attractions or stretched the travelogue with comic or dramatic scenes. (And, of course, tours like *Automobile Tours of the World* simply
moved the audience from its *Hale's Tours*esque fare to the variety format of an
electric theater.) For example, a 1906 *New York Clipper* advertisement for *Hale's
Tours* listed five "humorous railway scenes" that could be included in *Hale's
Tours* programs.[25] *Trip through the Black Hills* (Selig Polyscope, 1907) covered
"the difficulties of trying to dress in a Pullman berth."[26] In addition, the early
film classic *The Great Train Robbery* played in *Hale's Tours* cars. *Hale's Tours'*
latent content assumed a newly commercialized tourism—the traveler made
over into a spectator by taking a journey specifically to consume the exotic,
whether that was the city for the country "rube," the "primitive" for the west-
erner, or picturesque Nature for the urbanite. The subject did not require a
visual point-of-view literalism for the realism of the experience so long as a perceptual realism was being maintained because of the convergence of multiple
senses, especially including sound.

It therefore was not unusual for the films to cut regularly to the interior of a
railroad car, producing a "mirror image" of the social space in which the patron
was seated. These films were not purely travelogues then, but were also about
the social relations and expectations connected with the experience of travel.
What was fundamental to the illusion ride was never merely the sight of the
"destination" and the sensation of visual immersion in it, but the *experience*—
both physical and social—of being in that place. Thus, in addition to the ambient sound effects of wheels clattering or water swirling, whistles shrieking, and
bells ringing that attempted to cover the disparity between the physical sensation of motion and the visual perception of hurtling into space, the bang of a
revolver being fired in the hold-up films or musical effects could also have
enhanced narrative elements. In his discussion of *The Great Train Robbery,*
Charles Musser speculates that sound effects may have been used during those
portions of the story that depart from the viewer-as-passenger point of view.[27]
However, in his discussion of the film's landmark close-up, he notes that it
heightened realism because realism itself was associated not with greater pictorial naturalism but with increased identification and emotional involvement in
the drama. Although he does not comment on this, it is logical then that sound
effects would just as fully have contributed to this narrative sensibility of identification.

Two more examples of narrative *Hale's Tours* films reinforce this point. *The
Hold-Up of the Rocky Mountain Express* switches to the car interior not just once
but twice, to portray social interactions among the passengers and then a train
robbery. The first interior offers a comic bit involving an old maid: her attempts
at coy flirtations are answered by a tramp, and she reacts by getting him thrown
out of the car. The film later returns to the interior of the passenger car during

the hold-up, where passengers are robbed amid gunplay and one of the women faints. Both of these scenes offer ample opportunities for sound effects to underscore drama, comedy, and psychological identification. In fact, this film's return to a point of view of forward locomotion in order to depict the criminals getting away on a handcar and the train pursuing them overturns the original picturesque visual purpose with a narrative one. *Grand Hotel to Big Indian* is a variant of the same practice. After an extended traveling shot from a cowcatcher point of view, the film cuts to the train interior, where a sexual flirtation between comic characters results in a brawl among the male passengers.

Hale's Tours thus offered its customers vicarious long-distance journeys compressed into seven minutes while it poked fun at tourist travel. Whether Pullman car, steamship, or automobile, the conveyance was usually the domain of the wealthy and signified luxury travel and class status. Even though such actual tourist travel was beyond the economic means of most travelers, the *Hale's Tours* virtual leisure trip initiated men and women into their new status as consumers and tourists for the faraway, the exotic, and the modern alike. In this regard, *Hale's Tours* transformed the status of a mechanical conveyance into a seemingly limitless commodity of pleasure and excitement.

Of course, illusion rides extended the work of other amusement park rides. Like the roller coasters and scenic railways, illusion rides emphasized the traveler's body as the center of an environment of action and excitement as well as the illusion of travel in an actual worldly location outside the park. They extended a multiplicity of effects *on* the body—the novelty of moving images, loud sounds, and physical sensations of motion shocks and wind effects. Although confirmed only by scant anecdotal evidence (such as the moviegoer yelling "get out of the way"), the theater space may also have been punctuated by the calls and shouts of audience members.

This combination of spatial and perceptual program made for a kind of audience involvement that conflicts with models of passive spectatorship. Mary Ann Doane's recent description of the cinema's spectator position as one of "progressive despatialization and disembodiment [wherein] the spectator is increasingly detached and dissociated from the space of perception" simply does not fit this historical situation.[28] Spectator contemplation here might more aptly be labeled a "sensory fascination" with the event. Sensory fascination invokes an active commitment of multiple senses, a type of *jouissance* that is a physically grounded, self-aware pleasure in the bodily perception of visual sensations and information, environmental sound, touch, and kinesthetic stimuli. Whereas dominant models of cinema spectatorship have posited a rapt visual attention to and absorption in the events on the screen, illusion rides overturn that model. They even extend the notion of the phantasmagoric space of cinema from the screen to the theater itself.

Previously marginalized means of cinematic exhibition such as illusion rides best represent an experience unaccounted for by theories of cinema spectatorship that have generally represented movie-going as a passive experience in which spectators are increasingly drawn *out* of their bodies and into the screen.

They illustrate that cinema has covered the disjuncture between the materiality of the body and the body's de-emphasis in distracted cinema viewing. In this regard, illusion rides provide an important model for further work on the spectator's experience in general and for understanding, in particular, the spectatorial pleasures of porn, horror, action, melodrama, and other genres that coordinate addresses to out-of-the-body and in-the-body experiences. The consequence is that cinematic realism has never been purely about optical perception but has *always* been constituted in relationship to both social and sound phenomena.

Notes

1. See, for example, Noël Burch, *Life to Those Shadows*, trans. Ben Brewster (Berkeley and Los Angeles: University of California Press, 1990), 39; Raymond Fielding, "Hale's Tours: Ultrarealism in the Pre-1910 Motion Picture," in *Film before Griffith*, ed. John L. Fell (Berkeley and Los Angeles: University of California Press, 1983), 116–130; Lynn Kirby, *Parallel Tracks: The Railroad and Silent Cinema* (Durham, N.C.: Duke University Press, 1997), 46, 57; Charles Musser, *The Emergence of Cinema: The American Screen to 1907* (Berkeley and Los Angeles: University of California Press, 1990), 429–431.

2. It is likely that Hale was less the inventor of the illusion ride than a refiner of "Le Ballon Cinéorama" from the 1900 Paris Exposition, where the former Kansas City fire chief had presented Hale's Fire Fighters, his exhibition of American fire fighting (Musser, *The Emergence of Cinema*, 429). This seems especially so since one of the earliest *Hale's Tours* shows reported at Coney Island was "A Trip in a Balloon," an "imaginary sky voyage" that featured moving-picture views of New York made during aeronaut Leo Stevens's balloon trip, in a transparent imitation of the French illusion ride ("Dreamland and the Beautiful Is Pearl of Coney Island," *Billboard*, 9 June 1906, 6).

3. Hale and Gifford advertisement, *Billboard*, 17 February 1906, 19.

4. All descriptions are from the patent application; *The Official Gazette of the United States Patent Office*, vol. 118 (September 1905), 788–789.

5. Ibid.

6. For descriptions of Hale and Gifford's patents of an amusement device (patent no. 767, 281) and a pleasure-railway (patent no. 800,100), see: *The Official Gazette of the United States Patent Office*, vol. 111 (August 1904), 1577, and vol. 118 (September 1905), 788–789. In 1906, they sold the rights east of Pittsburgh to William A. Brady of New York and Edward B. Grossmann of Chicago for $50,000; *Billboard*, 27 January 1906, 20. They sold the southern-states rights to Wells, Dunne and Harlan of New York. They sold additional licenses to C. W. Parker Co. of Abilene, Kansas for traveling carnival companies. They sold the Pacific-Northwest–states rights to a group of men who incorporated as "The Northwest Hale's Tourist Amusement Company" in Portland, Oregon.

7. "Coney Island on the Outside," *Billboard*, 26 May 1906, 30.

8. Warren A. Patrick, "The Chicago Park Season Epitomized and Reviewed," *Billboard*, 22 September 1906, 9.

9. This installation was visited by Hale and Gifford shortly after it opened, and the trade paper reported that Hale and Gifford did not view it as an infringement on their patents; *Billboard*, 3 March 1906.

10. *Billboard,* 3 February 1906, 20.

11. "Parks," *Billboard,* 9 June 1906, 24.

12. See, for example: "Duluth's New Summer Park," *Billboard,* 28 July 1906, 28. At Riverview Park in Chicago, the nation's largest and best-attended amusement park, *Hale's Tours* was the fifth-biggest moneymaker of the fifty concessions there, earning $18,000 for the season. It was topped only by the Igorotte Village ($40,000), the Kansas Cyclone ($28,000), and the Figure 8 roller coasters ($35,000), Rollin's animal show and ostrich farm ($26,000), and the dance pavilion ($22,000). It even surpassed the revenues from the park's other moving picture venue, the electric theatre, which took in $16,000 for the year. "Riverview," *Billboard,* 1 December 1906, 28.

13. Hale and Gifford promptly brought a patent-infringement suit against the company [Scenic Novelty Co. advertisement, *Billboard,* 25 August 1906, 2] and, when it was dismissed, Hale and Gifford purchased the Citron patent, no. 845, 524, for the 1907 season. Hale and Gifford advertisement, *Billboard,* 16 May 1907, 29. Citron's patent no. 845,524 is described in *The Official Gazette of the United States Patent Office,* vol. 126 (January–February 1907), 3292. Interestingly, the patent application for a pleasure-railway that has fully operating curtained windows on the sides says nothing about showing movies through those windows as the above advertisement claims.

14. *Official Gazette of the United States Patent Office,* vol. 126, 3292.

15. Trolley Car Tours advertisement, *Billboard,* 26 March 1906, 39.

16. Their advertisement read: "The illusion of seeing the various countries and cities from an automobile is produced by a panorama of moving scenes attached to the wall beside the Sightseeing Auto upon which are seated the 'Sightseers,' and the throwing upon a screen in front of the Sightseeing Auto the moving pictures which were taken from a moving automobile, by this company, and which are the property of the Sightseeing Auto Co. By an original and clever idea the 'Sightseers' are given a side trip which enables them to view a variety of moving pictures, thus taking away from the patrons of the Sightseeing Autos that 'tired feeling' which is produced by a repetition of the same kind and character of moving pictures they would be forced to witness should they always remain on the auto." *Billboard,* 27 January 1906, 23.

17. Patent application no. 828, 791, *The Official Gazette of the United States Patent Office,* vol. 121 (July–August 1906), 2246–2247.

18. White and Langever's Steamboat Tours of the World advertisement, *Billboard,* 22 September 1906, 44.

19. Hruby and Plummer's Tours and Scenes of the World advertisement, *Billboard,* 3 March 1906, 25.

20. Ibid.

21. A Trip to California advertisement, *Billboard,* 31 March 1906, 31; 26 May 1906, 31.

22. Barbara Maria Stafford, *Good Looking: Essays on the Virtue of Images* (Cambridge: MIT Press, 1997), 212.

23. E. C. Thomas, "Vancouver, B.C. Started with 'Hale's Tours,'" *Moving Picture World,* 15 July 1916, 373.

24. Burch, 39.

25. Edison Manufacturing Company advertisement, *New York Clipper,* 28 April 1906.

26. Fielding, 128.

27. Charles Musser, *Before the Nickelodeon* (Berkeley and Los Angeles: University

of California Press, 1991), 265. See, for example, the following display advertisements: "Hale Tour Films, Selig Polyscope 'Latest Films,'" *Views and Films Index,* 20 April 1907, 5; "Hale Tour Runs," Biograph Bulletin no. 73, 30 June 1906, reprinted in *Biograph Bulletins 1896–1908,* ed. Kemp R. Niver (Los Angeles: Artisan Press, 1971), 250–252.

28. Mary Ann Doane, "Technology's Body: Cinematic Vision in Modernity," *differences: A Journal of Feminist Cultural Studies* 5, no. 2 (1993), 15.

Part Four: *Spectators and Politics*

17 The Noises of Spectators, or the Spectator as Additive to the Spectacle

Jean Châteauvert and
André Gaudreault

The type of space institutional narrative cinema creates between spectator and screen is, as a general rule, a decidedly private space, an intimate space of contemplation in which the screen addresses itself not to the multitude, but to a singular, individual, and personal spectator isolated in the intimate obscurity of the movie theater. "Addresses" is in this case rather strong insofar as the screen of the institutional cinema, as well as its sound additives, generally pretend to address no one in particular. By contrast, if we except specific exhibition practices of moving images,[1] early cinema commonly involved a resolutely public space between screen and spectator. It is not, then, an individualized spectator but an audience, a collective entity, that is implicated in the viewing situation specific to this period. Indeed, at the time, spectators were often invited to participate collectively in the spectacle of moving images. This participation by necessity implied sound occurrences (for instance, applause as certain actors like Méliès come back to bow to the audience at the end of some films, singalong to song slides, etc.) and accordingly turned individuals into members of an audience, that is, a community.

Our objective here will be, first, to identify the different logics of representation practiced in early cinema. To this end, we will draw up a basic inventory of various "spectatorial noises," which leads to the question of the pertinence of these noises. Secondly, we will attempt to isolate a few of the factors that contributed to what we will refer to as the structuration of the sound space.[2]

About Periodization

The long period referred to as *early cinema*, which customarily ends around 1913, should obviously not be thought of as undifferentiated muddle. For the purpose of our demonstration, we will consequently borrow from Eric de Kuyper's distinction between *first period cinema* and *second period cinema* (1908 being a turning point).[3] *First period cinema* is notably characterized, as far as exhibition conditions are concerned, by the primacy of a public space allowing for the free participation of spectators in the sound environment of the moving images. This public space stands in sharp contrast to the private space of institutional cinema (after 1913), where silence in the audience is generally valued. Between these two dates (1908–1913), consequently, there is an intermediary, buffer period, neither fish nor fowl, that of *second period cinema*, during which the sound space of the screening is being organized. In the course of this time span, the various "spectators' noises" begin to be subject to the constraints forced upon them by different mechanisms structuring the sound space —that is, the space of the screening, which will foster the emergence of an institutional mode of representation.

During each of these periods, a number of systems of representation of moving images are in favor, depending on, among other things, the site and type of exhibition. Our breakdown relies on the system of representation privileged during each period, as some of them clearly prevail at given moments. *Second period cinema* thus contrasts with *first period cinema*, though not as a set of exclusive practices, with the beginning of a period by necessity implying the disappearance of practices characteristic of the previous one. Rather, it qualifies as a period in terms of screening conditions, because it witnessed the gradual consolidation of practices that resulted in the organization of the sound space of the theater. These practices appeared in the course of the time span known as first period cinema but were not the result of a concerted effort until the second period. Similarly, screenings of moving images in a non-organized sound space did not disappear with the end of the first period, but the practice became marginal during the second period, at a time when the sound space of screenings tended to be organized.

Although the proposed distinction between *first period cinema* and *second period cinema* rests on the modes of reception of moving images and the context in which these are presented, it nevertheless has as its counterpart the "texts" themselves (*images* and *films*) or at least the analyses of these texts. Thus the distinction put forward here matches the one that was once advanced by Tom Gunning and one of the authors of this essay and that contrasted the *system of monstrative attractions* (typical of *first period cinema*) and the *system of narrative integration* (which dominated *second period cinema*).[4] The distinction *first period/second period* does not constitute, accordingly, a revision of the periodizations established on the basis of textual analyses, but partakes of a desire to support textual analyses with contextual ones.

Structured Sound Space vs. Non-structured Sound Space

First period cinema, the "first cinema" if you will, was characterized by the primacy of a system of representation in which the various kinds of sound accompaniment retained a relative level of autonomy in relation to the images featured in moving pictures. Not only were these sounds only loosely tied to the visual spectacle of the image track, but in addition, those producing these accompanying sounds did not have clear instructions to follow, nor did they answer to a clearly pre-established norm. The sound space of the theater, which then was not governed by any precise rules, was not structured. Such rules were progressively put into place with the process of institutionalization marking the second period.

As far as film exhibition is concerned, *second period cinema,* the "second cinema" if you will, essentially revolves around the gradual institution (we will later see how) of a *structured sound space.* We should nevertheless bear in mind that the dominant system of representation during *first period cinema* continued, throughout this second period, to claim its share in some exhibition venues (fairgrounds, neighborhood theaters, etc.). What characterizes *second cinema* (1908–1913), then, is among other things this co-existence, in various ratios (depending on the year and the country in question), of two systems of representation that suppose quite divergent types of reception:

- a first type, coming from *first period cinema* (yet enduring after 1908 in the form of increasingly marginal practices), which initiated a public, *spectacular* space between spectator and screen, the corollary of what has been called an exhibitionist confrontation (on this topic, see the article mentioned in endnote 4);

and

- a second type, typical of *second period cinema,* in which are set into place mechanisms structuring the sound space, some of which will have as a consequence the deployment of conditions of representation necessary to the emergence of institutional cinema.

It seems to us a reasonable assumption that the second portion of what is commonly called "early cinema," a portion corresponding to the period known as *second period cinema,* is an era of transformations that witnessed the shift from *early cinema* to *institutional cinema.* It is a time during which the agents typical of the sound space of *first period cinema* were diverted from their original function as additives to the spectacle of moving pictures into instruments in the structuration of the sound space. Besides the fact that just their presence in the theater implies a public space at the opposite pole from the intimate space later required by the institution, these agents contributed to the establishment of rules and customs surrounding film screenings. Spectators were invited to remain silent during the lecturer's speech, to sing along as song slides were projected, to applaud at the end of the film, and so on.

There would thus be, at one end of the spectrum, a public space fostered by the presence of the lecturer, a common, "spectacular" space, so to speak. It is, indeed, not to an individual spectator but to an audience (that is, a community of listeners and/or spectators) that the voice addresses itself, in the form of the lecturer's sound "close-ups," which in some way make up for the visual distance of long shots so characteristic of the image track of *first period cinema.*

At the other end of the spectrum, we would find *institutional cinema* (from 1913 on), whose main system of representation is founded on a cinema of silent films without lecture, interspersed with titles and accompanied by tailor-made music. This system no longer addresses itself to the multitude but to a singular, individual, and personal spectator isolated in the intimate obscurity of the movie theater. This individualized spectator thus consumes images and sounds from the private space of his/her seat, a decidedly intimate space of undisturbed contemplation whose correlate is the space induced by the close-up—a figure that is already present in *second period cinema* and that will become characteristic of *institutional cinema*. Indeed, it comes as no coincidence, in our opinion, that the close-up begins to play a crucial role in cinematographic expression at the time the lecturer declines in importance.

The Spectators' Applause

Within the context of the *spectacular representation,* a given spectator would thus have felt more easily licensed to manifest him-/herself through various noisy gestures, if only to answer the direct, constant, and systematic interpellation of the audience by the lecturer, who always already acted to some extent as an interlocutor. This probably explains why, as evidence bears out, collective sound expressions were very frequent in early cinema, especially during *first period cinema*. Our own collection of the journalistic commentaries provoked by the first years of film exhibition in a city such as Montréal is in this respect quite telling. Indeed, it is frequently reported that spontaneous behavior on the part of spectators often led them to applaud *jointly*. This contrasts with the spectator of institutional cinema, who was to applaud only under exceptional circumstances, for example when individuals participating in the production of the film were present in the space of the representation. Thus we noticed, on the basis of a summary sample of daily newspapers published between 1899 and 1907, that most "sound expressions" on the part of spectators reported by journalists involved applause,[5] probably the best sign of satisfaction at the end of a picture or filmed attraction. It could be read, for instance, that "moving pictures raised applause many times"[6] or that "each picture raised hearty applause from the audience."[7]

It is generally presumed that during the first period, spectators were not only allowed, but also encouraged, to applaud to express their contentment. Within their paradigm, spectators of early cinema could feel the exhibition system in all its thickness, and the presence of the lecturer notably made them aware of how the spectacle they were attending was a *unique event* that would never be exactly replicated anywhere else—it was happening here, in this very theater, *hic et nunc*. Everything converged to remind them of this specificity—obvious copresence of other spectators due to the slight obscurity, *in situ* presence of the additives to the exhibition, musicians, master of ceremony, lecturer, sound effects engineers, and the like.

It is then patent that the spectator of early cinema differed at least in this respect from the spectator of its institutional counterpart, who, notwithstanding some exceptions, did not deem it necessary to communicate his/her satisfaction at the sight of shadows and spots moving on the screen. It is then quite true that the *institutional screen* is a "fantasy screen," and that what is projected on it is perceived by the *institutional spectator* as a story whose enunciative and representational mechanisms s/he will readily forget.

Other Sound Interventions by Spectators

The spectators of *first period cinema* had more than applause at their disposal to express themselves through sounds. They could just as well burst out laughing, cry out, sing, or whisper. As to the occasional uncouth spectator speaking out loud and making untimely comments throughout the screening, it evidently was the common lot in the reception process during *first period cinema*. One may nevertheless imagine that such occurrences dramatically decreased during *second period cinema* and were to be later considered a breach of the code of conduct of the institutional spectator.

Laughter and cries (as well as whispering—unfortunately, some would have it) have as a particularity the fact they endured in the range of spontaneous reactions on the part of the film spectator after the shift to the paradigm of institutional cinema. Singing, applause, and speaking out have completely disappeared from usual screening conditions at this point. They nevertheless remain in certain cases, such as in neighborhood theaters or during the screenings of cult films, for example, when the film is the object of a collective appropriation. Thus, during screenings of *The Rocky Horror Picture Show* or *Hair*, spectators sing or shout in unison. Another instance is some *psychotronic* festivals dedicated to third-rate science-fiction or horror films, where screenings are generally punctuated with shouts and commentary. This shows how celebratory rituals inviting collective participation still occasionally take place at the margins of the mainstream consumption of films, where discretion and silence are the rule.

We should not believe, however, that codes of good conduct managed to establish uncontested domination during *second period cinema*. All audiences did not become subdued from the moment different strategies of sound structuring and silencing were put into place. In Great Britain, for example, spectators of popular theaters may have remained quite raucous until very late into the 1910s.[8]

The additives to the exhibition changed roles during *second period cinema*, as we have seen, by making room for, or at least by contributing to impose, within the space of the projection, moments during which the spectator had to (or could) sing and others during which s/he had to observe silence. Sound occurrences in the theater then came to be a part not so much of the spectator's relationship to the spectacle of moving pictures as of the integration of all elements taking part in film screenings. It could indeed be assumed that the shift from a *non-structured* to a *structured* sound space had as a consequence, in the course of *second period cinema*, the gradual imposition of silence for a spectator accustomed to the *spectacle of moving pictures* yet more and more frequently invited to attend *a representation of narrative films*, which were to become the bread and butter of institutional cinema. It would indeed appear quite inappropriate for the individualized spectator, merged in the darkness of the intimate space for contemplation created by institutional cinema, to license him/herself to intervene loudly through speech or noises during the screening, thereby somewhat intruding in the intimate space of his/her co-spectators.

The Factors in the Structuring of the Sound Space

From *second period cinema* on, the sound environment of the theater was structured on the basis of at least six factors, which are relatively easy to identify:

(1) The lecturer could now and then occupy the sound space in its entirety through speaking, which also enabled him to drown out possible untimely speech by spectators. Yet, as a figure of interlocution, he also called for and encouraged an (inter-)active participation on the spectators' part, a participation that could then translate into various forms of sound expressions just when needed.

(2) Slides and intertitles also participated in the structuring of the sound space insofar as they could bear explicit or implicit directions that led spectators to manifest themselves through sound (invitation to sing in chorus, to applaud, etc.).

(3) Music often served to discipline spectators—at the very beginning it was there only to fill the sound space of the representation, but later prescriptive texts regularly published in corporate newspapers advocated certain types of music based on the emotion or the genre in question. During *first period cinema,* music had imposed a first form of structuring by occupying the whole sound space of the theater; during *second period cinema,* it contributed to force silence in the space of the theater, especially in relation to drama as a genre.

(4) The sound space was also structured by the nature of the very site of the screening—the fairgrounds tent did not lend itself as easily to diegetic absorption as did the movie palace.

(5) The film's topic summoned up habits and behaviors linked to theatrical or spectacular genres (or even to cultural or religious referents) inside the movie theater. The screening of a *Passion* thus probably was attended to with a much more discreet participation on the part of the audience than was, say, a comedy.

(6) Finally, an analysis of the film corpus of early cinema brings out the existence, from the first years, of actual strategies of filmic mise-en-scène that serve as incentives for the spectators to participate through sound. Conceived in the very space of the direction, they may be read as authentic invitations to the spectators to laugh, applaud, even sing at a given time of the film and might have contributed to the structuring of the sound space characteristic of *second period cinema.*

Filmic Strategies That Call for Sound Participation

A first strategy to incite sound participation on the part of the spectators is employed in the shots where characters greet the audience watching them. A good instance of this is provided by the curtain-call shots that conclude many films and convey the impression that actors bow to listeners who are in all likelihood applauding their performance. Such invitations are also found in the Gaumont Chronophones, at whose end the artist comes back "on stage" for a virtual applause. Such applause is thus limited to the margins of the film text, at the very end of the "act," and represents the opportunity for the spectators to sanction the film.

Another, more subtle strategy may reside in those moments when, at the end of a particularly "theatrical" performance or an eminently spectacular gesture, an actor moves forward to *strike a pose* in front of the camera. Such greetings are found in a more discreet form in all trick films where conjuring acts end with a movement toward the camera or even a look toward it. This is the case with Méliès, when for instance he invites the newly appeared queen in *Les Cartes vivantes* (1905) to move to the fore and strike a pose just long enough for the applause to take place. Such applause crowns the success of the attraction captured by the camera, an attraction that is not *profilmic* but *filmed*. It isolates and sanctions the attractional surprise as a strong, successful moment of the picture.

Among these attractional surprises were pictorial quotations, that is, filmed tableaux whose mise-en-scène and duration pointed to the quotation of a famous painting in the moving image. This, according to Roberta Pearson and William Uricchio, enabled cinema to establish its pedigree by offering its spectators the live expression of famous paintings.[9] Thus in *Julius Caesar* (Vitagraph), the duration of the tableaux, in which actors evidently stop acting to strike a pose, functions to allow spectators to identify the painting but also, we believe, to give them the time and opportunity to express through applause their appreciation of the performance. Cinema then shared certain similarities with histrionic theater, where it was common for the actor to interrupt the action to get the audience to applaud.

A third strategy, the cinematographic adaptation of songs, relied on previous knowledge of the adapted song but also on vocal participation on the part of spectators. A forerunner to these adaptations, the illustrated song slides of the magic lantern had set the tone for the spectators of the *first period cinema*.

Noiseless Communication

With the hindsight of our first analyses, it appears that the famous opposition between spectatorial noises/screen noises, which today we take for granted, was inherited from the institutional mode of representation, with its emphasis on individual consumption and its requirement that the surrounding presence of other spectators be forgotten (or at least consigned to the background). In this type of moving pictures characteristic of *first period cinema*, in which the lecturer harangued the crowd of spectators, the latter took part in the sound environment of a representation played out in a collective fashion. Sounds made by spectators thus did not constitute, noisy as they were, *noises* in the communication process. They even were, in a spectacular regime, the sign of an active participation. They belong in the very definition of the said spectacle, a spectacle that is addressed to a group, a collective entity. This is the group the lecturer addresses himself to, this is the mass of spectators to which actors direct their first look when they turn to the camera. Through their inscription in the space-being-structured of *second period cinema*, which tended to discriminate between appropriate and inopportune sounds and noises, these expressions eventually found their purpose and coherence. At the end of *second period cinema*, spectators as a whole were in theory supposed to remain silent during the screening and could sing or applaud only when cued to do so.

The structuration of the sound space may have, in our opinion, increasingly circumscribed spectators' participation to the point where it imposed the silence necessary for diegetic absorption to happen. And with silence, the regime of film consumption may have let the spectator move imperceptibly from a *solidary* to a *solitary* mode of consumption!

TRANSLATED BY FRANCK LE GAC AND WENDY SCHUBRING

Notes

This text was written within the framework of GRAFICS (Groupe de Recherche sur l'Avènement et la Formation des Institutions Cinématographique et Scénique; Research Group on the Creation and Formation of Cinematographic and Theatrical Institutions) at the *Université de Montréal,* supported by the *Conseil de recherches en sciences humaines du Canada* (Canadian Council on Research in Human Sciences) and the FCAR fund (Quebec). GRAFICS and both authors of the present piece are part of the *Centre de recherche sur l'intermédialité* (CRI) at the *Université de Montréal.* We want to thank all those who, through their interventions and comments, have enabled us to improve our text and make it more precise; particular thanks to Donald Crafton, Ben Brewster, and Tom Gunning.

1. We will not deal here with particular exhibition contexts (private screenings, for example) that may have occurred at the time, or even, in some cases, have been documented (through contemporary testimony), except to emphasize that they probably involved spectatorial practices that differ from the ones we describe here.

2. Our research follows from Noël Burch's remark that music and lecturer contributed to organizing the sound space of the theater. See *La Lucarne de l'infini: naissance du langage cinématographique* (Paris: Nathan, 1991), 223–231.

3. We are thus keeping some distance from the breakdown proposed by de Kuyper, which includes the whole 1910s in the second period. See Éric de Kuyper, "Le cinéma de la seconde époque. Le muet des années dix," *Cinémathèque* 1 (May 1992), 28–35.

4. See André Gaudreault and Tom Gunning, "Le cinéma des premiers temps: un défi à l'histoire du cinéma?" in *Histoire du cinéma. Nouvelles approches,* ed. Jacques Au-

mont, André Gaudreault, and Michel Marie (Paris: Publications de la Sorbonne, 1989), 49–63.

5. This summary press sample from the two most important Francophone Montréal daily newspapers was put together by Karine Martinez and Églantine Monsaingeon, research assistants at the GRAFICS, whom the authors want to thank for their precious collaboration. It enabled us to identify twenty references (traced in the newspapers *La Presse,* from 1902 and 1907, and *La Patrie,* from 1899 and 1905), sixteen of which relate applause on the part of spectators attending a screening of moving pictures. It is worth noting that during the period under scrutiny, these daily newspapers regularly published accounts of cinematographic representations and that the representations mentioned in our examples are by no means exceptional.

6. *La Presse* 11 (November 1902), 7.

7. *La Patrie* 11 (May 1905), 14.

8. This is the argument defended by Nicolas Hiley in "The British Cinema Auditorium," in *Film and the First World War,* ed. Karel Dibbets and Bert Hogenkamp (Amsterdam: Amsterdam University Press, 1995), 160–170; as well as in "Fifteen Questions about the Early Film Audience," in *Uncharted Territory: Essays on Early Nonfiction Film,* ed. Daan Hertogs and Nico de Klerk (Amsterdam: Nederlands Filmmuseum, 1997), 105–118.

9. Roberta Pearson and William Uricchio, *Reframing Culture: The Case of the Vitagraph Quality Films* (Princeton: Princeton University Press, 1993). The two authors describe the effects of pictorial quotations as many "realizations": "literal recreation and translation" of the images "into a more real . . . vivid, visual, physically present medium" (86). On this topic, see also Martin Meisel, *Realizations: Narrative, Pictorial, and Theatrical Arts in Nineteenth-Century England* (Princeton: Princeton University Press, 1983).

18 Early Cinematographic Spectacles: The Role of Sound Accompaniment in the Reception of Moving Images
Jacques Polet

This essay means to adopt the perspective of the spectator addressed by early filmic representations. I hope to reconstruct, if only slightly, what constituted his/her horizon of expectations, to borrow Hans-Robert Jauss's concept.[1] In other words, I will attempt to identify the type of spectatorial relationship with moving images that a peripheral sound production (lecture, music, sound effects, and so on) could foster given the expectations, interests, and knowledge of the audience at the time.

Quite obviously, this comes close to an "irrecoverable object," and the reconstruction of parameters in a horizon of expectations is "always somewhat hypothetical."[2] Given the constraints of this forum and the state of my thought on the subject, we cannot proceed but cautiously and in a piecemeal fashion, all the more since the range of combinations between images and sounds may be considerable, just as attitudes of reception certainly vary. Indeed, we should also bear in mind that there is no such thing (and this also applies to the period under scrutiny) as a homogeneous audience. Noël Burch, among others, has shown this in his works on variations in audience make-up in France, Great Britain, and the United States.[3]

I am of course aware of the multiplicity of empirical as well as theoretical variables. Reception may be approached from a number of perspectives: psychological (identification), sociological (the structure of audiences), anthropological (calling for an intercultural analysis), and so on.

Here I intend to follow two methodological directions:

- On the one hand, through the relations between perifilmic images and sounds (to paraphrase François Jost, who originated the notion of *périfilm*),[4] I will try to infer the most common types of attitudes that the cinematographic spectacle solicited among early viewers and listeners, given their expectations and their assumed experience of shows, beyond the empirical variability of publics and spectatorial behavior;
- on the other hand, and similarly, I will attempt to go beyond the practical

diversity of *perifilmic* sound productions, among which our approach more fundamentally distinguishes between (a) the iconic representation and (b) the here-and-now[5] of the sound configuration.

The reflection I propose here thereby relies on this double methodology, one involving the object, the other dealing with the position chosen in relation to it. It has often been noted that sound accompaniment was used to reinforce the *reality effect* closely tied to the reception of early moving images. What's more, we know that early modes of representation induced spectators to *center* their gaze, at the same time as that gaze was being widely solicited by the multiple actions occurring simultaneously within the frame. This multiplicity, nicely described by Noël Burch as "topological swarming,"[6] was also referred to by Serge Daney about ten years ago when he observed that nowadays, "not only are film theaters less numerous and more empty, but the films themselves are also de-populated."[7] This "swarming" of early cinema staged, more or less, in any given image the very principle of the programmatic diversity that structured the representations of the time. Still, the frontal model and axial continuity made it possible to transcend this topological dissemination. Centering an action had as its principal consequence the visual subsumption of the other actions.

This is where early sound accompaniment comes into play, in the way its strongly *performative* character affected the contemporary spectator, when sounds were not yet fixed by recordings. Near the entrance stood the *tout,* whose enticing patter sometimes seeped in the space of the spectacle. There also was the *lecturer,* who, standing close to the screen, monitored the interpretation of the images but also the behavior of an audience little inclined to silence and itself an important source of non-filmic sounds. Not far away, on the other side of the screen, was the *pianist,* and on occasion the *orchestra* playing in the pit. Behind the screen, there could be some *speakers* or *singers,* and backstage *sound-effects engineers* performed various simulations. These were the main protagonists of sound production, who could work in various combinations. Their *heterogeneity,* but most of all their *pluri-localization,* are remarkable—sound could issue from virtually everywhere, from beside the screen, behind it, below it, backstage, outside the theater.[8]

Although it has often been noted that the sounds of silent film "self-effacingly served" the image, it would seem quite appropriate to me to make more of the specifically *presential* dimension of all these sound sources. The spectator of the time, it seems, was caught up in a double movement that hinged on a tension rather than a slavish allegiance. On the one hand, s/he was engaged, as if by transparency, by the centered iconic apparatus into the reality effect produced by it. On the other hand, that same spectator could not help but experience the physical presence of sound sources, which punctually manifested themselves from a plurality of places, with the effect of overdetermining their constitutive heterogeneity. This latter aspect stood in stark contrast to the *transparent* relationship with images, as it created a relationship to sounds based on *opacity.* This resistance of bodies was all the more perceptible by the audience since their experience of spectacles of attractions (circuses, fairs, music halls, *cafés-concerts*) was woven into their horizon of expectations and had accustomed them to powerful acts of "performative enunciation."[9]

In other words, spectators were caught between two opposite processes: one tied to images, which tended toward *centering* in a hegemonic manner; the other, associated with sounds, which *decentered* the audience's attention. Yet this decentering process was all the less unbearable at the time as the physical experience of noise was a completely legitimate one in the contemporary context. The right to noise was almost recognized as a "natural right," an assertion of individual autonomy subject to a minimum of coercion and, as Jacques Attali specified about France, not worthy of a significant campaign until 1928—well after the time period of interest to us.[10]

It is significant in this respect to make a note of the observations included in a number of teleological historical texts, which mention the "deplorable conditions" of cinematographic reception, precisely in regard to noise. As Jean-Louis Schefer remembered his preteen years (referring to a time as recent as the immediate post–World War II period), he described film-going experiences in which "viewing conditions were terrible" and "conversations went on during the screening," and so on.[11] Were these conditions so terrible, though, when approached from the perspective of early audiences, for whom noise was a defining element of space? It is only in retrospect, within a horizon that has shifted and where cinephilia has replaced attractional expectations, that such a judgment may be passed.

It seems a viable hypothesis to suggest that these non-filmic noises (such as conversational ones) could only accentuate the decentering of the spectator and the tension to which the famous iconic reality effect was submitted. It's not unlikely that silence could be heard only in the classical concert hall . . .

In terms of music, and of the most common instrument in this context, the piano, I will not expand on what has already often been underlined in the past, namely, that its phrasing bridged over iconic discontinuity by creating for the spectator an essentially emotional musical narrative. What is more of relevance to our topic is the *improvisational* register to which the pianist's discourse belongs. Certainly, it tapped into "sound libraries," into standardized musical frameworks, which constitute as many "moments": "mysterious," "sentimental," "comic," "tragic," or even "Chinese-like." Yet, within this set of rules the pianist, by his live improvisation, enjoyed a degree of freedom that came as a reinforcement of the performative dimension of sound production I have already underlined above.

It is significant to note in this respect the account of an eminent Belgian pianist who accompanied silent films, Fernand Schirren, who for so many years worked at the Cinémathèque Royale in Brussels and made a strong impression on all those who got to hear him annually at the Pordenone Silent Film Festival. In an interview published by the *Revue Belge du Cinéma*, he goes as far as to say (with the hint of amused provocation that will not surprise those who know him even slightly) that his best memory as a film piano accompanist is from the day when, playing along with a film without interest, he fell asleep: "That day, I was asleep for one hour and I kept playing mechanically, without seeing or knowing anything about the story that was unfolding."[12] This is of course an amazing limit case, beyond the period under scrutiny here, but one that sheds light on how the discourse of the film piano accompanist can be predictable to the point of abstracting itself from any conscious relationship to the images to yield to the play of fingers on the keyboard. Paradoxically, pure functionality in relation to images opens up a space of freedom, be it one of "play in a dreaming state," dreams about which Schirren says, in the conclusion to his interview, that they fill his sleep with wonder.

This anecdote, as symbolic as it is, exemplifies yet again a possible division in the way sound and image are experienced, a division that, again, was likely to be well received by early film audiences. Indeed, we should keep in mind that piano improvisations reached their peak during the nineteenth century with great performers and virtuosos traveling the country and crossing borders. At that time, in the classical form of the concerto, the passage known as the cadenza provided pianists with a part where they could give free rein to their creativity and virtuosity. Quite logically, this peak also marks the beginning of a decline, as the tradition of improvisation and the free cadenza tended to disappear at the end of the nineteenth century, when scores increasingly indicated a given cadenza—codified, fixed, rigid—putting an end to the improvisational inventiveness of the pianist. It seems as though this freedom was no longer compatible with the flourishing of the classical concert as it assuredly entered the era of mercantile logic and control. To paraphrase the famous aphorism according to which "war is too serious a matter to be left to the military," classical music then appears too serious a matter to be left to its performers.

Let me then venture a hypothesis—that everything then happened as though this sphere of improvisational freedom retreated into a new space, that of a so-called minor, marginal spectacle, a mere attraction. Cinema, indeed, through piano variations on a few tunes etched on the collective memory, did in a way reappropriate for itself this area of performative freedom and gave it a new lease on life, obscurely and in an artisanal manner, placing it on the horizon of attractional expectations at the turn of the century.

Various *sound effects* also contributed to this recognition of performance beyond their imitative function. Some accounts have been found of silent film spectators going backstage to have a look at "the thundermaker cart rolling its many-sided wheels."[13] Similarly, sound effects, which were sometimes written down in the music scores prepared for screenings, were also on other occasions left to the choice of the traveling showman or theater owner—as with the famous close-up of George Barnes in Edison's *The Great Train Robbery* (1903).

Just as with the improvisation of cadenzas and their reining in through a codification of their notation, cinema went through a process of regulation and control in the form of the fixing (recording) of sounds by different media and techniques (which are analyzed here by other contributors), as if its *haphazard* aspects had become somewhat heretical from an institutional perspective.

Yet while non-recorded sounds were received by spectators through the living performance of the speakers' bodies, fixed sounds divert reception from *direct listening* to a *natural source* to center it on *indirect listening* geared toward *relay sources.*[14]

Indeed, in contrast to early images, whose flicker and scintillation did not undermine transparency as a medium, fixed sounds do not seem to have benefited from the same effect. This is not to say, yet again, that theological or retrospective considerations made them pass as "mediocre" or "deplorable" compared, say, to Dolby stereo systems; rather, they fared poorly in comparison to the great tradition of natural sounds coming down from the spectacle of attractions, which constituted most of the experience of early audiences. Certainly, audiences admired the sound restitution of a "having-been-there." However, as the texture of natural utterances became more nasal or whiny, the technical mediation was foregrounded, obstructing once more the desired transparency. This prevented the spectator-listeners from fully giving themselves up to what Pierre Schaeffer and Michel Chion have termed *causal listening,*[15] in this case *secondary,* which refers to the suggested source, usually a character in the diegesis. Instead, their attention was redirected toward the relay source, the technical mediation, thus fostering *primary causal listening.*[16]

Everything occurred as though, in the relationship of non-fixed sounds to images, the performance of speakers was *too present* compared to iconic transparency, whereas in the case of fixed sounds, the reality effect of images seemingly prevailed over a body suddenly become *too remote.*

Nevertheless, in the shift from non-fixed to fixed sounds (I will avoid the notion of "progress" here because of its teleological character), a decisive step was taken. The *presential, heterogeneous, pluri-localized* nature of the former was replaced by the *replicative,*[17] homogenized, and *monolocalized* character of the latter, in which the assembly of sources through technical mediation was to have as its logical outcome the unified soundtrack.

The fixing enabled by sound reproduction had signaled the beginning of control over the uncertainties present in the original cinematographic spectacle. We have to assume that "tensions" in the relationships between images and sounds (not to mention desynchronization!), while they appeared acceptable in the early years of cinema within a reception context shaped by attractions, had gradually lost their justification for the *spectator* whose horizon of expectations moved away from attractional devices. Similarly, the budding film *industry* had everything to fear from the unpredictability of spectacles; the extent of its reach depended on an increasing control of the reception stage.

Since the strong presential dimension of early cinema acted as a stimulant for the reactivity of the audience, the *whole* apparatus of the cinematographic spectacle, not only images, had to conform to the formula according to which, in Christian Metz's words, "film is a non-interactive discourse achieved before its presentation."[18] Through diverse transformations of sound, early cinema allows us to gain a better understanding of what the *freedom* of the cinematographic spectacle once was.

TRANSLATED BY FRANCK LE GAC AND WENDY SCHUBRING

Notes

1. Hans-Robert Jauss, *Pour une esthétique de la réception* (Paris: Gallimard, 1978).

2. Patrice Pavis, *L'analyse des spectacles* (Paris: Nathan, 1996), 244.

3. Noël Burch, *La lucarne de l'infini: Naissance du langage cinématographique* (Paris: Nathan, 1990), especially chs. 3, 4, and 5.

4. François Jost, "Le cinéma dans ses oeuvres," in *Après Deleuze: Philosophie et esthétique du cinéma* (Paris: Editions Dis Voir, 1996), 124.

5. This is expressed in the French text by a neologism, *présentielle*, derived from the word *present*—the experience of the time and space of theater as opposed to that of film. [Translator's note]

6. Noël Burch, "Passion, poursuite: la 'linéarisation'," *Communications* 38 (1983), 36.

7. Serge Daney, *Devant la recrudescence des vols de sacs à main* (Lyon: Aléas, 1991), 147.

8. For a detailed analysis of diverse silent film sounds, see Pascale Bertolini and Jacques Polet, "Boniments, explications et autres bruits de scène: les accompagnements des spectacles cinématographiques muets en Belgique," *Iris* 22 (1996), 145–160.

9. According to the formulation of François Jost in "Des images et des hommes," *Recherches en communication* 8 (1997), 23.

10. Jacques Attali, *Bruits* (Paris: Presses Universitaires de France, 1997), 244–245.

11. Jean-Louis Schefer, "Arrimer des mots au fleuve des images," *Vertigo* 17 (1997), 19.

12. Philippe Marion, "Pianiste comme aux premiers temps. Rencontre avec Fernand Schirren," in Jacques Polet, ed., *Revue belge du cinéma* 38–39 (1995), 101.

13. Laurent Jullier, *Les sons au cinéma et à la télévision. Précis d'analyse de la bande-son* (Paris: Armand Colin, 1995), 34.

14. This notion comes from Jullier, 30.

15. Pierre Schaeffer, *Traité des objets musicaux* (Paris: Editions du Seuil, 1966), 126. Michel Chion, *L'audio-vision* (Paris: Nathan, 1990), 25–27.

16. Jullier, 187.

17. "Replicative" sound is a notion proposed by Jullier, 49–56, 197.

18. Christian Metz, "L'énonciation impersonnelle ou le site du film," *Vertigo* 1 (1987), 14–34.

19 Sounding Canadian: Early Sound Practices and Nationalism in Toronto-Based Exhibition

Marta Braun and Charlie Keil

The controversy that recent research on early sound practices has engendered underlines the centrality of such practices to an expanded understanding of early cinema as a cultural enterprise.[1] The increased attention to sound reinforces our understanding that cinema functions not only as a text, but also as an experience rooted within a particular cultural context. Moreover, as research on the *bonimenteur* has shown, investigating early sound practices in the context of regional exhibition can help specify how sound practices derive from social and political conditions particular to nations not known for indigenous production.[2] In the spirit of such investigation, we offer a case study of early sound practices in Toronto, in the belief that the circumstances of film exhibition in a large city in English-speaking Canada affect the role of sound in revealing ways. More specifically, we have found that sound practice proved instrumental in constructing a distinctive Anglo-Canadian cultural context for film reception, a context devised at a time of nascent national identity, whose characteristics were (and still are) not American, and, although neo-colonial, not British either. Indeed, given the precarious cultural specificity of English-speaking Canada, the existence of sound practices became crucial in establishing this identity. In Ontario, the provincial home of Toronto, establishment of cultural distinctiveness proved an especially daunting task. Ontario's proximity to the largest urban metropolises of the United States and its constitutionally reinforced links with Britain mark it as a region destined to absorb outside cultural influences quite readily. As the obvious linguistic distinctions that obtain in Quebec do not apply to Ontario, what elements of early sound practice are relevant to the establishment of a particularized English-Canadian film-going experience?

Because of its centrality to cultural life in English-speaking Canada, and Ontario in particular, Toronto seemed an ideal starting point to formulate an answer to this question. The hub of entertainment, trade, and provincial politics in Ontario, Toronto functions as a privileged site for the study of early cinema, as it was the largest English-speaking city in Canada at the turn of the century, with a population of over 200,000 (this would nearly double to 376,000 by 1911).[3] In the years 1895–1915, Toronto experienced substantial economic and cultural growth. The city's prominence as a banking center became established in these years, as did its utility as a branch-plant haven for expanding U.S. corporations. By and large, the city's corporate elite was involved in the financial sector, even if the bulk of the city's population was still engaged in manufacturing (65,000 versus 40,000 in commerce and finance). In fact, by 1911, Toronto employed 27 percent of the province's industrial force. During this period, centralized provision of hydro-electrical power and the expansion of existing streetcar lines facilitated the city's financial growth.

The first decades of the twentieth century also witnessed an increase in immigration, which contributed to Toronto's rapid rise in population Though the majority of immigrants continued to be from the British Isles, continental Europeans began to appear in greater numbers, changing the ethnic makeup of the city significantly for the first time. The Anglo-Celtic majority stood at 92 percent in 1901, but had declined to 86 percent by 1911. Of the non-British immigrants, the largest blocks came from Austria/Hungary or Italy, with the Italian population in Toronto quadrupling over the first ten years of the new century. Meanwhile, the Jewish community in Toronto grew to over 18,000 by 1911. Many of the more recent immigrants settled in the inner city, particularly St. John's Ward, located near the downtown entertainment core. Still, the majority of immigrants during these years came from Britain, and from 1901 to 1911, the share of Toronto's population that was native-born dropped to 63 percent, while those British-born rose to 28 percent. An important distinction between American and Canadian society derived from Canada's immigration policy. Canada's class structure at the turn of the century was indebted to a notion of society as a vertical mosaic: the American melting pot model was not adopted, and immigrants maintained their cultural identity much more easily in Canada. Nonetheless, vestiges of the class structure inherent to the European system still remained, and the hierarchical structure allowed those of Anglo heritage to assume a position of authority as Canada's cultural elite. This elite exerted influence in particular ways, such as approving proper Canadian ways of speaking, as we will describe below.

During this period, the city's growing affluence spurred the establishment of a variety of cultural institutions, including Massey Hall (1894), the Art Gallery of Toronto (1900), the Toronto Symphony Orchestra (1906–08), and the Royal Ontario Museum (1912). While music and fine art were created locally, theatrical performances tended to be traveling productions of American and British plays. Toronto had a live-entertainment corridor, consolidated in the southern portion of Yonge Street within the primary business district, and located near the early concentrations of immigrant housing. And it was in this downtown corridor that films were first shown. As Canada did not produce its own films to any significant extent, it relied upon the same imports that other countries did at the time, in venues whose owners' names might sound familiar to the American ear: the Shea and Schubert organizations among them. But there were distinctions that influenced the ways in which imported films were shown and received by Torontonians, such as the effects of municipal by-laws, the actions of local civic groups, advertising strategies, and the like. We contend that aspects of sound practices amplified whatever distinctions existed: such practices foregrounded a nationalist undercurrent, one articulated within their performative dimension.

Broadly speaking, of course, we can say that the nature of sound practices in Toronto mirrors what was typical within American cities of a comparable size at this time. A tradition of lectures in combination with stereopticon views preceded the appearance of cinema, and coincided with cinema's ascendance during the early years.[4] Eventually, motion pictures would be incorporated into these lectures, as is the case with Frederic Villiers' program at Massey Hall in 1901 and the combination of Reverend J. J. Lewis's lecture and the film of the Oberammergau Passion Play the following year at the same venue.[5] Lyman Howe's show, replete with sound effects, would make a stop in Toronto in 1909, followed by numerous others in subsequent years.[6] And musical performances often accompanied film showings, whether performed by an "expert lady pianist," as mentioned in connection with film showings of 1896, a series of bands, for a week of outdoor screenings at Munro Park, or "a big symphony organ" and a "9-piece orchestra," referred to more typically in the post-nickelodeon era.[7] Sports films and military-themed screenings appear to have been the occasion for more elaborate commentary and/or musical accompaniment, which might include some combination of lecturer, orchestra, and/or singer.[8]

None of this deviates from accepted practices within other locales. So how do sound practices contribute to a distinctive form of film-going in Ontario? Primarily in the details of performance, be it musical or lecture. Both musicians and lecturers had the opportunity to alter what, on a textual and visual level, were products of filmmakers from other nations. Aspects of regionally inflected identity derived from the presence of locally trained musicians and speakers, who existed within a cultural environment shaped by a network of musicians' unions, instrument makers, music publishers, elocution instructors, and exhibition-site owners.[9] To the degree that regional particularities might be supplied as a supplement to a foreign-based filmic text, they would reside in the performative dimension of the sound component of the experience. In the U.S., such regionalism might audibly manifest itself as identifiable forms of music and accents, but in Canada, this regionalism should be understood as a form of nationalism as well.[10] Sound as a signifier of national identity comes into play in numerous instances, not least with the insertion of Canadian melodies at opportune moments. Should a chosen film feature an identifiable Canadian locale, musicians could supply a Canadian tune, or Canadian-themed narratives could be accompanied by appropriate music. Even performers known to be Canadian by birth, like Mary Pickford, or Marie Dressler, could have their national origins signaled by local musicians inclined to foreground the Canadian connection. Indigenous popular songs certainly existed in abundance, and sheet-music sales indicate musicians and audiences alike would be more than familiar with such tunes. So the playing of "Land of the Maple" or "The Beaver Rag" would doubtless prove a welcome nationalist addition to an evening out. Moreover, Canadian songs might have been sung during reel changes, and certainly such tunes figure within the recruitment evenings featuring films and lectures that proliferated in the wake of Canada's involvement in World War I.[11] In certain instances, entire performances would celebrate the nation through a combination of indigenous music and films, as with *Living Canada,* advertised as "views of our country's splendid resources and great beauties" with "the 48 Highlanders Band [adding] to the impression."[12]

Similarly, Canadian lecturers possessed familiarity with local and national content, and traded on same whenever possible. In particular, the lecturer highlighted the nationalist aspirations of the Anglo-Canadian establishment. Films in Toronto, as elsewhere, were often accompanied by local and foreign experts on the subject matter of the film, for example, the Biblical scholar Prof. Smith Warner, who "increased the interest of the Passion Play by his masterly explanation" in 1899, the "Frisco lightweight fighter" Temple C. Grady, who came to Toronto with the Nelson-Wolgast fight in 1910, and the British and French military experts who described the films used in recruiting efforts during World War I.[13] Although such expertise seems to have been a marketable aspect of the film program, it is also true that the quality of the lecturer could actually affect the film's reception. An inept lecturer, in fact, could have a negative impact on the reception of the film. In 1909, for example, a report on the Burns-Johnson fight pictures in the *Toronto World* included the comment that "[t]he films worked poorly on opening night . . . the crowd accepted the lecture as of the baseball umpire type, and indulged in considerable guying."[14] Another report involved the Toronto singer and entertainer W. E. Ramsay, who provided his own ringside commentary for the earlier Corbett-Fitzsimmons fight pictures. Ramsay's commentary has passed unnoticed, but his extemporaneous addition of local color has not: "Later in the day it began to snow," said Ramsay in his opening speech describing the fight. "You're a damn liar," yelled a man in the gallery, who recalled the weather conditions and knew Ramsay was bluffing.[15]

Indeed, the most popular lecturers—the ones that found the greatest praise in the newspapers—were local; popular, therefore, because of their familiarity with their audience as well as with their subject. The audience who knew the lecturer trusted him to bring a knowledge of locale that made the films more relevant. "The views [of the Soldiers mobilizing for the Boer war] are appreciated more every day for being described and located by Mr. Owen Smiley [sic]," wrote a reporter in the *Toronto Star* in 1899; and similarly, in 1900: "Mr. Owen Smily announced and explained the pictures. His readings of a poem of his own—'Britisher and Boer'—and Kipling's 'The Flag of England' were well received."[16] If the number of times his name appears in the papers is any guide, Owen Smily became the most distinguished of the Toronto lecturers, and, for our thesis, he is the most interesting.

Born in England, Smily had come to Toronto and made a distinguished career on stage from 1888 to 1892, accompanying English-Canada's foremost poet, the native Mohawk Pauline Johnson. While Johnson declaimed her poems in England, the United States, and the east and west coasts of Canada, Smily's role seems to have been to recite other well-known British and American poetry.[17] It is from 1899 that Smily's name appears with some regularity as a film lecturer in Toronto, commenting on films of "great personages and events of the day," accompanying Biograph programs with "humorous musical sketches," and supplementing other programs with description, poetry, running commentary, and monologue.[18] (Smily announced and explained the pictures, and he often read poetry—including his own—after the program, as part of the evening's entertainment.) Although we do not know the full extent of his film-lecturing activities, we do know from the newspapers that he was the preferred lecturer for unusual and high-profile events and that his specialty was the patriotic. Smily performed primarily in places like Massey Hall, a locale for serious theater and symphonic concerts. His audience for the most part would therefore have come from the middle classes, the Toronto establishment. Since Smily was a resident of Toronto, he was, in other words, the equal of his audience.

Our initial assumption was that as an actor, poet, and member of the Anglo-Canadian establishment, Smily would have spoken with a British accent. But we were wrong. Smily not only spoke with a Canadian accent but he directed a school of elocution in which he taught his students the Canadian way of pronunciation. Smily's "Canadian" accent—neither British nor American but something in between—reflects the aspirations of his class at the beginning of the century. A Canadian accent was not an indigenous accent, but rather the product of trying not to be something else. It had of course developed under the influence of American English, but by the turn of the century it had also become a desirable inflection. A Canadian accent signaled a quiet attempt at self-definition, or identity, based on—as it is to this day—a notion of Canadians being neither British nor American. In general, the Anglo-Canadian establishment considered itself British, in that its political and social institutions were patterned for the most part on those of the British Isles, but it perceived itself as inherently more advanced because it had adopted a democratic ideal that ostensibly eliminated the baggage of the British class system. The middle-class "Canada First" movement, which began in the 1870s, aspired to a future in which English Canada would become the leader of the British Empire, supplanting the dissolute, worn-out, mother England. On the other hand, the Canadian democratic ideal was not a subscription to the American way. The capitalist excesses of our southern neighbor offended the British sense of decorum in us.

Smily's accompaniment of the Boer War Biograph films provides a most pertinent example of how an accent helped foster this growing Canadian spirit of self-identification. As they would in the First World War, Canadian forces fought as part of the British Empire. Yet there was a general understanding—evidenced in the literature, journalism, and poetry of the time—that Canadians wanted the Canadian forces to be recognized as distinct, and that their regiments had an important contribution to make to the war as Canadians. Smily seems to have been especially in demand for these films. And indeed he was able to speak with equal authority about the situation in South Africa, about the Toronto troops and the specific parts of the city in which they were mobilized, outfitted, housed, and moved before going overseas, and even about the city of Halifax, whence they embarked.[19] Smily's performances created an extra dimension to the film, an acoustic space in which Canadian identity was given, literally, a voice. With its "Canadian" accent, this voice typified the sound of nascent Canadian self-awareness for the film viewer in turn-of-the-century Toronto.

The coming of the sound film many years later put an end to the possibility of relocating American and British images in an English-Canadian acoustic landscape. As a result, the spirit of nationalism that had inflected the films through the voices of lecturers such as Owen Smily was forced to find more overt and concrete forms of expression.

Notes

The authors are grateful to Peter Steven for his contribution to this paper and to the Social Science and Humanities Research Council of Canada for its support. This is part of a larger project on the history of early cinema in Ontario.

1. For a particularly provocative examination of early sound practice that challenges the assumption that silent exhibition was never silent, see Rick Altman, "The Silence of the Silents," *Musical Quarterly* 80, no. 4 (Winter 1996), 648–718.

2. For a representative sampling of work outlining the premises inherent in the concept of the *bonimenteur,* see the special issue, *Iris* 22 (1996), devoted to this topic.

3. Most of the statistics cited in this section derive from census reports; a convenient source for this information can be found in J. M. S. Careless, *Toronto to 1918: An Illustrated History* (Toronto: James Lorimer and Company, 1984).

4. For a representative sampling, see *Evening Telegram,* 24 January 1898, and *Toronto World,* 3 February 1899.

5. *Daily Mail and Empire,* 3–5 April 1901, and 16–18 January 1902; see also *Toronto Globe,* 8 July 1900.

6. Royal Alexandra Theatre Account Books, May 1909, May 1911, August 1911, Toronto Reference Library.

7. *Toronto Evening News,* 23 September 1896; *Daily Mail and Empire,* 8 and 11 June 1901; *Toronto World,* 5 July 1914, 31 August 1909. See also *Toronto Evening Telegram,* 20 September 1915; and *Toronto World,* 24 June 1914, and 15 September 1915.

8. On sports, see *Toronto Daily News,* 10 January 1900; *Toronto Globe,* 10 May 1909; and *Toronto World,* 19 April 1910. On patriotic evenings, see *Toronto Globe,* 1 March 1900; *Toronto World,* 27 February 1900; and *Toronto Star,* 26 November 1910.

9. For an overview of the development of music culture in Canada, see Helmut Kallman, *A History of Music in Canada 1534–1914* (Toronto: University of Toronto Press, 1987). For the role of the musicians' union, see coverage of the theater orchestra strike in *Toronto World,* August 1912.

10. For a study of American motion picture exhibition that highlights the significance of regionalism, see Gregory A. Waller, *Main Street Amusements: Movies and Commercial Entertainment in a Southern City, 1896–1930* (Washington, D.C.: Smithsonian Institution Press, 1995); for a consideration of nationhood and American early cinema,

see Richard Abel, *The Red Rooster Scare: Making Cinema American* (Berkeley and Los Angeles: University of California Press, 1999).

11. See *Toronto Mail,* 13 May 1911; *Evening Telegram,* 2 November 1915; Kallman, 259; and Gerald Lenton, "The Development and Nature of Vaudeville in Toronto from 1899–1915" (Ph.D. dissertation, University of Toronto, 1983), 433.

12. *Daily Mail and Empire,* 28 December 1903, and 4 January 1904. See also *Daily Mail and Empire,* 16 May 1904; *Evening Telegram,* 26 May 1904.

13. *Toronto Star,* 29 August 1899; *Toronto World,* 19 April 1910; *Evening Telegram,* 4, 11, 24 December 1915.

14. *Toronto World,* 11 May 1909.

15. Hector Charlesworth, *More Candid Chronicles* (Toronto: Macmillan, 1928), 102; a different Ramsey lecture is described in *Daily Mail and Empire,* 21 August 1899.

16. *Toronto Star,* 13 June 1899, and 27 February 1900. See also *Daily Telegram,* 27 February 1900.

17. Johnson's biographer, Betty Keller, notes that Smily was a music hall artist and actor—see *Pauline: A Biography of Pauline Johnson* (Vancouver: Douglas and McIntyre, 1981), 66–67.

18. *Toronto Star,* 13 June 1899. See also *Daily Mail and Empire,* 6 June 1899, and 6 November 1900.

19. See, for example, *Toronto World,* 26–28 February, and 1 March 1900.

20 The Double Silence of the "War to End All Wars"

Germain Lacasse

One of the strangest and most tragic films that can be viewed today is 1916's *The Blind Fiddler*, in which blinded soldiers dance to the sound of an instrument that the muteness of the film prevents us from hearing.[1] Intertitles give the following explanation: "Heroes who have lost their sight in the service of the country, dance with their nurses with a courage that defies affliction." This naive outpouring of patriotism may have been accepted at the time, but today it seems to surround these already silent films with yet another, dense silence. Of course, the absence of a soundtrack makes it impossible to hear the music of the violin and the dancers' steps, yet the commentary makes this silence even more unbearable and above all suggests that it not be broken, that nothing be said about the war unless expressed through a suppressed experience.

Another extremely strange audiovisual experience is summoned up by the screening of a film depicting "recruiting gramophones"—a soldier walking in London's streets with a gramophone on his back, playing the patriotic speech of an officer seeking recruits.[2] The film, an aberration by the standards of 2000, requires some contextualization in order to be understood. The gramophone, probably still a novelty in 1914, could capture the bystanders' attention and facilitate the work of military recruiters. Hanging from a soldier's back, it must have drawn even more attention, the oddity of the gear adding to the novelty of the device. This method, where man was only the prop for a machine calling for enlistment, was employed repeatedly. A similar film titled "Recruiting by Graphophone" even showed men training following instructions played on a gramophone; an actual recruiter then called the roll.[3]

Still, the strangest of these experiences might be listening to the patter of one of these recruiters. Frenchman Émile Barlatier said as he showed films to a Montréal audience in 1916, "Spent outdoors, the life of a soldier is healthy and fortifying. I have met with former office clerks who used to be in frail health and who now are stronger and manlier than ever after a year or six months of their life spent in the trenches. The food is good and healthy and you live continually in open-air. There's nothing better to give a man his lost vitality back."[4]

Health through war! This commentary sounds so incongruous as to appear unbelievable and lead us to ascribe it to a rather excessive outburst of patriotism. And yet if the commentary seems completely aberrant, so do the films screened in which war was all but invisible and soldiers were shown training by practicing team sports as well as marching and parading. Official Canadian films of the First World War, which had long disappeared but were recently brought back to light,[5] are in fact mostly devoted to this kind of demonstration, with its attendant training sessions, sports, and parades. The dead are nowhere to be seen, and when wounded soldiers are shown, they are convalescing and are playing various games. An operator filmed a day of sporting events organized for Canadian troops at the beach at Deauville in 1915. The day obviously starts with a parade. Then, some men are shown competing, running or horse-racing, in obstacle or sack races, individually or in teams, with a presentation of trophies and joyful salutes to the camera closing the day.[6]

The film quite obviously seeks to present the cheerful life of Canadian soldiers in France, and does not neglect to integrate into the picture the army's female auxiliaries as well as the French women brought to the beach for the occasion. One may even wonder whether the whole film was not staged, with the soldiers being taken to Deauville to emphasize the pleasures of life on leave. In order to do so, the operator would have had to spend a few days on location with the battalions, since the sequences involved too much preparation and shooting to be finished in just a day. The high cost of transporting the soldiers and organizing the shooting tells how much military authorities were ready to pay for a reassuring piece of propaganda. The least one could do was to procure the whole regimental band for a screening, while it was self-evident to add a commentary praising life in the trenches as a therapeutic experience!

This experience belongs to what could be termed oral cinema, or cinema of orality, in which silent films are commented on by a speaker or a lecturer. In silent cinema as accompanied by such a narrator, spoken commentary seems indeed crucial to the interpretation—it is now established that this type of discourse could even completely change the meaning of the film. Consequently, it seems appropriate to use the term *cinema of orality* insofar as the image track is integrated into a representation where the commentator's discourse holds equal importance. This type of representation is also related to orality through other characteristics, primarily the presence of an individual who is known to the audience and whose performance may take the show into an infinite number of directions.[7]

This theory coincides with Rick Altman's hypotheses on sound during the silent era. Altman points out the recent shift in sound research toward reception and conceives a model of the "cinema as event," which makes it possible to account for the material heterogeneity of sound and the variability of performance.[8] The film text is no longer considered as a center of gravity but as an object floating between the sphere of production and that of reception. Instead of a dialectics of pre- and post-institutional contexts, sound's evolution is described along the lines of a "crisis model" in three phases (identity crisis, jurisdictional conflict, and negotiated settlement).[9] The stage of development I have termed oral cinema belongs mostly to the first two phases, since the lecture gradually disappeared with the standardization of sound and persisted only in non-producing countries, in minority groups, and in a number of specific contexts. War was one of these contexts.

The Lecturer's New Lease on Life

The First World War witnessed a revival of oral cinema, and even gave it a new lease on life, as speakers, who had almost disappeared from bourgeois film exhibition for a few years, made a forceful comeback to serve recruiting efforts. The numerous films produced by the Canadian government were offered or rented at a very low price to exhibitors, but they also were widely used in highly publicized special screenings commented on by an army speaker and accompanied by a regimental band. For instance, such a screening, sponsored by the daily newspaper *La Presse,* took place at the Casino theater in Montréal on Wednesday, December 15, 1915. Among the films mentioned, only one features Canadian soldiers, "unloading sandbags to protect their friends' lives in the trenches."[10] Such screenings took place all over Canada, where recruiting drives were often conceived as large public entertainments including concerts, lectures, and films. An entire arsenal of seduction methods was employed to attract the audience and move potential recruits.[11] The double silence of the films was attenuated by a noisy staging of the cinematic spectacle meant to stir patriotic feelings in the extreme.

It remains to be demonstrated that the popular lecturer commented critically on propaganda films, but the surviving documents on the theaters where lecturers exercised their talents, upon examination, point to a context of strong resistance and suggest that they took part in a resistant reading of war films. Like the military speaker, the popular lecturer seems to have met with renewed success during the war in a type of show developing at the time in Quebec. A variant of the American vaudeville, Quebecois burlesque was made up of dance numbers, sketches, comic monologues, and moving images commented on by a lecturer.[12] The opposition of French Canadians to the war stimulated nationalist feelings, and historians of the burlesque often underline the desire of artists to emphasize the use of French in the shows. Several of the French lecturers who worked on Quebec stages went back to France to enlist, and were replaced by their Quebec peers. The various reports on stage events of the time became very different from what they were when military speakers were involved.

The pièce de résistance in this regard is the monologue written in 1917 by Armand Leclaire and simply titled "Le conscrit Baptiste." It tells of the blunders made by a Quebecois from the country who proves incapable of carrying out the instructions given to him by recruiting officers. Skilled in farm work but clueless when it comes to military maneuvers, he exasperates recruiters, who send him back:

> "Baptist, th'officer tells me, you better go work in your fields. You're discharged, you'll never make a soldier . . . "—"Well, I say, let me tell ya, I'd rather stay livin' than being a soldier o' even worse clown 'bout with guns that cudn't kill a fly! 'n

don't ya come bother me at home, 'cuz I got a gun too, and lemme tell ya, that one's loaded!" Then I made off, and when the girls saw me come back, I tell ya, them gave me a wa'm welcome! See, me and the parish father, we are the only men left around, the others got conscriptionated or them got killed.[13]

The monologue cleverly draws its irony from the skills of the Quebec farmer in cultivating the earth and his indifference to military drills; it valorizes civilian work while ridiculing hawkish mindsets. Its author, Armand Leclaire, was an actor and playwright who worked in the "scopes" with lecturers Alex Silvio and Hector Pellerin, among others. His text was read aloud in theaters but was also published in *Le Passe-temps* (The Pastime), a popular magazine on songs and music with a wide circulation. The reading by Leclaire of conscription and of the recruiters' work was certainly shared in large part by Montréal's francophone audience, to whom the many films showing soldiers being trained must have appeared laughable. The audience had evolved somewhat along the same lines as Leclaire, who had also written a play a few years earlier in protest against the elimination of French from Ontario's school curriculum. His concerns were not only national, as he also attacked capitalist war profiteers:

> Poor Canadians
> From every corner
> Pressed by the war
> When everyone else gets richer
> That the country's burdened
> It should come as no surprise
> That the pay's cut off
> The rich have every right
> We have to starve
> Or enlist "Oversea"![14]

This piece did not manifestly attract the attention of the censor or one of his collaborators, as war is openly criticized as a political tool whereby some get richer at the expense of the lives of others. While official propaganda addresses a homogeneous audience to which it proposes one interpretation, the popular song divides the world into two opposed camps, only one of which endures the throes of war. Leclaire was far from being the only one to thrive in the genre of sarcastic criticism. An author by the pseudonym of Paul Rosal, who also wrote extensively for *Le Passe-temps,* composed several satirical poems about conscription. He first published a poem titled "Le Service National," in which he ridiculed the census promulgated in preparation for compulsory enlistment:

> With insight the government
> Wants to card us
> To make an assessment
> Of our stock and age. [. . .]
> Everyone's cautious
> Because everyone's convinced

That conscription will
Come out of this paperwork.[15]

The national service was a compulsory census deemed necessary by the government in order to know the state of the available workforce on the national territory and thus plan wartime production. Yet in Quebec civilians quickly assumed that this militarization of the economy would also provide the information required for lists of possible conscripts to be drawn up. Rosal did not stop there, and like Leclaire he showed that public opinion on the war would never be as unanimous as the government and their censors trumpeted. In another text titled "Nos braves conscriptionnistes" (Our Brave Conscriptionists), Rosal proceeded to take on the draft-dodgers who called for conscription for others. He underlined that patriotism was shared by the French Canadians but had to be consented to in the first place:

> The ones who shout the loudest
> Want to have the others sent
> They can lie low
> These unbounded moralizers! [. . .]
> We are first and foremost Canadians,
> As loyal as they are to the Crown,
> And if we do not proclaim it loudly,
> It is just that we will not force it upon anyone.[16]

Despite the massive opposition of French Canadians, the conscription bill was eventually passed and came into effect in January 1918. Antiwar and antimilitarist texts then became completely illegal and seem to have disappeared at that time, yet other voices carried on the resistance by evoking the fate of conscripts. Their tone was less polemical, and they tended to draw inspiration from the genres of the lament or the melodrama, but theater and songs continued to qualify the discourse of military films, whose production had increased tenfold by 1918 to stir patriotic feelings. Paul Gury, a Breton actor and playwright who lived in Montréal, thus staged a revue titled *Le Petit conscrit*[17] (The Young Draftee). On that occasion he wrote an eponymous ritornello:

> He was a young draftee
> Taken from his country
> Because in a distant land
> More blood needs to be shed for an inhuman war
> It is a very sad fate
> To go and risk being killed
> So far from one's family
> So far from one's country
> The eldest the young draftee
> The eldest the young draftee

Leclaire's and Rosal's sarcastic tone is no longer present, but we are a far cry from Barlatier's patriotic bursts on the soldiers' health. Instead of an enthusiastic combatant ready to die under the bombs, the soldier of this song is forced to enlist and fight for a foreign cause and an "inhuman" war.

These speeches and songs, heard in the same theaters where official films were screened, possibly constitute the only realistic commentary on the war. Read or heard in scopes or elsewhere, told and sung before or after the films, they could not fail but create a striking contrast. In fact, the Canadian censorship commissioner Ernest J. Chambers complained about it early on. His report particularly insisted on numbers and plays and stated that

> Men in high places and with a sound judgment (. . .) have brought to attention that the songs in some vaudevilles expressed with much pathos a longing for peace at all costs and evidently had as their objective to foster feelings of weariness towards the war.[18]

The repression of these dissenting texts occurred through the newspapers' theater critics, whom the censor asked to help dissuade the presentation of such shows. When the shows at stake continued, the information gathered by the newspapers was forwarded to the police, who then intervened. However, a share of the dissenting texts probably escaped the censor's attention, since the audience of people "in high places and with a sound judgment" attended vaudeville theaters infrequently, and theater critics rarely mentioned them. It is therefore not unlikely that resistance to the propaganda took place in popular spectacles. It was probably more allusive than explicit, but it was accessible for whoever had been accustomed to it. The censor, who had a long arm, still did not dare meddle in certain matters.

Blind Scores

Silent films from the First World War call for a particular reading, not only contextual but also performative. They need to be understood not in terms of showing the war, but rather as representing its least forbidding aspects. We also need to assume that they were not always read in this manner by some audiences, who instead performed a resistant reading of them. These readings can be reactualized through the paratexts that have come down to us and offer a partial reconstruction of the sound environment of the films. These texts recount more or less seditious words for their time and give us access to a version of reality about which the films remained silent.

If indeed silent film sound was strongly marked by performance, as Altman and others have pointed out, we need to assume that in the context of a military conflict the variants of these performative readings evolve according to the extremely severe restrictions of the war. Propaganda cinema relies on naive and epic lectures, while resistant performances occur quietly through paratextual interventions such as the ones I have mentioned. The double silence of official representations had as its counterpart the second degree of resistant readings.

Walter Benjamin wrote that after the conflict such a silence was a necessity because the experience of the war was not translatable:

With the [First] World War a process began to become apparent which has not halted since then. Was it not noticeable at the end of the war that men returned from the battlefield grown silent—not richer, but poorer in communicable experience? (...) And there was nothing remarkable about that. For never has experience been contradicted more thoroughly than strategic experience by tactical warfare, economic experience by inflation, bodily experience by mechanical warfare, moral experience by political power.[19]

One may think that authorities had come to an understanding of this, as they eventually made films where no regimental bands could be heard or seen: "The Great Silence Filmed [...] most impressive vistas of the great multitude thronged round the base of the Cenotaph—hushed and silent in remembrance of the Glorious Dead."[20] This official silence, however, did not bode well; in fact, it meant to keep silencing the horror and reviving the epic, and the silence of trumpets and bands had simply succeeded that of cannons and recruiters.

The history of silent cinema should not be limited in order to make images speak, since the images in question often were the reflections of a silenced experience. Lived and heard experience is preserved, rather, in oral memory as well as in the few texts that give an account of it. While it is true that the so-called silent films should be termed deaf, war films more particularly give the expression its full meaning—they are deaf to the din of war, and their spectators are as deaf to this conniving silence as they are to a commentary too naively eloquent to be true. History needs to take these silences and these sounds into account.

TRANSLATED BY FRANCK LE GAC AND WENDY SCHUBRING

Notes

1. Topical Budget film #248-2 (27 May 1916): *The Blind Fiddler.* Several other films showed blind soldiers: *Sightless Soldiers' Recreation* (#247-2), *Blind Men's Boat Races* (#255-1), *Blind Soldiers Typewriting* (#271-2), etc. This information was communicated to us by English historian Luke McKernan, who is preparing a filmography of the company Topical Budget, to which he has already devoted a book: *Topical Budget. The Great British News Film* (London: British Film Institute, 1992).

2. Topical Budget film #290-1 (14 March 1917): *Motor Volunteers Graphophone Band.*

3. Topical Budget film #208-1 (18 August 1915).

4. Anonymous, "Une jolie soirée au Monument," *La Presse,* 8 October 1915, 2.

5. The original films were destroyed in 1967 during the fire at the location of the Office National du Film. Copies had been made but had then been forgotten, and the bulk of the collection remained invisible for a few decades. On this topic, see Germain Lacasse, "Les films 'perdus' de la guerre oubliée" (The "Lost" Films of the Forgotten War), *Canadian Journal of Film Studies* 7, no. 1 (Spring 1998).

6. Film record #FG-14-38, Office National du Film, Montréal.

7. These notions were developed in my doctoral dissertation: *Le Bonimenteur et le cinéma oral: Le cinéma muet entre tradition et modernité* (The Lecturer and Oral Cinema:

The Double Silence of the "War to End All Wars" 211

Silent Film between Tradition and Modernity) (Département de littérature comparée, Université de Montréal, 1996).

8. Rick Altman, "General Introduction: Cinema as Event," in Rick Altman, ed., *Sound Theory Sound Practice* (New York: Routledge, 1992), 1–14.

9. Rick Altman, "The Silence of the Silents," *Musical Quarterly* 80, no. 4 (Winter 1996), 688.

10. Publicity, "La Guerre en France" (War in France), *La Presse,* 14 December 1915.

11. Paul Maroney, " 'The Great Adventure': The Context and Ideology of Recruiting in Ontario, 1914–17," *Canadian Historical Review* 77 (March 1996), 75.

12. Chantal Hébert, *Le Burlesque au Québec: Un divertissement populaire* (Burlesque in Quebec: A Popular Entertainment) (Montreal: Hurtubise HMH, 1981).

13. Armand Leclaire, "Le conscrit Baptiste" (Baptist the Conscript), *Le Passe-temps,* 8 September 1917. The French text reads: " 'Baptiste, que m'dit l'z'officier, t'es mieux d'aller travailler dans tes champs. T'es déchargé, tu feras jamais un soldat . . . '—'Ben, j'vas dire là, toé que j'y répercute, j'aime mieux rester habitant que d'être soldat pis faire des singeries avec des fusils qui sont tant seulement pas capables de quer une mouche! Pis r'viens pas me badrer cheu nous, toé, parce que j'en ai un fusil moi itou, pis j't'avartis qu'y est chargé c'lui-là!' Là-dessus, j'ai pris le bord. Quand les criatures m'ont vu arriver, vous parler qu'y m'ont fait une fête! Faut vous dire qu'y avait pus rien que moé pis mossieu le curé dans la paroisse en fait d'hommes, les autres ont été conscriptionnés ou ben y sont morts."

14. Armand Leclaire, "La Valse des Piastres" (The Dollar Waltz), *Le Passe-temps,* 10 March 1917.

15. Paul Rosal, "Le Service National" (The National Service), *Le Passe-temps,* 27 January 1917.

16. Paul Rosal, "Nos braves conscriptionnistes" (Our Brave Conscriptionists), *Le Passe-temps,* 5 May 1917.

17. Anonymous, "Dans nos théâtres" (In Our Theaters), *Le Pays,* 16 November 1918.

18. Ernest Chambers, "Rapport sur le service de la censure de la presse canadienne" (Report of the Censorship Service for the Canadian Press), reprinted in *Cahiers d'histoire politique* 2 (Winter 1996), 276.

19. Walter Benjamin, "The Story-Teller: Reflections on the Works of Nicolai Leskov," translated from the German by Harry Zohn, *Chicago Review* 16, no. 1 (Winter–Spring 1963), 80–101.

20. Topical Budget film #429-1 (13 November 1919).

Part Five: *Film Music*

21 Domitor Witnesses the First Complete Public Presentation of the [*Dickson Experimental Sound Film*] in the Twentieth Century

Patrick Loughney

The 1998 Domitor conference closed at 5:00 P.M. on Friday, June 5, 1998, with a demonstration of the surviving artifacts of an early 1890s Edison laboratory experiment in motion picture sound synchronization, in which a 35mm film and simultaneously recorded wax cylinder sound track were recombined for their first public presentation in the twentieth century. The event was not previously announced by the conference host, the Library of Congress, and came at the end of a long week of excellent papers and demonstrations on the relation of sound to motion picture production and exhibition practice in the early days of cinema. The screening of the film known most widely as [*Dickson Experimental Sound Film*] was accompanied by the original sound track, played via an audiocassette copy over the sound system of the Coolidge Auditorium. The presentation energized those suffering the effects of conference fatigue and, for many, left an afterglow of wonder and surprise.[1]

The known and speculative facts about the making of [*Dickson Experimental Sound Film*] and the surviving film copies and sound track are these. The production was made sometime during the mid-1890s as one of a series of collaborative experiments by the Edison laboratory staff to perfect the kineto-phonograph, a device intended to combine the separate technologies of the phonograph and the kinetoscope into a single peephole mechanism for the presentation of motion pictures with synchronized sound.[2] Charles Musser has speculated that production probably occurred during the period September 1894 to early April 1895.[3] When a 35mm nitrate print was acquired from the Edison Historic Site and preserved by the Library of Congress in 1964, the preliminary cataloging research completed by the Library in 1968 indicated a production date of circa 1895. It is possible, however, that the film may have been produced at an earlier date. While Dickson and his colleagues worked on developing the phonograph and kinetoscope during the period 1889 to 1894, they conducted many experiments attempting to link the sound and motion picture technologies that they were perfecting separately. Contemporary published accounts describe demonstrations of the kineto-phonograph prior to 1894, including Dickson's claim of producing a welcome-home demonstration for Edison, on his return from the 1889 Paris Exposition in October of that year, of a synchronized film in which "Mr. Dickson himself stepped out on the screen, raised his hat and smiled, while uttering the words of greeting, 'Good morning, Mr. Edison, glad to see you back. I hope you are satisfied with the kineto-phonograph.'"[4]

The note appended to the filmographic entry for [*Dickson Experimental Sound Film*] in *Edison Motion Pictures, 1890–1900*, speculates that, due to the appearance of the "R" (for Raff and Gammon) in the lower right corner of the film frame, production may have occurred in late 1894 or early 1895, with a possible intention for commercial distribution. The LC print of [*Dickson Experimental Sound Film*] shows an apparent mark or letter card in the lower right-hand corner in the last few frames; however too small a portion of it can be seen to definitively declare it to be an "R." Also, the casual nature of the actions recorded, especially that of the workman who walks into the frame behind the recording horn toward the end, indicates the film's purpose was probably wholly experimental. The same note also observes that the violinist in the film might be a Dickson look-alike named Charles D'Almaine, then employed in the Edison phonograph department as a musician. Yet a comparison of the clearest 35mm prints of [*Dickson Experimental Sound Film*] with contemporary photographs leaves no doubt that Dickson is the violinist in the film. The identities of the two men dancing while Dickson fiddles are as yet unknown. Further evidence that Dickson was one of the on-screen talent comes from the fact that, in addition to his responsibilities as an inventor, he also doubled as violinist for the experimental recordings made while developmental work on the phonograph was underway. In the March–April 1893 issue of *Phonogram*, in an article that lauds those most responsible for aiding Edison in perfecting the phonograph, Dickson is specifically described as the "artist" who worked closely with Dr. Wangemann, the musical expert in charge of the recording department.[5]

The existence of the [*Dickson Experimental Sound Film*] and its related sound track have been known to a relative handful of interested archivists and researchers since at least the 1960s.[6] The physical separation of the film and sound artifacts first occurred when the Museum of Modern Art acquired a 35mm nitrate print, measuring forty feet in length, from the Edison Historic Site and preserved it to safety film in 1942. The sound track lay dormant until the U.S. National Park Service began the task of inventorying and cataloging the holdings of the Edison Historic Site (EHS) in 1960. At that time the EHS staff found and cataloged a brown wax cylinder in the Music Room of the Edison Laboratory in a metal canister labeled "*Dixon—Violin by W. K. L. Dixon with Kineto.*"[7] In 1964 it was discovered that the cylinder had broken into two pieces. In the same year, the EHS staff arranged the transfer of all surviving nitrate film materials at the Site to the Library of Congress for preservation. Included in that collection was a nitrate print, measuring thirty-nine feet and fourteen frames, which the Library staff cataloged in 1968 as [*Dickson Violin*], probably after the title information found on the EHS cylinder container.[8] That was the second occasion when the film and sound artifacts were separated to two different institutions.

Efforts to reunite the film and sound track for preservation and research purposes, prior to the 1998 Domitor conference, were hampered by the usual obstacles: the difficulties of effecting cooperation between different governmental branches, lack of funding and technical resources, and insufficient common interest in the early film research community to motivate the necessary restoration effort by the involved archives. In early 1998, during final planning of the conference demonstrations, it was realized that most of those obstacles were no longer insurmountable. A call to EHS curator George Tselos led to Jerry Fabris, curator of sound recordings at the EHS, who became enthusiastic about undertaking the restoration of the broken wax cylinder and the prospect of rejoining it with the film. Lacking the necessary sound restoration equipment, Fabris contacted Peter Dilg and Adrian Cosentini and arranged, with funding support from the Library of Congress, to recover the cylinder sound track in the laboratory of the Rodgers and Hammerstein Archive of Recorded Sound of the New York Public Library for the Performing Arts at Lincoln Center. According to Fabris' notes,

> Dilg, Cosentini, and Fabris pieced the cylinder together on the phonograph mandrel, secured the parts with thin tape around the outer edges of the cylinder (outside the groove area), then carefully filled the open crevices in between the cracks with small shavings from another broken wax cylinder. The cylinder was played back at 120 rpm with a 2-minute Edison ball stylus on an electrical pick-up mounted on Dilg's modified Edison recording lathe phonograph.[9]

The resulting preservation re-recording was made, with no equalization, on a BASF Studio Master 911 analog, one-quarter inch, 15 ips, open-reel tape.[10] The recording played while the [Dickson Experimental Sound Film] was projected on June 5 was a DAT audiocassette, made from the open-reel master.

Absolute synchronization of the DAT audiocassette with the projected image of the [Dickson Experimental Sound Film] could not be accomplished on June 5 for several reasons. First, the variable-speed film projectors in the Coolidge Auditorium, which are designed to run at speeds up to 30 frames per second, could not accommodate the 46 frames per second speed at which the [Dickson Experimental Sound Film] was originally recorded by the Kinetograph. Second, rehearsal time was limited due to the fact that Fabris and his colleagues finished their recording work on June 3 and the DAT audiocassette copy was received in the Library on the afternoon of June 4. Third, and most challenging, was the length and condition of the recovered sound track, which is nearly two minutes long and understandably in bad condition, compared to the much shorter running time of the projected 35mm print. Since the LC print measures thirty-nine feet, plus fourteen frames, the normal running time would amount to 13.86 seconds if it was projected at 46 fps. If the track and the moving image material for [Dickson Experimental Sound Film] do match, then it is apparent that approximately nine seconds, or about twenty-five feet, of the original film are lost.

21.1. [*Dickson Experimental Sound Film*], ca. 1894–1896 (frame enlargement). W. K. L. Dickson plays a violin waltz into an acoustical recording horn attached to a standard Edison two-minute, brown wax cylinder recording phonograph. The Library of Congress and the Edison Historical Site are cooperating in the restoration of the film and sound track.

The fragmentary nature of the LC print is suggested by the abrupt beginning and end of the recorded action.

Two screenings were presented on June 5. On the first run-through, the film started much too soon to match the sound, so the film and sound track were rewound for a second pass. The second attempt was more successful, and, even though the film ran too slowly and the track had many distracting defects, a moment from more than one hundred years in the past seemed to come alive. In spite of the worn grooves and loud pops caused by the cracks between the broken pieces, the Domitor audience heard what sounded like Dickson warming up with a few impromptu bars of operatic and waltz selections, some unintelligible talking between technicians in the background, more violin playing and, finally, an audible command to "Go ahead," followed by a clear segment of unidentified violin waltz music, lasting twenty-three seconds. It is the twenty-three-second violin waltz segment that seemed to all who heard and saw the film in the Coolidge Auditorium that day to be the original sound track for the [*Dickson Experimental Sound Film*].[11]

Much work remains to be done before it can be claimed that the two industrial artifacts that comprise the [*Dickson Experimental Sound Film*] have been successfully restored. First, a thorough comparison of surviving film elements—the 1942 copy at MoMA and the 1964 copy at Library of Congress—needs to be made to determine which is most complete. Even a few extra frames will add much to our understanding of the historic experiment recorded in this film. Second, the sound track will need the benefit of the most sophisticated sound restoration technology available to see if additional aural information can be recovered from under the present surface noise of the wax cylinder. Third and most important, once the track has been restored to the highest possible level, its content will have to be analyzed and compared to the motion picture to verify the supposition that it is the original sound track for the [*Dickson Experimental Sound Film*]. And finally, if it is confirmed, a technological method will have to be devised for reuniting the sound and image in a way that will make it readily available to researchers and the public. The effort will require the cooperation of the Edison Historic Site, the Museum of Modern Art, and the Library of Congress, and discussions are now underway to realize that goal.

The author is indebted to Jerry Fabris, of EHS, for his efforts to restore the [*Dickson Experimental Sound Film*] sound track and for making it available in time for the Domitor conference, and to Steven Higgins for information about the film elements at MoMA.

Notes

1. [*Dickson Experimental Sound Film*], in the parlance of formally trained catalogers, is a "supplied title." Brackets are used at the beginning and end to indicate a supplied title. A supplied title is given to a work for which there is no official or published title known to the research community and is meant to stand only as a temporary descriptive title until broad agreement is reached on a credible permanent title.

2. Writing in 1895, Dickson defined *kineto-phonograph* as "the comprehensive term for this invention. The dual *taking* machine is the *phono-kinetograph,* and the *reproducing* machine is the *phono-kinetoscope*" (italics mine). W. K. L. Dickson and Antonia Dickson, *History of the Kinetograph, Kinetoscope, and Kineto-Phonograph* (New York: Albert Bunn, 1895), 8.

3. Charles Musser, *Edison Motion Pictures, 1890–1900* (Washington, D.C.: Smithsonian Institution Press, 1997), 178.

4. Dickson and Dickson, 19.

5. O. K. Davis, "Some Facts Relating to the Early Development of the Phonograph," *Phonogram,* March–April 1893, 385.

6. The preface to the 16mm compilation of *Early Edison Shorts* in the MoMA collection, which includes the [*Dickson Experimental Sound Film*], informs viewers that the wax cylinder sound track for that film survives at the Edison Historic Site.

7. National Park Service (NPS) catalog number: EDIS 30142; E-number: E-6018-1.

8. Two frames short of 40 feet. (One foot of 35mm film contains 16 frames.)

9. Memo from Jerry Fabris to Patrick Loughney, June 3, 1998.

10. ips = inches per second.

11. Experts in the LC Music Division and American Folklife Center were unable to specifically identify the melody, beyond that it is a violin waltz typical of the late nineteenth century.

22 A "Secondary Action" or Musical Highlight? Melodic Interludes in Early Film Melodrama Reconsidered

David Mayer and Helen Day-Mayer

The mail train has been robbed. Armed men, boarding the moving train, have broken into the mail car, shot dead the guard, and, using the violent technique developed in the labor wars of the 1890s, dynamited the safe. The robbers have also murdered the fireman, throwing his body on the rails, and shot dead a fleeing passenger. But the outrage has been discovered. The telegrapher, who was knocked unconscious and bound by the bandits, has been found by his small daughter and revived to give the alarm. We—spectators to these criminal acts as we watch Porter-Edison's *The Great Train Robbery*—are eager to see justice done and done swiftly.

But pursuit isn't immediate. Rather, and perhaps to our frustration, there is instead what an intertitle informs us is "A lively quadrille." In the setting of a frontier saloon, a square dance begins. Four couples, in square-dance parlance, honor their corners and their partners, balance, form a ring and circle left, join a grand right and left, and allemande until a dude in fancy city clothes breaks into their square to interpolate a nimble, fast-jigging step-dance. The cowboys and cowgirls, wary and only briefly amused, drive off this intruder with blasts of gunfire into the floor, then re-form in couples to dance a reel: corner-to-corner, saluting, balancing and swinging, do-si-do-ing. Only when this third dance, with its complicated figures, is nearing its conclusion does the newly freed telegrapher burst into the saloon to report the crime and remind his rifle-toting posse that justice is waiting. Our impatience will be mollified. Justice will be done and the train-robber outlaws hunted down, but not until those three discrete—compacted, but nonetheless distinct—dances have been performed.

Some more episodes from another familiar film drama made by Edison and Porter: A riverboat, the side-wheeler *Robert E. Lee,* pulls into the levy to allow St. Clair, Eva, and their slave Tom to disembark. The arriving river-steamer is greeted by a group of six black dancers. Later, before Tom and Eva have a quiet evening in the plantation garden, we are treated to a cakewalk by the same six male and female dancers and a further reprise by two child dancers emulating their elders. We might even suspect that the purpose of the interlude in the garden is the dance, not the quiet repose of the old man and the child. Like the dancers on the levy, these dancers are authentic African Americans, not white actors blacked-up like Tom and Topsy. The eight dancers perform a further, final jigging and shuffling dance at a slave market where Tom is sold to the slave-driver Simon Legree, who will be his killer.

We, of course, recognize these moments from *Uncle Tom's Cabin* as well as *The Great Train Robbery*, but how do we account for them? What have these episodes—the barn dances and the several African-American dances—in common? Why are these episodes, which apparently interrupt the narrative flow of the film melodramas in which they appear, allowed to intrude? Film historians either don't mention the dance-hall episode in *The Great Train Robbery* or, embarrassed for Edwin Porter, describe it as something extraneous to an otherwise integrated narrative. Vardac, in particular, makes no attempt to interpret or justify this scene and somewhat dismissively explains away the dance-hall intrusion as a "secondary action,"[1] as if, somehow, this digression was a forgivable lapse on the part of Porter and the Edison crew or merely lazy embroidery. A similar reticence meets the several scenes of black slave dances in Porter's *Uncle Tom's Cabin* and, seventeen years later, the sleigh-ride and barn-dance episodes in D. W. Griffith's *'Way Down East.*

We suggest answers other than "secondary actions" or clumsy inserts for these moments. The reason why we largely fail to appreciate Porter's "lively quadrille" is that its presence is dictated not by a demand of film narrative, but by earlier theatrical considerations and lingering audience expectations. What we see in both early and later narrative film melodramas is a practice particular to American stage melodrama—indeed, a practice that has been uniquely developing in American melodrama since 1873. This theatrical practice, which places musical and dance interludes within dramatic performance, arises from the so-called Panic of '73, a severe financial depression stemming from unpaid American Civil War debts, the calling-in of European loans, fraud, and overspeculation.[2] One of the major crises in American history, the Panic of '73 and its aftermath so altered the structure of American theater company management as to have direct and lasting impact on the shape and content of entertainments offered from the mid-1870s until the second decade of the present century.

We further contend that the resulting structural changes in form and content, regularly introducing music and variety elements, became so embedded in American melodramatic theatrical practice that recognition of these changes is essential to the understanding of that genre. Further, audience reception and acceptance of these newer melodramatic conventions—even the expectation of musical and variety interludes—consequently brings to early narrative film similar musical and variety elements, which remain in American film melodrama into the 1920s. Indeed, these elements are still found in features made by Thanhouser in the mid-teens and by D. W. Griffith in 1920 when he films Lottie Blair Parker's stage play, *'Way Down East.*

And so to 1873. At that date, American theater companies and the theaters in which they performed were largely indivisible. Theaters were owned locally by share-, or stock-, holders. And these stock theaters, as they were called, employed, season-by-season rather than play-by-play, a permanent company of actors, each engaged to play roles predictable by the actors' ages, appearance, growing and practiced skills, years and experience in the profession, and favor with the local audience. This was the so-called stock company.[3] Some members of the stock company were related, filling positions in the acting company, scene-shop, the theater pit-orchestra, and front-of-house. Theater was a family business affording a small measure of stability, permanence, and regular—if seasonal—employment.

The stock company supported touring star actors, who arrived alone or with an acting partner. The usual stock leads stood aside or took supporting parts while the visitors performed the role or roles that brought in audiences for a night or a week, then departed, to be followed at some interval by another touring star. Plays were chosen from a large existing and gradually accumulating repertoire of comedies, melodramas, burlesques, farces, and occasional classics —often Shakespearean pieces. New plays gradually filtered in from New York or London. Scenery, too, was stock. The front parlor, cottage, forest, grand ballroom, and castle-keep settings all made frequent appearances throughout the season. New scenery was a rarity, important enough to be lavishly announced in handbills and programs.

All of this was to change with the Panic of '73. Stock companies, like ma-and-pa stores, were small family businesses without sufficient capital reserves, and were too dependent upon daily trade to withstand financial shocks. Of fifty urban American stock companies in 1870, only one survived by 1885.[4] As money became short in the community, other theaters failed. Falling victim to the same depression were the nation's other popular theaters: local variety and vaudeville houses, hippodromes and circuses, and establishments offering musical entertainments. Entertainment—serious and comic plays, variety and musical pieces alike—was in short supply, but then few people, pinched by the depression, could afford regular and varied theater-going.

One of the circumstances that had brought the Panic of '73 was over-expansion of the railroads. Some rail companies went into liquidation, but miles of track and rolling stock—passenger and freight cars—remained to inspire further speculators and recapitalization as the larger financial institutions, less demoralized by the depression, fought back. It is to the railroads and their almost desperate need to create paying traffic that we look for the next theatrical development. Here were scattered legitimate and variety theaters sitting empty and the availability of cheap rail fares to make it possible to move entire shows from theater to theater. Theatrical managers soon realized that a new approach to financing ventures, staging, and touring would save their bacon.

The result was the "combination" company, or as it was sometimes known and advertised, the "united" or "amalgamated" company. Combination companies—which were directly to influence film form, content, and reception—were formed around a temporary company to present a single new entertainment or—sometimes—a group of entertainments. Some of the combination's performers were actors engaged to perform the entertainment's dramatic and narrative segments. Some were variety performers with musical, dancing, and miscellaneous talents who performed their routines in gaps deliberately inserted in the dramatic action to exhibit their skills. Audiences now got drama and music and variety in the same entertainment. Now here was value for money, and American audiences came to expect their melodramas and comedies to be leavened with music, dancing, and variety. Tom Gunning might name this leavening of music and variety a "theater of attractions." We say it emphatically: the deliberate combining of light musical variety entertainments with strong emotional drama is what distinguishes late-Victorian American stage melodrama and American film melodrama into the 1920s from all other national melodramas.[5]

Thus actors and musical-variety entertainers, along with new scenery and new musical numbers especially created for the entertainment, were toured along the expanded rail networks, performing in theaters that were gradually renovated to accommodate standard sizes of scenery and to facilitate quick company change-overs. If the combination drew audiences and prospered, then the play continued to tour; if audiences stayed at home and hoarded their pennies, the combination failed. Money was lost, but the initial capital outlay was far less than in maintaining an urban theater with a permanent company of actors and a deteriorating inventory of tired scenery. Two distinct groups might be yoked together on a single tour. Edwin Porter's *Uncle Tom's Cabin* is based on just such a combination, which toured the theaters of New Jersey with new sets created for the tour, as Cooper Graham has pointed out, by a scene shop in Battle Creek, Michigan: a company of white actors playing the lead parts, including the blackface roles of Tom, Topsy, and Cassie, and a company of African-American dancers and singers, also playing supporting roles, united while the good days and good audiences lasted. As local repertory or stock companies vanished, touring combinations increased. In 1876–77, there were one hundred such companies on the road; by 1880, there were three hundred; by 1900, as many as five hundred companies were touring.[6] It was the combination company that gave late-nineteenth-century American melodrama its distinctive structure, and it is this same combination company structure that passed directly, frequently, and for some decades into American film melodramas.

As the dance-hall episode in *The Great Train Robbery* has hitherto been a problematic moment in Porter's film, it is useful to observe the degree to which Scott Marble, the author of the 1893–96 stage play, fulfilled his obligation to create spaces for musical and variety numbers as his melodrama toured the Midwest with Thomas H. Davis's and William T. Keogh's combination company. Equally, we may observe and infer how Edwin Porter, in adapting parts of Marble's play for the screen and adding certain elements of his own, similarly met that continuing obligation. Toward the end of Act II, set in the Never-Shut Saloon of an unnamed frontier settlement, the script sets up conditions for Broncho Joe, U.S. marshal and saloon proprietor, without stepping out of character, to act as master-of-ceremonies and to introduce variety specialties, the acts cast from a pool of artistes in any given section of the tour:

(Enter Supers, Ballet-Ladies, Sol, Gordon, and Louise—all seated. Gordon at bar. Broncho shakes hands with all when all seated.)

Broncho	Boys and Gals, we're going to have an entertainment tonight. The first man that pounds on the table with a beer glass or shoots out the lights will have to answer to me. Got that?
	Specialties Introduced by Broncho.
Broncho	(*After specialties*)
	(*Takes Frank to C L*) Gents and Ladies, this is my boy Frank, and I want everyone to respect him. Got that?
Sol	(*Rises—comes to C*) As a veteran of three wars and meeting a great many people, I will say that Frank is the best people I ever met. When I stood with Gen. Jones at the siege of Pompeii—
Broncho	What?
Sol	I mean the fall of Richmond.
Josh	Gol darn you, sit down.
Broncho	Frank, give the gals and boys a song.
	(*Frank's specialty*) . . .

Thus Broncho Joe can introduce, as the Davis-Keogh program and its penciled-in amendments suggest: whip acts, knife-throwers, trick-shooters, and rope-spinners. When these turns finish, we have a song, "Frank's specialty," performed in male drag by a female member of the company. A further variety turn, introduced as Sergeant Flynn of the U.S. Cavalry, brings on a dancing bear, which wrestles first with its trainer and then, comically, with the character Joshua Glue—who has previously boasted of his no-holds-barred wrestling prowess:

	(*At end of specialty enter Flynn door in flat*)
Broncho	Hello! Sergeant.
Flynn	How do, yes do, Joe?
Broncho	Ladies and gents, my old friend, Sergeant Flynn.
Everybody	Hello! Sergeant.
Sol	Salute.
Josh	Shut up.
Flynn	I salute you, ladies and gentlemen, I salute you. No doubt you all wonder why I am in this costume de character. There's going to be a grand entertainment over at the camp tonight. I take part myself.

Thos. H. Davis and William T. Keogh,

PROPRIETORS AND MANAGERS.

"On the Bowery," "On the Mississippi," "Down in Dixie," "The Sidewalks of New
York," "Girl Wanted," "Fallen Among Thieves," "Lost in Siberia,"
"The Black Cat," Etc.,

Present their Stupendous Dramatic Spectacle,

The Great Train Robbery.

Written by SCOTT MARBLE.

CAST.

Tom Gordon, Cashier U. S. Express Co	W. C. Holden
Sam Carter, Chief Clerk U. S. Express Co	Wm. De Setley
Dan Hollis, Clerk, alias, Jack Baker	Frederick DeVere
Broncho Joe, Deputy Marshal, owner of the Never Shut Saloon	Thos. J. Quinn
Wm. Bennett, Supt. of U. S. Express	Maurice Brennan
Sergeant Flinn, of the 6th U. S. Cavalry	Chas. Robinson
Joshua Glue, sooner wrestle than eat	Frank R. Jackson
Solitaire, a weary son of Mars, champion liar of the world	Frank O'Brien
Peanuckle Schlitz, trying to express a telephone	Edward McWade
Tip Porter	Dan Sullivan
John Sherley, Telegraph Operator and Station Agent	Ed. Adams
Jim Judson, Barkeeper	H. B. Williams
Black Snake Pete, a terror	Frank Wilbur
Expressman	W. H. Warner
Express Messenger	Amzi Newton
Louise Gordon	
Frank Vashell	Miss Kitty Wolf
Alice Bennett	Miss Helen MacGregor
Maggie Murphy	Miss Ada Boshell
Rose Wilson	Miss May Allen
Fanny Knight	Miss Lucy Browne
Laura Dorn	Miss Mary Barnes
Mary Lee	Miss Nellie Melton

Indians—Chief Running Deer, Crazy Dog, Split-Bark, Long Feather, Black Eagle,
Red Spear, Lone Wolf.
Cow Boys—Dashing Charlie, Dead Shot Harry, Alkali Ike, Cherokee Jake.
——Also Introducing——
The Star Bruins of the Bear World, "Phillip" and "Peter," Champion Wrestlers,
——And——
Ex-Deputy United States Marshal and Scout, George E. Bartlett, of the Pine
Ridge Indian Reservation, and—"Wild Burt" Williams, Champion Short Range
Lightning Rifle and Revolver Shot of the World. Capt. Williams Sends 12 Revolver
Shots into One Bullet Hole in 6 Seconds and Challenges any Man in the World to a
Match Contest with Rifles and Revolvers for a Purse of $100 a Side.

SYNOPSIS OF SCENES.

ACT I—Attempted Robbery of the Express Company. Innocent condemned.
ACT II—The frontier. On the trail for vengeance.
ACT III—The hold-up. Explosion of the Express car.
ACT IV—Caught in the Mountains. Retribution.

EXECUTIVE STAFF FOR DAVIS & KEOGH.

Edward J. Nugent	Acting Manager
Wilbur M. Bates	Advance Representative
Fred Devere	Stage Director
Indian Agent and Interpreter	George E. Bartlett

22.1. Playbill for the Thomas H. Davis and William T. Keogh combination company
tour of *The Great Train Robbery* through the Midwest, 1896–1897. Emendations to the
cast list and to the specialty acts offered indicates that these were subject to change as
performers became available or left the company.

Broncho	What part do you take?
Flynn	I don't know, but I'll tell you anyhow.
	(*Flynn's Specialty*)

Finally, we have an unspecified square dance or reel ("casting-off" is another standard move in country dancing) from the ballet company.

	(*at Finish of Flynn's Specialty*)
Broncho	Take your partners for a dance. (*Music cue. No. 11*)
	Music. (*All rise, put tables and chairs aside. Clear stage for dance*)
Sol	That reminds me of a dance I had just before the Battle of—
Josh	Shut up.
Flynn	Here, here, respect that man, he's the finest liar the army ever produced.
	(*Wild yell outside. All look toward door. Enter Peter with a rush down C*)
Pete	Well, this is a fine mob. Hello, Gals! (*throws kiss*) Divide that among you. Hand out your poison. (*Pea. hands out bottle. Pete takes six drinks then drinks out of bottle, places it on bar.*)
Sol	I wish that was me.
Pete	(*C*) You dont know who I am. I'm Black Snake Pete, a bad man from Dead Man's Gulch. I'm looking for blood. Who wants to lose an ear—Come speak up, and I'll kill one of you for luck—Aint had a killing in three days, Whoop! I'm hungry for gore
	(*Swaggers about stage closely followed by Pea. Turns and sees Pea. Points gun at him*) Don't follow me around; don't follow me, or I'll drop you where you stand.
Pea	(*R C*) Wont you shake hands, Peter?
Pete	(*L C*) Well you're too small to waste a cartridge on, so shake, Dutchy, shake. (*Gives Pea his hand who squeezes it. Pete hollers and writhes about until the door in flat is reached, then Pea kicks him out and struts about*)
Sol	(*Pushes up to door then down to Broncho*) Did you see me look at him? If I hadn't been a friend of yours, I'd a thrown him right through the ceiling.
Broncho	(*Pushes Sol.*) Oh, get out. Take your gals. Let her go. (*Music cue. No. 14 ff*)
Dance	(*When the dancers cast off, Crazy Dog appears in door on flat and as Broncho is going down stage Crazy Dog leaps at him to stab him. Is caught by Gordon held C. picture*) (*Music cue. Segue. No.11p*)
Gordon	What do you mean—stab a man in the back—you treacherous cur.

Everybody	Lynch him. Kill him.
Broncho	Stand back, everybody, let no man interfere. This injun tried to kill me once before, but now he's got to fight right yer.
Louise	Don't Joe, he may kill you.
Broncho	Don't be scared Frank, this is my regular business. Come on you dog-eating injun. (*No. 15 ff till curtain*)
	Fight
	(*When Broncho Joe kills Crazy Dog he gives a war whoop. Indian jumps to C covered by Joe. One inside door in flat covered by Peanuckle, one in window covered by cowboy, one in door R covered by cowboy, one in R 1 E covered by cowboy. Capt. Clark L 1 E covered by cowboy. 2 ladies C in front of Joe, 2 ladies R of C.*)
	(*During the Black Snake Pete Exit, Hollis has entered X ex to door L. Exit during fight he watches. When warwhoop given, grabs Louise and is carrying her off. Gordon knocks him on table L holding him at bay with gun. 6 supers as road agents appear 2 at door D, 2 at window 2 with Indian door in flat. Picture formed, quick CURTAIN*)[7]

It is this last, non-verbal square dance, the most pictorial of the musical numbers, that best enacts and affirms the comradeship and unity of the frontier community who will avenge the murders and recover the stolen loot. Edwin Porter—being neither expedient nor lazy, but fulfilling the expectations of a 1903 audience honed by thirty years' accumulated experience of stage melodrama[8]—places this reel on the screen. And, we must emphasize, Porter doesn't stint on dance and music. He intentionally foregrounds variety. Three discrete dances, perhaps difficult for us to recognize, but obvious to American spectators in 1903, and presumably all three accompanied—appropriately enough—in the theater by the house musicians, whose presence Porter takes for granted and whose availability to support this variety turn he exploits—offer us enjoyment altogether distinct from watching the train robbers pursued to final justice.

It would be altogether incorrect to insist that cinema invariably absorbed theatrical structures wholesale or uncritically or, for that matter, that combination comedy and melodrama translated intact from stage to screen. Sometimes the influence was small and obscure. Domitor members who saw 1908 Griffith screenings at Pordenone or who otherwise recall Griffith's *The Romance of a Jewess* will remember that this otherwise lachrymose Biograph film has a comic episode in which a succession of unlikely clients bring to Mr. Simonson's pawnshop counter various items to pledge in exchange for cash loans. This episode repeats the way in which combination companies learned to build plays around successions of variety players. The probable source for Griffith, often imitated and elaborated by the touring combinations, is the final act of George H. Jessop's comic melodrama, *Sam'l of Posen; or, The Commercial Drummer* (1883), where much activity occurs around the arrivals and importunities of both the genuinely needy and the comically eccentric at a New York pawnbroker's. Similarly, in another widely toured comic melodrama, Leonard Grover's *Our Boarding House* (1877),[9] numerous characters arrive and depart from a dilapidated Midwest rooming house populated by eccentric transients. These roles necessarily included variety and musical performers who, in ethnic character—the stage Irishman in battered bowler, the Irish "biddy" (a drag role), the Italian in the conical felt we associate with Chico Marx—or in American stereotypes, such as the Yankee "rube" paying his first city visit, were all given pretext and space to display their stage personae. Farce, music, and pathos can in such circumstances stand together. Griffith and Biograph were not obliged to seek emotional or generic consistency in environments such as *The Romance of a Jewess.* The legacy of the theatrical combination absolved them from that constraint.

At other times filmmakers kept the musical and dance elements of the combination, but chose to foreground the dramatic or overlapped musical elements with the dramatic. We see such an instance as a key episode in the Thanhouser-Pathé 1915 *The World and the Woman* (again shown in Pordenone). Edwin Thanhouser was, as we know, a theatrical producer on the Ohio circuit before he turned to film, and the successes of his own combinations financed his ventures into motion pictures, so it is understandable that his films will draw on the vocabulary of his first profession. An episode runs for much of the first reel of this film in which Jeanne Eagles, playing the role of a prostitute down on her luck, is tempted into a café, where she is offered money to attend a party at a luxurious country home and impersonate a society guest. At a table sit the smug males who would bribe her and perpetrate a hoax. She joins them. The principal action is thus across the table. But behind them, always in shot and always in clear focus, is the cabaret where a series of distinctive and spectacular dances engage our eyes and make, serially, quite different demands on the theater musicians: a French *apache* dance in which a girl is thrown between two men, a Russian *gopak* where the squatting male dancers kick forward and to the sides, a country reel, and, finally and more appropriate to the venue, a foxtrot performed by a skilled pair.

The influence of the combination company actually lasted into the sound era. One of the most popular combinations of the last century, Charles Dazey's 1893 sporting or horse-racing melodrama, *In Old Kentucky,* which was performed on the same circuits as Thanhouser's dramas and on numerous other American circuits, was in 1935 one of the early dramatic pieces adapted for sound. Most of Dazey's plot and dialogue were cast aside. However, musical variety—in the stage play a black singing quartet, the Woodlawn Whangdoodles[10]—was retained by requiring numerous and frequent tap dances from Bill "Bojangles" Robinson, three comic dances from Will Rogers, and some abridged Rogers monologues.

We close with a further instance of the legacy of combination company melodrama, choosing as our example the 1898 stage play *Way Down East,* authored by Lottie Blair Parker and further developed into a touring combination by William Brady and Joseph Grismer. You are more likely to be aware of this

play as a 1920 motion picture by D. W. Griffith, recalling, if little else, the almost final moments of the film with Lillian Gish as Anna Moore, floating unconscious on the ice of the Connecticut River, heading for certain death at
the nearing waterfall until rescued by Richard Barthelmess's young farmer. In
Lottie Parker's first draft, brought in 1896 by her husband to the theatrical
manager William Brady,[11] the play is set in rural Nebraska and has only the
voices of off-stage berry-pickers and a rudimentary on-stage harmonic group.
By the 1898 third draft, the result of constant experimentation before theater
audiences on the rural circuits hosting combination companies, the play has
been translated from the Western plains to the New England of the American
"B'gosh" play, and a cluster of further musical elements have been cleverly
integrated—not superimposed as with Scott Marble's *The Great Train Robbery*
—into the Parker-Brady-Grismer script.[12]

As extracts from the final printed-not-published script of *Way Down East*
reveal, there are substantial musical occasions in the first two acts and an extensive musical entr'acte—a sleigh-ride full of happy singing revelers heading for
a rural barn dance, which literally carries happiness away from the Bartlett farm
into the deep woods. In these two acts, we have frequent singing from a mixed
quintet, the "Village Choir." Some of their songs are specified by the script, but
Brady also gives them latitude to interpolate their own numbers and to adjust
their repertoire to current favorites and regional tastes. Additionally, we find the
character of Rube Whipple. "Whipple" was the invention of the variety actor
Charles Seamon and made his earliest appearance in a vaudeville sketch that
Brady described as "a small-time hick act"[13] in which Seamon, cast as a village
constable, reported in Yankee dialect that the rural post office had been robbed
of a handful of stamps and postal cards. Brady engaged Seamon, placed him
and his variety turn into the first act, but then divided the turn into three parts
to extend Seamon's comic performance for a further act. Thus, it is in the second
act that Seamon's Rube Whipple performs an eccentric dance and, moments
later, when he has caught his breath, sings his composition "Big Hat, All Bound
'Round with a Woolen String," one of numerous variations on the anonymously
written American song, "The prettiest gal I ever saw was sippin' cider through
a straw."

Griffith, arriving on the scene sixteen or seventeen years later, honors these
musical antecedents and intentionally amplifies them. He makes large musical
and dance moments of the hayride to the barn dance and even more of the
stopover at the Bartletts' farm when the revelers " . . . warm up . . . with an old-
fashioned barn dance." Watching *'Way Down East,* we might experience déjà vu
because Griffith's barn dance is composed of discrete squares and reels interrupted by duets and solos. Rube Whipple's eccentric solo dance is now one of
several subsumed into the frenetic impromptu revels. Louis Silver's score for this
segment of the film draws on such specific airs as "Arkansas Traveler," "Pop
Goes the Weasel," "Little Brown Jug," and even a few bars of Charles Seamon's
"All Bound 'Round."[14]

Again, at the drama's end, when the various couples wed, the setting for these festivities is a dance. Here, as before, music and the spectacle of dancing deliberately call attention to themselves, both elements standing on their own, even as they again assist in the overall action. Music and dance in silent film melodrama, we contend, more than meet their obligation to reinforce the drama's thematic needs. And as much to the point—as the combination company tradition encouraged them to do—music and dance entertain in their own right and are enjoyed for the pleasure that they bestow.

Notes

1. Nicholas A. Vardac, *Stage to Screen, Theatrical Method from Garrick to Griffith* (Cambridge, Mass.: Harvard University Press, 1949), 183.

2. Peter A. Davis, "From Stock to Combination: The Panic of 1873 and Its Effects on the American Theatre Industry," *Theatre History Studies* 7 (1988), 1–10.

3. Rosemarie K. Bank, "A Reconsideration of the Death of Nineteenth-Century American Repertories and the Rise of the Combination," *Essays in Theatre* 5, no. 1 (November 1986), 61–75.

4. Alfred Bernheim, *The Business of the Theatre: An Economic History of the American Theatre, 1750–1932* (New York: Benjamin Blom, 1964, reprint), 31. See also M. B. Leavitt, *Fifty Years of Theatrical Management, 1859–1909* (New York: Broadway Publishing, 1912).

5. We refer to the last quarter of the nineteenth and first quarter of the twentieth centuries. It was pointed out to us at the Domitor conference that much Asian cinema, conspicuously the "Bollywood" action-film of India, also unites musical variety with melodrama.

6. Frank Rahill, *The World of Melodrama* (University Park: Pennsylvania State University Press, 1967), 179.

7. The text is from the full prompt script held in the New York Public Library.

8. The frontier saloon as locus for a sequence of combination company variety acts is not at all unique to *The Great Train Robbery*. Typically, we find in touring melodramas, as in James McCloskey's frequently revived *Across the Continent* (1871), stage directions such as the following for II,2: "Bar with bottles and glasses, sandwiches and apples, seltzer bottles and a couple of Indian clubs made to look like bottles all on bar. Curtains painted to resemble back of bar. Window in curtain. Chairs, table-doors. When curtain rises, Dolores and other young women seated in chairs, chair in front of bar is dummy representing young woman. Bill is behind the bar. Young woman comes in and sings. Dutch song-and dance does a turn and waltzes with dummy from the chair, and retires with it under his arm. He also comes out with a coat on in which the sleeves are six or eight feet long and have large hands sewed on the ends. Inside the sleeves and fastened to the hands, are sticks by which he can hold the hands up and make them look very natural. He sings 'Only to See Her Face Again,' and at each pause lets the arms out a little way until finally they are stretched to their full limit. Very funny. After this a nigger song and dance, and the play goes on. . . . "

9. Both Jessop's *Sam'l of Posen* and Grover's *Our Boarding House* are reprinted in Hubert Heffner, ed., *America's Lost Plays,* vol. IV, Barrett H. Clark, series ed. (Princeton: Princeton University Press, 1940), 1963.

10. Charles T. Dazey, *In Old Kentucky,* ed. Barrett H. Clark (Detroit: Fine Book Circle, 1937).

11. William A. Brady, *Showman* (New York: E. P. Dutton, 1937), 185–189.

12. Typescript early versions of *Way Down East* are held in the Billy Rose Collection, New York Public Library. The final printed-not-published text is the copyright copy held by the Library of Congress and the Lord Chamberlain's Collection, British Library.

13. Brady, 188.

14. This score is heard on the American print released on the NTSC video-format by Kino Video, New York.

23 The Living Nickelodeon
Rick Altman

The study of silent film sound stands at the threshold of a new era. Just as recent breakthroughs in the realm of early cinema required recognition that early films are not primitive, failed attempts at producing cinema as we know it, but the product of systems and logics quite different from those that we now identify with cinema, so current revelations in the domain of early film sound have been fostered by a series of new assumptions and practices:

- instead of assuming that silent film sound is coherent and unitary, scholars have begun to consider the possibility of multiple silent film accompaniment styles;
- instead of extrapolating to cinema's first two decades the accompaniment style of the1920s, film specialists now approach early film sound as a separate and perhaps quite different question;
- instead of heavy dependence on the reminiscences of cinema musicians (who remember most vividly the practices of the 1920s), film historians anchor their conclusions regarding early film sound practices in contemporary evidence (1895–1914);
- instead of deferring to secondary accounts of silent film sound, historians now increasingly attend to primary materials, which often contradict secondary reports;
- instead of concentrating exclusively on film music, film scholars now pay close attention to narrators, sound effects, and films with synchronized sound;
- instead of limiting their attention to sounds produced in the theater during film projection, researchers now consider a wider range of sound practices, including music played in the theater between films and music played outside the theater during film projection.

While these new assumptions and practices have yet to achieve universal acceptance, they have already begun to revolutionize the field of silent film sound. In particular, they have brought new light to the previously neglected domain of early film sound.

A Little Lexicon of Misunderstood Terms

The strongest impediment to new understanding of early film sound lies in our tendency to ascribe post-1915 meanings to terms that meant something quite different before 1915. Widespread, this tendency most notably affects simple terms that are so familiar as to remain above suspicion. How could the meaning of such basic words as "film" and "music" possibly be in doubt? Because the key to new understanding lies in our ability to recognize fundamental shifts in the meaning of a few crucial terms, I offer this little lexicon of words commonly misunderstood by students of silent film accompaniment.

film: Today, film is defined by opposition to a series of similar yet specifically different cultural products. As now conceived, film involves the chemical registration of an image on a transparent, continuous support, along with moving, large-size projection of that image. As such, film differs from theater (which is live rather than recorded), television (which involves electronic instead of chemical recording), photographs (which record only a single image), slides (which are projected as still frames rather than as moving images), and filmstrips (which are projected as a series of stills rather than as a continuously moving image). What we now confidently describe as films were defined and understood quite differently before 1910. No one today would confuse theater and cinema, yet in the early period the terms "theater" and "drama" were regularly applied to live and recorded entertainments alike. Today the law carefully differentiates between film and photographs, yet at the beginning of the century no such legal distinction was made. Whereas we now clearly distinguish films from slides (a term designating a stationary projectable transparency), the two were once regularly conflated as "views" (a term whose meaning was inflected by the existence of slides with moving parts). Over the last century, a shifting mediascape has radically changed both the status and the definition of those artifacts known today as films.

film projector: Ask what a film projector looks like and you will invariably be given a description of a one-piece instrument, dedicated to film projection alone, including light source, intermittent film drive, and lens. Yet throughout the early period, projectors were systematically built in two parts: a "motion head" (through which the film is fed) placed in front of a standard magic lantern projector consisting of a light source and a slide transport. No wonder that films were considered just a different form of "view," since the film portion of the projector was nothing more than an add-on to the familiar projector of views. Note that the bivalent nature of early projectors (for instance, their capacity to project two types of view, slides as well as films) makes it possible for a single projector to support what we would now think of as a mixed program.

film program: In a world like ours, where the words "film" and "film projector" clearly exclude still images, the term "film program" is also restricted to moving images. The terminological instability characteristic of early cinema led to a constant mixing of (what we would call) different media in the same program: live theater and films (both labeled "drama"), short acts and films (both labeled "vaudeville"), lantern slides and films (both labeled "views"). Until the teens, all-film programs were the exception. Nickelodeons, for example, thrived on a combination of films and illustrated songs.

film music: In modern usage, references to film music assume wordless (and often titleless) instrumental music. Decades of film music designed to evoke or reinforce specific emotional states have led to unconscious restriction of our understanding of the term "music" itself, when used in conjunction with the term "film." Yet early musical practices often mobilized the very popular songs (with great emphasis on lyrics and titles) shunned by modern understanding. Whereas our notion of film music depends heavily on the musical conventions of late romantic tone poems and songs without words, early cinema musicians often made their choices among the substantial and well-publicized popular song corpus. In fact, the regular use of automatic musical instruments (especially phonographs and player pianos) usually limited early film music to song-length selections (since early cylinders, records, and piano rolls rarely surpassed three minutes). Whether it was played in the theater or outside, whether it was played during the film or between films, whether it was meant to accompany the film, to provide a rest from it, or even to compete with it, early film music typically involved popular songs rather than the later light classical selections. Whereas today the term "film music" is restricted to music that is both played during a film and specifically meant to accompany that film, an understanding of early film sound requires attention to many types of music that are specifically not designed to accompany the film.

film accompaniment: Current standards of film accompaniment, as established by decades of concertizing former silent film organists and years of modern scores for silent films, involve the matching of musical rhythm and texture to a film's narrative components. Contemporary sources suggest that standards of accompaniment during film's early years depended far more heavily on the matching of a song's title or lyrics to a film's narrative situations. For example, *Vitagraph Bulletin* 222 suggests playing selections from "The Telephone Girl" (one of many telephone songs popular at the time) to accompany Vitagraph's film, *The Telephone* (October 1910). This suggestion is entirely based on a concordance between the song title and the film topic; indeed, the upbeat tempo and melody of the song provide no match at all for the film's suspenseful narrative. This type of verbal matching remains a major accompaniment principle until the teens.

musical cue: The term "cue sheet" became so widespread during the late teens and twenties that it has obliterated an important prior usage of the term "cue." In modern terminology, a musical cue is the point at which, according to the score or cue sheet, a particular musical entry is to be made. Referring to accompaniment instructions provided for a particular film, this usage of the term "cue" designates a practice that was not generalized until the mid-teens. Before that time, the term "cue" (as in the expression "cue music") regularly referred to on-screen reference to the making of music or noise. Pictures of the blowing of a bugle, the playing of a violin, or the firing of a rifle are all, in the language regularly employed during cinema's early period, "cues" for the film musician. Note that this usage implies a direct relationship between film images and the appropriate accompaniment, whereas the later use of the term "cue" systematically applies to the moment when music recommended by the film and music industries should be played.

This little lexicon might well be expanded to include such terms as *talking pictures* (which since the late 1920s have included synchronized recorded sound, but during the late 1900s depended on live, behind-the-screen speaking of the words mouthed by the on-screen characters), *drummer* (for us the musician who plays the drums, but around 1910 the employee responsible for playing the "traps," that is, for providing sound effects), or even *sound effects* (today a separate category of sound, but virtually undifferentiated from music during the nickelodeon period).

Reading early uses of these terms as if they had today's meaning invariably condemns modern scholars to radical misunderstanding of early film sound practices. When early texts are properly understood with their contemporary meanings, however, they clearly reveal a variety of accompaniment practices that differ as widely among themselves as they do as a group from the post-1915 traditions typically referred to in secondary literature about silent film accompaniment.

Four Early Accompaniment Modes

Careful scrutiny of contemporary documents suggests that early film sound was dominated not by the light classical music typically chosen for film accompaniment in the post-1915 period, but by four practices that have received next to no scholarly attention.[1]

Silence. Scholars have systematically assumed that the presence of a piano in a nickelodeon indicates musical accompaniment of all films. Even rudimentary understanding of the importance of illustrated songs in nickelodeon programs quickly dispels this assumption. In fact, strong evidence suggests that until about 1910 many theaters preferred music between films, covering reel changes and extending the program, to music during the films. As early as 1900, Biograph distributed music to be used between films:

> Dear Sir:—We will furnish you with a Biograph and . . . religious views. . . . The charge for the Biograph for one evening is $50. The only other charge will be for music to be given during the time that the reels are being changed. The Biograph views and music will give an entertainment lasting about two hours.[2]

By 1909, the process was fully codified in a listing of the nickelodeon projectionist's duties first published in *Nickelodeon* and quoted extensively in David Hulfish's influential *Cyclopedia of Motion Picture Work*:

> What, then, are the total duties . . . which are required of the operator? . . .
> In the intermission the pianist is on duty. The operator, having his picture film in readiness,
> 1) lights his arc and
> 2) rings for the singer. He then

23.1. Song slide from "My Lovin' Picture Man" (DeWitt C. Wheeler, 1913). Marnan Collection, Minneapolis, Minnesota.

3) turns out the lights in the auditorium,

4) turns off the ventilating fans,

5) turns off the automatic "barker" and

6) projects the song slides in proper order and at the proper instant for each. At the conclusion of the song he

7) shifts to the motion head and begins to turn the crank of the kinetoscope, and at the same time, with his free hand

8) turns on the ventilating fans and

9) turns on the automatic "barker." This is the time for the accompanist's period of rest, and as the operator nears the end of the reel of film he

10) rings for the accompanist to be in readiness for the intermission. At the end of the motion pictures he

11) projects the "Please Remain" slide; then

12) turns on the auditorium lights,

13) cuts off the current from his arc light,

14) rewinds the film and

15) adjusts the carbons of his arc. Now, last but by no means least

16) the operator decides the length of the intermission before repeating his routine of 16 separate duties.[3]

As many a contemporary text demonstrates, the only music playing during films was often the ballyhoo phonograph, typically located in the projection booth, with its horn extending through the wall above the ticket booth so that the music could be heard in the street. Strikingly, and in contradiction to decades of film scholarship, it would appear that most early "film music" was actually distanced from the film either in time (played between films rather than during them) or in space (played outside rather than inside the theater).

Cue music. Because they concentrate on sounds implied by film images, early commentators on film accompaniment rarely make clear distinctions between music and sound effects. Though historians have regularly assumed that film music derives directly from the musical practices of stage melodrama, it now seems likely that sound cues within films constitute an even more important—

and far more complex—originary instance. Even the earliest reports of film music involve a characteristic mixing of music and non-musical sound effects, both serving cinematic realism rather than contributing the emotional overtones typical of later film music. For example, the *Philadelphia Record* reports a November 1897 film showing as follows:

> Not content with showing the living picture, Manager Keith furnishes with every view the noises which accompany the scene. . . . At the Bijou the roar of the waves, splashing of water, the playing of bands of music, a locomotive whistle, bell, stream, etc., are accompaniments that have played no small share in the 48 weeks success of the biograph.[4]

This is not musical accompaniment as we know it, but rather the production of what is now called "source music." It is hardly surprising that the list of "noises which accompany the scene" mixes music willy-nilly with what we now think of as something quite different, namely sound effects. Even dialogue, during the short-lived vogue of "talking pictures," is treated as a form of sound effect required by the image.

As late as 1910, critics continue to conflate multiple types of sound under the general rubric of sound effects:

> A character enters the picture, seats himself at a piano and runs his fingers over the keys, the pianist in the orchestra imitating him. This is a "sound effect" and is a part of the picture. . . . Imagine the "Swan Song" or "The Violin Maker of Cremona" without the violin sound effects. Nearly every battle scene . . . needs trumpet calls.[5]

A year later, the *New York Dramatic Mirror* still defines cue music as "the bugle calls and other such loud alarums demanded by the action on the stage."[6] Only later will the term "cue" begin to refer to the cue sheets that flourished during the teens and twenties.

Song films. During the first decade of this century, close ties were established between the thriving music industry and the nascent film industry. The early years of the decade depended primarily on connections between songs popularized by live renditions and filmic attempts to capitalize on that popularity. Edison's *Down Where the Wurzburger Flows* (1903) was one of many films built around a vaudeville hit, in this case the song that carried Nora Bayes to fame. By mid-decade, films and illustrated songs began to play an active role in advertising new songs and their cylinder, disc, piano roll, and sheet music commodified forms. Based on a recent Lew Dockstader hit, Biograph's *Everybody Works But Father* (in whiteface and blackface versions, 1905), rapidly followed by the comedy spin-off *Everybody Works But Mother* (1905), made Jean Havez's song into one of the decade's greatest financial successes. Still later in the decade, the popularity of synchronized sound systems (Cameraphone, Cinephone, Chronophone, and many others) led to the synchronized film and disc recording of many vaudeville hits, including Vesta Victoria's 1907 *Waiting at the Church* (Belcher and Waterson, 1907).

In many cases, we know that these song films were meant to be used just like illustrated songs, with the audience joining in. Of *Everybody Works But Father,* for example, *Biograph Bulletin* 57 says: "The great popularity of illustrated songs has led us to introduce a novelty in the form of a film which covers the entire action of the verses and choruses of a well-known song. . . . No slides are necessary. Anyone can sing it, and if you sing it just as it is written you can't get away from the pictures." In many cases, however, we do not yet know exactly how musicians and audiences were expected to react to song films. Suffice it to say that the tendency to build films around the titles, lyrics, and actions of popular songs obligates early film sound researchers to gain active knowledge of the period's substantial corpus of successful popular songs.

Accompaniment by title or lyrics. The extraordinary spread of the popular song business during the nickelodeon era went hand in hand with a tendency to base film accompaniment on the titles and lyrics of popular songs. Today it would strike us as a bad pun to play "Love Me Tender" during a scene showing a housewife tenderizing a steak; around 1910, however, purely verbal matches to on-screen action were frequent. In March of 1910, for example, the Edison *Kinetogram* suggested a dozen popular songs to be played with the recent Edison release, *A Western Romance.* Repeatedly, it is the title of the song that matches the action, not the music. Musicians are urged to play "I'm Going Away" while the son is packing to go away, followed by "On the Rocky Road to Dublin" when he is on the train, then "Pony Boy" when he meets the girl on a horse. When Indians appear, "Wahoo" is recommended; when the villain arrives, "I'm a Bold Bad Man" is proposed, with "Everybody Works but Father" accompanying the hero's eventual return home.[7] That same year, Clyde Martin's "Playing the Pictures" column makes similar recommendations:

> You can use several popular tunes during the showing [of Edison's 1910 *The Valet's Vindication*]. About the third scene in the picture is where Kirby, the valet, is await-ing the arrival of a number of friends. . . . The table is well supplied with refresh-ments, cigars, poker chips, etc., and the audience will repeat the lines with you "It Looks Like a Big Night To-night," you have won your first point. The next scene shows the Valet the morning after the party and asleep at the table. If you will play just a few strains from "The Morning after the Night Before" it will make every man in the audience, want to hand Kirby a cold towel and a pitcher of ice water. . . . [When] Beekman and Miss Bradley have been married and are enjoying their first home breakfast . . . then play "The Waning Honeymoon" from "The Time, the Place and the Girl" until the close of the picture.[8]

A month later, Martin himself took the time to explain to his readers the danger of this approach to film accompaniment. Half of the country's musicians, he says, "will pick up a publisher's catalogue and get names of songs that corre-spond with the scenes portrayed and they never consider that to make their point, the audience must know what they are playing."[9] Shortly, Martin and his *Moving Picture World* colleague, critic Clarence E. Sinn, would begin to cam-paign actively and systematically against accompaniment by title and lyric, pre-

PROGRAM II

Source music ("cue music") only

DRESS PARADE OF SCOUTS, ST. LOUIS EXPO (Biograph, 1904, 1'08")
   Shot like hundreds of others at the Louisiana Purchase Exposition, this film records the
   maneuvers of U.S. scouts (in military uniforms) and their Filipino counterparts.
accompaniment: "You're a Grand Old Flag" (1906)
   Words & music by George M. Cohan

THE COWBOY AND THE LADY (Biograph, 1903, 1'19")
   Shot by Billy Bitzer in Biograph's New York City studio, this film borrows motifs from
   the contemporary cowboy craze.
accompaniment: "Champagne Rag" (1910)
   Music by Joseph F. Lamb

Illustrated Song Slides:
   "Only a Message from Home Sweet Home" (1905)
      Words by Carroll Fleming, music by Edmond M. Florant
      Slides by DeWitt C. Wheeler

A DISCORDANT NOTE (Biograph, 1903, 38")
   Also shot by Bitzer, this is one of many period films portraying the making of music--if
   you can call it that!
accompaniment: "Wait Till the Sun Shines Nellie" (1905)
   Words by Andrew B. Sterling
   Music by Harry Von Tilzer

THE MELOMANIAC (Méliès, 1903, 1'58")
   "Just listen to those telephone wires sing!" goes the saying, but this film brings new
   meaning to the expression, as the bandmaster (played by Méliès himself) introduces a
   heady new form of musical transcription.
accompaniment: "America" ("God Save the Queen")
   Words by Samuel F. Smith, music source unknown

Illustrated Song Slides:
   "Sunbonnet Sue" (1906)
      Words by Will D. Cobb, music by Gus Edwards
      Slides by A. L. Simpson

THE MERRY WIDOW WALTZ CRAZE (Edison, 1908, 57")
   In late 1907 Lehar's Merry Widow opened first on stage then as a Kalem film. This
   April 1908 fragment, depicting Mr. Lightfoot's final frenzy, is all that remains of a
   longer film lampooning the craze surrounding Lehar's famous waltz.
accompaniment: "The Merry Widow Waltz" (1906)
   Music by Franz Lehar

23.2. Page four of The Living Nickelodeon program, Library of Congress, 3 June 1998.

ferring matches of on-screen emotion to the rhythm and texture of light classical music. Until their campaign succeeded later in the teens, however, film accompaniment would continue to be heavily marked by popular songs and their
titles and lyrics.

The Living Nickelodeon

These four practices are exemplified by the four separate programs of
The Living Nickelodeon, a research-driven entertainment first performed during the 1998 Library of Congress Domitor conference.[10] Unlike most early film

programs presented at festivals and conferences, The Living Nickelodeon includes illustrated songs and employs the four modes of film accompaniment introduced in the previous section rather than the light classical emotive approach commonly practiced during the late teens and twenties. Many of the contemporary statements quoted above are taken from the Living Nickelodeon program notes distributed at the Library of Congress performance.

During the Domitor conference, The Living Nickelodeon provoked a great deal of heated debate. From utterly basic questions (Were films really ever projected without musical accompaniment?) to matters of detail (Where exactly would the trap drummer have been located?), The Living Nickelodeon led conference participants to question in creative ways accepted notions about early film accompaniment. This is precisely the purpose envisioned by the creators of The Living Nickelodeon. By actually experiencing programs more like those typical of the pre-feature era, today's viewers are invited to ask the many questions about early film accompaniment that decades of scholars have avoided, preferring instead simply to extrapolate 1920s accompaniment practice back to the previous decades. If The Living Nickelodeon can induce a new generation of scholars to consider problems circumvented by their predecessors, then it will have served its role as an important moment in the 1998 Domitor conference, and an essential experiential complement to archival research and scholarly articles.

Notes

1. To my knowledge, the sole exception to this statement is my "The Silence of the Silents," *Musical Quarterly* 80, no. 4 (1997), 648–718. Thanks to the generosity of Tom Gunning, copies of this article were distributed to 1998 Domitor conference participants.

2. American Mutoscope and Biograph letter, 22 November 1900—quoted in Kemp Niver, *Biograph Bulletins 1896–1908* (Los Angeles: Locare Research Group, 1971), 53.

3. L. Gardette, "Conducting the Nickelodeon Program," *Nickelodeon,* March 1909, 79; quoted in David Hulfish, *Cyclopedia of Motion Picture Work,* vol. 1 (Chicago: American Technical Society, 1911), 136–137. Instructions reformatted for clarity.

4. *Philadelphia Record,* 23 November 1897, 2;—quoted in Musser, *The Emergence of Cinema* (New York: Scribner's, 1990), 178.

5. Clarence E. Sinn, "Music for the Picture," *Moving Picture World,* 10 December 1910, 1345.

6. *New York Dramatic Mirror,* 30 August 1911, 3.

7. *Kinetogram,* 15 March 1910, 11.

8. Clyde Martin, "Playing the Pictures," *Film Index,* 29 October 1910, 7.

9. Clyde Martin, "Playing the Pictures," *Film Index,* 19 November 1910, 27.

10. Personnel for the Library of Congress Living Nickelodeon performance were Rick Altman, director and pianist; Corey Creekmur, trap drummer (sound effects); Ann R. Lamond, song illustrator (soprano); and Lauren Rabinovitz, projectionist.

24 Music for Kalem Films: The Special Scores, with Notes on Walter C. Simon

Herbert Reynolds

In 1907, its first year of operation, the Kalem Company prepared a music score for its production of *The Merry Widow;* thereafter, the company commissioned an unusually enterprising series of scores for films from 1911 to 1916. Any consideration of the Kalem scores naturally draws our attention to the work of Walter C. Simon, who was responsible for the majority of the scores and thereby stakes his claim as America's first regular composer of film music.

From the longer list that concludes this report, I can identify four cases where a Kalem film survives (at least in part) along with the music score written specifically to accompany it. All four scores are for piano solo, were composed in 1912 by Walter Simon, and are among the Copyright Office holdings of the Music Division of the Library of Congress in Washington. In recent years we have had presentations of each of these films with its score. A highlight of the Fifth Domitor Conference at the Library of Congress in June 1998 was the first modern exhibition of all four, which derived special interest from their historic venue, the newly restored Coolidge Auditorium in the Jefferson Building, and from the gifted pianism of Martin M. Marks.[1]

The archival sources for the surviving films, each in 35mm and one reel long, are given below; prints were gathered for the conference by Patrick G. Loughney, Head of the Motion Image Section at the Library. *Captured by Bedouins* was directed by Sidney Olcott, his unit traveling in Egypt (Cairo and Luxor) and on the Mediterranean Sea, with a cast including Gene Gauntier, J. P. McGowan, Jack Clark, and Robert Vignola. The other three films, all American Civil War subjects exploiting the fiftieth anniversary of that conflict, were directed by Kenean Buel in the vicinity of Kalem's Jacksonville, Florida, production site, and feature Anna Q. Nilsson, Miriam Cooper (except in *Susanna*), Guy Coombs, and Hal Clements.

Captured by Bedouins	(released June 26, 1912). British Film Institute, London (Roles Collection), and Library of Congress, Washington; both prints derive from the same negative at the BFI. The BFI copy is edited clean of repeated footage caused by laboratory "pullbacks" during printing. A

second BFI print (Scottish Film Council/James Graham Collection) is catalogued as being less complete.

The Siege of Petersburg (July 22, 1912) was originally two reels, of which Reel 1 survives. The British Film Institute print (Bert Langdon Collection) is just slightly more complete than a second print of the same reel at the Library of Congress (AFI/Cromwell Collection).

The Soldier Brothers of Susanna (July 31, 1912). British Film Institute.

The Confederate Ironclad (October 5, 1912). George Eastman House, Rochester, N.Y. A 16mm reduction of this print is distributed by the Museum of Modern Art Circulating Film Library, New York.

Through his practical experience of rehearsing and performing these four, Marks discovered that Simon's scores contain more than enough measures of music to fill individual scenes in the films, so that a comfortable pacing of film projection with piano accompaniment requires the film to be run as slowly as possible, while avoiding noticeable flicker onscreen. For Marks's playing of these scores at the Library of Congress, David Reese, the Library's Film Technician, achieved the requisite balance with a projection speed of 14 to 15 frames per second. To my eyes and ears, this minimal rate proved ideal for presenting these films with their scores—and it offers empirical testimony (however unexpected) to the projection speeds of 1912. For an audience observing the films in the sequence of their original release, the synthesis of music and image seemed to grow increasingly effective with every work, reaching a peak in the rousing melodrama of *The Confederate Ironclad*, a film whose action I had always found too frenetic at higher velocities.

In November 1999, the Museum of Modern Art in New York screened the same film at a more conventional rate, close to 18 frames per second, with Stuart Oderman playing Simon's score.[2] While the choice of projection speed may remain a subjective decision for the best viewing of this picture (Steven Higgins, Curator in the Museum's Department of Film and Video, takes issue with my preference for the slower rate for these films), this new occasion brought fresh insight and corroboration to the experience of its performance with Simon's music. As a professional accompanist for silent films for forty-two years, thirty of them at the Museum, Oderman is an heir to the legions of pianists who played in early cinemas and can offer a living example of the routine and vicissitudes of performing practice such as must have obtained during the early period. To begin with, he performed Simon's score for *The Confederate Ironclad* all but "cold," having had no opportunity to see the score, nor the film itself, before arriving for the evening's presentation; a short review of the score beforehand was his only preparation. It's easy to believe that such must often have been the case with contemporary pianists, if only for the first of several traversals during a commercial run of the picture. That challenge notwithstanding, Oderman has related to me his excitement and gratitude for the rare chance to play music specifically intended for a film of 1912—this is the earliest original film score he has seen—and so I take his misgivings about Simon's method of composition as a telling observation.

Oderman points out that Simon introduces as many as four themes to be played with a given segment of the film when a single theme would have sufficed: a pianist can find himself playing for the duration of a scene without using all the material the composer supplied. Of the superabundance of music to go with the picture, Oderman drolly recalled the emperor's alleged admonishment to Mozart: "Too many notes, Mr. Simon." If Simon's musical capabilities are decidedly more earthbound than Mozart's, his ambitions may still have placed uncomfortable demands on pianists of his day, many of whom, Oderman believes, would have been unable to sight-read the music, with or without the luxury of a rehearsal. (As accomplished a musician as Marks still made sure to preview each film and note carefully where cues given in its score correspond to scene changes in the film.) Regular accompanists grow accustomed to using themes they like and know by heart. Moreover, it's difficult to imagine that the motion picture pianist could have dictated the speed of the projector, when a faster rate was certain to guarantee extra shows every day.[3] The projection rate could also vary widely through the duration of the film, and throughout its run. In the absence of a standardized speed (which would enable later movie composers to time segments with a stopwatch), Simon could only guess the length of any scene.

Walter Cleveland Simon joined the American Society of Composers, Authors, and Publishers in 1924. During his lifetime, his entry in *The ASCAP Biographical Dictionary of Composers, Authors, and Publishers* gave his place of birth on October 27, 1884, as Cincinnati, Ohio. Later editions report his death in New York City on March 5, 1958, and in the most recent, his native city is said to have been Lexington, Kentucky. It is in Lexington that Simon recalled "many years [as] pianist & organist in motion picture theatres, beginning [in] 1896, specializing in sound effects." (He would have celebrated his twelfth birthday that year.) Educated at Pittsburgh College of Music and the New England Conservatory, he claimed to have been "first to play pipe organ in [a] motion picture theatre, Bronx, N.Y., 1912."[4] It is near the end of the previous year when we can be sure he began composing "Special Music" for the Kalem office in New York.

As distinguished from cue-sheets or suggested titles of pre-existing themes, "special music" and "special score" were the terms used within the American film industry of the early 1910s for a music score specifically prepared and supplied by the producing firm (or perhaps by a distributor) to accompany an individual film. Such scores may have been original compositions, arrangements of music compiled from other sources, or a combination of the two (as seems likely to have been the usual case). A score might be cued to a film for performance by piano solo, other solo instrument, or instrumental group (piano and drums being especially popular). As will be clear from my ensuing catalogue of

THE CONFEDERATE IRONCLAD

24.1. Page one of Kalem's copyrighted piano score for *The Confederate Ironclad* (5 October 1912), composed by Walter C. Simon, its original music blended with borrowed tunes (here, "That Railroad Rag") and cued to changes of scene. (U.S. Copyright Office holdings, Music Division, Library of Congress).

Kalem's prepared music scores, Walter Simon can be identified as the composer of the great majority. It is tempting to think he was responsible for virtually all of them, for only one score can definitely be attributed to anyone else. In spite of the challenges illuminated by recent performances discussed above, a recurring refrain below, as throughout Kalem's announcements, is that the music was "simply arranged, so any pianist can play it."

The Kalem "Special Music" Scores
and the Contribution of Walter C. Simon

Martin Marks provides a model for this roster in *Music and the Silent Film* (New York: Oxford University Press, 1997), Appendix 4, 194–196. His list for 1911–1913 offers strict chronology; data on copyright registration, length, and the number of musical segments for almost all of the surviving scores; and references to *Moving Picture World* (hereafter, abbreviated *MPW*). The following groupings by category, on the other hand, violate chronology in only three instances—designated by (a), (b), (c), and where they occur chronologically by (*a*), (*b*), (*c*)—and expand Marks's list with additional scores and references.

All scores are for piano solo, with four exceptions as noted (for *Arrah-Na-Pogue* and *War's Havoc*); and the length of each release is one reel (1000 feet), unless specified. Following a title is the film's release date (or, on two occasions, the date of its first showing); "Special" before a release date denotes a film distributed exclusively by the General Film Company rather than directly through exchanges (a few other films evidently were distributed both ways). In addition, I have inserted each film's director, based on my own recognition during a period before such credit was regularly acknowledged. Where a score is mentioned in the *Kalem Kalendar* (the company's distribution bulletin, abbreviated as *KK*), this is indicated, in order to establish here the record of Kalem's most direct communications to exhibitors. Where it is necessary to look beyond the *Kalendar* for information that contributes substantially to our knowledge, I have added another source. Each entry concludes with the price of the score, and further remarks as appropriate. Surviving films are highlighted by an asterisk (*).

1907–08: 1 score by an unidentified arranger, no © application on file.
  The Merry Widow (first shown Jan. 20, 1908, released Jan. 25; director uncertain, possibly Sidney Olcott). Predates publication of *KK*. Kalem ad, *MPW*, 28 Dec. 1907, p. 704: "Accompanying the film will be *a complete musical score* [for] a pianist and a singer" (emphasis in the original). Price, if any, unknown. This score's arranger may have been Theodore Lipscher, the music director for the performers Kalem filmed.[5]

1911: 1 score by Simon, 1 questionable case (*The Colleen Bawn*, q.v.); no © applications on file.

For *The Colleen Bawn** (Oct. 16, 1911, 3 reels; Sidney Olcott), the evidence at hand suggests that Kalem endorsed (perhaps even prepared) a list of "music suggestions" or cue-sheet, but not a full score. The film was released two months before publication of the *Kalem Kalendar* began, but "News Items" in the issue of 22 Dec. 1911, p. 6, recalls "the recommendation of old Irish airs to be played" with it, as distinguished from the "special arrangement" composed for *Arrah-Na-Pogue*. These "airs" may be the ones published by the music columnist Clarence Sinn, crediting them "courtesy of Mr. Grover Kayhart"—who therefore would seem to have been their compiler ("Music for the Picture," *MPW*, 21 Oct. 1911, p. 200). Months later, Sinn mentions *The Colleen Bawn* within a group of films, others of which had "special scores" ("Music for the Picture," *MPW*, 25 May 1912, p. 717), but (if he is not wholly in error) he could be thinking of a printed list of recommendations, such as *KK* implies. As to the unconventional possibility of a score composed subsequent to the release of the film, no such score was cited in *KK*, not even when the film was re-released early in 1914 (and then announced in *KK*, 15 Feb. 1914, p. 20; 1 March 1914, pp. 2–3, 4; in *MPW*, 31 Jan. 1914, p. 557; 7 March 1914, pp. 1202, 1210; and posted on an extant lithograph in the Theater Collection, Philadelphia Free Library). In the *ASCAP Biographical Dictionary*, Walter Simon referred to himself as "composer of first original music score published for a motion picture, *Arrah Na Pough* [*sic*]."[6]

> *Arrah-Na-Pogue* (Dec. 4, 1911, 3 reels; Sidney Olcott). *KK*, 15 Dec. 1911, p. 16, and 22 Dec. 1911, p. 16: "the work of a well known composer . . . carefully cued . . . a piano score and four-piece orchestration"; 22 Dec. 1911, p. 6. *MPW*'s note, 18 Nov. 1911, p. 536, and Kalem's ad, 25 Nov. 1911, p. 613, credit "Walter C. Simons [*sic*]." 50¢

1912: 14 scores copyrighted (for 16 film titles), all extant; 13 by Simon, the exception (*"Fighting Dan" McCool*) by M. Komroff. See explanation following this group.

> *A Spartan Mother* (March 11; Kenean Buel). *KK*, 12 Feb., 3: "by an eminent composer"; 19 Feb., 2: "by Mr. W. C. Simon, a well known composer . . . accurately cued for each change of scene and simply arranged, so any pianist can play it"; 2 March, pp. 4, 10; 1 May, p. 8 (among group of four); 1 June, p. 12 (group of six). Report in *MPW*, 2 March 1912, pp. 770–771: "a careful blending of a number of patriotic airs with other appropriate music." 25¢

> *The Spanish Revolt of 1836* (April 3; George Melford). *KK*, 2 March, p. 15; 30 March, p. 16; 1 May, p. 8 (among group of four); 1 June, p. 12 (group of six). 25¢ Simon is named on Kalem's © application.

> (*a*) *"Fighting Dan" McCool* (May 13; Buel). *KK*, 13 April, p. 15: "simply arranged and accurately cued"; 1 May, p. 8 (among group of four); 1 June, p. 12 (group of six). 25¢ This score is by M. Komroff (see paragraph following).

> *Under a Flag of Truce* (May 24; Buel). *KK*, 1 May, p. 7; 1 June, p. 12 (among group of six). 25¢ The correct © assignment is Cl[ass] E 284865.

> *The Fighting Dervishes of the Desert* (May 27; Olcott). *KK*, 13 April, p. 10: "[By] an eminent composer . . . arranged so that any pianist can play it"; 1 May, p. 10, 15 May, p. 10, and 1 June, p. 10: "The arranger of Kalem's special music has quite outdone himself in preparing this score"; 1 June, p. 12 (among group of six). Report in *MPW*, 1 June 1912, p. 826: "The composer, Mr. W. C. Simon, presided at the piano" at an exhibition screening. 25¢

(*b*) *The Drummer Girl of Vicksburg* (June 5; Buel). *KK,* 15 May, p. 15: "'fine music with a fine picture' . . . simply arranged." 25¢

An Arabian Tragedy (June 19; Olcott). *KK,* 1 June, p. 14. 25¢ Simon is named on Kalem's © application.

*Captured by Bedouins** (June 26; Olcott). Score not noted in *KK* (1 June, p. 11) but in Kalem ad, *MPW,* 15 June, p. 1002. 25¢

Tragedy of the Desert (Special, July 1, 2 reels; Olcott). *KK,* 13 April, p. 10 (under an earlier title, "Dust of the Desert"): "[By] an eminent composer . . . arranged so that any pianist can play it"; 15 June, p. 16: "'fine music with a fine picture.'" 25¢ (The title change is confirmed by Gene Gauntier, "Blazing the Trail," typescript, 155, Film Study Center Special Collections, Museum of Modern Art) [omitted as published in *Woman's Home Companion,* February 1929].

The Bugler of Battery B. and *Hungry Hank's Hallucination* (July 10, split reel; *Bugler* directed by Buel; *Hank* uncertain, possibly by P. C. Hartigan). *KK,* 15 June, p. 10. 25¢

A Prisoner of The Harem and *Egyptian Sports* (July 19, split reel; Olcott.) *KK,* 1 July, p. 10. 25¢ Simon is named on Kalem's © application.

*The Siege of Petersburg** (Special, July 22, 2 reels; Buel). *KK,* 15 July, p. 16: "two complete piano scores—one for each reel . . . [with] no increase in the regular rate for feature music." 25¢ (Only the first reel of this film is extant.)

*The Soldier Brothers of Susanna** (July 31; Buel). *KK,* 1 July, p. 12. 25¢

(*c*) *The Confederate Ironclad** (Oct. 5; Buel). *KK,* 1 Sept., p. 14. 25¢

In the U.S. Copyright Office files at the Library of Congress, Washington, I have located the original application card that Kalem filled out for each of the fourteen scores above. (These cards are the basis for the published compilations, the *Catalogue of Copyright Entries.*) In 1912, the application asked, "State exactly on what new matter copyright is claimed (see Sec. 6 of Act of 1909)," to which Kalem's response, without exception, was "Re-arrangement and new matter." To the application's inquiry, "Author of new copyrighted matter," Kalem simply replied, "U.S. Citizen," adding the name "Walter C. Simon" in only three cases, as shown above. Far more importantly, because copyright law required that copies of these scores be deposited with the Copyright Office, copies of all now survive among the Copyright Office holdings of the Library's Music Division, and these scores all name their composers. In his examination of Kalem's copyrighted scores, Marks corroborates Gillian B. Anderson, *Music for Silent Films, 1894–1929: A Guide* (Washington: Library of Congress, 1988): thirteen acknowledge "Music by Walter C. Simon"; the exception, *"Fighting Dan" McCool,* reads "Music by M. Komroff." (For Komroff, I found no copyright applications submitted directly by anyone of this name, nor of any name beginning with "Komr," for the period 1898–1937.)[7] Beyond these fourteen, the only copyright application on file for Kalem is for *The Black Crook* in 1916 (below). As was idiomatic within the film industry of the time, the contents of a split reel formed a single release and were regarded as an entirety; thus, both titles on each of the two split reels above are included on a single copyright application, and the score for the entire reel was issued a single copyright number.

1912–13: scores for 5 or 6 films, composer(s) unknown; no © applications on file. (*From the Manger to the Cross* is the uncertain case, q.v.)

(a) *War's Havoc* (April 15, 1912; Buel). *KK*, 16 March 1912, p. 8: "'exceptional music with an exceptional picture'"; 30 March 1912, p. 16; 1 May 1912, p. 8 (among group of four); 1 June 1912, 12 (group of six). Scores for piano, 25¢; piano and drums, 35¢; piano and orchestration for violin, clarinet, cornet, and drums, 50¢

(c) *The Prison Ship* (Aug. 16, 1912; probably Buel). *KK*, 15 July 1912, p. 12. 25¢

From the Manger to the Cross* (shown Oct. 14, 1912, prior to General Film release; Olcott). *KK*, 15 Oct. 1912, p. 8: Music presented for special screening, New York. Gene Gauntier, "Blazing the Trail," *Woman's Home Companion* (March 1929): 146, and its typescript, 217: "a musical score [was] prepared." W. Stephen Bush, *MPW,* 26 Oct. 1912, p. 324: "A musical program has been compiled." Whether a full score or a cue-sheet, this unique performance at least included organ and vocal quartet. Other gala exhibitions featured differing musical accompaniment, however, and no score is known to have been offered for distribution with the film.[8]

The Shaughraun (Dec. 23, 1912, 3 reels; Olcott). *KK*, 1 Dec. 1912, p. 10: "Kalem's famous composer . . . prepare[d] an unusually impressive musical arrangement." 50¢ (I cannot confirm the assignment of this score to Simon by Kevin Rockett, *The Irish Filmography* [Dublin: Red Mountain Media, 1996].)

The Cheyenne Massacre (Special, May 9, 1913, 2 reels; Melford). *KK*, 1 May 1913, p. 6. 15¢

The Battle for Freedom (Special, May 17, 1913, 2 reels; Melford). *KK*, 1 May 1913, p. 12; 15 May 1913, p. 7. 15¢

Beginning in June 1912, Kalem announced it would offer special music with *all* its "features." (See "Special Music for the Features," *KK*, 15 June 1912, p. 14; p.14 in subsequent issues; "Fine Music with a Fine Picture!" 15 July 1912, p. 8; and, e.g., Kalem's ad for *Captured by Bedouins,** *MPW,* 15 June 1912, p. 1002.) Yet the evidence of actual scores is lacking. Following Kalem's announcement, here are the first seven films billed as "Coming Features" in *KK* with no proof of an accompanying score (with more examples to come in 1913): *The Darling of The C.S.A.* (Sept. 7, 1912), *The Street Singer* (Sept. 13, 1912), *The Grit of The Girl Telegrapher** (Sept. 21, 1912), *The Rival Engineers* (Oct. 19, 1912), *The Kerry Gow* (Nov. 18, 1912), *The Indian Uprising at Santa Fe* (Dec. 21, 1912), and *The Wives of Jamestown* (Jan. 10, 1913). (*KK*, 1 Aug.–16 Dec. 1912, *passim;* the one exception within this run of *KK* is *The Confederate Ironclad** [Oct. 5, 1912], which was billed as "A Coming Feature" along with a notice about its piano score: *KK*, 1 Sept. 1912, p. 14.)

1912–15: 4 scores credited to Simon by contemporary sources; no © applications
on file.
  (b) *Missionaries in Darkest Africa* (June 3, 1912; Olcott). Score not noted in
     KK (15 May 1912, p. 12) but in Kalem ad, *MPW,* 25 May 1912, p. 702.
     Report in *MPW,* 1 June 1912, p. 826: "The composer, Mr. W. C. Simon,
     presided at the piano" at a private screening. 25¢
  The Tragedy of Big Eagle Mine (Special, June 7, 1913, 2 reels; Melford). *KK,* 1
     June 1913, p. 7: "arranged by Walter C. Simon, the originator of special
     photoplay scores." 15¢
  Motion Picture Dancing Lessons (29 Oct. 1913, 3 reels; director uncertain,
     possibly Robert Vignola). *KK,* 15 Oct. 1913, pp. 2, 10; 1 Nov. 1913, p. 4.
     Featured review in *MPW,* 18 Oct. 1913, p. 248: "Assisted by Prof. Walter
     Simon at the piano," with photograph. Price unknown.
  Midnight at Maxim's (July 12, 1915, 4 reels; George L. Sargent) *KK,* Aug.
     1915, p. 26: "Two Dollars' Worth. . . . This is the music which is played
     nightly at Maxim's, Rector's, and Bustanoby's Cabarets[,] and which was
     used when the[se] dance numbers . . . were filmed. . . . 37 pages"; July
     1915, p. 18, Aug. 1915, p. 24, and Sept 1915, p. 6: "arranged." Note in
     MPW, 24 July 1915, p. 630: "an elaborate piano score . . . written by
     Walter C. Simon." 50¢

1916: 1 score copyrighted and extant; by Simon.
  The Black Crook (Jan. 10, 1916, 5 reels; Robert Vignola). Score not mentioned
     in *KK* (Nov. 1915, p. 16; *KK* ceased publication with the subsequent
     issue) but noted in Kalem ads, *MPW,* 25 Dec. 1915, p. 2324, and 1 Jan.
     1916, p. 16. Simon's performing his score on organ is reviewed in *MPW,*
     15 Jan. 1916, p. 430. Simon is named on Kalem's © application, as well as
     the surviving score, © Cl. E 376817. Price unknown ("at cost price": ad,
     MPW, 1 Jan. 1916, p. 16).

Besides *Arrah-Na-Pogue, The Black Crook* is the only score for Kalem that
Simon listed among his credits in the *ASCAP Biographical Dictionary.*

From 1915 to 1922, Walter C. Simon copyrighted four additional works in his own
     name within the copyright period of 1898–1937.
  "Society Dramas; special music for one reel motion pictures; piano"; pub-
     lished 7 April 1915, © Cl. E 361006.
  "The Phototune; piano"; published 25 July 1916, © Cl. E 387690.
  "Progress studies, no. 5; piano"; unpublished, copy received 8 July 1919, ©
     Cl. E 453186.
  "Original organ works, combinations and imitations"; unpublished, copy
     received 21 Feb. 1922, © Cl. E 529811.

The latter application, in the name of Walter Cleveland Simon, bears a signature that is recognizably consistent with the previous three: highly cursive,
with a looped beginning and bottoms on its *W,* a curled start to its *C,* and exe-
cuted in a single stroke without lifting the pen from the page. Each application

gives a different address, so, while all are in the vicinity of New York City, it is the unmistakable handwriting that unites them and distinguishes this Walter Simon from other copyright applicants during this period: a Walter C. Simon of New Orleans ("The Sponge; two step; piano," 1910), who may be the W. C. Simon of Detroit with two 1912 copyrights (a song, "I Don't Want You No Mo'," and "Sponge Rag [Revised Edition]"); and a Walter C. Simon of York, Pennsylvania ("March Continental; p[iano]f[orte]" in 1926), who printed his name in capitals in lieu of a signature. (There is a Walter B. in St. Louis with copyrights in 1929 and 1930.)

Walter Cleveland Simon renewed the copyrights for many of his Kalem scores beginning in 1940.[9] None of the four copyrighted works immediately above is among his compositions in the *ASCAP Biographical Dictionary*, where he cited three works for piano, "Jack in the Box," "Fleur de Lys," and "Gay Cavalier," and one for violin, "Ecstasy," besides a half dozen titles from a "large catalogue of mood music used in motion picture productions." In later life, he "specialized in recitals of traditional movie music, demonstrating with old silent films [the] technique of the nickelodeons." The film scores he wished to be remembered for are *Arrah-Na-Pogue* and *The Black Crook* (both for Kalem), *The Hunchback of Notre Dame, Ben Hur,* and *The Last Days of Pompeii.*[10]

Notes

A longer version of this text, "Aural Gratification with Kalem Films: A Case History of Music, Lectures, and Sound Effects, 1907–1917," which places music scores within a broader historical context of all varieties of sound accompaniment, appears in *Film History* 12, no. 4 (2000), where the present catalogue of special music scores is included, in a slightly different form, as Appendix 2. The author would like to thank the editors as well as all those, too numerous to reiterate here, whose assistance is acknowledged within the longer work.

1. Marks first recognized the originality of Simon's music, reporting on the composer and his score for Kalem's *An Arabian Tragedy* (1912) in *Music and the Silent Film* (New York: Oxford University Press, 1997). Of the scores for surviving films, he offered his insights into *Captured by Bedouins* and *The Confederate Ironclad* in "The First American Film Scores," *Harvard Library Bulletin*, new series 2, no. 4 (Winter 1991), 78–100.

2. The specific event at the Museum of Modern Art was a lecture I gave on 19 November 1999, entitled "Just Off the Stage?: The Theater and the Camera in *Ben Hur* and Other Kalem Productions," which functioned as a component of the large exhibition organized by Steven Higgins, "From Automatic Vaudeville to the Seventh Art." I am grateful to Steven Higgins for making this presentation possible, and to Stuart Oderman for sharing his comments on the score to *The Confederate Ironclad.*

3. There are 16 frames to the foot on 35mm stock; *The Confederate Ironclad* was advertised at the standard 1000-foot length. At 15 frames per second (56

feet per minute), this reel runs just under 17.8 minutes, whereas at 18 frames per second (67 feet per minute) it requires only 14.8 minutes, saving 3 minutes and allowing six performances in place of five for every 89 minutes of actual projection. (With additional time required for any other items on the bill and clearing the house between shows.)

4. Early editions of *The A[merican] S[ociety of] C[omposers,] A[uthors, and] P[ublishers] Biographical Dictionary . . .* (1st and 2nd eds., New York: Thomas Y. Crowell, 1948 and 1952; 3rd ed., New York: ASCAP, 1966) give Cincinnati. The 3rd and 4th editions (New York: Bowker, 1980) cite his death, the latter amending his birthplace to Louisville, Kentucky. Catherine A. Surowiec alerted me to the usefulness of this source.

5. Theodore Lipscher, affidavit, 18 March 1908, *Henry W. Savage v. Kalem Co., Inc. and Miles Bros., Inc.,* U.S. Circuit Court, Southern District of New York, Equity Vol. 2–187, National Archives—Northeast Region, New York.

6. My conclusion about *The Colleen Bawn* differs with Marks's, *Music and the Silent Film,* 76ff. and 194 (Appendix 4).

7. For more on Komroff, see Marks, 260, n.54.

8. See Herbert Reynolds, "Aural Gratification with Kalem Films: A Case History of Music, Lectures, and Effects, 1907–1917," *Film History* 12, no. 4 (2000), n.44, also n.22.

9. Gillian B. Anderson, *Music for Silent Films, 1894–1929: A Guide* (Washington, D.C.: Library of Congress, 1988), indicates Simon's copyright renewals of his scores for Kalem.

10. *ASCAP Biographical Dictionary . . .* (the 4th edition varies in its inclusion of details). Simon's actual contribution to the three non-Kalem films remains uncertain.

25 The Orchestration of Affect: The Motif of Barbarism in Breil's *The Birth of a Nation* Score

Jane Gaines and Neil Lerner

The controversy over Griffith's *The Birth of a Nation*, the documented social strife and turmoil that followed in its wake from its 1915 premiere until the present, has largely been considered only in relation to its images. Generally discussions of the controversy have singled out particular images, often focusing on the censored shots or sections ("leering Negroes" or the "Gus chase scene"). Surprisingly, there has been no real discussion of either the melodramatic structure or that aspect of the melodramatic that would be so significant in this case: the orchestral score. While understanding that the most famous of the *Birth of a Nation* scores was a compiled score, consisting of a pastiche of borrowed tunes together with original music,[1] our interest here will be particular features of Joseph Carl Breil's original composition.[2] We want to single out for analysis one of the musical motifs written by Breil, that motif that has, on at least one occasion, been referred to as the "Negro theme." In the excerpts from the piano score published in 1916 (for domestic use), this melody is identified as the "Motif of Barbarism."[3]

Martin Marks, in his monumental work on silent film music, has already helped us to identify this motif, calling it to our attention as the identifying title given to the musical theme in the J. D. Chappell publication of selections from Breil's score.[4] Further, Marks notes the way the term "primitive" was so often used as an adjective to describe the film itself and suggests that another connotation lurks here in the film's attitude toward its black characters. But whereas Marks implies that "primitive" is assigned to the black characters as an attribute, he never really comes out and says that the film, through the use of the musical motif of barbarism, would have helped to characterize the black characters as "barbaric."[5] What we have tried to do in the following analysis of the Breil score is to show where and how this happens, for in our analysis, we have discovered that the use of this musical formation in conjunction with each of the key black characters is systematic and extreme. We cannot hope to understand the way in which this film divided and tore apart American communities in the early years of its reception without careful consideration of this particular musical motif, which most likely made such a significant contribution to the heating of passions. It is astounding that with so much written about the

NAACP (National Association for the Advancement of Colored People) protest and the threat of riots around the film that no one has suggested a linkage between social unrest and the performance of the Breil score in any of its several forms.[6] Breil's score was clearly an "orchestration" of the melodramatic effect, and we need to consider the ways it might have manipulated feelings in these early audiences.

Before we go on to consider this motif, however, we need to deal with the problem of the multiple scores for *The Birth of a Nation*. The problem begins with the fact that the renowned score was not the very first score that accompanied the film in 1915. Marks has clarified the situation for us, arguing that it was probably Carli D. Elinor who contributed significantly although not exclusively to the production of the score that accompanied the film, then called *The Clansman*, at its Clune's Auditorium premiere in Los Angeles on February 8, 1915.[7] The Breil score was used at the March 3, 1915 premiere at the Liberty Theatre in New York, where the film played for the first time as *The Birth of a Nation*.[8] A third score may have been produced for the revival of the film at the Capital Theatre in New York in 1921, but scholars know the least about this score, and it only takes on significance here as we attempt to consider who heard it when.[9] Even the existence of a printed musical score—the MOMA-LC piano conductor score—does not normally (there is, however, a notable exception in this score) provide definitive information on precisely what music would have accompanied which image, because, as was often the case with early printed scores, there was not enough printed music to sound throughout the visual sequence in each cue. A musical director (or pianist or organist, depending on the venue) would have made decisions on what parts of the music to repeat, and what tempos to take, in order to provide continuous music within a given cue (but this is to assume that music, whenever present, was always continuous, a premise problematized by Rick Altman).[10] The original film to which the Breil score corresponds no longer exists. But perhaps it is better to say that the *films* no longer exist, since in the early years of the film's release, the years in which the Breil score would have been performed in key cities, slightly different versions of the film may have been featured in the theatrical road show. We will momentarily return to this question of the censorship and cutting of the film, but suffice it to say, the historical instability of this film presents contemporary challenges for the analyst.

Given that the musical "text" for *The Birth of a Nation* is never fixed and singular—just as there is no single filmic version—one should exercise considerable caution when drawing interpretive significance from the correspondence between images and musical motifs. For instance, the musical motifs that correspond with certain images on the Kino version are occasionally different from the motifs prescribed by Breil in the MOMA-LC score. This question of which precise images were seen in conjunction with which sounds is a relatively new issue, one important for scholars writing histories of silent film accompaniment that attempt to reconstruct original reception conditions. Further, we have attempted to work as well with a published version of *The Birth of a Nation*'s

Continuity Script (hereafter CS), a version that corresponds with the Museum of Modern Art's 16mm circulation print.[11] While based then on documentary sources (the continuity script and the earliest surviving printed score), our analysis of the "Motif of Barbarism" should be tempered with the understanding that variations would, could, and will exist between image and music.

The unmistakable "Motif of Barbarism" is particularly crucial to our understanding of the Breil score performances because it so literally "sets the tone" (see Fig. 25.1). Intended for use under the introductory title, "The bringing of the African to America planted the first seed of disunion," (CS 7), the motif reappears throughout the entire film score. It could be seen (or heard?) as the overarching premise that guides the entire narrative. The next image (CS 8) is identified as "tableau of a minister praying over manacled slaves to be auctioned in a town square. Fade out." The musical motif encapsulates the narrative in other terms. As closer analysis will show, it can be heard to say, "First there was black African barbarism and then it was conquered by white European forces."

Breil's own account of the derivation of the musical ideas that became this motif only confirms the political implications of these particular musical structures. But perhaps more interestingly, it suggests the process through which musics are transmitted from folk culture to high culture to mass culture, a transmission that always involves an elaborate filtering. In his unfinished essay, "On Motion Picture Music," Breil recalls the difficulty he had in formulating the musical themes that were to accompany Griffith's photograph images of his black characters.[12] So it was from Griffith that he pulled the musical ideas, since the director "had spend [sic] his boyhood days on a Kentucky plantation." Breil listened to the director "hum and chant some of the old croons of [the] mammies and [the] loose jointed young plantation negroes which he still remembered in a vague sort of way." And it was after listening to Griffith sing his version of black folk music that Breil was able to compose "the theme which opens the film . . . and which is thereafter ever applied to the description of the primitive instincts of the blacks."[13] It is interesting to note Breil's choice of the word "applied" to the relationship between the music and the images, an interesting avoidance of any terminology that might suggest music-image equivalence or even confirmation of the connotations of barbarism. It would seem that the barbarism music is not "applied" directly to the imagery but is rather "applied" to the description. Breil wants to think that his music works at the connotative rather than the denotative level—that is, it is added on top of the meanings exuded by Griffith's characterizations (and understanding that music seems only to work at the connotative level, as a second order signifying system). Breil may have thus found a way of distancing his music from certain aspects of the film while at the same time acknowledging the formulaic function of the score.

It is not surprising that Breil would not think in terms of elementary semiotics in his own understanding of how he might have encoded his music to produce a particular meaning. This cultural studies approach, which separates encoding from decoding, would be basic to film studies but has only recently been

25.1. "Motif of Barbarism," first appearance (MOMA-LC, p. 1).

applied to music.[14] The question as to how far apart musicology stands from film theory is beyond the scope of this essay, but immediately when we talk about the production of musical stereotypage or the encoding of a cliché, we encounter two different understandings that overlap and diverge. Whereas in film theory the emphasis on popular culture has produced the concept of stereotype as purely descriptive of the employment of cultural codes, in musicology the concept may still carry an evaluative overtone. There seems no way around this dilemma since to insert the more neutral concept of "typage" may cause confusion. Nevertheless, the encoding of the motif that carries the connotation of "primitivism" works like a traditional characterological stereotype, as in the example of Austin Stoneman's music (see Fig. 25.2). Such a musical stereotype points forward as well as backward in the narrative. As Marks's analysis of this music reveals (152–155), Austin Stoneman's minor-mode motif contains musical elements that reveal unseen dimensions of his character: its continuously rising melodies match his political ambition, and its turn to the unexpected harmony of D-flat minor (in measure 4 of Fig. 25.2) hints at something unpredictable, even ominous. The weightiness of Austin's motif stands in stark contrast to the lightness of his daughter Elsie's motif (there are musical contrasts in tempo, timbre, meter, and mode), and as Marks points out, the elision of Austin's theme directly into Elsie's "seems to symbolize the kinship between father and daughter" (153). Breil's reliance upon traditional harmonic syntax, in particular the powerful relationship of the dominant and tonic chords, serves to emphasize further the father/daughter connection in the film; no matter what other musical/character contrasts exist, Elsie's motif is unmistakably connected to her father's. Clearly Breil's motifs are rich in signifying potential and are fully deserving of closer musical analysis.

While we may be able to establish that Breil and Griffith encoded the musical premise that connotes "primitivism," it is somewhat more difficult to understand exactly how the music would have been decoded by audience members, even though we are assuming shared cultural references. Politics inserts itself here since it is clear that we are talking about a highly ideological musical encoding, one that characterizes Negro characters as less than human. That the "Motif of Barbarism" would have been *heard* as distinct from other motifs and would have been "read" as carrying particular connotations may not be that difficult to establish since several historical accounts of hearing the Breil score performed as part of the film exhibition do exist. There is, of course, tremendous difficulty in relying on written accounts of music recollected over time for any theory of musical reception (and even without the passage of time, verbal descriptions of music are infamously ambiguous and elusive). To the factor of dimming memory we would need to add the factor of selective reception, or, better, political receptivity, that aspect of reading we hesitate to call simply subjective, particularly since these listening accounts have fallen so clearly on one or the other side of the political divide. A reviewer for the *New York Independent* clearly signaled out the "Motif of Barbarism" when he thus described and criticized the score:

> Music lends insidious aid to emphasize the teaching of the screen, for the tom-tom beats from time to time convince us that the colored man, well drest and educated though he may be, came from Africa.[15]

On top of his basic reading of the music, this listener adds an astute political analysis. In direct contrast with the interpretative hearing of the reviewer for the *New York Independent* is that of Thomas Dixon, author of *The Clansman* and *The Leopard's Spots,* the two novels that it is well known provided the basis for much of Griffith's narrative. Dixon recalls hearing this score at New York's Liberty Theatre with a small group of seventy-five, apparently just before the March 3 premiere of the film in New York, the premiere that featured Breil directing his newly composed score.[16] As Dixon remembers the impact of the film on him, "the last light dimmed, a weird cry came from the abyss below—the first note of the orchestra, a low cry of the anguished South being put to torture." The score for him was "the throb through the darkness . . . raising the emotional power to undreamed heights." It was, to him, "uncanny."[17] We will return to the question of the significance of this piece of music for Dixon, but more immediately we want to know what musical signifiers carried the connotations that were read by Dixon as "uncanny."

What did Dixon see and what did he hear? The "Motif of Barbarism," you will recall, accompanies the first moving images of the entire film: the tableau of a minister standing in prayer above African slaves who kneel before him (CS 7). In this first occurrence, the normally four-measure motif has a three-measure phrase added to it (mm. 5–7 in Fig. 25.1), a phrase that occurs only

T. In 1860 A great parliamentary leader

25.2. Motifs for Austin and Elsie Stoneman (MOMA-LC, pp. 1–2).

during this first iteration of the motif and that could be read as signifying the alleged "civilizing" influence of the minister. Several features of this music contribute to the signification of "primitivism," the meaning heard by the New York reviewer. Most noticeable in its first appearance is the insistent tom-tom beating underneath a mildly syncopated melody, a rhythmic effect (syncopation) created by the accenting of the weak part of the first beat in measure one. The origins of this kind of syncopation are important to recall since they draw our attention to the question of the cultural history of musical connotations. African musical traditions are rich in their use of cross-rhythms and polyrhythms, rhythms that produce syncopations, and it has been widely argued that African syncopation has had a profound influence on American popular music from the nineteenth century to the present.[18] As we will see, in *The Birth of a Nation*, syncopation becomes attached to connotations of "primitive" sexual instincts, instincts that are thought to have the potential to become predatory and violent. Although at the outset the motif is attached to all Africans in general, it will later become attached just to those who are specifically positioned as sexually threatening. It is also heard briefly during some of the battle scenes, as though to reiterate that "the bringing of the African to America" produced the war itself, as well as to stress the proximity between "warlike" and "primitive."[19]

The first occurrence of Breil's "Motif of Barbarism" sets up several contrasting oppositions, creating musical signifiers for "primitivism" as defined against European art-music norms.[20] Thus, syncopation is opposed to the "smoothness" of European rhythms. In addition, musical textures (i.e., the ways melodies are positioned against each other, as in monophony, homophony, or polyphony) are contrasted. Breil's "barbaric" melody is first given in octaves lacking the more complex homophonic or polyphonic underpinnings so prized in European music since the rise of polyphony (European art music privileges the trained coordination of multiple, simultaneous melodic lines, as in a Bach fugue). In contrast, the gapped melody of the "Barbarism motif" (in which there is a jump of a minor third between the fifth and sixth melodic notes) and a flat seventh scale degree establishes a pentatonic pitch collection, a scale frequently found in folk music. Furthermore, the use of D minor, a traditionally sad and tragic key, is notable through the first four measures, through both the arrival on D and through its restatement (after a brief upper neighbor) in measure two, as well as through repeated modal cadences in measures three and four. Measures five through seven move to the parallel key of F major and a fuller homophonic texture. Finally, in this introductory laying out of the "Barbarism Motif," the suspension in measure six helps add to the hymn-like character of this final part of the cue, the part "attached" to the image of the minister. The entire first statement of the Barbarism theme therefore uses musical binaries (such as major/minor and contrasts in texture) to set out the primary black/white binary of the film's central ideological position.

This, then, is the "Motif of Barbarism," the memory motif that is recontextualized throughout the film, consistently in relation to black male characters (with the exception of its use in relation to the blacker moments of the Civil War). One could also make a case for understanding related melodies in the music associated with Austin Stoneman's mistress, Lydia Brown, music titled "Lust and Passion" in the Chappell and Co. published selections.[21] Indeed, these motifs (the "Motif of Barbarism" and "Lust and Passion") are juxtaposed in the scene in which Silas Lynch first gazes at Elsie Stoneman in Eric Beheim's arrangement of the score.[22] Most consistently, however, the "Motif of Barbarism" is shared by Lynch and Gus. It introduces Lynch to us when Stoneman announces: "I shall make this man, Silas Lynch, as a symbol of his race, the peer of any white man living" (CS 664). Then, the motif occurs prominently at the title, "Gus, the Renegade, the product of vicious doctrines spread by the carpetbaggers" (CS 879), whereafter we see Gus stalking the innocent and oblivious Flora. Breil's composed score frequently consists of a rapid alternation between two or more motivic ideas, the musical equivalent of cross-cutting. In this section, Breil alternates between motifs already heard, including those identified in Chappell as the "Motif of Barbarism" and "Violent Anger" as well as the "Flora Cameron" theme that Marks identifies and analyzes for its "darker implica-

25.3. Excerpt from "The Rape of Flora."

tions."²³ Here also are motifs transformed (a development of the theme Marks discusses as the Stoneman theme and a new motif that Marks called "The Rape of Flora.")²⁴ Through this technique of musical cross-cutting, Breil links the musical signifiers for Africans, for Flora, for violent anger, and for the scene so often called Flora's "rape." This linkage is set up even before the tragedy takes place on the screen; perhaps it is a kind of preface.

What of the notorious scene itself? Can a close analysis of the Breil score help us in our analysis of the scene the NAACP called the "Gus Chase" scene, the scene that community censorship boards so often asked to have cut from the local screenings in the early years of the film's release? Why was the scene originally called the "Gus Chase" scene and later referred to, as Marks does, as "The Rape of Flora"?²⁵ Griffith's most infamous sex scene, the encounter between Little Sister and Gus, has often been referred to as the "rape" scene, although viewers will at the same time observe that the girl throws herself off the cliff "rather than submit" to the overtures of the importunate Gus. The titles would seem to support the "rather jump than submit" reading: "For her who had learned the stern lesson of honor we should not grieve that she found sweeter the opal gates of death" (CS 1093). One could also argue, however, that death was pride's response to the shame of violation. Why, then, is this a "rape" (after all these years), if Flora jumps to avoid being violated?²⁶ Again, can an analysis of the music here help us with this question? Curiously, at least one account of a response to the music at this point in the film survives, quoted in an NAACP pamphlet attacking *The Birth of a Nation.* NAACP member Francis Hackett recalls what was most likely the same "Motif of Barbarism," prescribed for nearly all of Gus's appearances. The music emphasizes the way the lurking Gus stands in contrast to Flora's innocent play in the scenes before he chases her to the cliff's edge:

> Encouraged by the black leader, we see Gus the renegade hover about another young white girl's home. To hoochy-coochy music we see the long pursuit of the innocent white girl by this lust-maddened Negro, and we see her fling herself to death from a precipice, carrying her honor through "the opal gates of death."²⁷

Granted, "hoochy-coochy" music does not exactly describe the "Motif of Barbarism" that would have been played at this point in the film, nor does it seem to refer to the unmistakable ripping and tearing produced by the strings during the chase to the edge of the cliff (see Fig. 25.4).²⁸ But remember that this all-purpose "Barbarism" motif draws on rhythms and melodies that are meant to be read as characteristically un-European. At the time of its release, more important than the enactment of a rape in this film was the *threat* of it. The most threatening music for American audiences, the music most strange to the European-bred ear and therefore aligned with the terrifying sexuality of the African, is the "Motif of Barbarism," the theme heard before Gus corners and chases Flora. The barbarism theme from "The bringing of the African to America" introduction has here been repositioned against new images and with other motifs, strongly tied up with Gus's latent sexual violence.

The MOMA-LC piano conductor score has occasional notes in the score indicating what image or action should appear with that particular musical cue (a performance aid to help the conductor synchronize the music). The music for the sequence from shots 986–1001 (page 102 of MOMA-LC; Fig. 25.4) contains several of these descriptive notes; no other cue in the score has such detailed instructions. Breil evidently had a clear and precise idea of how to accompany the scene where Gus stalks Flora, alternating between happier, lighter music for Flora and an insistent descending semitone for Gus. Nearly every shot receives its own musical idea. In this sequence, Flora walks out to a spring, fills her bucket, and plays on a log with a squirrel, all while being covertly observed by Gus.[29] When we first see Gus, spying on Flora and Elsie in shots 880–890, we "hear" barbarism. Breil creates even more musical tension for Gus's second appearance, while spying on the lone Flora. Between brief snippets of the song "Listen to the Mockingbird" and Flora's motif, Breil calls for an ominous, descending semitone (from F to E) each time the film cuts to shots of Gus.[30] In Breil's musical world, the descending semitone for Gus is continually recontextualized in this sequence. The local tonics change nearly each time we hear Gus's semitone, causing the tones to adopt different active tendencies. (Tendency tones are scale degrees that our ear wants to hear resolve to another tone, usually a semitone or tone away. Because of these specific tendencies in functional tonal harmony, tonality contains repeating patterns of voice leading and harmonic syntax.)[31] In example four, Breil opens in E major, so Gus's semitone of F to E creates the severest dissonance of the example, a minor ninth to an octave (see Fig. 25.5 for a harmonic reduction of Fig. 25.4). The music then shifts to one of Flora's motifs in A minor, at which point the semitones are reconfigured as a less dissonant sixth resolving to a fifth. Finally, the music moves to C major, wherein the semitones, as scale degrees 4 and 3, become the milder dissonance of a fourth and the imperfect consonance of a third. In each case, the half steps represent moments of tonal instability, constantly recast, moving from the harshest dissonance (to emphasize the shock of Gus's first leering appearance) to less extreme sonorities, as Gus's position in the landscape becomes more familiar. The changing tendency tones are a particularly apt and even insidious musical signifier for Gus's unsettling presence.

Yet the most insidious combinations of music and Gus's character may come with the evidence pointing to missing footage representing Gus's castration scene in the film as released in 1915, footage that at one time was probably cut in between the title "Guilty" and the image of Gus's body thrown over a horse (CS

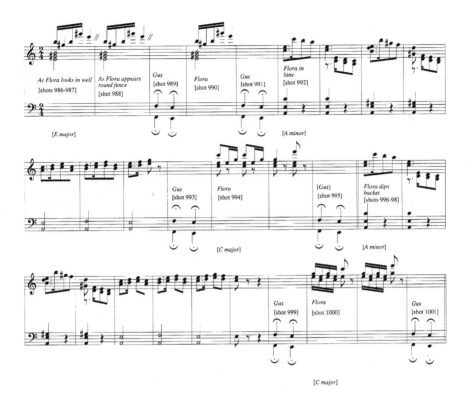

25.4. Flora and Gus (MOMA-LC, p. 102).

Harmonic reduction of example three, showing the continual recontextualization of the descending *f - e* semitone.

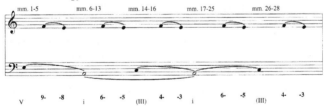

25.5. Harmonic reduction of Figure 25.4, showing the continual recontextualization of the descending *F–E* semitone.

1153–1154). Much more work needs to be done to confirm the lone account (by Seymour Stern) of having heard the fourth movement (the "thunderstorm") of Beethoven's Sixth Symphony, the "Pastoral" (opus 68).[32] The thunderstorm music was not only present but apparently—in at least the one performance discussed by Stern—timed to the plunging of the Klansman's knife into Gus's (unseen) body. If there is doubt about the existence of the castration sequence (which may not have been seen since 1933), the existence of the music from Beethoven's "Pastoral" Symphony in the surviving piano score (pages 111–115 of MOMA-LC) may be seen as corroborating evidence for Stern's account.[33] This evidence also points to the possibility that the political offense produced by the scenes containing the Gus character (the scenes cut in so many U.S. cities) would have been perhaps exacerbated, if not produced, by the musical reinforcement of the connotations of lechery in the image.[34]

The encounter between Gus and Flora is not the only interracial encounter in the film that is judged harshly by the musical commentary in the Breil score. Not surprisingly, the final sexual encounter, Lynch's proposal of marriage to Elsie, also makes extensive use of the "Barbarism Motif." Almost as soon as Lynch enters the office room where Elsie has been waiting at the end of the film, the motif returns (CS 1306; MOMA-LC page 122) (see Fig. 25.6), this time repositioned against a different musical cue, the one identified as "Fear" by Marks (215). As Lynch's advances against Elsie mount in intensity—providing the narrative "excuse" for the Klan's final ride—the "Barbarism Motif" alternates with the "Fear" motif, paralleling the back and forth between the two characters. While Elsie's half of this "dialogue," the "Fear" motif, rises with each successive statement, Lynch's "Barbarism" is made more terrible by its calculatedly unwavering statements of the melody. Elsie's "Fear" is restated at a higher pitch level while Lynch's "Barbarism" remains stable for its first two iterations (it then undergoes an extension and development in its third statement). This whole musical series (the dialectic between Barbarism and Fear) leads into a transformation of the "Elsie Stoneman Motif," an alteration that alerts us to the character's mood shift. Earlier in the film (as in example two), Elsie's theme had been light and happy, in a major key and orchestrated with flutes and violins, but here Breil transforms it into a dark and minor version, heard first by a mournful cello, next by a plaintive oboe, and cadencing on an unexpected major chord (see Fig. 25.7).

The effect of this alternation, coupled with the transformation of Elsie's theme into a darker version of itself, would be to reiterate the message of the scene in which Gus stalks Flora—this is a message of warning to white women about the sexual threat posed by black men. Recall that the function of the "Barbarism Motif" throughout is, in the words of the very first intertitle, to warn about the kinds of "seeds" planted by the "bringing of the African to America," to associate the black male characters with a particularly wild and inexplicable menace, a menace that is made all the more horrible through its connection with the sexual strangeness of Africa. Certainly there is confirmation here that the white woman is threatened by a kind of beast.[35] Of all of the analyses of the Breil score on this count, Seymour Stern's, based on significantly later viewing, is the most vivid:

> The effect of Breil's Negro-theme is that of a black penis pushing into the vagina of a white virgin. The Breil theme occurs throughout the score and "cuts into" the

[Motif of Barbarism]   [Fear]   [Motif of Barbarism]   [Fear]

25.6. "Motif of Barbarism" combined with "Fear."

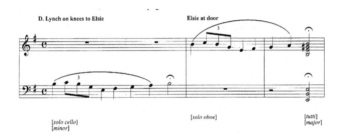

25.7. Elsie's motif in minor (MOMA-LC, p. 124).

heart of the Klan-music in those climactic sections of Part Two which relate to thematic scenes and subtitles on racial intermarriage.[36]

At least one account from the 1915 Boston run of the film would seem to support this interpretation that the film is a cautionary tale directed at white women in a particular way. William Monroe Trotter, editor of the black newspaper *The Guardian,* predicted that the film would "make white women afraid of Negroes" and would "stir up" white men.[37] Unfortunately, Thomas Dixon, in a famous interview, went on record as having said that his express purpose was, "to create a feeling of abhorrence in white people, especially white women against colored men." The interviewer went on to report that Dixon's ultimate goal was to "prevent the mixing of white and Negro blood by intermarriage."[38] With high expectations that he would see and hear a narrative that conveyed this message—his message—Dixon watched and listened that evening before the New York premiere, and where others might have apprehended the "Motif of Barbarism" as an insulting characterization of the Negro, Dixon heard instead a crying out to be saved; that is, he heard an opportunity for white fathers to rescue the anguished woman-South, and heard as well in the first measures of the symphonic overture, the resolution that signified the European as victorious. The "throb against the darkness," the tom-tom call to the white imperialist that underscored every Empire film thereafter, conveyed something wondrous to him—the "undreamed heights," the promise of glory. To claim victory over barbarism was the white man's elevated mission. It is no mystery that he heard this music as "uncanny," that is, strange and yet familiar, for although the music was strange, the feeling of superiority was familiar.

In contrast, in the "Barbarism Motif" Francis Hackett, the NAACP member, heard "hoochy-coochy" music, familiar to him because of its associations with the exotic, and he strenuously objects to its use in relation to the scene in which Gus, the "lust-maddened Negro" pursues the "innocent white girl."[39] To restate the question we have been asking, what was the function of the music in the production of feelings of outrage against the film and what contribution did it make to the effort to outlaw it? We need to go on here to raise the more difficult question of the relationship between musical performance and social unrest. It is well known that *The Birth of a Nation* was banned in eighteen states and in many cities, an action often based on local codes addressing the problem of disturbance of public order. One of the best sources of the articulated rationale for banning or otherwise cutting this film is the finding in *Mutual v. Ohio* (1915), the Ohio Supreme Court case in which it was found that motion pictures, because of their "attractiveness and manner of exhibition," were "capable of evil."[40] Is it that the music "makes" some people do things they can't help doing, or does the music suggest to others that it will make certain people (notably blacks and women) do things?

Whether one or the other, it is worthwhile mentioning here something of the legacy of music and social disturbance, a legacy that has characterized modernist music in particular.[41] One should recall the fascination during the early part of the twentieth century, in both high and low art, with non-European folk styles, coincident with the discovery of what was labeled "primitivism" in modernist artists like Picasso and Stravinsky. In fact, Stravinsky's *Le Sacre du printemps,* a ballet filled with (so-called) primal sexual themes, unexpected rhythmic eruptions, and grinding bitonalities, prompted an infamous riot at its Paris premiere in May 1913. This ballet and its score moved an audience to shout out and strike others in the crowd, enacting the very situation that so many American city fathers feared the most about performances of *The Birth of a Nation.* And we should not forget the other great trouble-making film at the opposite end of the political spectrum—Sergei Eisenstein's *The Battleship Potemkin* (1925), which was censored, cut, and banned around the world.[42] Testimony to the power of the modernist musical accompaniment, in Germany, Edmund Meisel's famous *Potemkin* score itself was scrutinized by censors who passed the film on condition that it be screened without Meisel's "provocative" score.[43]

But to study Breil's score for Griffith's film in isolation from the other aspects of the melodramatic aesthetic would be to fail again to understand the reasons for this film's enormous impact, an exercise that will still need to meet halfway a deeper study of the powder keg of historical conditions in 1915. *The Birth of a Nation* was, after all, the first feature film melodrama to be mounted as spectacular attraction on such a *scale* for so many U.S. towns and cities both in 1915 and in its re-release in the early 1920s. Several new studies of the film by African-American as well as Euro-American critics offer illuminating angles on the film, the most recent of which has linked the film with the lynching of Leo Frank in 1913.[44] Linda Williams, in a new work that considers D. W. Griffith and the origins of melodrama in American cinema, will hopefully lead us to a much greater understanding of the power of silent melodrama.[45] We are only just beginning to talk about the way the music helps to carry the insistent force of the melodrama—it is remarkably the iteration of the "Barbarism Motif" that produces this force as terrible. In the style of the melodramatic compiled score of the time, the Breil score is characteristically obsessive in its melodies. Perhaps the obsession is more recognizable in the performed score, where the *same* melodies recur (although with variation) while the image is giving us infinite variety. The power of the music here is in its remarkable repeats, its pairings, its characterizing typologies. But melodrama *is* an obsessive form—depending upon overstatement, repetition, and return as well as upon a stubbornly dualistic version of the world. Not surprisingly, James Baldwin once described *The Birth of a Nation* as exhibiting the "Niagara force of an obsession."[46]

Notes

1. By the mid-1910s, it was increasingly common for American films to be distributed with scores or cue sheets that utilized a compilation of original and borrowed (popular and concert-hall) music as accompaniment. Breil's score for *The Birth of a Nation* is an exemplar of the compiled score, containing original themes as well as borrowed tunes and symphonic excerpts. See Martin Miller Marks, "Film Scores in America, 1910–14," in *Music and the Silent Film: Contexts and Case Studies, 1895–1924* (New York: Oxford University Press, 1997), and Gillian B. Anderson, "A Warming Flame: The Musical Presentation of Silent Films," in *Music for Silent Films: 1894–1929* (Washington, D.C.: Library of Congress, 1988).

2. Consider Harlow Hare's important early review of the music (*Boston American*, July 18, 1915), reprinted in *The Birth of a Nation*, ed. Robert Lang (New Brunswick, N.J.: Rutgers University Press, 1994), 186–189. After commenting on the "really brilliant musical setting" that combines borrowed and original tunes, Hare relates three "distinctive strains or motifs run[ning] through the second half of the picture," which he identifies as: one, Breil's "Perfect Song" (the love theme for Ben Cameron and Elsie Stoneman); two, "the wild, chaotic-seeming tune that marks the entry of the negro carpet-bagger mobs and the racket of the rioters"; and three, "the welcome [sic] Ku-Klux-Klan call" (188). Perhaps Hare's second distinctive strain was the "Motif of Barbarism."

3. *Selections of Joseph Carl Breil's Themes from the Incidental Music to "The Birth of a Nation"* (London: Chappell and Co., 1916).

4. Marks, 128–129, discusses the six piano pieces and identifies them as "The Motif of Barbarism," "The Elsie Stoneman Motif," "Stoneman and Lydia Brown, the Mulatto," "The Ku Klux Clansmens' [sic] Call" and "Flora's Death," in addition to "The Perfect Song," which had already been published as a sheet-music arrangement. It is important to note that the "Motif of Barbarism" is not identified as such on the orchestral score.

5. Marks, 109–111.

6. For the most comprehensive overview see Thomas Cripps, *Slow Fade to Black: The Negro in American Film, 1900–1942* (New York: Oxford University Press, 1977), especially ch. 2.

7. Marks, 131. See Marks, 132–133, on the question of the authorship of the score that *The Clansman* used in the twenty-two-week run at Clune's Auditorium.

8. Marks, 131.

9. Marks reads the evidence as pointing to the probability that the score was not related to either of the earlier scores and that neither Breil nor Elinor worked on it; see Marks, 132, also 280, n. 35.

10. "The Silence of the Silents," *Musical Quarterly* 80, no. 4 (1997), 648–718.

11. The "Continuity Script" is found in Lang. See also John Cuniberti, *"The Birth of a Nation": A Formal Shot-by-Shot Analysis Together with Microfiche* (Woodbridge, Conn.: Research Publications, 1979).

12. Marks, 286, n. 76.

13. Marks, 286, n. 76, describes Breil's incomplete essay, noting as confirmation that the composer was writing a motif to correspond with "primitive instincts," that the author has transcribed the opening melody in the essay on a single staff. Seymour Stern, "Griffith: *The Birth of a Nation* Part I," *Film Culture* 36 (Spring–Summer 1965), 119, adds another twist to Breil's account, recalling that Madame Sul-Te-Wan, a black actress who appeared in *The Birth of a Nation* but was also under contract to Griffith, claimed that she had helped Griffith and Breil with the plantation melodies. As Stern describes a meeting she had with Griffith in 1947, she danced and sang (as he transcribed it):

> Jigaboo, jigaboo—zis-boom-bah!
> Jigaboo, jigaboo—rah, rah, rah!

14. For a succinct overview of the recent shifts within musicology as a discipline, see Nicholas Cook, *Music: A Very Short Introduction* (New York: Oxford University Press, 1998).

15. As quoted in Stern, 108.

16. Marks, 135–141.

17. Raymond Allen Cook, *Fire from the Flint: The Amazing Career of Thomas Dixon* (Winston-Salem, N.C.: John F. Blair, 1968), 168.

18. Gilbert Chase is one of the earliest writers to connect the African tradition of syncopation with American popular music; see *America's Music: From the Pilgrims to the Present* (New York: McGraw-Hill, 1955), 73–76. Eileen Southern writes that "Since the mid-19th century there has been a continuous absorption of Afro-American music into the mainstream of American music, so that in many instances, for example, jazz, the two have become indistinguishable"; see "Afro-American Music," *The New Grove Dictionary of American Music,* vol. 1, ed. H. Wiley Hitchcock and Stanley Sadie (New York: Macmillan Press, 1986), 13.

19. As Seymour Stern reads the "Motif of Barbarism," it is "a theme expressing barbarism, insolence, lust and nihilism, played during the film-prologue, over the scenes depicting the introduction of Negro slavery into colonial American, and more especially, during Part II, in virtually all scenes depicting the rise to power of the Negroes, after the Civil War." "The Birth of a Nation," *Cinemages* 1, no. 1 (1955), 6.

20. Our analysis here does not differ significantly from that of Marks, 156–157.

21. Marks, 129, 212; Marks, 150, notes that Lydia's theme is in a "tango rhythm" and observes a connection between Lydia and another female character represented by a tango—Flora. The characteristically lurching rhythm of the tango has become a musical

signifier for a particularly exotic type of passion, a passion connoting an erotic exoticism more appropriate for Lydia Stoneman than for Flora Cameron. Marta E. Savigliano writes that "As a powerful representation of male/female courtship, stressing the tension involved in the process of seduction, the tango performance has gone through successive adjustments as it was adopted and legitimized by higher classes and by Western hegemonic cultures." ("Tango and the Postmodern Uses of Passion," in *Cruising the Performative: Interventions into the Representation of Ethnicity, Nationality, and Sexuality,* ed. Sue-Ellen Case, Philip Brett, and Susan Leigh Foster [Bloomington: Indiana University Press, 1995], 131.)

22. Kino Video, 1992.

23. See Marks, 149–150. In his view, "the effect of this music is comic but unsettling; in hindsight, the entire number can be heard to contain omens of Flora's misfortune."

24. Marks, 152, 215.

25. Marks, 152, lists "The Rape of Flora" as beginning Act II; for his analysis of this scene, see 162. He also refers to "The Rape of Flora" in Part II of the appendix, 215.

26. See Jane Gaines, "*The Birth of a Nation* and *Within Our Gates:* Two Tales of the American South," in *Dixie Debates: Perspectives in Southern Culture,* ed. Richard E. King and Helen Taylor (London: Pluto Press, 1995), 187.

27. "Fighting a Vicious Film," NAACP pamphlet (1915), as quoted in Gerald Mast, *The Movies in Our Midst* (Chicago: University of Chicago Press, 1982), 126. For more on the history of "hoochy-coochy" music, see Charles A. Kennedy, "When Cairo Met Main Street: Little Egypt, Salome Dancers, and The World's Fairs of 1893 and 1904," in *Music and Culture in America, 1861–1918,* ed. Michael Saffle (New York: Garland Publishing, 1998), 271–298.

28. In Figure 25.3, this two-measure excerpt from "The Rape of Flora" features the strings repeatedly racing quickly up the interval of a tritone, creating a sound that imitates ripping and tearing. The musical technique and effect are not far removed from Bernard Herrmann's famous underscoring of the brutal shower murder scene from *Psycho* (1960). For detailed discussion of Herrmann's music, see Graham Donald Bruce, *Bernard Herrmann: Film Music and Film Narrative* (Ann Arbor: UMI, 1985); and Royal S. Brown, "Herrmann, Hitchcock, and the Music of the Irrational," in *Overtones and Undertones: Reading Film Music* (Los Angeles: University of California Press, 1994), 148–174.

29. Beginning with shot 986 and continuing through shot 1001, the descriptions in the score match shot for shot with the continuity script. The first instruction ("As Flora looks in well") must have come about from someone (perhaps Breil) confusing Flora's actions in shot 987; what the musical score calls "look[ing] in [the] well," the script more correctly calls "stop[ping] to admire the roses." Beheim's arrangement for the Kino release substitutes this music with the "Lust and Passion" cue.

30. The retrograde of this semitone (E to F) in similarly low registers forms the basis for John Williams's famous shark motif in *Jaws* (1975).

31. See Edward Aldwell and Carl Schachter, *Harmony and Voice Leading,* 2nd ed. (New York: Harcourt Brace Jovanovich, 1989), 8–9, for a brief introduction to active and stable tones.

32. Stern, 122–124. Marks comments on Stern's unreliability on page 279.

33. See MOMA-LC Piano score, Sec. 17D. "As horse shows on screen," 111–113. For further discussion of this scene in detail see our forthcoming essay, "Mutilation and *The Birth of a Nation,*" in *Cinema and Nation,* ed. Mette Hjort and John MacKenzie (New York: Routledge, forthcoming).

34. For a comprehensive overview of the censorship in U.S. towns and cities see

Nickieann Fleener-Marzec, *D. W. Griffith's The Birth of a Nation: Controversy, Suppression, and the First Amendment As It Applies to Filmic Expression, 1915–1973* (New York: Arno Press, 1980). See also Jane Gaines, *Fire and Desire: Mixed Blood Relations in Early Cinema* (Chicago: University of Chicago Press, 2000), ch. 7.

35. See Michael Rogin, "'The Sword Became a Flashing Vision': D. W. Griffith's *The Birth of a Nation*," *Representations* 9 (Winter 1985), 150–195, for a discussion of the visual contrast between the blonde Elsie Stoneman and the dark and beast-like Lynch.

36. Stern, 118.

37. As quoted in Richard Schickel, *D. W. Griffith* (New York: Simon and Schuster, 1984), 295.

38. As recalled by Rolfe Cobleigh, associate editor of *The Congregationalist* and *Christian World,* in Boston Branch, The National Association for the Advancement of Colored People, "Fighting a Vicious Film: Protest against *The Birth of a Nation*" (1916), in *The Movies in Our Midst,* ed. Gerald Mast (Chicago: University of Chicago Press, 1982), 128.

39. Music signifying exotic sexualities must have been prevalent in the repertoire of musical accompaniments for silent film. Vachel Lindsay, *The Art of the Moving Picture* (New York: Macmillan, 1915), in his discussion of the frequent mismatch between music and scene, refers to the "hoochey koochey strains" played in the wrong place in silent film exhibition in general during the early years (192). He recalls seeing both *Cabiria* and *The Birth of a Nation,* and complains about the musical performances in his home town of Rochester, Illinois, comparing the small town with the city exhibition, which for him is a question marked by the difference between projection and the musical accompaniment. The "local orchestra cannot play the music furnished in annotated sheets as skillfully as the local operator can turn the reel (or watch the motor turn it!)" (191).

40. *Mutual Film Corporation v. Industrial Commission of Ohio,* 236 U.S. (1915), 244.

41. Suggestive here is Jacques Attali, *Noise: The Political Economy of Music,* trans. Brian Massumi (Minneapolis: University of Minnesota Press, 1985), 10, who says that "every major social rupture has been preceded by an essential mutation in the codes of music, in its mode of audition, and in its economy."

42. See, for instance, "Censor Once Again Shreds Film," in *The Battleship Potemkin,* ed. Herbert Marshall (New York: Avon Books, 1978).

43. Marian Hannah Winter, "The Function of Music in Sound Film," *Musical Quarterly* 27, no. 2 (April 1941), 146–164.

44. Manthia Diawara, "Black Spectatorship: Problems of Identification and Resistance," *Screen* 29, no. 4 (Winter 1988), 66–76; Mary Ann Doane, "Dark Continents: Epistemologies of Racial and Sexual Difference in Psychoanalysis and Cinema," in *Femmes Fatales* (New York: Routledge, 1991); Janet Staiger, "*The Birth of a Nation:* Reconsidering Its Reception," in Lang; Clyde Taylor, "The Re-Birth of the Aesthetic Cinema," *Wide Angle* 13, no. 3–4 (July–October 1991), 12–30. On the relation between the film and the Leo Frank lynching, see Cedric Robinson, "In the Year 1915: D. W. Griffith and the Whitening of America," *Social Identities* 3, no. 2 (1997), 161–192.

45. Linda Williams, "Melodrama Revised," in *Refiguring American Film Genres: Theory and History,* ed. Nick Browne (Berkeley and Los Angeles: University of California Press, 1998), 42–88.

46. James Baldwin, *The Devil Finds Work* (New York: Dell, 1976), 53.

Appendixes: *Original French Texts*

Appendix A
Les Voies du silence
François Jost

A travers l'examen de la presse française de 1908, j'ai acquis la conviction que la multiplicité des situations sonores offertes par le cinéma, qu'a bien mise en lumière R. Altman, n'est pas un simple foisonnement proliférant au hasard selon les installations ou les contingences matérielles, mais qu'elle a une logique propre, qui repose sur le statut conféré aux films projetés, et que le film d'art joue dans la constitution de cette axiologie du sonore un rôle déterminant.

La relation du son à l'image connaît, en ce début de siècle, plusieurs modes théoriques fort différents sémantiques ou syntaxiques. L'hypothèse que je développerai est qu'elle est largement dépendante de la valeur artistique que l'on accorde aux images projetées. Pour le montrer, je me concentrerai sur ce moment de l'histoire du cinéma où le silence devint un enjeu esthétique: le lancement du film d'art.

Quoi qu'on en ait, un bruit ne sera jamais produit par une image. D'où un obstacle que tout le cinéma s'efforcera d'aplanir: comment ancrer un son dans une image? Pour ce faire, trois opérations doivent être accomplies avec succès:

- l'iconicité: le son produit doit suffisamment ressembler à l'objet qu'il représente pour être identifié par le spectateur: il faut un savoir-faire du bruitage;
- la redondance: pour que l'ancrage visuel fonctionne, il faut que le spectateur puisse trouver dans l'image des sèmes communs avec ceux du signe sonore
- la coïncidence temporelle d'un mouvement visuel—geste ou liping—fixera cette relation de l'image au son.

Les bruits de coulisses travaillent les deux premières dimensions. Mais peut-être pas, comme on le soutient souvent, dans le seul but d'accroître le réalisme. Reconnaît-on vraiment le tonnerre dans ces dispositifs à jalousie "dont on laisse vivement retomber les lames de bois retenues"? Peu importe. En fait, comme le suggère un auteur de *Ciné-Journal*, ces sons ont surtout pour fonction d'impressionner[1]: il faut entendre la brusque irruption du tonnerre dans *Amadigi di Gaula* de Haendel, détonnant si l'on peut dire, avec le contexte proprement musical, pour imaginer le sursaut du spectateur absorbé par l'image qui sort brusquement de son silence intérieur en raison du vacarme suscité par un "appareil fait de douves de tonneaux et de plaques de tôles alternées, enfilées à un cordage," qui tombe du haut d'un cintre. L'iconicité est moins affaire de ressemblance entre les sons que de ressemblance entre les peurs provoquées par l'émergence d'un bruit impromptu.

Quant au critère du synchronisme, l'inventaire des sons soumis au spectateur par certains cinémas montre qu'il s'agit plutôt de bruits continus, plutôt horizontaux que ponctuels et qui s'étalent dans le temps. Pour dire les choses en termes modernes ils constituent ce que nous appelons des *ambiances,* c'est-à-dire des masses sonores qui ont pour particularité de ne pas être véritablement orientées et de ne s'ancrer en aucun point précis de l'image.

Alors que, dans le modèle théâtral, l'imitation dépendait de l'habileté d'un homme et variait donc largement suivant le bruiteur, le "meuble portatif à bruits de coulisses" marque une coupure dans l'histoire du cinéma. D'abord, parce qu'il permet de fabriquer des bruits reproductibles à l'identique ("Naguère, et maintenant encore, on faisait ces bruits en coulisses selon la formule et les traditions du théâtre . . . "). Les rivages de la performance s'éloignent, de même que la forte composante autographique du cinéma: à l'instar des cartons qui assureront l'itérabilité absolue du récit verbal (vs le bonimenteur), le meuble portatif, éventuellement loué et, donc, transportable, assurera une continuité de spectacle quel que soit l'interprète, voire le changement de lieu.

L'autre déplacement important réside dans la nature des bruits et dans la façon dont ils peuvent être reproduits: "la pierre qui tombe fait du bruit en tombant, l'enfant qui agite une sonnette est entendu . . . " Aux ambiances fondées sur des durées sonores, s'ajoute la possibilité de produire facilement des *effets,* ponctuels et liés par synchronisme à des aspects visuels: "le bruit naît du mouvement comme dans la vie." On passe d'un accompagnement à une extraction des détails visuels par le son.

Dans ce contexte bruissant de sons de toute sorte, quelle place tient le silence? C'est la question que j'examinerai à présent. Une chose est sûre: le silence est souvent valorisé par les penseurs du cinéma. Encore faut-il préciser que, dans ce cinéma, le silence n'est pas l'absence de tout bruit: il serait plus juste de dire qu'il est le résultat d'une action de l'une des sources sonores sur les autres, dont le succès se solde par la réduction au silence.

En premier lieu, il est probable qu'il accompagna la projection de certains films à visée informative. Il n'est pour s'en convaincre que d'écouter M. Louis Fabry, Président de l'association des projectionnistes de Marseille, qui se plaint auprès du *Fascinateur* des problèmes que posent, pour sa profession, "les vues mal repérées": "les opérateurs qui lui servent d'aides placent alors les vues à l'envers, font paraître à droite ce qui devrait être à gauche, le conférencier est obligé d'interrompre son discours pour placer les vues dans le sens voulu ou, s'il ne dit rien, les personnes qui connaissent *les paysages font des réflexions tout haut,* ce qui distrait l'auditoire et diminue naturellement la portée des conférences."[2] Manifestement, les genres requièrent des attitudes différentes, les plus instructifs imposant au public de se taire.

Mais, pour observer la valorisation du silence ou pour comprendre véritablement ce qui put apparaître à un moment donné comme "the sound of silence"; il est fructueux de s'arrêter sur la première projection des films d'art et, plus spécialement, de *L'Assassinat du duc de Guise.* Fidèle à mon hypothèse que le genre, loin d'être une catégorie définissable en soi, est plutôt le lieu où se rencontrent, et parfois s'affrontent, les divers acteurs de la communication cinématographique, j'examinerai successivement le rôle qu'occupa le silence dans la réception de l'œuvre et dans son écriture.

Tournons-nous d'abord du côté de la critique. L'article de G. Dureau du 19 novembre 1908, intitulé "Visions d'art," est d'autant plus intéressant qu'il n'a pas assisté à la séance du 17 novembre 1908, salle Charras, et qu'on peut donc supposer qu'il fait état de ce qui se dit à Paris après la projection du film.

D'emblée, *L'Assassinat du duc de Guise* est présenté comme une "pièce silencieuse," par opposition au terme "pellicule," dont le directeur de *Ciné-Journal* précise qu'il est péjoratif. Cette expression concentre le paradoxe artistique de ce qu'il appelle aussi une "vision d'art": la valeur tient à la fois à sa théâtralité et à son silence. Mais à un silence qui est moins une infirmité qu'un choix artistique. En cela, il n'encourt pas les reproches que l'on fait couramment au cinématographe d'être "un spectacle pour sourds."[3]

A en croire G. Dureau, les comédiens mimeraient "la mort de ce pauvre duc de Guise," et ce mime irait à l'encontre de l'expression de la pensée: "Que va-t-il demeurer de la *pensée* dramatique de M. Lavedan à peine perceptible sans l'expression verbale?" Si le simple fait de poser la question présuppose une méfiance quant au résultat, que l'auteur de ces lignes, je le répète, n'a pas vu, il n'en reste pas moins qu'elle surgit pour ce film-là, et pour la première fois dans *Ciné-Journal,* ce qui laisse à penser que, dans un contexte où il est admis que les films sont muets (cf. l'article cité *supra*), le silence de *L'Assassinat du duc de Guise* est plus assourdissant qu'un autre.

Pourquoi ce silence serait-il à craindre? Sans doute d'abord parce que, comme le notera Victorin Jasset, "des artistes jouaient sans courir, restaient immobiles[4]," l'absence de mouvement se trouvant en quelque sorte soulignée *a contrario* par l'absence de son (dont on a vu qu'il était par ailleurs lié au mouvement). Mais, surtout, parce que ce film apparut aussi comme l'émergence de la psychologie à l'écran et que G. Dureau imagina mal que celle-ci s'accommodât du silence. "Que seront devenus les gestes de M. Albert Lambert, la splendeur de Mlle Robinne, réduits tous deux à s'agiter dans le tumulte de *leurs passions veuves de mots?*"

Or ce qui retient ici, c'est que Dureau va trouver la solution à ce problème qui, selon lui, était d'ailleurs senti par les auteurs du film, dans l'existence de la musique de Saint-Saëns: "les promoteurs de ces œuvres ne les conçoivent pas sans le secours d'une *musique puissante* qui remplacera pour le public la *voix humaine* dans les infimes ressources de son expressivité." (je souligne). On voit se mettre en place, dans ce texte, un usage de la musique qui rompt avec ceux que mobilisent généralement le spectacle cinématographique. Alors que les genres mineurs sont dotés d'un accompagnement musical, souvent bien mis en évidence par l'architecture de la salle, dans le cas de *L'Assassinat du duc de Guise,* "il y a le grand jeu, tout le grand tralala de la musique *invisible* et *présente,* du mystère qu'il convient *[sic]* à des évocations cinématographiques." Cette invisibilité présente tranche avec cet autre type de spectacles, où l'orchestre accueille le spectateur, comme à l'Hippodrome, où il introduit et conclut tout le programme. Il semble que, dès lors, ces deux usages de la musique alterneront d'ailleurs: d'un côté, l'accompagnement avec ce qu'il comporte de stéréotypes et de clichés aidant à la compréhension du sens de l'action, et la musique de scène à laquelle sont dévolues d'autres fonctions que je vais préciser dans un instant.

Mais, auparavant, il me faut insister encore sur le silence qui parut bien constituer la révolution esthétique du film d'art. A en croire le célèbre article de Brisson[5], qui a visité les usines Pathé de Vincennes, les plateaux auraient été de petits théâtres ouvrant sur "un monde muet, où tout s'accomplit dans le silence et c'est dans ce cadre que se serait élaborée une "forme de théâtre neuve," "la pièce cinématographique," dont Lavedan et Le Bargy auraient "codifié l'esthétique," conférant au silence un sens particulier, à l'opposé de la production de "pellicules" de consommation courante.[6]

Si j'ai pu avancer tout à l'heure que la musique est la continuation du silence par d'autres moyens, c'est que, pour ces codificateurs du film d'art, il n'entre en opposition paradigmatique qu'avec la parole. Alors que celle-ci est le support de la pensée et de l'abstraction, avec le silence "nous sommes dans le concret." Et l'on trouve chez Brisson une définition des contraintes du muet qui n'est pas sans rappeler la première règle de la méthode cartésienne. "La première était de ne recevoir jamais aucune chose pour vraie que je ne la connusse évidemment être telle: c'est-à-dire éviter soigneusement la précipitation et la prévention, et de comprendre rien de plus en mes jugements, que ce qui se présenterait si *clairement* et si *distinctement* à mon esprit que je n'eusse aucune occasion de le mettre en doute": "Il faut que les personnages agissent et qu'ils agissent *clairement* et non point *confusément* et que chacun de leurs mouvements soit *expressif* et que ces mouvements soient émis ensemble par une perpétuelle relation de cause à effet." Pour l'occasion, les "raisons" de Brisson sont plus artistiques que scientifiques, bien que le style soit conçu à l'instar du raisonnement, pour le philosophe, comme une simplification de la nature.[7] A cette valorisation quasi-rationnelle du silence, se surajoute un argument dicté par une conception quasi-rousseauiste de la communication, pour laquelle la transparence entre les âmes ne serait possible qu'aussi longtemps que les hommes communiquent sans avoir recours à la langue. "Dans le théâtre parlé, le détail du dialogue, la variété des intonations suppléent en quelque mesure à la précision du geste. Ici le geste étant nu est obligé d'être *vrai*."

Que cet art "d'où le verbe est retranché" soit en deçà du langage, on en trouverait la confirmation dans le fait que Brisson l'oppose à la pantomime "parce qu'elle possède une langue, une grammaire spéciale, des signes immuables dont le sens ne varie point," alors que "le cinématographe s'abstient d'user de son alphabet; son but est la vie."

A cette vertu quasi heuristique d'un silence qui aide à comprendre l'action, à sa valeur d'authenticité s'ajoute enfin ce qu'on pourrait appeler sa force communicationnelle, son efficacité sur le spectateur: "Ce récit visuel que Lavedan a reconstruit avec une dévotion minutieuse et passionnée, se grave dans l'esprit en des traits inoubliables." Et Brisson de conclure: "Rien ne vaut l'enseignement des yeux." Ainsi, le silence libérerait l'œil de la confusion où le plongeait le récit verbal.

Pour bien comprendre le discours qui accompagne la projection de *L'Assassinat du duc de Guise,* il faut le prendre pour ce qu'il est: non un compte-rendu exact de la pratique effective d'une époque, mais une argumentation en faveur d'une poétique du silence qui n'eût peut-être d'autres réalités que discursives. Comme une prescription plus que comme une description.

En effet, bien que, selon la presse spécialisée, les auteurs du premier film d'art revendiquassent l'idée de "pièce silencieuse," la lecture du scénario convainc qu'au stade de l'écriture, la parole y occupait une place importante. Qu'on en juge par quelques extraits: "Le cardinal de Guise s'est levé à demi, de l'effroi sur la face, comme pour rejoindre son frère. Mais de la main, celui-ci l'immobilise et le rassoit. Le cardinal se laisse retomber terrifié. Tout le monde le regarde. Il les regarde aussi, brave, énigmatique, narquois . . . *il a l'air de leur dire . . .* " où est-ce que je vais? Qu'est-ce qui m'attend? Je m'en doute. Vous aussi. Eh bien pourtant j'y vais. Et nous allons bien voir."

La vision du film confirme d'ailleurs cette omniprésence du dialogue, puisque, loin de se contenter de mimer, comme le laissait entendre G. Dureau, les comédiens ne cessent de parler, donnant assurément raison à Isabelle Raynauld, qui a insisté sur les sons présupposés par le film.

D'où vient alors que ces films paraissent silencieux? D'où vient l'illusion de ceux qui se focalisent sur le récit visuel?

D'abord du fait que la multitude des paroles qui parsèment le scénario sont moins des répliques que les personnages prononcent que des commentaires que le spectateur pourrait se faire en son for intérieur: "le cardinal lui dit tout bas un mot rapide *qu'on devine* être un mot d'inquiétude, de recommandation ou 'prenez garde, faites bien attention.' Guise y répond évasivement par un sourire et un haussement d'épaules." Ou encore: "Il a l'air de leur dire: où est-ce que je vais? Qu'est-ce qui m'attend? Je m'en doute. Eh bien pourtant, j'y vais. Et nous allons bien voir . . . "

En d'autres termes, la lettre importe moins que l'esprit. Si le spectateur ne connaît pas les mots exacts qui sont énoncés par le comédien, il doit en restituer le sens grâce à la situation construite par l'ensemble du scénario ou par le geste de l'acteur. Aussi, après la mort du Duc de Guise, pourra-t-il reconstituer ces échanges: "Tous s'écartent pour lui faire voir le corps de loin: "Voyez Sire, c'est fait." Le roi, tenant toujours son petit chien s'avance, tout doucement . . . Quand il a fait trois pas, il s'arrête, demande craintif: "Etes-vous bien sûr que . . . —Oh tout à fait sûrs, répondent plusieurs."

Récit visuel, *L'Assassinat du duc de Guise* l'est aussi parce que les cartons, peu nombreux, il est vrai, ne transcrivent presque aucune de ces répliques reconstruites par identification spectatorielle aux méfaits des conjurés. Et, à cet égard, deux remarques s'imposent:

- d'une part, le metteur en scène a abandonné l'idée d'un rendu visuel des paroles qui avait été imaginé au stade du scénario. Aussi, pour la requête de Pétremol au roi en faveur des pauvres soldats écossais qui attendent leur paye depuis 6 mois, le scénario précise: "les mots s'inscrivent sur l'écran au fur et à mesure que les prononce Pétremol." Cette idée de visualisation du dit est d'autant plus notable qu'à ce stade de l'écriture ne figure aucun carton.
- d'autre part, aucun de nos critiques ne fait référence à l'existence de carton, justement, et, donc, au rôle d'un récit verbal visualisé.

Sans doute frappèrent-ils moins que l'absence en cette séance de Charras de tout boniment ou de tout conférencier: "Eh bien, le croirez-vous? Après une heure et demie de ce spectacle [. . .] nous éprouvions l'impérieux besoin d'entendre le son d'une voix humaine." Quoi qu'il en fût des mentions écrites, qui devaient bien figurer sur le film projeté, la présence de la musique et l'absence de la parole de la salle dut mettre les spectateurs dans une situation de lecture silencieuse qui incita à ne plus voir le son que le film pourtant présupposait. En un sens, le sentiment du silence, l'illusion peut-être, résulte d'abord d'un accroissement de l'activité visuelle du spectateur, elle-même résultat de la conjonction de l'écrit et de la musique.

Dans la période où *L'Assassinat du duc de Guise* crée l'événement à Paris, *Ciné-Journal* reproduit deux articles de la *Revue internationale de photographie,* dont on peut penser qu'ils sont choisis pour leur capacité à accompagner la rupture esthétique revendiquée par le film d'art, vu l'intérêt que *Ciné-Journal* manifeste pour ce phénomène.

Le premier milite pour la "musique à programme, c'est-à-dire la musique qui est de caractère purement instrumental et qui a pour raison d'être un thème littéraire ou artistique nettement défini." Contrairement à la musique d'accompagnement qui, comme son nom l'indique, va avec l'image, cette musique à programme "ne nous émeut pas seulement par des sons, mais éveille en nous d'autres sentiments, par évocation spontanée d'images, des scènes de caractère ou d'actions nettement définies." Pour caractériser cette musique qui est capable de créer des images dans l'esprit du spectateur, l'auteur, pictorialiste, emploie curieusement le même mot que le poéticien de film d'art: "la composition musicale n'est pas forcément *abstraite,* elle peut créer des paysages ou des thèmes, en sorte que "celui qui écoute même sans connaissance de la musique, mais qui y prête attention, finit par y découvrir les tableaux qu'elle contient."[8] De là à penser que cette virtualité synesthésique de la musique pourra servir la compréhension silencieuse— c'est-à-dire sans l'aide de la linéarisation iconique du bonimenteur—il n'y a qu'un pas que l'on pourra franchir en détournant le synchronisme de l'utilisation linguistique qu'il connut au début du siècle pour l'appliquer aux relations de la musique et de l'image. Le synchronisme ne sera plus au service du réalisme, mais de l'intelligibilité spectatorielle:[9] "La musique aide la compréhension du cinématographe. M. Camille de Saint-Saëns a écrit la partition de *L'Assassinat du duc de Guise* devant l'écran où était projeté le film. La musique doit souligner, accompagner, préciser la mimique. Il faut que les phrases musicales coïncident parfaitement avec l'action." En termes plus sémiologiques, on dirait qu'à la musique sont confiées trois missions qui incombaient au bonimenteur: *ponctuer* les mouvements et gestes, constituer les unités syntagmatiques et opérer leurs démarcations.

Et l'auteur du texte de révéler à son public que, pour veiller à ce synchronisme, au moment du tournage, M. Lavedan a adjoint au "directeur de la scène," un directeur musical et un chef d'orchestre. Utilisant une méthode assez proche de nos play-back modernes, "l'artiste rythme ses gestes sur la musique écrite en même temps que le scénario. Il s'y essaie avec un phonographe."

L'apparition de la musique de film en tant que telle renverse donc la logique de l'accompagnement musical: alors que celui-ci suivait le résultat filmé du jeu de l'acteur, celui-là modèle au contraire ses gestes et ses mimiques, lui imposant son rythme. Du même coup, on doit bien admettre que la hiérarchisation parole-son est renversée, puisque l'acteur doit se couler dans le temps musical. On peut se demander si cette articulation image-musique n'est pas responsable de cette impression de rapidité qui nous étonne un peu aujourd'hui: "ses images se succèdent, un peu trop rapides parfois et fiévreuses, parfois trop ramassées, trop compactes, mais étrangement suggestives."[10]

Parallèlement à ce souci d'articulation syntaxique de l'audio et du visuel, *Ciné-Journal* met aussi l'emphase sur la composition visuelle comme en témoigne cet article intitulé sobrement "De la composition," qui insiste sur le fait que le parcours du spectateur dans l'image peut être contraint par l'organisation de la scène: "il faut admettre qu'on peut exercer l'œil à choisir, dans un paysage, certaines parties qui, disposées de telle ou telle façon, se conforment à ces lois qui sont la base de l'art sainement entendu."[11] (la prédominance, la balance, la répétition).

Quelle portée eut ce type de théorie sur le travail de Lavedan, Calmette et Le Bargy? En l'état actuel de nos connaissances, c'est difficile à dire. Ce que nous savons de son esthétique musicale laisse à penser néanmoins qu'il n'est pas improbable qu'il les connût ou, même, qu'il se souciât de s'y conformer. Quoi qu'il en soit, la vision silencieuse de *L'Assassinat...*, c'est-à-dire, on l'a compris, sans la linéarisation iconique imposée par le bonimenteur et avec sa linéarisation musicale, dût non seulement amplifier l'activité de l'œil, mais aussi la conscience, pour le spectateur, de se retrouver face à cet écran. La parole de la salle disparue, l'œil fut conduit par les déplacements des personnages dans l'écran et par les fixations oculaires imposées par la lecture.[12] A titre d'exemple—et pour finir—observons le parcours de l'œil au moment où le carton vient interrompre l'action visuelle.

L'insertion du premier billet, qui prévient la marquise de Noirmoutiers de prendre garde à ce qui peut arriver au duc de Guise coupe l'action de la lectrice en deux, mais la fin du texte, déterminée par le sens de lecture occidental, amène le spectateur vers la droite de l'écran où se trouve la marquise. De ce fait, l'entrée en scène du Duc, par la gauche, marque une rupture perceptive qui lui confère *de facto* une importance particulière. Quand le duc de Guise ayant lu le billet et ajouté "Il n'oserait !" se lève pour sortir, il quitte en revanche la scène du côté où nous a dirigé son point d'exclamation. Ainsi surgit l'hypothèse que l'absence du son et la "présence invisible de la musique" confèrent une importance singulière aux mouvements du regard et à la composition de l'image.

Il est difficile d'aller plus loin dans cette direction pour l'instant. Je me contenterai de souligner, pour conclure, que la présence de la musique a deux conséquences: l'une cognitive, l'autre émotive.

Du point de vue cognitif, comme on vient de le voir, la musique renforce paradoxalement l'activité de l'œil.

Du point de vue émotif, la musique ne se contente pas de souligner ou d'illustrer des sentiments. Elle donne au film une dimension tragique. N'y a-t-il pas quelque chose de forcément tragique dans ses personnages qui évoluent silencieusement pendant que la musique nous emporte avec son mouvement et sa logique propre, dans un monde dont ils ne sont pas conscients et qui les englobe malgré tout?

Notes

1. "Au moment où nos Directeurs de cinémas-théâtres se préoccupent d'accompagner les vues cinématographiques des divers bruits qu'elles comportent pour impressionner le public, nous croyons devoir citer ici quelques-uns des moyens de coulisses les plus communément employés," lit-on dans *Ciné-Journal* (1 septembre 1908).

2. *Ciné-Journal,* 10–16 avril 1909.

3. "Visions d'art," *Ciné-Journal,* 19 novembre 1908.

4. "Well-known artists acted by standing still instead of running around; they achieved an increasing intensity of effect," "Etude sur la mise en scène en cinématographie," *Ciné-Journal* 165 (21 octobre 1911), traduction américaine, Richard Abel, *French Film Theory and Criticism, 1907–1939: A History/Anthology,* vol. I (Princeton: Princeton University Press, 1993), 56.

5. *Le Temps,* repris dans *Ciné-Journal,* 10 décembre 1908.

6. Delluc notera d'ailleurs qu'il "est difficile de mimer sans parler quand on ne vous a pas éduqué pour l'écran" et il déplorera que "les comédiens sans expérience cinématographique parlent en tournant, et comme le dialogue qu'ils emploient est entièrement laissé à leur soins, vous imaginez le style." Et d'ajouter une anecdote: "Récemment, j'assistais à la prise de vue d'un film mondain où un couple aristocratique se querellait avec de grands airs. Le mari clamait *Grande salope! . . . Dégoûtation! Morue! etc.*" *Le cinéma des cinéastes* (Paris: Cinémathèque française, 1985), 59.

7. "Dès que la nature est simplifiée par l'effort du cerveau humain, le style apparaît." Brisson, *op. cit.*

8. *Ciné-Journal,* 3 décembre 1908.

9. Cf. ce que dit Altman de l'utilisation des micros au début du "parlant," qui va dans le même sens, dans "Technologie et représentation: l'espace sonore," *Histoire du cinéma. Nouvelles approches,* J. Aumont, A. Gaudreault, M. Marie eds., Paris: Publications de la Sorbonne, 1989.

10. Brisson, *op. cit.*

11. *Ciné-Journal,* 16 août 1909 (signé L. F. et repris de la *Revue Internationale de Photo*).

12. On peut expérimenter cette impression en visionnant la version musicale de *L'Assassinat* restaurée par les Archives du Film du Centre National de la Cinématographie français.

Appendix B
L'Événement et la série: le déclin du café-concert, l'échec du Chronophone Gaumont et la naissance de l'art cinématographique
Edouard Arnoldy

"*Ça fait rire les enfants,
ça dure jamais longtemps . . .* "
Pour Alex, Nathalie, et le futur déjà présent

Histoire(s) du cinéma et *séries (de séries)*.

Penser l'histoire du cinéma (parlant)? Autant couper court et, à l'instar de Paul Veyne, l'affirmer d'emblée: *l'histoire du cinéma (parlant) n'existe pas.* Peut-être mieux vaut-il davantage privilégier une formule cette fois empruntée à Michel de Certeau: *l'histoire du cinéma (parlant) est à la limite du pensable.* Ces deux (ou trois) bons mots n'ont pour autre souci que de dévoiler *l'esprit directeur* de mon article. La première interrogation est d'abord là pour dire que les pages consécutives ne satisferont sans doute pas complètement le lecteur avide de découvrir une nouvelle histoire du cinéma (parlant) qui réhabiliterait des films méconnus, ferait surgir de l'ombre des documents inédits, additionnerait les découvertes ou encore dresserait une liste de faits historiques et d'événements importants, comme autant de chaînons manquants à une histoire globale, complète et *définitive* du cinéma (parlant). Cette histoire-là, effectivement, n'existe pas. Ou plutôt, elle est *sans fin* parce que, ne sachant pas vraiment ce qu'elle cherche, elle refuse de reconnaître sa partialité, sa dimension parcellaire et fragmentaire, *sui generis. Un effet pour une cause:* il ne sera en aucune manière question pour moi de dévoiler l'hypothétique origine de la "révolution du parlant," ou d'accorder une valeur singulière aux seuls faits (prétendument) signifiants de l'histoire du cinéma (parlant). Une phrase des *Combats pour l'histoire* de Lucien Febvre enceint ce qui pourrait constituer le programme d'une histoire du cinéma (parlant), juste effleurée en ces pages: *donner une Histoire non point automatique, mais problématique.*[1]

Trop souvent coupée de ses racines ou artificiellement circonscrite à une période de transition, *au passage d'un cinéma à un autre,* démesurément pensée en termes de progrès ou de révolution, l'histoire du cinéma (parlant) va plutôt en ces pages se penser par entrecroisements et entrelacs, et—pour reprendre Gilles Deleuze à propos de Michel Foucault—"ne jamais se contenter de dérouler les phénomènes et les énoncés suivant la dimension horizontale ou verticale, mais former une transversale, une diagonale mobile."[2] Envisagée sous cet angle, l'histoire du cinéma parlant aura pour souci permanent de ne jamais fonder son discours sur une date de naissance (en l'occurrence la sortie du *Jazz Singer* le 6 octobre 1927), un (heureux) événement reléguant tout le reste au rayon des faits divers. Dans cette perspective, *The Jazz Singer* ne constituera invariablement le point de départ (ou d'arrivée) de cette histoire mais bien un élément d'une série (de séries).

Ce terme de *série* constitue un *concept opératoire* autour duquel l'histoire du cinéma (parlant) peut être, selon moi, en mesure de se décliner avantageusement. Le souci récurrent de cette "mise en séries" serait—comme l'a suggéré André Gaudreault—de "travailler sur une problématique plutôt que sur une période ou, plutôt, ne travailler sur une période que si elle provient d'une *périodisation problématisée.*[3] *Enveloppant* l'histoire du cinéma (parlant), les *séries (de séries)* pourraient se répondre, se préciser, et s'enchâsser comme les tuiles d'un toit. Déploiement de la "multiplicité des temps" conçue par Fernand Braudel, *l'histoire en séries* est, avant toute autre considération, là pour s'inscrire radicalement en faux face aux prétentions illusoires d'une histoire totale (du cinéma parlant). Postuler dès lors *l'analyse de séries* ne consiste aucunement à démembrer l'histoire en des unités toujours plus petites, sous le couvert d'une fallacieuse précision historienne, et à constituer des tranches d'histoire (comme on parle de "tranches de vie") de plus en plus resserrées, imperméables à des séries connexes. Dans les années soixante-dix, François Furet l'a dit très clairement:

> L'histoire sérielle décrit . . . des continuités sur le mode du discontinu. En distinguant par nécessité les niveaux de la réalité historique, elle décompose par définition toute conception préalable d'une histoire "globale" en mettant précisément en question le postulat d'une évolution supposée homogène et identique de tous les éléments d'une société . . . Elle atomise la réalité historique en fragments si distincts qu'elle compromet en même temps la prétention de l'histoire classique à la saisie du global . . . [. . . .] Ce n'est pas à dire qu'elle doive se borner à l'analyse microscopique d'une seule série chronologique; elle peut regrouper plusieurs de ses séries et proposer dès lors l'interprétation d'un système, ou d'un sous-système.[4]

Penser l'histoire du cinéma et ses séries (de séries), c'est, à l'instar de Michel Foucault, refuser la "description globale [qui] resserre tous les phénomènes autour d'un centre unique."[5] C'est, *in fine,* ouvrir une brèche dans l'histoire des arts du XXe siècle, où il devrait être question de cinéma, d'arts institués et de spectacles de divertissement, de *technique,* d'*art* et de *pratiques culturelles (populaires), tout à la fois* car, comme l'a suggéré avec force Paul Veyne, "il est impossible de décider qu'un fait est historique et qu'un autre est une anecdote digne d'oubli, parce que *tout fait entre dans une série et n'a d'importance relative que dans sa série.*[6] Plurielle, l'histoire du cinéma (parlant) appelle *des séries (de séries).* En ce sens, André Gaudreault a judicieusement postulé une histoire du cinéma(tographe) qui serait (aussi) *l'histoire de séries culturelles.* Particulièrement attentif aux rapports étroits qui lient solidement les "films chantants et parlants" des années dix et les spectacles des cafés-concerts en France, il ne s'agira jamais ici d'établir une stricte relation de cause à effet entre l'échec (relatif) des premiers et le déclin (partiel) des

seconds, ni—comme l'a écrit Marc Bloch—de "confondre une filiation avec une explication," mais plutôt de regarder sous un jour nouveau l'histoire des "projections parlantes"
au temps du cinéma muet.[7] Dans cette perspective, mon attention va ici essentiellement
se concentrer sur les liens presqu'indéfectibles qui unissent, comme les maillons d'une
chaîne, deux éléments d'une série culturelle: les phono-scènes Gaumont et les spectacles
(chantés) des cafés-concerts parisiens.

Le déclin du café-concert et l'échec (relatif) des phono-scènes Gaumont: L'événement et la série.

A l'aube des années dix, le cinéma semble subir les effets d'un séisme sans épi-
centre. L'art et l'industrie cinématographiques sont ballottés de toutes parts, affectés
de profonds mouvements, sans qu'un événement majeur soit apparemment à l'origine
de ces glissements de terrain. Les secousses sont multiples, de plus ou moins grande
ampleur, et de conséquences diverses: les premières revues corporatives voient le jour
(*Phono-Ciné-Gazette, la Revue du Phonographe* et *du Cinématographe,* puis *Ciné-Journal*), le *Film d'Art* paraît promis à un bel avenir, le cinéma se structure en industrie et se
sédentarise pour peu à peu s'affranchir des salles populaires qui inscrivaient régulièrement depuis 1903 des projections à leurs programmes, etc. En 1908, en plein cœur de
cette tourmente, Gaumont publie un catalogue presqu'essentiellement consacré à ses
"films pour projections parlantes" et au Chronophone, le système de synchronisation (du
son et de l'image) mis au point dans ses laboratoires. Journalistes, scientifiques ou exploitants s'accordent pour souligner l'extrême perfection technique du procédé. Eu égard
à ces témoignages, l'énigme posée par l'échec (relatif) du Chronophone paraît plus largement s'inscrire dans la tourmente des années 1905–1910. A l'inverse d'une compagnie
comme Pathé dont on connaît les "scènes phono-cinématographiques," la compagnie à
la marguerite ne disperse pas ses films "chantants et parlants" au hasard de catalogues
dévolus à sa production silencieuse. Ce traitement privilégié est à la hauteur de l'importance qu'octroie alors Léon Gaumont aux phono-scènes.

Scènes représentatives de classiques du théâtre, de la chanson populaire et de l'opéra,
sans hiérarchie de valeur apparente, genres nobles et moins nobles se succèdent au gré
de la liste des phono-scènes mises en vente dans les catalogues Gaumont. En proposant
côte à côte des extraits d'opéras et des chansons populaires, la société à la marguerite
paraît, à première vue, faire un grand écart audacieux entre la grandiloquence ronflante
des uns et le côté polisson des autres. Cet aspect disparate et composite du catalogue
constitue un héritage direct de la programmation parfois bigarrée des cafés-concerts, où
des genres complètement différents s'entremêlent, où des spectacles variés se croisent sur
scène. Bien que Gaumont s'en défende, le Chronophone entre ainsi en concurrence directe avec les cafés-concerts, ces salles de spectacle qui ont favorisé l'essor du cinématographe.[8] Puisant directement dans le répertoire des cafés-concerts, Gaumont—qui, littéralement, *leur vole la vedette*—paraît en 1908 assuré du succès de ses "films chantants
et parlants." Bien que la compagnie annonce "un répertoire enrichi de plus en plus de
sujets toujours plus artistiques," sans doute ne tient-elle pas suffisamment compte des
débats qui agitent la presse à pareille époque. Emanant des plus farouches défenseurs du
théâtre et de l'art cinématographique, de nombreux journalistes fustigent les spectacles
des cafés-concerts dont s'inspirent manifestement les phono-scènes.

A partir de janvier 1907, *Phono-Ciné-Gazette,* la revue fondée en 1905 par Edmond
Benoît-Lévy, répercute les déclarations émises dans *L'Intransigeant* ou *La Patrie.* Fidèle
à "l'évolution du goût du public," soucieux de pratiquer des tarifs très bas, le cinéma-

tographe est maintenant un concurrent redoutable tant pour le théâtre que pour le café-concert. A la mi-janvier, Fernand Divoire note dans *Phono-Ciné-Gazette* que "les théâtres s'émeuvent de la concurrence que leur fait le cinématographe, comme ils se sont émus aussi, sans pouvoir rien y faire, du développement pris par le café-concert."[9] Dans un contexte particulièrement défavorable, une alliance—en un sens paradoxale—va pourtant être scellée entre les théâtres et les cinématographes, les ennemis avoués du moment. Sans qu'une coalition ne se constitue entre les directeurs de salles et les intercesseurs de la photographie animée, les premiers se réjouissent à l'idée que l'essor du cinématographe puisse asséner un coup fatal aux cafés-concerts.[10] Le succès du cinématographe profite aux directeurs de théâtres au moins sur ce point: les cafés-concerts, dont ils n'avaient jamais réussi à empêcher l'ascension depuis leur éclosion dans la première moitié du XIXe siècle, trouvent là un rival de dimension.[11] Propriétaires de théâtres ou de cinématographes, fervents défenseurs du *vrai* répertoire ou du jeune cinéma, tous s'accordent pour saluer une telle émulation, contraignant les cafés-concerts à proposer des divertissements de "meilleur goût," comme l'opérette, un genre (populaire) socialement plus acceptable que les traditionnels pots-pourris d'origine foraine. Désormais, les cafés-concerts qui soignent leur réputation excluent la grossièreté et les mauvais mots, trop souvent décochés en direction de l'Eglise et de la Patrie. Le café-concert participe à une plus large diffusion de pièces sérieuses *pour le peuple.* Particulièrement condescendante et élitiste, la grande presse loue occasionnellement le souci de certains grands artistes de vouloir partager leur art (noble) avec le peuple. Aux alentours de 1908, *Le Temps, Le Figaro* et *Comœdia,* jusqu'alors les chantres d'une culture d'élite, professent les bienfaits de la vulgarisation des grands classiques.[12]

Les trop fortes accointances d'un théâtre prétendument populaire et d'un café-concert repenti de ses fautes sont vilipendés par les amateurs du cinéma. Le 1er septembre 1908, *Ciné-Journal* fait grand cas de l'émotion suscitée auprès des directeurs de cinématographes par une circulaire promulguée à la date du 10 août. *Ciné-Journal* relève un passage du texte officiel où "les établissements ont été départagés sur des bases différentes de l'ordonnance de 1898, qui divisait les spectacles en théâtres et cafés-concerts." Désormais les salles se distinguent les unes des autres "suivant les dangers que peuvent présenter les installations et les aménagements de la scène."[13] Pour la rédaction de *Ciné-Journal,* cette ordonnance met noir sur blanc le théâtre et le café-concert sur un pied d'égalité. Pour les avocats du cinématographe, la confusion entre théâtre et café-concert, déjà perceptible dans les programmes proposés par les salles de spectacle, est rendue effective depuis la promulgation de cette ordonnance du 10 août 1908. Georges Dureau se fait un malin plaisir d'écrire alors que "le théâtre et le café-concert c'est tout un."[14] Le journaliste fustige l'hypocrisie des indécrottables pourfendeurs du cinématographe qui osent remettre en question sa moralité, alors qu'eux-mêmes fréquentent assidûment d'affreux bouis-bouis. L'éditorial que signe Georges Dureau le 11 juin 1909 dans *Ciné-Journal* trace une ligne de démarcation franche entre le cinéma et le théâtre. Dans ce manifeste, la rupture est consommée:

> La presse quotidienne qui est une grande redresseuse de torts ne manque pas de s'élever périodiquement contre ce qu'elle appelle d'un mot pompeux l'immoralité du cinématographe. [. . . .] Comme [les grandes revues d'honnêteté] ont la garde du goût français, elles déplorent que le public oublie le chemin des théâtres pour aller voir passer quelques films au pays du silence, dans la joie des gestes expressifs ou des paysages évocateurs. [. . . .] Dimanche dernier, en bon français qui sait ce qu'il se doit, je suis allé au café-concert. La salle—une des plus belles du genre—

était pleine de gens qui étaient venus pour se réjouir en suçant des cerises "après le turbin" hebdomadaire. Il n'y eut pas de cinématographe. Par contre, le comique spécial de l'établissement se recommandait de la plus remarquable "cochonnerie" parisienne. Plus les chanteurs, plus les diseurs soulignaient la saleté de leurs couplets, appuyaient sur leurs effets, plus les dames et les jeunes filles—on était en famille—semblaient heureuses. Aucune gêne dans cette atmosphère écœurante. Cette aimable bourgeoisie élégamment endimanchée nageait à l'aise dans cette pourriture. [. . . .] Mais voilà ! De cette prodigieuse sottise, de cette pornographie qui exclut tout esprit, la grande presse éducative ne parle pas. Elle émarge aux communiqués des bouis-bouis, elle a des entrées qui la dispensent de crier à l'immoralité. Pour elle qui ne connaît qu'une cloche, la cloche d'argent, le café-concert et le théâtre c'est tout un. C'est le grand art. [. . . .] Et c'est contre le cinéma que [la presse] se retourne pour faire diversion.[. . . .] La neutralité obligatoire [des scénarios] dépouille le film de tout ce qui pourrait le rendre pernicieux et l'oppose nécessairement à la pornographie qui s'épanouit au café-concert. Au surplus, le vent est au cinématographe d'art. Le succès ira de plus en plus au comique délicat, au drame sobre et bien joué, aux voyages et aux grandes actualités. Si la gravelure de quelques bouis-bouis en souffre . . . tant mieux![15]

Au pays du silence et de l'art cinématographique.

La "Première Sensationnelle de *L'Assassinat du Duc de Guise*" correspond pour les rédactions de *Phono-Ciné-Gazette* ou *Ciné-Journal* à la naissance d'un "art cinématographique nouveau" et d'un "cinéma artistique." En décembre 1908, Edmond Benoît-Lévy saluera le retour "de ces spectateurs [qui] n'avaient pas revu le cinématographe depuis les premiers spectacles du Café de la Paix et ne se doutaient pas des progrès accomplis dans ces dernières années."[16] En septembre 1908, Georges Dureau, le fondateur de *Ciné-Journal*, allait déjà dans ce sens lorsqu'il dressait un premier bilan de la courte histoire du cinématographe. Pour le directeur de *Ciné-Journal*, les spectateurs, encore sous le charme presqu'hypnotique de l'invention de la photographie animée, se seraient jusqu'alors satisfaits "des facéties d'un *Toto Gâte-Sauce*, des poursuites effrénées mises à la mode par la maison Pathé, des drames servis en abondance, des féeries diverses et plus ou moins coloriées et des comédies et des pièces de fantaisie et de voyages et des actualités."[17] A ses yeux, ce temps est bel et bien révolu. Deux mois à peine avant la sortie de *L'Assassinat du Duc de Guise*, Georges Dureau ne cachait pas son goût pour les "vues réelles," mais pensait devoir:

louer les rapports du Cinéma avec le vrai Théâtre parce que, en se rapprochant de la vie dramatique et de l'art, les scénarios et les artistes qui les interprètent vont nécessairement s'ennoblir. Il y a là comme une dignité nouvelle pour le Cinéma naguère attardé dans de médiocres aspirations.[18]

Vues réelles, comique délicat bien joué, actualités, décors et scénarios soignés, voilà *le pays du silence cinématographique* dont rêve, en ces termes là, le directeur de l'*Organe hebdomadaire de l'Industrie cinématographique*. Sans dénigrer "les mélodrames à grosse sensation, les pièces chères au Grand Guignol, les vaudevilles plaisants ou la pièce policière [qui] entre brillamment au Cinéma avec les aventures de *Nick Carter*, roi des détectives," Georges Dureau reconnaît ne guère porter dans son cœur le comique facile, les poursuites effrénées ou les féeries, bref "la cinématographie de composition [qui] marche avec la mode, à la façon des revuistes de nos music-halls [et] s'inspire des goûts passagers de la vie parisienne dont elle devient peu à peu comme une manifestation expresse, aussi fugitive."[19] Georges Dureau accepte bien quelques écarts mais refuse assez radicalement les films qui conservent des liens de parenté avec le monde du spectacle et du café-concert. A cette "cinématographie de composition," aux attractions et aux films qui conservent des affinités trop grandes avec les représentations des foires et des cabarets parisiens, Georges Dureau préfère désormais le *Cinéma*.[20] Lui qui s'évertue depuis quelques temps à convaincre "*les gens de bonne compagnie*" de devenir les "*spectateurs ordinaires du cinéma,*" début 1910, Georges Dureau "félicite les fabricants d'avoir rivalisé d'efforts artistiques."[21] Au printemps 1911, Georges Dureau l'admet avec un certain désappointement: "les gens de culture un peu soignée ne sont pas encore les clients assidus de nos salles de projection."[22] "Le vent du cinématographe d'art" par lui annoncé en juin 1909 perd de sa superbe. Dans un tel climat, au *pays du silence cinématographique*, les films trop proches de "la gravelure des bouis-bouis"—à l'image des phono-scènes mises en vente dans le catalogue Gaumont 1908—pouvaient difficilement échapper au sarcasme des amateurs de l'art cinématographique, ni bénéficier de leur clémence.

En 1908, Emile Maugras (avocat, administrateur délégué de l'Omnia-Pathé et Président du Conseil du Cinéma-Théâtre Pathé) et M. Guégan (docteur en droit et administrateur du Cinéma National Pathé) rédigent un document de cent quarante pages sèchement intitulé *Le Cinématographe devant le droit*. Dans cet ouvrage, il est tout à la fois question de protéger le "génie" et les droits de l'auteur, de défendre les intérêts des sociétés productrices de films et de barrer la route à la contrefaçon et au contrefacteur. Afin de définitivement faire admettre le cinématographe parmi les beaux-arts, l'art cinématographique naissant doit, selon les deux avocats, tout mettre en œuvre pour se distinguer radicalement des spectacles de réputation parfois peu amène. Pour eux, il y va, ni plus ni moins, de sa survie. Reconnaissant au cinématographe des origines populaires (son bon marché, son goût pour les histoires simples et vite résolues, etc.), Maugras et Guégan lui accordent néanmoins—au contraire du théâtre et de la littérature—le bénéfice d'une *valeur morale ajoutée*:

> La cinématographie a été jusqu'alors des plus morales, que jamais on y trouve de scènes scabreuses, de situations équivoques. Il semble que cet art, au milieu de l'immoralité ambiante et toujours grandissante du théâtre, ait voulu s'affranchir des goûts dépravés et des idées dangereuses de la littérature moderne. Les scènes cinématographiques sont des pantomimes, mais des pantomimes courtes, admirablement jouées, toujours d'une conception honnête, souvent d'un esprit fin. [. . . .] Dans ces conditions, il nous paraît encore plus aisé de classer parmi les arts, les films cinématographiques dont le triomphe tient aussi bien à la perfection des scènes ou paysages qu'à la moralité des spectacles.[23]

En 1908 (encore et toujours), quand les intérêts de Pathé et Gaumont paraissent conduire les deux puissantes firmes sur la voie d'un cinéma d'art, un poète italien, admiré par Guillaume Apollinaire, rédige un texte d'un grand lyrisme: Ricciotto Canudo y exhorte au *triomphe du cinématographe*. Le poète a bon espoir, mais affirme alors que "le cinématographe n'est pas *encore* de l'art, car lui manquent les éléments du choix typique, de l'*interprétation* plastique et non de la *copie* d'un sujet. *Le Cinématographe n'est donc pas un art, aujourd'hui.*"[24] Lorsqu'il prédit le triomphe du cinématographe, Ricciotto Canudo entérine le divorce entre l'art cinématographique et la cinématographie-attraction, entre le cinématographe d'art et les spectacles de variétés. Envisageant incidemment le 7e Art au cœur de séries (de séries), l'article du poète consomme la rupture—contenue en germe dans les éditoriaux de *Ciné-Phono-Gazette* ou *Ciné-Journal*—entre un *Art plastique en mouvement* et le *théâtre filmé,* entre le cinéma et le Verbe:

> Et cette expression d'art sera une conciliation entre les Rythmes de l'Espace (les Arts plastiques) et les Rythmes du Temps (Musique et Poésie). Le théâtre a réalisé jusqu'ici cette conciliation; mais elle était éphémère, parce que la plastique du Théâtre dépend étroitement de celle des acteurs, et elle est par conséquent toujours très diverse. La nouvelle expression de l'art devrait être au contraire, précisément, *une Peinture et une sculpture se développant dans le temps,* comme la Musique et la Poésie qui prennent vie, rythment l'air pendant le temps de leur exécution. Le Cinématographe—il est inutile d'en changer le nom, mais il n'est pas beau— indique la voie. Un génie pourrait créer un courant énorme d'émotion esthétique nouvelle, avec un *Art plastique en mouvement.*[25]

En 1908, Ricciotto Canudo invente le cinéma muet.

Notes

1. Febvre, Lucien, *Combats pour l'histoire* [1952] (Paris: Armand Colin, 1992), 42.
2. Deleuze, Gilles, *Foucault* (Paris: Les Editions de Minuit, 1986), 30.
3. Gaudreault, André, "Les *Vues cinématographiques* selon Georges Méliès, ou: comment Mitry et Sadoul avaient peut-être raison d'avoir tort (même si c'est surtout Deslandes qu'il faut lire et relire) . . . ," in Malthête, Jacques, Marie, Michel, eds., *Georges Méliès l'illusionniste fin de siècle?* (Paris: Presses de la Sorbonne Nouvelle, 1997, 117. Ce texte d'André Gaudreault s'articule entièrement autour de l'interrogation qui inaugure le présent article: *Penser l'histoire du cinéma ?* Par ailleurs, Rick Altman a, lui aussi, déjà proposé de "Penser l'histoire du cinéma autrement: un modèle de crise," in *Vingtième siècle* 46 (1995), 65–74. *Penser l'histoire:* il faut en convenir la question hante la "Nouvelle Histoire" depuis près d'un demi-siècle . . .
4. Furet, François, "Le quantitatif en histoire," in Le Goff, Jacques, Nora, Pierre, *Faire de l'Histoire,* vol. 1 (Paris: Gallimard, 1974), 54–55. Ce terme de "série" n'est pas sans correspondre ici au sens (précis) que lui donne Michel Foucault dans *L'Archéologie du savoir* et dans *L'Ordre du Discours.*
5. Foucault, Michel, *L'archéologie du savoir* (Paris: Gallimard, 1969), 19.
6. Veyne, Paul, *Comment on écrit l'histoire* [1971] (Paris, Seuil, 1996), 35.
7. Bloch, Marc, *Apologie pour l'histoire ou Métier d'historien* [1943] (Paris: Armand Colin, 1997), 56.
8. Dans la revue espagnole *Archivos,* j'ai eu l'occasion de revenir plus en détail sur ce qui unit les phono-scènes et la mise en scène des spectacles dans les cafés-concerts. J'y analyse notamment un commun "travail d'inclusion" du spectateur, en convoquant trois phono-scènes des catalogues Gaumont: *Le frotteur de la Colonelle* [Polin, no 134, cat. 1908], *Questions indiscrètes* [Mayol, no 154, cat. 1908] et *Le vrai jiu-jitsu* [Dranem, no 167, cat. 1908].
9. Divoire, Fernand, "Cinéma & Théâtre," *Phono-Ciné-Gazette* 42 (15 janvier 1907), 32.
10. Eu égard à la place de choix occupée par les chants ou la musique dans la programmation des cafés-concerts parisiens (dont l'essor remonte à la première moitié du XIXe siècle), conjuguée à l'installation d'une estrade, les cafés-chantants prennent, vers

1860 en France, le nom de *cafés-concerts*. Dès ce moment, les *clients* des *cafés-chantants* sont les *spectateurs* des *cafés-concerts*. Concernant l'histoire du café-concert, un ouvrage est, à mes yeux, incontournable: Chadourne, André, *Les Cafés-Concerts,* Paris, E. Dentu, 1889. Riche de près de quatre cents pages, le livre d'André Chadourne aborde le café-concert sous des angles multiples. Il en retrace l'histoire, s'intéresse aussi bien aux clauses des contrats des artistes et à leurs appointements qu'aux œuvres et à leur mise en scène, au droit d'auteur et à la censure. Plus récemment, Lionel Richard a publié un livret consacré aux différents types de cabarets en Europe: *Cabarets. Cabaret,* Paris, Plon, 1991. Voir également: Georges d'Avenel, *Le Mécanisme de la vie moderne* (1902); Edmond et Jules de Goncourt, *Idées et sensations* (1893); Alfred Delvau, *Les Plaisirs de Paris (Guide Pratique)* (1867); Jules Lemaître, *Impressions de théâtre* (1900); et les articles de *Comœdia, Le Figaro, Le Temps, Phono-Ciné-Gazette* et *Ciné-Journal* (publiés en gros entre 1890 et 1915). Par ailleurs, dans les ouvrages de Jacques Deslandes et Jacques Richard—*Histoire comparée du cinéma,* 2 tomes, Tournai: Casterman, 1966–1968—et de Jean-Jacques Meusy —*Paris-Palaces,* Paris, CNRS Editions, 1995—il est notamment question du passage du Cinématographe dans les cafés-concerts parisiens.

11. Voir, entre autres: Vallery, François, "La fin du beuglant," *Phono-Ciné-Gazette* 79 (1 juillet 1908), 644.

12. Les programmes proposés par les salles de spectacle entre 1906 et 1910 paraissent régulièrement dans *Le Temps, Le Figaro* ou *Comœdia.* J'y renvoie le lecteur intéressé. Voir également les articles alors publiés dans *Le Figaro* (8 janvier 1908), et Bernheim, Adrien, "Trente ans de théâtre," *Le Figaro* (5 juin 1907), 6.

13. Toutes ces citations sont extraites d'un même article paru dans *Ciné-Journal:* "Le nouveau régime des Théâtres et Cinématographes," (1 septembre 1908), 4–5 [non signé].

14. Dureau, Georges, "Littérature de Bouis-Bouis et Cinématographe," *Ciné-Journal* 42 (5 juin 1909), 1–2. Voir aussi: Dureau, Georges, "Le Cinéma et le Théâtre," *Ciné-Journal* 5 (15 septembre 1908), 1–2.

15. Dureau, Georges, "Littérature de Bouis-Bouis et Cinématographe," art. cit., 1–2.

16. Convoquant à la barre *Le Temps, Gil-Blas, Le Matin, Comœdia* et *Le Gaulois,* Edmond Benoît-Lévy donne la parole aux éditorialistes à l'accoutumée hostiles au Cinématographe, dont Jules Clarétie et Adolphe Brisson. Comme une note discordante face à une apparente unanimité, Victor Jasset ne dira pas en 1911 que le *Film d'Art* fut *le* fait historique ou l'événement-charnière du "tournant des années dix." Voir: Benoît-Lévy, Edmond, "Une Première Sensationnelle," *Phono-Ciné-Gazette* 90 (1 décembre 1908), 804–806; "M. Clarétie et le Cinématographe," *Ciné-Journal* 15 (26 novembre 1908), 5–7; "Ce que M. Brisson pense du Film d'art," *Ciné-Journal* 17 (10 décembre 1908), 7–9; Jasset, Victor, "Etude sur la mise en scène," *Ciné-Journal* (21 octobre-25 novembre 1911), repris in: Lapierre, Marcel, ed., *Anthologie du cinéma* (Paris: La Nouvelle Edition, 1946), 82–99. [The Jasset text also is translated in Richard Abel, *French Film Theory and Criticism, 1907–1929: A History/Anthology* (Princeton: Princeton University Press, 1988), 55–58.]

17. Dureau, Georges, "Le Cinéma et le Théâtre," art. cit., 1–2.

18. Dureau, Georges, art. cit., 2.

19. Dureau, Georges, art. cit., 1–2.

20. A cet égard, un *artisan* comme Georges Méliès a sans doute aux yeux des fervents promoteurs de l'Art Cinématographique le tort de d'abord se présenter comme un *opérateur* hors-pair. Les quelques textes et l'œuvre filmique de Georges Méliès gagneraient sans doute à être envisagés sous cet angle. Voir notamment: Méliès, Georges, "Les vues cinématographiques," *Annuaire Général et International de Photographie* (Paris, Librairie

Plon, 1907), 363–392. [This text is translated in Abel, *French Film Theory and Criticism,* 35–47.]

21. Dureau, Georges, "Soignons le public," *Ciné-Journal* 74 (16 janvier 1910), 1–2.

22. Dureau, Georges, "Le Cinématographe, Théâtre du peuple," *Ciné-Journal* 143 (20 mai 1911), 1–4.

23. Maugras, Emile, Guegan M., *Le Cinématographe devant le droit* (Paris, V. Giard & E. Brière, 1908), 17–19. Je remercie mille fois André Gaudreault de m'avoir transmis une copie de cet ouvrage. Nous n'avons pas fini—je pense—d'en discuter (avec enthousiasme).

24. Canudo, Ricciotto, "Lettere d'arte. Trionfo del cinematografo ["Triomphe du Cinématographe"]," *Il Nuovo giornale,* Firenze (25 novembre 1908); repris dans: Canudo, Ricciotto, *L'Usine aux images,* (Paris: Séguier/Arte Éditions, 1995), 27.

25. Canudo, Ricciotto, art. cit., 24–25.

Appendix C
Les transi-sons du cinéma
des premiers temps[1]
Bernard Perron

Cet article découle encore beaucoup plus d'une réflexion théorique sur le cinéma des premiers temps que d'une recherche historique. Je dis "encore" parce qu'il se veut un prolongement du texte que j'ai rédigé pour le dernier colloque de Domitor sur la firme Pathé Frères [Perron, à paraître]. À cette occasion, j'ai fait une analyse comparative du *Médecin du château* (ou *The Physician of the Castle*)—une production distribuée par Pathé en 1908—et de *The Lonely Villa*—réalisé par Griffith en 1909 —, deux films qui exploitent l'intrigue grand guignol de la famille menacée par des voleurs ayant au préalable éloigné le père de la maison. Considérant *Le Médecin du château* comme un paradigme de l'état du récit cinématographique au début du système d'intégration narrative (1908-1915)[2], j'ai voulu rendre compte avec lui de l'une des étapes de la systématisation du montage alterné. Toutefois, tel que l'a souligné Richard Abel lors d'une discussion subséquente, j'ai négligé un élément essentiel: le son intradiégétique. Je me propose donc de combler cette lacune de mon analyse du film de Pathé et d'envisager des propositions théoriques plus générales.

En me référant à la figure suivante [figure 1], je résumerai d'abord les conclusions que j'ai tirées au sujet du *Médecin du château*. Le mode de représentation ainsi que l'articulation entre les plans du film de Pathé relèvent d'une conception théâtrale. Les plans d'ensemble prennent explicitement modèle sur la scène à l'italienne. Les changements de plans sont largement motivés par l'entrée ou la sortie de personnages. Lorsqu'elles s'effectuent en profondeur, ces dernières se conforment à la convention théâtrale voulant qu'un personnage qui quitte à droite fasse aussi son entrée à droite, ce qui empêche la création d'une ligne d'action simple et cohérente (de gauche à droite comme dans *The Lonely Villa* de Griffith par exemple). Ces entrées et sorties de scène sont enfin ponctuées par des champs vides qui instituent une certaine distance entre les lieux de la diégèse. En ce sens, *Le Médecin du château* n'est pas en mesure d'établir que les deux pièces de la *maison* du médecin qu'il nous présente, soit le salon et le cabinet [voir ci-après les photogrammes 1, 2, et 3], sont contiguës. Il ne relie pas ces pièces, il les juxtapose. Il n'est pas à même d'articuler des disjonctions proximales entre un champ (*ici*) et un hors-champ (*là*) et de créer une alternance antérieure au sein du même lieu (du type *A1–A2*) [voir la figure 1]. Le hors-champ (*offscreen space*) demeure une région métonymique flottante qui n'entoure pas le champ et qui n'exerce pas encore une pression continuelle sur ce dernier. Chaque plan est plutôt considéré comme une unité autonome, comme un cadre locatif où se déroule un événement, bref comme une scène. Les prolongements hors du champ ne sont pas tant spatiaux (le *là* d'un *ici*) que narratifs. J'appelle "hors-scène" (*off-screen scene*) cette portion d'espace diégétique non visible et non contiguë (*là-bas*) au cadre locatif mais rattaché à celui-ci par le développement du récit.

Parce qu'il existe toujours un écart entre les espaces diégétiques, *Le Médecin du château* n'articule que des disjonctions distales entre une scène (*ici/là*) et un hors-scène (*là-bas*). Marquant bien, par un trajet de voiture et par un carton ("Arriving at the Castle"), la distance qui sépare la *maison* du *château* où est faussement entraîné le médecin, le film n'a cette fois-ci aucune difficulté à tirer profit d'une alternance supérieure entre ces deux segments narratifs (du type *A-B*) [voir la figure 1]. En fait, cette alternance est constituée de trois séries:

A) le médecin au *château,*
B) la femme et le fils dans le cabinet de la *maison;* et
C*) les deux malfaiteurs dans le salon de la *maison.*

Si une disjonction proximale avait été établie, les séries A-C* seraient alors considérées comme une alternance A1–A2. On s'explique mieux que seul le rapport de corrélation scène/hors-scène a pu être considéré lorsqu'on sait que le montage alterné était désigné en 1908 par l'expression "scènes alternées." N'empêche que le film de Pathé réussit à situer et à relier les lieux du drame. Une fois les termes posés, l'alternance se déroule comme suit:

Carton: "Arriving at the Castle."
A) chateau: grille—La voiture du médecin arrive au château (plan 13).
             Salon—Le médecin rejoint la famille qui se porte finalement bien (plan 14).
B) maison: cabinet—L'épouse et le fils du médecin entrent à droite et barricadent la porte. Ils restent tout ouïe près de cette dernière (plan 15).
C*) maison: salon—Les deux malfaiteurs entrent dans le salon et tendent l'oreille afin de localiser le cabinet. Ils sortent en arrière-plan à droite (plan 16).
B) maison: cabinet—L'épouse cesse d'écouter mais le fils reste attentif près de la porte du cabinet. L'épouse trouve le numéro du château et téléphone (plan 17).
A) château: salon—Le médecin est toujours avec la famille. Un serviteur l'informe de l'appel de son épouse (plan 18).
B) maison: cabinet—L'épouse du médecin au téléphone (plan rapproché 19).
A) château: salon—Le médecin au téléphone (plan rapproché 20).
             salon—Le médecin quitte la famille (plan 21).
             grille—La voiture du médecin quitte le château (plan 22).

Isabelle Raynauld l'a noté à propos des scénarios et des films de Méliès [1997] et de ceux de Pathé d'avant 1914, "le son fait partie intégrante de la mise en scène et influence la façon de raconter l'histoire. C'est un élément dramaturgique essentiel du récit cinématographique de cette époque [muette]" [Raynauld, à paraître]. *Le Médecin du château* étaye cette observation. Au sein de l'alternance ci-haut décrite, il y a deux grands événements sonores intradiégétiques, c'est-à-dire deux actions à caractère sonore qui apportent une information narrative et qui font changer le cours de la situation narrative [Raynauld, 1997: 204].

Le premier grand événement sonore est sans aucun doute le plus intéressant. Il concerne l'écoute des personnages dans la MAISON. Celle-ci est explicitement visualisée dans les plans 15, 16 et 17 [photogrammes 1, 2 et 3]. Les trois auteurs qui se sont suffisamment intéressés au *Médecin du château* pour en décrire l'action, c'est-à-dire Barry Salt [1985–86: 285], Tom Gunning [1991a: 197][3] et Richard Abel [1994: 194][4], ne notent ni l'un ni l'autre cette écoute explicite qui, pourtant, constitue la pierre angulaire de la première alternance supérieure (salon/cabinet). À l'instar des entrées et des sorties de personnages, la visualisation du son autorise l'investissement graduel du champ aveugle car elle décentre l'image. Dans cette optique, et pour reprendre une expression deleuzienne qu'utilise Livio Belloï dans sa *Poétique du hors-champ* [1992], s'il n'y a pas encore de "fil" unissant le champ au hors-champ, il y a certes une "onde" qui part de la scène et qui la relie au hors-scène. L'articulation de disjonctions proximales et les transitions spatio-temporelles franches et serrées au sein d'un même lieu ne sont peut-être pas encore possibles parce que difficiles à comprendre pour le spectateur. Mais ce que j'appellerai des transi-sons (*transi-sounds*[5]), elles, sont fort concevables [figure 2].

Le cinéma dit muet, et c'est une donnée fondamentale qu'il est nécessaire d'accentuer, ne fait peut-être pas réellement appel à l'oreille, mais il s'adresse beaucoup à l'entendement. *Le Médecin du château* fait fond sur les attentes d'un public formé au théâtre ainsi que sur la perception quotidienne et ordinaire du son. À l'instar de ce que l'on retrouve au théâtre, c'est par l'utilisation d'un procédé sonore intradiégétique marquant la résonance des pièces cachées que la mise en scène du film de Pathé suggère la réalité qui se déroule en dehors du champ de vision du spectateur et qu'elle transforme les coulisses (*offstage*) en hors-scène (*offscene*) [cf. PAVIS, 1987: 193]. Le son appartient tout aussi bien à l'*ici* qu'au *là* ou qu'au *là-bas*. Les personnages écoutent des bruits produits au-delà de la scène. L'audible, écrit Mikel Dufresne dans son livre *L'oeil et l'oreille,* possède deux dimensions co-présentes:

> le son à la fois m'investit de tous côtés, m'entoure, m'englobe en lui, et d'autre part se situe dans une certaine direction qui donne quelque indication sur sa source [Dufresne, 1991: 86].

Par la spatialité de son champ qui déborde les données visibles ainsi que par l'attention portée à la localisation de sa source, le son permet de combler la distance séparant les espaces diégétiques. Il rend surtout possible la réalisation de transitions intelligibles entre lesdits espaces [d'où la flèche de la figure 2]. De la sorte, la supposée proximité des scènes à l'intérieur de la maison du médecin (le salon et le cabinet) est établie par l'action des personnages qui tendent l'oreille vers une source hors-scène. L'événement sonore pose les tenants de l'alternance. Celui-ci demeure un indice fourni au spectateur afin qu'il puisse comprendre le film et combler les espaces blancs entre les plans ou les scènes. Dans *Le Médecin du château,* l'écoute sert littéralement de point de transi-son [d'où le point gris qui déborde et englobe tout à la fois l'espace du cadre dans la figure 2].

Parler de transi-son permet de mettre l'accent et sur l'idée de passage et sur l'importance du son. À mon avis, cela éclaire de nouvelle façon la réflexion d'Eileen Bowser au sujet de la systématisation du montage alterné au cinéma.

> It seems significant to me that the early examples of parallel editing deal with adjacent space and not distant ones. This is evidently the first step in the development of the concept [Bowser, 1983a: 338].

Et elle note ailleurs que plusieurs de ces premiers exemples "might be interpreted as the need to show visual equivalents of sounds, sounds to which the characters react" [1983b: 370]. Les scènes alternées de *The Mill Girl,* le film de Vitagraph (1907) qu'étudie

Bowser en détail et à partir duquel elle déduit ses conclusions, sont éloquentes. L'action se déroule près d'une fenêtre à l'intérieur et à l'extérieur d'une maison. N'étant pas plus en mesure d'articuler des disjonctions proximales, Vitagraph prend soin, comme le note Bowser [1983a: 338], de laisser la fenêtre de la maison hors du champ de vision du spectateur. À l'instar des malfaiteurs du *Médecin du château*, le héros du film approche sa main près de son oreille afin d'écouter les bruits extérieurs et de situer les agresseurs dans le hors-scène. De leur côté, ceux-ci font du bruit en plaçant une échelle contre le mur et sont réprimandés par leur chef qui commande le silence en gesticulant. L'empiétement sonore intradiégétique joue un rôle important. L'alternance repose derechef sur des transi-sons. C'est également le cas d'un autre exemple canonique cité par Bowser. Il s'agit de *The Trainer's Daughter; or, A Race for Love*. Dans ce film d'Edison (1907), le plan d'un homme qui sonne l'appel des jockeys en soufflant dans un cornet est inséré dans une scène à l'écurie où ladite fille de l'entraîneur doit se préparer pour la course. Ici, la compréhension du lien entre les espaces beaucoup plus éloignés est rendue possible par la grande portée du cornet. Ce type de communication sonore amplifiée[6] m'amène à discuter rapidement du second événement sonore de l'alternance que j'ai décrite plus tôt.

La deuxième alternance supérieure du *Médecin du château* (maison/château) met en scène un coup de téléphone à suspense. Il s'agit d'un autre dispositif sonore que plusieurs films de cette époque ont exploité. On aura compris que l'utilisation d'un instrument qui permet de transmettre à distance des sons et de relier des espaces éloignés sert de manière parfaite mon propos. Je ne veux donc pas m'étendre sur la représentation des conversations téléphoniques. Toutefois, je noterai à la suite d'Eileen Bowser [1985] et de Tom Gunning [1991b] que l'introduction de cette nouvelle technologie a permis de naturaliser le pouvoir du cinéma de se déplacer à travers le temps et l'espace. Curieusement, c'est à ce moment que Pathé se déplace dans l'espace de la scène du *Médecin du château* afin de nous offrir deux exceptionnels plans rapprochés de l'épouse et du médecin au téléphone. La visualisation de l'écoute produit un puissant effet dramatique. Mais si toutes les conversations téléphoniques étaient reproduites par un montage alterné après 1908, on sait qu'elles ont d'abord relevé d'une conception théâtrale. Les cinéastes recréaient les coups de téléphone dans des plans d'ensemble en utilisant des décors ou des écrans divisés. La scène et le hors-scène étaient directement juxtaposés. Pour exprimer la simultanéité, on n'effectuait alors pas des transitions spatio-temporelles entre des plans en disjonction distale, mais des transi-sons entre deux aires de jeux distinctes. Le fameux *College Chums* de Porter (1907) est un remarquable exemple d'une telle pratique. À l'intérieur d'iris insérés aux deux extrémités du cadre et situés au-dessus de l'image d'une ville, un couple converse au téléphone. Pour traduire leur échange, Porter anime des lettres qui flottent dans les airs vers l'homme et vers la femme. Une "onde" relie les interlocuteurs. Quelle belle transi-son littérale !

Le néologisme que je viens d'introduire et la conception que j'ai exposée permettent de mieux nommer et de bien définir l'un des procédés utilisés lors des premières articulations spatio-temporelles. Évidemment, les transi-sons ne constituent pas la seule manière d'effectuer des passages entre deux espaces diégétiques (il existe des transitions "muettes"[7]). Elles ne se limitent ni à l'alternance ni au cinéma des premiers temps puisqu'elles prendront de plus en plus d'importance dans un cinéma qui s'institutionnalise et dans le cinéma sonore. Mais force est d'avouer que, dès 1907/08, la visualisation du son et de l'écoute a joué un rôle important dans la suture de l'espace (particulièrement au sein d'un même lieu) et dans la systématisation du montage alterné. Il fallait tout simplement y prêter l'oreille pour mieux la voir.

Notes

Note de rédaction: Pour les deux figures et les photogrammes, voir la version en anglais, pages 79–86.

1. Cet article a été écrit dans le cadre des travaux du GRAFICS (Groupe de recherche sur l'avènement et la formation des institutions cinématographique et scénique) de l'Université de Montréal, subventionné par le Conseil de recherches en sciences humaines du Canada et le Fonds FCAR du Québec.

2. *Le Médecin du château* (1908) est à la charnière de deux modes de pratique filmique: le système d'attractions monstratives (1895–1908) et le système d'intégration narrative (1908–1915) [Gaudreault et Gunning, 1989: 57].

3. Bien que Tom Gunning m'expliquât après mon intervention au colloque que son analyse visait l'articulation des plans du *Médecin du château* et non le son, il est intéressant de constater que lorsqu'il décrit les plans de *The Lonely Villa* de Griffith (1909), Gunning note cette fois-ci les bruits entendus [1991a: 198]. À mon avis, cela est symptomatique du statut des deux films et de l'attention que l'on porta plus à l'un—le Griffith —qu'à l'autre—le Pathé. Voir à ce sujet l'introduction de mon analyse du *Médecin du château* [Perron, à paraître].

4. Puisque c'est lui qui m'a mis sur la piste du son en me signalant l'écoute des malfaiteurs, il est tout de même curieux qu'Abel ne note pas l'importance du son dans le film de Pathé alors qu'ailleurs, il prend soin de noter certains "sound cues" [1994: 131, 135 et 147]. Quoi qu'il en soit, après mon intervention, lui aussi me confia s'être beaucoup plus intéressé aux plans rapprochés du film qu'à la mise en scène du son.

5. Bien que je traduise mon néologisme, je suis conscient qu'il fonctionne beaucoup moins bien en anglais. L'intérêt en français réside évidemment dans le jeu de mots (il ne manque que le "i" entre transi-son et transition), alors qu'en anglais "sound" et "tion" (prononcé d'ailleurs "shun") sont assez différents. Je crois tout de même que le terme *transi-sound* exprime aussi bien, sinon mieux, que *sound link* (lien sonore) ou *sound bridge* (pont sonore) l'idée que je veux exposer. Ceux-ci, même traduits ou utilisés en français, insistent uniquement sur ce qui sert de lien et non sur la notion de transition.

6. "Il y a disjonction *proximale* toutes les fois que le spectateur peut supposer, à partir des informations de nature spatiale émise par le film, une possibilité de communication visuelle ou sonore non amplifiée (la lunette d'approche, par exemple, est un moyen d'amplification visuelle et le téléphone, d'amplification sonore) entre deux espaces *non contigus* rapprochés par le montage . . . " [Gaudreault et Jost, 1990: 95].

7. D'ailleurs, tout juste avant l'extrait du *Médecin du château* que j'ai décrit, il y a des transitions spatio-temporelles directes "muettes" entre la maison et le château. Il s'agit cependant de deux lieux entre lesquels la distance a bien été marquée.

Bibliographie

Abel, Richard [1994]. *The Ciné Goes to Town; French Cinema, 1896–1914,* Berkeley: University of California Press.

Belloï, Livio [1992]. "Poétique du Hors-champ," *Revue belge du cinéma,* 31.

Bowser, Eileen [1983a]. "Toward Narrative, 1907: *The Mill Girl,*" *Film Before Griffith,* édité par J. L. Fell, Berkeley: University of California Press, 330–338.

—— [1983b]. "Griffith's Film Career Before *The Adventures of Dollie*," *Film Before Griffith*, édité par J. L. Fell, Berkeley: University of California Press, 367–373.

—— [1984]. "*Old Isaacs the Pawnbroker* et le raccordement d'espaces éloignés," *David Wark Griffith*, sous la direction de J. Mottet, Paris: L'Harmattan, 31–43.

—— [1985]. "Le coup de téléphone dans les films des premiers temps," *Les Premiers ans du cinéma français*, sous la direction de Pierer Guibbert, Perpignan: Institut Vigo.

—— [1990]. *The Transformation of Cinema 1907–1915*, New-York: Charles Scribner's Sons.

Chion, Michel [1990]. *L'audio-vision*, Paris: Nathan.

—— [1992]. *Le son au cinéma*, Paris: Éditions de l'Étoile/Cahiers du cinéma.

Dufresne, Mikel [1991]. *L'oeil et l'oreille*, Paris: Édtions Jean-Michel Place.

Gaudreault, André et Tom Gunning [1989]. "Le cinéma des premiers temps: un défi à l'histoire du cinéma?" *Histoire du cinéma. Nouvelles approches*, sous la direction de J. Aumont, A. Gaudreault et M. Marie, Paris: Publications de la Sorbonne, 49–63.

Gaudreault, André et François Jost [1990]. *Le Récit cinématographique*, Paris: Nathan.

Gunning, Tom [1991a]. *D. W. Griffith and the Origins of American Narrative Film*, Urbana et Chicago: University of Illinois Press.

—— [1991b]. "Heard over the phone: *The Lonely Villa* and the de Lorde tradition of the terrors of technology," *Screen*, 32. 2, 184–196.

Pavis, Patrice [1987]. *Dictionnaire du théâtre*, Paris: Messiaor.

Perron, Bernard [1992]. "Au-delà du hors-champ: le hors-scène," *Communication* (Spectateurs), 13.2, p. 85–97.

—— [à paraître] "L'alternance du *Médecin du château* (1908): scène/hors-scène," *La firme Pathé Frères (1896–1914)*, Paris: L'Association française de recherche en histoire du cinéma.

Raynauld, Isabelle [1997]. "Présence, fonction et représentation du son dans les scénarios et les films de Georges Méliès (1896–1912)," *Georges Méliès, l'illusionniste fin de siècle?*, sous la direction de Jacques Malthête et Michel Marie, Paris: Presses de la Sorbonne Nouvelle/Colloque de Cerisy.

—— [à paraître]. "Importance, présence et représentation du son dans les scénarios et les films Pathé dits muets," *La firme Pathé Frères (1896–1914)*, Paris: L'Association française de recherche en histoire du cinéma.

Salt, Barry [1985–1986]. "*The Physician of the Castle*," *Sight and Sound* 54, hiver, 284–285.

Appendix D
Les bruits des spectateurs ou: le spectateur comme adjuvant du spectacle[1]
Jean Châteauvert et André Gaudreault

Le type d'espace que le cinéma institutionnel narratif instaure entre le spectateur et l'écran est, règle générale, un espace résolument privé, un espace intime de recueillement, dans lequel l'écran *s'adresse* non pas à la multitude, mais à un spectateur singulier, individuel et personnel, isolé dans l'intimité de la salle obscure. "S'adresser" est d'ailleurs un bien grand mot, dans la mesure où, justement, l'écran du cinéma institutionnel, de même que ses adjuvants sonores, fait généralement mine de ne s'adresser directement à quiconque. À l'opposé, nonobstant certaines pratiques particulières d'"exhibition" des vues animées,[2] le cinéma des premiers temps instaure, règle générale, un espace résolument public entre son écran et le spectateur. Ce n'est alors pas un spectateur individué, mais un auditoire, une entité collective, qui est impliqué par le dispositif spécifique à cette période. En effet, à cette époque, les spectateurs étaient souvent invités à participer de façon collective au spectacle de vues animées. Une participation qui, par nécessité, se traduisait par des manifestations sonores (par exemple, à applaudir des acteurs comme Méliès qui reviennent saluer à la fin de certains films, à accompagner les chanteurs des chansons illustrées, etc.) et, de la sorte, à agir comme individus participant d'un auditoire, soit une collectivité d'individus.

Il s'agira ici, dans un premier temps, d'identifier les logiques de représentation qui avaient cours à l'époque du cinéma des premiers temps, Pour ce, nous établirons un recensement sommaire des divers "bruits des spectateurs" et, de là, soulèverons la question de la pertinence de ces bruits. Dans un second temps, nous tenterons d'identifier quelques-uns des facteurs qui ont contribué à ce que nous appellerons la structuration de l'espace sonore.[3]

Du côté de la périodisation

La longue période dite du *cinéma des premiers temps*, qui s'étend, par convention, jusqu'aux environs de 1913, ne doit, bien entendu, pas être pensée comme un magma indifférencié. Aussi reprendrons-nous, pour les besoins de notre démonstration, la distinction proposée par Eric de Kuyper entre *cinéma de la première époque* et *cinéma de la deuxième époque* (en prenant comme charnière l'année 1908).[4] Le *cinéma de la première époque* se caractérise notamment par des conditions d'exhibition où prévaut un espace public admettant une libre participation des spectateurs à l'univers sonore des vues animées. Cet espace public s'oppose à l'espace privé du cinéma institutionnel (après 1913) où, de façon générale, l'on prisera le silence parmi les spectateurs. Entre les deux (1908–1913, donc), il y a un espace intermédiaire, mi-chair mi-poisson, un espace tampon, celui du *cinéma de la seconde époque,* durant lequel on assiste à une organisation de l'espace sonore de la projection. Au cours de cette période, les divers "bruits de spectateurs" commencent à subir les contraintes que leur imposent les divers mécanismes de structuration de l'espace sonore, de l'espace de la projection s'entend, laquelle favorisera l'émergence du mode de représentation institutionnel.

Au cours de chacune de ces périodes, une diversité de systèmes de représentation sont à l'honneur, en ce qui a trait à l'exploitation des vues animées, dépendant notamment du site et du type de l'exploitation en question. Les périodes que nous délimitons se différencient les unes des autres notamment par le privilège qu'elles accordent à tel ou tel système de représentation, dont certains occupent, à certaines époques, une place prépondérante. Le *cinéma de la seconde époque* s'oppose ainsi au *cinéma de la première époque* non pas comme un ensemble de pratiques exclusives où le début d'une époque impliquerait de façon nécessaire la disparition des pratiques caractéristiques de la précédente, mais comme une période durant laquelle les conditions de projection sont marquées par la mise en place de pratiques qui ont eu pour résultat d'organiser l'espace sonore de la salle. Ces pratiques font leur apparition au cours de la période dite du cinéma de la première époque, mais elles ne s'opèrent de façon concertée que lors de la seconde époque. Pareillement, les projections de vues animées dans un espace sonore non organisé ne disparaissent pas avec la fin de la première époque, mais deviennent des pratiques marginales au cours de la seconde époque, à un moment où l'on tend à organiser l'espace sonore des projections.

Si la distinction proposée entre *cinéma de la première époque* et *cinéma de la seconde époque* s'établit sur la base des modes de réception des vues animées et du contexte dans lequel celles-ci sont présentées, elle n'en trouve pas moins son pendant dans les "textes" eux-mêmes (soit les *vues* et les *films*), ou du moins dans l'analyse que l'on en fait. Ainsi la distinction proposée ici va-t-elle de pair avec celle qui avait naguère été proposée par Tom Gunning et l'un des auteurs du présent texte, et qui distinguait le *système des attractions monstratives,* caractéristique de la production du cinéma de la première époque, du *système d'intégration narrative* qui dominait le cinéma de la seconde époque[5]. La distinction *première époque/seconde époque* ne constitue donc pas une révision des périodisations établies sur la base des analyses textuelles mais participe d'une volonté d'étayer les analyses textuelles par des analyses contextuelles.

Espace sonore structuré versus espace sonore non structuré

Le *cinéma de la première époque,* le "premier cinéma" si l'on veut, se caractérise par le privilège qu'il accorde à un système de représentation au sein duquel les accompagnements sonores restent relativement autonomes par rapport aux images présentées par les vues animées. Non seulement ces sons ne sont-ils pas intégrés de façon ferme au spectacle visuel offert par la bande-images, mais encore ceux qui produisent ces sons d'accompagnement n'ont-ils pas de directives claires pour leur production, et ne répondent-ils généralement à aucune norme clairement pré-établie. L'espace sonore de la salle, qui n'est alors pas régi par des règles précises, y est non-structuré. De telles règles seront progressivement mises en place, au cours du processus d'institutionnalisation du cinéma qu'amorce la seconde époque.

Sur le plan de l'exploitation cinématographique, le *cinéma de la seconde époque,* le "second cinéma" si l'on veut, se caractérise essentiellement par le fait que commence à s'y instituer, on verra plus loin comment, un *espace sonore structuré.* Il ne faut cependant pas oublier que le système de représentation qui était dominant à l'époque du *premier cinéma* continue, tout au long de cette deuxième période, à faire des siennes dans certains types de sites d'exploitation (fêtes foraines, salles de quartier, etc.). Il faut donc convenir que ce qui caractérise le *second cinéma* (1908–1913), c'est, entre autres choses, cette co-existence, selon des ratios fort variables d'un pays à l'autre et d'une année à l'autre, de deux systèmes de représentation qui supposent des types tout à fait divergents de réception:

> un premier type, hérité du *premier cinéma* (mais qui perdure au-delà de 1908 sous forme de pratiques qui tendent à devenir marginales), qui instaure, entre le spectateur et l'écran un espace public, un espace *spectaculaire,* corollaire de ce que l'on a appelé la confrontation exhibitionniste (voir notamment sur le sujet l'article cité en note 5);

et

> un deuxième type, typique du *second cinéma,* dans lequel s'instaurent des mécanismes de structuration de l'espace sonore, lesquels se traduiront par la mise en place des conditions de représentation nécessaires à l'émergence du cinéma institutionnel.

On peut ainsi convenir, nous semble-t-il, que la deuxième portion de ce qu'il est convenu d'appeler le "cinéma des premiers temps," et qui correspond à la période dite du *second cinéma,* est une période de mutation, qui se traduit par le glissement du *premier cinéma* au *cinéma institutionnel.* Il s'agit d'une période au cours de laquelle les agents propres à l'espace sonore du *premier cinéma* ont été détournés de leur fonction première d'adjuvants du spectacle de vues animées pour devenir des instruments de la structuration de l'espace sonore. Nonobstant le fait que leur seule présence active dans la salle infère un espace public aux antipodes de l'espace intime qui sera requis par l'institution, ces agents contribuent à l'établissement des règles et des usages qui entourent la projection des films: les spectateurs sont invités à se taire pendant le discours du bonimenteur, à chanter lors des chansons illustrées, à applaudir à la fin du film, etc.

Il y aurait donc, à un bout du spectre, un espace public, nourri par la prestation du bonimenteur, un espace commun, un espace "spectaculaire" pourrait-on dire. C'est en effet, non pas à un spectateur individuel, mais à un auditoire, soit une communauté d'auditeurs et / ou de spectateurs, que s'adresse la voix, en "gros plans" sonores, du bonimenteur, des "gros plans" sonores qui viennent en quelque sorte compenser la distance visuelle des *plans d'ensemble* de la bande-image caractéristiques du *premier cinéma.*

À l'autre bout du spectre, il y aurait le *cinéma institutionnel* (à compter de 1913), dont le système de représentation dominant est fondé sur un cinéma de films muets, sans boniment, "entrelardés" d'intertitres et nourris d'une musique qui leur colle à la peau, un système qui s'adresse alors non plus à la multitude, mais à un spectateur singulier, individuel et personnel, isolé dans l'intimité de la salle obscure. Un spectateur individué, donc, qui consomme les images et les sons à partir de l'espace privé de son siège, de cet espace résolument intime de recueillement que rien ne vient déranger, un espace intime qui trouve son corrélat dans l'espace induit par le gros plan, cette figure déjà présente dans le *second cinéma,* qui deviendra caractéristique *du cinéma institutionnel.* À noter, d'ailleurs, que le gros plan commence à jouer un rôle-clé dans l'expression cinématographique au moment, justement, et cela ne saurait être un hasard nous semble-t-il, du retrait du bonimenteur.

Applaudissements des spectateurs

Ainsi le spectateur se sentirait-il plus aisément autorisé, dans le cadre de la *représentation spectaculaire*, à se manifester par divers gestes porteurs de bruits, ne serait-ce que pour répondre à l'interpellation, directe, du spectateur à laquelle se livre, de façon constante et systématique, le bonimenteur, qui agit en quelque sorte toujours-déjà comme une figure d'interlocution. C'est probablement ce qui explique que les manifestations sonores collectives aient été, selon toute évidence, fort fréquentes à l'époque du cinéma des premiers temps, surtout au moment du *premier cinéma*. Notre propre collecte de commentaires journalistiques suscités par les premières années de l'exhibition cinématographique dans une ville comme Montréal est, à cet égard, fort éloquente. On y rapporte en effet assez souvent que le comportement spontané des spectateurs des premiers temps amenait ceux-ci à favoriser, de façon toute *solidaire*, les applaudissements. Au contraire du spectateur du cinéma institutionnel, qui n'applaudira que de façon exceptionnelle, lorsque des individus participant de la production du film sont par exemple présents dans l'espace de la représentation. Ainsi avons-nous constaté, sur la base d'un échantillonnage assez sommaire de quotidiens publiés entre 1899 et 1907, que la plupart des "manifestations sonores" d'origine spectatorielle rapportées par les journalistes, concernent les applaudissements[6], sans doute le meilleur signe de contentement des spectateurs qui vient clore la projection d'une vue ou d'une attraction filmée. On y lit par exemple que: "les vues animées ont à maintes reprises soulevé les applaudissements";[7] ou, encore: "les applaudissements de l'auditoire étaient nourris à chaque vue."[8]

On présume généralement qu'il était admis, et même souhaité, que les spectateurs de la première période applaudissent pour manifester leur contentement. Au sein de son paradigme, le spectateur des premiers temps sent bien toute l'épaisseur du dispositif d'exhibition, et la présence du bonimenteur, notamment, lui fait ressentir que le spectacle auquel il assiste est un *événement unique*, qui ne se reproduira jamais de la même façon nulle part ailleurs au monde, et que c'est ici même, *hic et nunc*, dans cette salle qu'il se produit. Tout est là d'ailleurs pour le lui rappeler: co-présence appuyée des autres spectateurs en raison de la faible obscurité, présence *in situ* des adjuvants de l'exhibition, musiciens, maître de cérémonie, conférencier, bruiteur, etc.

Où l'on voit que le spectateur des premiers temps diffère au moins en cela de son homologue institutionnel qui, sauf exceptions, ne juge pas utile d'essayer de communiquer son degré de contentement aux ombres et taches qui s'agitent sur la toile. Comme quoi, aussi, il est bien vrai que la *toile institutionnelle* est un "écran du fantasme," et que ce qui s'y projette est perçu par le *spectateur institutionnel* comme une histoire dont il oublie volontiers les dispositifs énonciatifs et de représentation.

Autres interventions sonores des spectateurs

Le spectateur de l'époque du *premier cinéma* n'avait pas que les applaudissements pour se manifester, sur le plan sonore. Il pouvait tout aussi bien s'esclaffer de rire, pousser des cris, chanter ou chuchoter. Quant à la prise de parole, à haute voix, de la part d'un spectateur sans gêne, qui n'hésite pas à ponctuer la projection de commentaires intempestifs, il s'agit d'une manifestation sonore qui a vraisemblablement dû régner sans partage sur l'activité de réception filmique du *premier cinéma*. On peut cependant imaginer qu'elle a diminué de façon dramatique durant la période du *second cinéma,* et qu'elle sera, plus tard, considérée comme une pratique en infraction au code de conduite du spectateur institutionnel.

Les rires et les cris (de même que, malheureusement diront d'aucuns, les chuchotements . . .) ont ceci de particulier qu'ils ont continué, par-delà le passage au paradigme du cinéma institutionnel, à faire partie du répertoire des réactions spontanées du spectateur de films. Le chant, les applaudissements et la prise intempestive de parole sont aujourd'hui disparus des conditions courantes de projection. Ils demeurent néanmoins présents dans certains cas, dans certaines salles de quartier, de même que lors de la projection de films-culte, par exemple, lorsqu'il y a appropriation collective du film. Ainsi, lors des projections de films comme *The Rocky Horror Picture Show* ou *Hair,* les spectateurs chantent-ils et crient-ils en chœur. Ainsi aussi, dans certains festivals *psychotroniques,* consacrés aux navets du cinéma de science-fiction ou du cinéma d'horreur, la projection est-elle, de façon générale, ponctuée de cris et de commentaires. C'est dire qu'en marge de la consommation courante des films, où l'on se tapit et se tait, des rituels de célébration qui invitent à la participation collective ont encore parfois lieu.

Il ne faut cependant pas croire que les codes de bonne conduite auront réussi à s'imposer sans partage au cours de la période du *second cinéma.* Tous les "spectatorats" ne se sont pas assagis dès lors que, au cours de cette période, furent mises en place les différentes stratégies de structuration sonore et de mise au silence du spectateur. Ainsi, pour ne prendre qu'un exemple, les spectateurs des salles populaires de Grande-Bretagne auraient-ils été particulièrement bruyants jusque très tardivement dans les années 10.[9]

Les adjuvants de l'exhibition changent de rôle, avons-nous dit, au cours de la période du *second cinéma,* en ménageant, ou à tout le moins en contribuant à imposer, dans l'espace de la projection, des moments durant lesquels le spectateur doit (ou peut) chanter, d'autres durant lesquels il lui faut applaudir, et d'autres encore durant lesquels il doit, en principe, observer le silence. Les interventions sonores dans la salle trouvent alors leur pertinence moins dans la relation du spectateur au spectacle des vues animées que dans l'intégration de tous les éléments qui participent de la projection des films. On peut d'ailleurs supposer que le passage d'un espace sonore *non structuré* à un espace sonore *structuré* a eu comme conséquence l'imposition progressive, au cours de la période du *second cinéma,* du silence chez un spectateur qui, habitué au *spectacle de vues animées,* sera de plus en plus fréquemment convié à une *représentation de films narratifs,* dont le cinéma institutionnel fera son pain et son beurre. Il paraîtra en effet peu indiqué pour le spectateur individué, tapi dans l'ombre de l'espace intime de recueillement du cinéma institutionnel, de s'autoriser à intervenir bruyamment, en paroles ou en bruits, en cours de projection, et de s'immiscer ainsi en quelque sorte, bruyamment, dans l'espace intime de ses co-spectateurs.

Les facteurs de structuration de l'espace sonore

À partir de la période dite du *second cinéma,* l'environnement sonore de la salle de projection a été structuré à partir d'au moins six facteurs assez aisément identifiables:

1) Premier élément de structuration de l'espace sonore, le bonimenteur qui, en prenant la parole, peut par moments arriver à occuper tout l'espace sonore, et couvrir par le fait même les éventuelles paroles intempestives des spectateurs, mais qui, paradoxalement, appelle et attise, à titre de figure d'interlocution, une participa-

tion (inter)active des spectateurs, laquelle se traduira à point nommé en manifestations sonores de divers types.

2) Les cartons projetés, et les intertitres, participent eux aussi de la structuration de l'espace sonore dans la mesure où ils peuvent supporter des directives explicites ou implicites suscitant une participation sonore des spectateurs (invitation à chanter en chœur, à applaudir, etc.).

3) Autre facteur de structuration de l'espace sonore, la musique, qui sert souvent à discipliner les spectateurs. Au tout début, elle n'est là que pour meubler l'espace sonore de la représentation mais par la suite, des textes prescriptifs, paraissant régulièrement dans les journaux corporatifs, préconisent tel type de musique en fonction de telle émotion ou de tel genre. À l'époque du *premier cinéma,* la musique aura imposé une première forme de structuration en occupant tout l'espace sonore de la salle; au cours de la période du *second cinéma,* elle aura participé, dans le genre dramatique notamment, à imposer le silence dans l'espace de la salle.

4) L'espace sonore est aussi structuré par la nature du site même de la projection—la tente de foire ne prête pas aussi bien à l'absorption diégétique que le *Movie Palace.*

5) Autre facteur de structuration de l'espace sonore, le sujet du film, qui convoque dans la salle de projection des habitudes et des comportements liés à des genres théâtraux ou spectaculaires, voire à des référents culturels ou religieux. La projection d'une *Passion* devait de la sorte sans doute s'accompagner d'une participation beaucoup plus discrète de l'auditoire que, disons, une comédie.

6) Enfin, une analyse du corpus filmique du cinéma des premiers temps permet de remarquer la présence, dès les premières années, de véritables stratégies de mise en scène filmique qui sont autant d'appels à la participation sonore des spectateurs. Conçues dans l'espace même de la réalisation, elles peuvent être lues comme de véritables incitations et invitations lancées aux spectateurs à rire, à applaudir, voire à chanter, à un moment précis du film, et elles auraient contribué à la structuration de l'espace sonore propre au cinéma de la seconde période.

Les stratégies filmiques d'appel à la participation sonore

Une première stratégie d'incitation à la participation sonore des spectateurs est mise en œuvre dans les plans où des personnages saluent l'auditoire qui les regarde. Ainsi en est-il des plans-emblèmes qui viennent ponctuer la fin de nombreux films, et où l'on sent que les acteurs saluent des auditeurs qui sont vraisemblablement en train d'applaudir leur prestation. On trouve aussi de telles invites dans les Chronophones Gaumont, à la fin desquels l'artiste revient "en scène" pour les applaudissements virtuels. De tels applaudissements sont ainsi circonscrits aux marges du texte filmique, vers la toute fin de l'"acte," et représentent l'occasion pour les spectateurs de sanctionner le film.

Une seconde stratégie, plus subtile, tiendrait à ces moments où, au terme d'une performance particulièrement "théâtrale" ou d'un geste éminemment spectaculaire, un acteur s'avance, pour *prendre la pose* devant la caméra. On trouve de tels saluts, plus discrets, dans tous les films à trucs où le numéro de prestidigitation se clôt par un mouvement en direction de la caméra, voire un regard envers celle-ci. Ce sera par exemple Méliès qui invite la dame nouvellement apparue dans *Les Cartes vivantes* (1905) à s'avancer au premier plan et à tenir la pose, le temps des applaudissements. De tels applaudissements couronnent alors la réussite de l'attraction captée par la caméra, une attraction non pas *filmique* mais *filmée.* Les applaudissements viennent alors isoler et sanctionner la surprise attractionnelle, comme un moment fort et réussi dans la vue.

Parmi ces surprises attractionnelles, soulignons les citations picturales, soit ces tableaux filmés où la mise en scène et la durée du tableau donnent à lire dans l'image animée la citation d'une toile célèbre, et qui permettait au cinéma, selon Roberta Pearson et William Uricchio, de se donner ses premières lettres de noblesse en offrant à ses spectateurs la traduction vivante de tableaux célèbres.[10] Ainsi dans le *Julius Cæsar* de la Vitagraph, la durée des tableaux, où manifestement les comédiens interrompent leur jeu pour prendre la pose, est-elle là pour permettre au spectateur d'identifier le tableau mais aussi, croyons-nous, pour leur offrir l'occasion et le temps de manifester, par des applaudissements, leur appréciation de la performance. Le cinéma s'apparentait alors au théâtre histrionique, où il est de mise que l'acteur interrompe son jeu pour inciter l'auditoire à applaudir.

Troisième stratégie enfin, l'adaptation cinématographique de chansons reposant sur une connaissance préalable de la chanson adaptée mais aussi sur la participation sonore des spectateurs. En amont de ces adaptations filmiques, les chansons illustrées de la lanterne magique, qui avaient donné le ton aux spectateurs du *premier cinéma*.

La communication sans bruit

À la lumière des premières analyses que nous avons menées, il semble que la fameuse opposition bruits des spectateurs / bruits de l'écran, qui nous apparaît aujourd'hui comme allant de soi, soit héritée du mode de représentation institutionnel, lequel implique une consommation individuelle requérant l'oubli (ou, du moins, la secondarisation) de la présence environnante des autres spectateurs. Dans ce type de spectacle de vues animées caractéristique notamment du *premier cinéma*, au sein duquel le bonimenteur harangue la foule des spectateurs, ces derniers participent à l'environnement sonore d'une représentation qui se conjugue sur un mode collectif. Leurs manifestations sonores ne constituent ainsi pas, si bruyants soient-ils, des *bruits* dans le processus de communication. Elles sont même, dans un régime spectaculaire, le signe d'une participation active au spectacle. Elles font partie de la définition même du spectacle en question, un spectacle qui se donne à un groupe de spectateurs, à une entité collective. C'est à ce groupe que le bonimenteur s'adresse, c'est à cette masse de spectateurs que les comédiens lancent leur premier regard à la caméra. Or, en s'inscrivant dans l'espace-en-train-de-se-structurer du *second cinéma*, qui tend à discriminer les sons et les bruits jugés appropriés de ceux jugés peu opportuns, ces manifestations finiront par trouver leurs usages et leur cohérence. À la fin de la période du *second cinéma*, le groupe des spectateurs devra en principe se taire pendant la projection, et il ne devra chanter ou applaudir que lorsqu'on l'incite à le faire.

La structuration de l'espace sonore aurait, croyons-nous, circonscrit de plus en plus la participation des spectateurs jusqu'à leur imposer le silence nécessaire à l'absorption diégétique. Et avec le silence, le régime de consommation filmique aurait permis au spectateur de glisser de façon subreptice d'une consommation sur un mode *solidaire* à une consommation sur un mode *solitaire*...

Notes

1. Ce texte a été écrit dans le cadre des travaux du GRAFICS (Groupe de recherche sur l'avènement et la formation des institutions cinématographique et scénique) de l'Université de Montréal, subventionné par le Conseil de recherches en sciences humaines du Canada et le fonds FCAR du Québec. Le GRAFICS et les deux auteurs du

présent texte sont membres du CRI (Centre de recherche sur l'intermédialité) de l'Université de Montréal. Les deux auteurs tiennent à remercier toutes celles et ceux qui, par leurs interventions et commentaires, leur ont permis de préciser et d'améliorer leur texte. Des remerciements tout particuliers à Donald Crafton, Ben Brewster et Tom Gunning.

2. Nous ne nous occuperons pas ici des situations d'exhibition particulières (projections dans un cadre privé, par exemple) qui ont pu intervenir à l'époque, et dont certaines peuvent être documentées (par divers témoignages contemporains), sinon pour souligner qu'elles ont dû s'accompagner de pratiques spectatorielles différentes de celles que nous décrivons.

3. Notre recherche prolonge une remarque de Noël Burch à l'effet que la musique et le bonimenteur ont contribué à l'organisation de l'espace sonore de la salle. Cf. *La Lucarne de l'infini* (Paris, Nathan, 1991), 223-231.

4. Nous prenons ainsi une certaine distance avec le découpage proposé par de Kuyper, pour qui la seconde époque recouvre, grosso modo, l'ensemble des années dix. Voir Éric de Kuyper, "Le cinéma de la seconde époque. Le muet des années dix," *Cinémathèque* 1 (mai 1992), 28-35.

5. Voir André Gaudreault et Tom Gunning, "Le cinéma des premiers temps: un défi à l'histoire du cinéma ?" *Histoire du cinéma. Nouvelles approches,* sous la direction de Jacques Aumont, André Gaudreault et Michel Marie (Paris: Publications de la Sorbonne, 1989), 49-63.

6. Cet échantillonnage sommaire des mentions de la presse dans les deux plus importants quotidiens francophones de Montréal a été réalisé par Karine Martinez et Églantine Monsaingeon, auxiliaires de recherche au GRAFICS, que les auteurs tiennent à remercier pour leur précieuse collaboration. Il nous a permis de repérer vingt mentions (retracées dans le journal *La Presse* de 1902 et 1907 et dans *La Patrie* de 1899 et 1905), dont seize rapportaient des applaudissements de la part de spectateurs assistant à une séance de vues animées. Il est à noter que, dans la période sous observation, ces quotidiens publiaient sur une base régulière des comptes rendus de représentations cinématographiques et que les représentations qui sont mentionnées dans nos exemples ne revêtent aucun caractère exceptionnel.

7. *La Presse* (11 novembre 1902), 7.

8. *La Patrie* (11 mai 1905), 14.

9. C'est ce que soutient Nicholas Hiley dans "The British Cinema Auditorium," *Film and the First World War*, sous la direction de Karel Dibbets et Bert Hogenkamp (Amsterdam: Amsterdam University Press, 1995), 160-170; ainsi que dans "Fifteen Questions about the Early Film Audience," *Uncharted Territory. Essays on Early Nonfiction Film,* sous la direction de Daan Hertogs et Nico de Klerk (Amsterdam: Nederlands Filmmuseum, 1997), 105-118

10. Roberta Pearson et William Uricchio, *Reframing Culture. The Case of the Vitagraph Quality Films,* Princeton, Princeton University Press, 1993. Les deux auteurs décrivent ces effets de citations picturales comme autant de "realizations" soit une: "literal recreation and translation" of the images "into a more real . . . vivid, visual, physically present medium" (86). Voir aussi, à ce chapitre, Martin Meisel, *Realizations: Narrative, Pictorial, and Theatrical Arts in Nineteenth-Century England,* Princeton: Princeton University Press, 1983.

Appendix E
Le spectacle cinématographique des premiers temps : fonctions des accompagnements sonores dans la réception des images animées
Jacques Polet

Notre intervention entend s'inscrire dans la perspective de celui qui fut le destinataire de la représentation cinématographique selon le mode de représentation primitif. Le but est de tenter de retrouver une petite part de ce qui pouvait constituer son *horizon d'attente,* pour reprendre le concept forgé par Hans-Robert Jauss.[1] Autrement dit, il s'agira d'essayer de repérer le type de rapport aux images animées que pouvait induire auprès du spectateur l'existence de toute une production sonore périphérique (boniment, musique, bruitages . . .) et cela compte tenu des attentes, des intérêts et des connaissances du public de l'époque visée.

Bien sûr, il y a là quelque chose d'un *objet introuvable* et la reconstitution de paramètres de l'horizon d'attente est "toujours un peu hypothétique."[2] Dans le temps imparti et selon l'état de ma réflexion en la matière, je ne saurais qu'être prudent et fragmentaire, ce d'autant que le nombre de combinaisons entre images et sons peut être considérable, et que les attitudes de réception sont évidemment diversifiées. Il ne s'agit pas de perdre de vue non plus qu'il n'existe pas—et qu'il n'existait pas plus aux premiers temps—un public rigoureusement homogène. Noël Burch, notamment, l'a bien mis en évidence dans ses travaux qui ont nuancé la composition du public selon qu'il s'agissait de la France, de la Grande-Bretagne ou des États-Unis.[3]

Nous sommes bien entendu conscient de la multiplicité des variables empiriques autant que théoriques, la réception pouvant être étudiée des points de vue psychologique de l'identification, sociologique de la structure des publics, anthropologique appelant une analyse interculturelle, etc.

Nous opérons en fait deux coupes méthodologiques:

— d'une part, à travers les rapports des images et des sons périfilmiques (pour reprendre une notion de François Jost qui parle de "périfilm"),[4] nous essayons d'induire les types d'attitudes que le spectacle cinématographique pouvait le plus communément solliciter auprès du regardeur/auditeur des premiers temps, compte tenu des attentes et de l'expérience des spectacles qui devaient être les siens, au-delà de la variabilité empirique des publics et des conduites spectatorielles;

— d'autre part, et de la même façon, nous nous attachons à aller au-delà de la diversité pratique des productions sonores périfilmiques, lesquelles peuvent être regroupées dans l'optique que nous adoptons et qui distingue, plus fondamentalement :
- d'un côté, la *re-présentation* iconique ;
- et de l'autre côté, la dimension *présentielle* de la configuration sonore.

La réflexion repose donc sur cette double coupe, l'une concernant l'objet, l'autre, l'angle d'attaque.

On a souvent fait remarquer que les accompagnements sonores étaient là pour renforcer l'*effet de réel* tout particulièrement associé à la réception des premières vues animées. Par ailleurs, on sait que le mode de représentation primitif induisait le centrement du regard spectatoriel, même si celui-ci était largement stimulé par la multiplicité des actions qui se déployaient en s'étageant dans le cadre: une pluralité déterminante dans ces plans d'ensemble des origines que Noël Burch disait "grouillant de monde" et appeler "une lecture topologique,"[5] alors qu'il y a quelque dix ans Serge Daney observait que, de nos jours, "ce ne sont pas seulement les salles qui sont moins nombreuses et plus vides, ce sont aussi les films qui sont plus dépeuplés."[6] Ce "grouillement" des premiers temps mettait en quelque sorte en abyme au sein d'une image donnée le principe même de la diversité programmatique qui structurait les représentations de l'époque. Il n'empêche que le modèle frontal et les raccords dans l'axe permettaient de transcender cette dissémination topologique: la centralité entraînait la subsomption visuelle de la variété des actions.

Mais c'est ici qu'intervient le rôle des accompagnements sonores dans ce que pouvait susciter auprès du spectateur de l'époque le caractère fortement *performantiel* de l'acte sonore des premiers temps, lorsque les sons n'étaient pas encore fixés (enregistrés): il y a près de l'entrée le *bonisseur* dont les propos racoleurs sont encore parfois perceptibles dans l'espace du spectacle; il y a le *bonimenteur* qui non loin de l'écran dirige la lecture des images et . . . la discipline d'un public qui, peu enclin lui-même au silence, se révèle un gros producteur de sons afilmiques ; de l'autre côté de l'espace latéral de l'écran, se tient le *pianiste,* ou alors c'est *l'orchestre* qui joue dans la fosse; derrière l'écran, il peut y avoir des *diseurs* ou des *chanteurs ;* et dans les coulisses, ce sont les *bruiteurs* qui s'exercent à de multiples simulations. En tout ou en partie, voilà donc présents beaucoup d'acteurs de la production sonore. Non seulement celle-ci frappe par son *hétérogénéité* mais aussi par sa *pluri-localisation* : le son peut surgir de partout—à côté de l'écran, derrière celui-ci, en contrebas, dans les coulisses, de dehors.[7]

On a beau avoir maintes fois souligné que les sons du muet étaient d'"humbles serviteurs" de l'image, il nous paraît qu'il y aurait lieu de prendre davantage en considération la dimension proprement *présentielle* de toutes ces sources sonores. Le spectateur de l'époque se trouve, semble-t-il, pris dans un double mouvement qui articule une tension plutôt qu'une inféodation servile: il est, d'une part, saisi par l'effet de *centration* du dispositif iconique qu'il traverse comme par transparence dans l'effet de réel qui se trouve induit ; d'autre part, ce même spectateur ne peut pas ne pas ressentir la présence physique des sources ponctuelles du son, perçues à travers une *pluri-localisation* qui vient surdéterminer leur hétérogénéité constitutive: le tout, à l'opposé du rapport de *transparence* aux images, donne à éprouver une relation *d'opacité* aux sons. Et le spectateur ressent d'autant plus cette résistance des corps que la trame de son horizon d'attente se trouve être tissée de son expérience des spectacles d'attractions (cirque, foire, music-hall, caf'conc') qui l'ont accoutumé à une puissante manifestation de l'*énonciation performantielle*.[8]

Autrement dit, le spectateur se voit pris entre deux processus contraires : l'un, lié à l'image, qui tend hégémoniquement vers la *centration;* l'autre, associé aux sons, qui le tire vers le *décentrement.* Mais ce décentrement sonore constitue d'autant moins une conduite vécue insupportable à l'époque, que la manifestation physique du bruit bénéficie d'une totale légitimité dans le contexte du temps : le droit au bruit est quasiment reconnu comme un "droit naturel," une affirmation de l'autonomie de chacun, soumise à un minimum de coercition, ainsi que l'a fait observer Jacques Attali qui—dans son ouvrage intitulé "Bruits," justement[9]—précise, s'agissant de la France, que la première campagne réellement significative contre le bruit eut lieu en . . . 1928, donc bien au-delà de la période qui nous concerne.

Il est significatif à ce propos de noter les observations contenues dans beaucoup de textes historiens de type téléologique qui ont fait état de "conditions déplorables" de la réception cinématographique, eu égard précisément au bruit. Jean-Louis Schefer se remémore des souvenirs de pré-adolescence qui ne remontent pourtant pas plus loin que l'après-deuxième guerre, dans lesquels il évoque—encore à l'époque—des visions de films où "les conditions de projection étaient terribles: les conversations dans la salle, etc."[10] Mais l'étaient-elles réellement "terribles," ces conditions, à l'égard du spectateur des premiers temps pour lequel le bruit était définitoire de son espace ? Ce n'est que rétrospectivement, à partir d'un horizon qui s'est déplacé et où la cinéphilie a remplacé l'attente attractionnelle, que l'on peut sans doute porter ce genre de jugement.

Il est sans doute légitime de se dire que ces bruits afilmiques (conversationnels) ne faisaient que renforcer le décentrement du spectateur et la tension, évoquée plus haut, à laquelle était soumise la fameuse impression de réalité iconique. Ce n'est probablement que dans la représentation musicale du concert classique que l'on pouvait entendre le silence . . .

Une forte dimension performantielle

Parlons-en de la musique, et plus particulièrement du piano qui correspond, dans l'espèce qui nous occupe, à son instrument le plus usuel. Nous ne reviendrons pas sur ce qui a déjà été souvent mis en exergue, à savoir sa fonction de liaison, de montage: c'est son phrasé qui relie la discontinuité iconique en créant pour le spectateur un narratif musical de type essentiellement émotionnel. Ce que nous retiendrons plus particulièrement par rapport à notre propos, c'est le registre de *l'improvisation* dans lequel s'inscrit le discours du pianiste. Certes, il se coule dans des "kinothèques," des cadres musicaux standardisés qui constituent autant de "moments": "mystérieux," "sentimental," "comique," "dramatique," voire d'"ambiance chinoise." Mais, à l'intérieur de ce schéma régulé, le pianiste, en improvisant en direct, jouit d'une marge de liberté qui vient conforter cette dimension performantielle de la production sonore qui a été soulignée précédemment.

Il est significatif de noter à ce sujet le témoignage d'un éminent pianiste accompagnateur de films muets, le Belge Fernand Schirren, qui a œuvré pendant tant d'années à la Cinémathèque Royale à Bruxelles et impressionné tous ceux qui l'ont entendu annuellement aux "Giornate del cinema muto" de Pordenone. Dans une interview publiée dans la "Revue belge du cinéma," il va jusqu'à dire—avec le zeste de provocation amusée qui ne surprend pas ceux qui le connaissent un peu—que son plus grand souvenir de pianiste de cinéma est celui où, accompagnant un film dépourvu d'intérêt, il s'est . . . endormi. Je le cite: "Ce jour-là, je me suis endormi pendant une heure tout en continuant à jouer machinalement, sans rien voir, ni rien savoir de l'histoire qui se déroulait"[11] C'est bien sûr un étonnant témoignage-limite, qui est certes hors du temps étudié, mais qui permet d'éclairer combien le discours du pianiste accompagnateur de films muets peut être conduit par une ligne de prévisibilité telle qu'elle l'incline à s'abstraire de tout rapport conscient aux images pour s'abandonner au pur jeu digital—la simple fonctionnalité iconique ouvrant paradoxalement un espace de liberté, fût-elle celle du "jeu rêvé," ces rêves dont Schirren dit d'ailleurs, en conclusion de son interview, combien ses sommeils en sont peuplés de merveilleux . . .

C'est un exemple évidemment symbolique mais qui atteste, ici encore, d'un possible détachement expérientiel du son par rapport aux images, lequel, une fois de plus, était susceptible d'être bien reçu par le spectateur des premiers temps. Il ne faut en effet pas perdre de vue que le régime de l'improvisation pianistique connaît son apogée au XIXème siècle, avec les grands interprètes-virtuoses qui sillonnent les routes et traversent les frontières. Déjà dans la forme classique du concerto, le passage dit de la "cadence" a réservé un temps de liberté où le pianiste a tout loisir de déployer sa créativité et sa virtuosité. Mais justement : on constate que l'apogée est aussi le signe du déclin et que la tradition de l'improvisation et le moment de la libre cadence tendent à disparaître à la fin du XIXème siècle, alors que les partitions notent de plus en plus un type de cadence donné, codifié, fixé et figé, mettant fin à l'inventivité improvisatrice du pianiste. Comme si ce régime de liberté n'était plus compatible avec l'extension florissante du concert classique et du contrôle marchand. Pour paraphraser le fameux aphorisme de "la guerre qu'il ne faut pas laisser aux militaires," la musique classique apparaît alors une affaire trop sérieuse pour la laisser à ses interprètes . . .

Tout se passe alors comme si—permettons l'hypothèse—cette sphère de liberté improvisatrice se déplaçait et refluait vers un nouvel espace de spectacle réputé mineur, marginal, une simple attraction : le cinéma, qui, à travers ses variations pianistiques sur quelques airs inscrits dans la mémoire sociale, va en quelque sorte reprendre un peu à son compte, relayer, "dans l'ombre" et à un niveau artisanal, cette région musicale de liberté performantielle située à l'horizon des attentes attractionnelles du tournant du siècle.

Les différents *bruitages,* eux aussi, participaient de cette reconnaissance de la performance par-delà leur fonction imitative. C'est dans cet esprit qu'il faut comprendre—rappelée par Laurent Jullier—la démarche du spectateur du cinéma muet qui allait "regarder dans les coulisses rouler le chariot à roues polygonales faiseur de tonnerre"[12] De même, le bruitage, "parfois noté dans les partitions musicales que l'on devait exécuter à la projection," était, parfois aussi—comme l'emplacement du fameux gros plan de George Barnes dans "The Great Train Robbery" (Porter, 1903)—"laissé à la libre appréciation des exhibiteurs et exploitants,"[13] ce qui ne pouvait que surdéterminer leur caractère présentiel.

Tout comme pour l'improvisation des cadences jugulée par la codification de leur notation musicale, le cinéma—avec un temps de retard—va connaître, par analogie, la régulation du contrôle, sous la forme de la fixation (l'enregistrement) des sons par différents supports et techniques, comme si *l'aléatoire* devenait institutionnellement insupportable.

Mais alors que les sons non enregistrés sont reçus par le spectateur à travers la performance vivante des corps des locuteurs sonores, les sons fixés détournent la réception d'une *écoute directe* orientée vers une *source naturelle,* pour la focaliser sur une *écoute indirecte* dirigée vers les *sources*-relais.[14]

Car contrairement à l'image dont le tremblotement et le scintillement primitifs n'ont pas porté atteinte à son statut de transparence, les sons fixés ne semblent pas avoir bénéficié du même effet. Non pas, une fois de plus, en raison de considérations téléologiques/ rétrospectives qui les ont jugés "médiocres," "déplorables"—confrontés, par exemple, aux acquis ultérieurs du procédé Dolby stéréo . . . —mais en comparaison, précisément, de la grande tradition des sons naturels du spectacle des attractions qui a nourri le fonds expérientiel du public des premiers temps. En effet, celui-ci ne peut qu'admirer la restitution sonore d'un "avoir-été-là," mais en même temps le côté nasillard ou pleureur, transformant le grain supposé de la profération naturelle, entraîne auprès du spectateur la conscience de la médiation technique qui fait une fois de plus résistance à la transparence : ce qui empêche le spectateur-auditeur de s'abandonner pleinement à ce que Pierre Schaeffer et Michel Chion ont appelé *l'écoute causale,*[15] en l'occurrence de *second niveau,* laquelle porte sur la source suggérée (qui est supposée renvoyer généralement à un personnage de la diégèse), pour faire peser sur elle tout le poids de *l'écoute causale* de *premier niveau,* dirigée, quant à elle, vers la source-relais, la médiation technique.[16]

Tout se passe comme si, dans la relation des sons non fixés aux images, la performance des locuteurs sonores se trouvait être *trop présente* par rapport à la transparence iconique—alors que, dans le cas des sons fixés, c'est cette fois l'effet de réel des images qui semblait l'emporter sur un corps devenu tout à coup *trop lointain.*

Il n'empêche que, du son non fixé au son fixé, une étape a été franchie (nous ne parlerons pas de "progrès," notion "finalisante"). Au *caractère présentiel, hétérogène, pluri-localisé* du premier va se substituer, chez le deuxième, le caractère *réplicatif,*[17] *homogénéisé* et *mono-localisé* par le groupement des sources dans la médiation technique, qui aboutira logiquement à terme à l'unicité de ce qu'on appellera la *bande-son.*

La fixation de la reproduction sonore avait permis un début de contrôle des aléas du spectacle cinématographique originel. Il faut croire que les "tensions" observables dans les rapports images/sons—et cela sans même parler des désynchronisations !—ces tensions, qui apparaissaient acceptables dans les premières années au sein d'un contexte de réception façonné par les spectacles des attractions, étaient devenues progressivement moins justifiables pour le *spectateur* dont l'horizon d'attente s'éloignait petit à petit des dispositifs attractionnels, comme elles étaient surtout devenues intolérables pour l'*industrie* cinématographique naissante qui ne pouvait, dans sa logique, que redouter l'imprévisibilité des spectacles : la maîtrise croissante de l'instance de la réception conditionnait l'extension même de son empire.

La puissance présentielle du cinéma des premiers temps induisant—stimulant—la réactivité des spectateurs, il fallait donc ensuite, pour *normaliser* la réception, que non seulement les images mais *tout* le dispositif du spectacle cinématographique se conforment à la formule qui veut, selon Christian Metz, que "le film est un discours non interactif achevé avant d'être présenté."[18]

A travers les avatars du son, les premiers temps nous font mieux comprendre ce que fut la *liberté* du spectacle cinématographique.

Notes

1. Hans-Robert Jauss, *Pour une esthétique de la réception,* Paris, Gallimard, 1978.

2. Patrice Pavis, *L'analyse des spectacles,* Paris, Nathan, 1996, p. 244.

3. Noël Burch, *La lucarne de l'infini. Naissance du langage cinématographique,* Paris, Nathan, 1990 (voir les chapitres 3, 4 et 5).

4. François Jost, "Le cinéma dans ses œuvres," in *Après Deleuze. Philosophie et esthétique du cinéma,* Paris, Éd. Dis Voir, 1996, p. 124.

5. Noël Burch, "Passion, poursuite : la 'linéarisation'" in *Énonciation et cinéma, Communications,* n° 38, 1983, p. 36.

6. Serge Daney, *Devant la recrudescence des vols de sacs à main,* Lyon, Aléas Éditeur, 1991, p. 147.

7. Pour une analyse détaillée de ces diverses manifestations sonores, voir Pascale Bertolini et Jacques Polet, "Boniments, explications et autres bruits de scène : les accompagnements des spectacles cinématographiques muets en Belgique," in *Le bonimenteur de vues animées / The Moving Picture Lecturer, Iris,* n° 22, automne 1996, pp. 145-160.

8. Selon la formulation de François Jost, "Des images et des hommes," in *Image et narration, Recherches en communication,* n° 8, Louvain-la-Neuve, 1997, p. 23.

9. Jacques Attali, *Bruits,* Paris, Presses Universitaires de France, 1977, pp. 244-245.

10. Jean-Louis Schefer, "Arrimer des mots au fleuve des images," in *Lector in cinema, Vertigo,* n° 17, 1997, p. 19.

11. Philippe Marion, "Pianiste comme aux premiers temps. Rencontre avec Fernand Schirren," in Jacques Polet (dir.), *Les premiers temps du cinéma en Belgique, Revue belge du cinéma,* n° 38-39, mars 1995, p. 101.

12. Laurent Jullier, *Les sons au cinéma et à la télévision. Précis d'analyse de la bande-son,* Paris, Armand Colin, 1995, p. 34.

13. *Ibid.,* p. 27.

14. Pour reprendre des notions évoquées par Laurent Jullier, *ibid.,* p. 50.

15. Pierre Schaeffer, *Traité des objets musicaux,* Paris, Éd. du Seuil, 1966, p. 126. Michel Chion, *L'audio-vision,* Paris, Nathan, 1990, pp. 25-27.

16. Laurent Jullier, *op. cit.,* p. 187.

17. La *réplicativité* est une notion proposée par Laurent Jullier et qui renvoie à un "original" sonore hypothétique et absent, favorisant l'écoute causale de second niveau : *op. cit.,* pp. 49-56 et 197.

18. Christian Metz, "L'énonciation impersonnelle ou le site du film," in *Le cinéma au miroir, Vertigo,* n° 1, Paris, 1987, pp. 14-34.

Appendix F
Le double silence de la "dernière" guerre
Germain Lacasse

Un des films les plus étranges et tragiques que l'on puisse projeter est certainement celui de 1916 intitulé *The Blind Fiddler* où l'on voit des militaires devenus aveugles mais qui dansent au son d'un instrument que la mutité du film empêche d'entendre.[1] Les inter-titres offraient l'explication suivante: "Heroes who have lost their sight in the service of the country, dance with their nurses with a courage that defies affliction." Ce naïf débordement de patriotisme était peut-être accepté à l'époque, mais aujourd'hui il nous semble ajouter une dense zone de silence à ces films appelés muets: l'absence de bande sonore empêche évidemment d'entendre la musique du violon et les pas des danseurs, mais le commentaire rend ce silence bien plus intolérable et suggère surtout de n'en rien répéter, de ne plus rien dire sinon parler de la guerre comme d'une expérience tue.

Une autre sensation audio-visuelle extrêmement étrange est suscitée par le visionne-ment d'un film montrant des "gramophones recruteurs": un soldat se promène dans les rues de Londres en portant sur son dos un gramophone faisant entendre le discours pa-triotique d'un officier sollicitant des recrues.[2] Complètement aberrant pour un spec-tateur de l'an 2000, ce film n'est compréhensible que par contextualisation. Le gramo-phone était probablement encore en 1914 une nouveauté pouvant capter l'attention des passants et faciliter le travail des recruteurs militaires. Accroché au dos d'un soldat, il devait certes attirer encore plus d'attention, l'étrangeté de l'attirail s'ajoutant à la nou-veauté de l'appareil. On répéta ce procédé où l'homme n'était que le support d'une ma-chine appelant au combat. Un film similaire intitulé "Recruiting by Graphophone" mon-trait même des hommes s'entraînant en suivant les ordres émis par un gramophone; un vrai recruteur faisait ensuite un discours d'appel.[3]

La plus étrange de ces expériences pourrait cependant être l'écoute du boniment d'un de ces recruteurs. Voici le propos de l'un d'entre eux, le Français Émile Barlatier, montrant des films à un auditoire montréalais en 1916: "Toujours au grand air, la vie d'un soldat est saine et réconfortante. Le conférencier a rencontré d'anciens employés de bureaux qui traînaient jadis une santé chancelante et sont aujourd'hui plus forts et plus virils qu'ils ne l'ont jamais été après un an ou six mois de vie dans les tranchées. La nour-riture est bonne et saine et on a le grand air continuellement. Rien de meilleur pour rendre à un homme la vitalité éteinte et perdue."[4]

La santé par la guerre! Ce commentaire semble si incongru qu'on en croit à peine ses oreilles et on conclut volontiers à un patriotisme pour le moins excessif. Si le commen-taire semble complètement aberrant, les films qu'on montrait le paraissent tout autant. On faisait projeter des films où la guerre était absolument invisible et où les soldats s'en-traînaient en pratiquant des sports d'équipe et en faisant des marches et des parades. Les films canadiens officiels de la guerre 14–18, longtemps disparus mais récemment remis à jour,[5] sont d'ailleurs surtout consacrés à ce genre de démonstration: entraînement, sports, parades. On n'y voit jamais de morts et quand on y voit des blessés, ils sont en convalescence et s'amusent à divers jeux. Un opérateur a filmé une journée de compétitions sportives pour les troupes canadiennes sur la plage de Deauville en 1915. La journée commence évidemment par un défilé. On y voit ensuite des hommes s'affronter dans des courses, à pied et à cheval, en sac ou à obstacles, individuellement ou en équipe, le tout couronné par une remise de trophées et de joyeux saluts à la caméra.[6]

Ce film veut de toute évidence montrer la joyeuse vie que mènent les soldats canadiens en France, et on ne manque pas d'y intégrer les auxiliaires féminines de l'armée ainsi que les Françaises amenées à la plage pour l'occasion. On peut même se demander si tout ce film n'a pas été mis en scène, les soldats étant amenés spécialement à Deauville pour souligner les plaisirs de la vie en permission. Pour ce faire, l'opérateur a dû passer quelques jours sur place avec les bataillons, car ces séquences représentent trop de préparation et de tournage pour une seule journée. La dépense importante occasionnée par le transport des soldats et l'organisation de ce tournage montre le prix que l'autorité militaire était prête à payer pour une propagande rassurante. Faire venir toute la fanfare du régiment pour une projection était ensuite la moindre des choses, et y ajouter un commentaire vantant la vie de tranchée comme thérapie allait alors de soi!

Cette expérience appartient à ce qu'on peut appeler cinéma oral ou cinéma de l'oralité: des films muets commentés par un conférencier ou un bonimenteur. Dans le cinéma muet accompagné par un tel narrateur, le commentaire verbal semble en effet déterminant dans l'interprétation, la preuve étant maintenant établie que ce discours pouvait même changer complètement la signification du film. Il semble dès lors approprié de parler de cinéma de l'oralité dans la mesure où la bande image est intégrée à une représentation où le discours du commentateur est un élément tout aussi important. Ce genre de représentation tient aussi de l'oralité par d'autres caractéristiques dont la principale est la présence d'un agent connu du public et dont la performance peut faire varier à l'infini la portée du spectacle.[7]

Cette théorie concorde avec les hypothèses de Rick Altman sur le son de la période muette. Altman souligne le déplacement récent de la recherche sur le son vers la réception et propose un modèle appelé "cinema as event" permettant de rendre compte de l'hétérogénéité matérielle du son et de la variabilité de l'exécution.[8] Le texte filmique n'est plus considéré comme un centre de gravité mais comme un objet flottant entre la sphère de la production et celle de la réception. Au lieu de la dialectique pré- et post-institutionnelle, le son aurait évolué selon un "crisis model" en trois phases (crise d'identité, conflit de juridiction et règlement négocié).[9] L'étape que nous appelons cinéma oral correspond surtout aux deux premières phases, car le boniment disparaît graduellement à mesure que le son est standardisé, mais persiste dans les pays non producteurs, dans les communautés minoritaires, et dans certains contextes particuliers. La guerre est une de ces circonstances extraordinaires.

Le second souffle du bonimenteur

La guerre 1914–18 fut l'occasion d'une recrudescence du cinéma oral, ou de son second souffle, parce que les conférenciers presque disparus de la pratique bourgeoise depuis quelques années y revinrent en force pour appuyer les efforts de recrutement. Les nombreux films produits par le gouvernement canadien furent offerts gratuitement ou à prix très avantageux aux exploitants, mais ils furent aussi abondamment utilisés dans des projections spéciales annoncées avec tambours et trompettes, commentées par un orateur militaire et accompagnées par la fanfare d'un régiment. Par exemple, une telle projection commanditée par le journal *La Presse* a lieu au théâtre Casino de Montréal le mercredi 15 décembre 1915; parmi les films mentionnés un seul montre pourtant les soldats canadiens, "déchargeant des sacs de sable pour protéger la vie de leurs camarades dans les tranchées."[10] De telles projections avaient lieu partout au Canada, où les assemblées de recrutement étaient souvent conçues comme de grands divertissements publics comportant des concerts, des conférences et des films. Tout l'arsenal de séduction était employé afin d'attirer le public et d'émouvoir les recrues potentielles.[11] Le double silence des films était atténué par une bruyante mise en scène sonore destinée à faire vibrer à l'extrême la fibre patriotique.

Il n'est pas établi que le bonimenteur populaire se livrait à un commentaire critique des films de propagande, mais l'examen des traces sonores des salles où il exerçait montre un contexte fortement résistant et laisse penser qu'il a pu participer à une lecture résistante des films de guerre. Comme le conférencier militaire, le bonimenteur populaire semble avoir connu un regain de popularité pendant la guerre dans une forme de spectacle qui se développa à ce moment au Québec. Variante du vaudeville américain, le burlesque québécois était constitué de numéros de danse, de sketches et monologues comiques et de vues animées bonimentées.[12] L'opposition des Canadiens français à la guerre stimula le sentiment nationaliste et les historiens du burlesque soulignent la volonté des artistes d'accentuer l'usage du français dans les spectacles. Plusieurs des bonimenteurs français qui pratiquaient leur métier sur les scènes du Québec repartirent en France pour s'enrôler et cédèrent la place à des collègues québécois. Les échos des spectacles de l'époque devinrent bien différents de ceux des soirées avec conférencier militaire.

La pièce de résistance à cet égard est certainement le monologue écrit en 1917 par Armand Leclaire et intitulé simplement "Le conscrit Baptiste." Il raconte les bévues commises par un campagnard québécois incapable d'exécuter les exercices que lui commandent les officiers recruteurs; habile aux travaux des champs, il ne comprend rien aux manoeuvres militaires et décourage les recruteurs qui le renvoient:

Baptiste, que m'dit l'z'officier, t'es mieux d'aller travailler dans tes champs. T'es déchargé, tu feras jamais un soldat . . . "—"Ben, j'vas dire là, toé que j'y répercute, j'aime mieux rester habitant que d'être soldat pis faire des singeries avec des fusils qui sont tant seulement pas capables de quer une mouche! Pis r'viens pas me badrer cheu nous, toé, parce que j'en ai un fusil moi itou, pis j't'avartis qu'y est chargé c'lui-là!" Là-dessus, j'ai pris le bord. Quand les criatures m'ont vu arriver, vous parlez qu'y m'ont fait une fête! Faut vous dire qu'y avait pus rien que moé pis mossieu le curé dans la paroisse en fait d'hommes, les autres ont été conscriptionnés ou ben y sont morts.[13]

Le monologue ironise adroitement sur l'habileté du paysan québécois pour les travaux agricoles et son indifférence aux manoeuvres militaires; il valorise les travaux civils au détriment de l'esprit guerrier qu'il ridiculise. Son auteur, Armand Leclaire, était un comédien et dramaturge travaillant dans les "scopes" avec les bonimenteurs Alex Silvio, Hector Pellerin et autres. Son texte fut récité dans les théâtres, mais il fut aussi publié dans *Le Passe-Temps*, magazine populaire de chanson et de musique largement répandu. La lecture que fait Leclaire de la conscription et du travail des recruteurs était certainement partagée par une grande partie de l'auditoire francophone de Montréal, lequel

devait trouver assez ridicules les très nombreux films montrant les soldats à l'entraînement. Le public avait évolué un peu comme Leclaire, qui avait aussi écrit quelques années
plus tôt une pièce protestant contre la suppression du français dans les écoles de l'Ontario.
Ses préoccupations n'étaient pas seulement nationales, il s'en prit également aux capital-
istes qui profitaient de la guerre:

> Les pauvr's Canayens
> Par tous les moyens
> Sont pressés par la guerre
> Quand tout renchérit
> Qu'on grève le pays
> Faut n'être pas trop surpris
> Si on coupe les salaires
> Aux rich's tout est permis
> Faut manger d'la misère
> Ou s'enrôler "Oversea"![14]

Ce texte n'a manifestement pas été soumis à l'attention du censeur ou de ses collabo-
rateurs, car on y critique ouvertement la guerre comme une politique destinée à enrichir
les uns aux dépens de la vie des autres. Tandis que la propagande officielle s'adresse à un
public homogène auquel est offerte une seule interprétation, la chanson populaire divise
le monde en deux camps opposés dont un seul subit les affres de la guerre. Leclaire était
loin d'être le seul à proférer ce genre de critique sarcastique. Un auteur dont le pseud-
onyme était Paul Rosal et qui écrivait beaucoup pour *Le Passe-Temps* composa plusieurs
poèmes satiriques traitant de la conscription. Il publia d'abord un poème intitulé "Le
Service National" où il tournait en ridicule le recensement promulgué pour préparer
l'enrôlement obligatoire:

> Le gouvernement perspicace
> Veut faire, au moyen de cartons,
> L'inventaire de notre race
> Et des ans que nous portons.
> (. . .) Chacun fait preuve de prudence
> Car on à la conviction
> Que de cette correspondance
> Sortira la conscription.[15]

Le Service national était un recensement obligatoire dit nécessaire par le gouvernement pour connaître l'état de la force de travail disponible sur le territoire national et
planifier la production de guerre. Mais au Québec les civils devinèrent rapidement que
cette militarisation de l'économie fournirait également l'information nécessaire à l'établissement des listes de conscrits éventuels. Rosal ne s'arrêta pas là et comme Leclaire il
montra bien que l'opinion publique sur la guerre n'atteignait jamais la belle unanimité
prêchée par le gouvernement et ses censeurs. Dans un autre texte intitulé "Nos braves
conscriptionnistes" Rosal s'en prenait ensuite à ceux qui réclamaient la conscription pour
les autres mais voulaient eux-mêmes y échapper; il souligne que les Canadiens français
sont patriotes mais non quand ils y sont forcés:

> Ce sont ceux qui crient le plus fort
> Qui veulent envoyer les autres,
> Mais ils savent "faire le mort"

Ces enthousiastes apôtres!
(. . .) Nous sommes Canadiens d'abord,
Loyaux comme eux à la Couronne,
Et si nous le clamons moins fort
Nous n'y voulons forcer personne.[16]

Malgré l'opposition massive des Canadiens français, la loi de conscription finit par être adoptée et entra en vigueur en janvier 1918. Les textes antibellicistes et antimilitaristes devenaient alors carrément illégaux et semblent avoir disparu, mais d'autres paroles perpétuèrent la résistance en parlant du sort des conscrits. Le ton est moins réfractaire et l'inspiration tient plutôt de la complainte ou du mélodrame, mais le théâtre et la chanson continuent d'apporter un bémol aux films militaires dont la production a décuplé en 1918 pour tenter d'intensifier le patriotisme. Paul Gury, acteur et dramaturge breton vivant à Montréal, monte ainsi en 1918 une revue appelée *Le petit conscrit*,[17] pour laquelle il compose une ritournelle coiffée du même titre:

C'est un petit conscrit
Qu'on prend à son pays
Parce qu'il faut sur une terre lointaine
Encore bien du sang à une guerre inhumaine
C'est un bien triste sort
D'aller risquer la mort
Si loin des siens
Si loin de son pays
L'aîné le p'tit conscrit
L'aîné le p'tit conscrit

Le ton sarcastique de Leclaire et Rosal est disparu, mais on est bien loin des élans patriotiques de Barlatier sur la santé du soldat. Au lieu d'un combattant plein d'entrain prêt à mourir sous les bombes, le soldat de cette chanson est un enrôlé de force condamné à lutter pour une cause étrangère et une guerre "inhumaine."

Ces monologues et ces chansons, entendus dans les mêmes salles qui projetaient les films officiels, constituaient peut-être le seul commentaire réaliste de la guerre. Lus et entendus dans les scopes ou ailleurs, dits et chantés avant ou après les films, ils ne pouvaient manquer de constituer un contraste frappant. Le censeur canadien, Ernest J. Chambers, trouva d'ailleurs assez tôt raison de s'en plaindre. Son rapport insiste particulièrement sur les "numéros" et pièces de théâtre, disant que:

des hommes haut placés et de jugement (. . .) ont fait remarquer que les chansons de certains vaudevilles exprimaient une envie pathétique de la paix à tout prix et visaient de toute évidence à provoquer un sentiment de lassitude à l'égard de la guerre.[18]

La répression de ces textes résistants fut faite par le biais des critiques dramatiques des journaux, auxquels le censeur demanda de décourager la présentation de tels spectacles. Lorsque les représentations suspectes se poursuivaient, les renseignements fournis par les journaux étaient transmis à la police qui intervenait, mais une partie des textes réfractaires échappait probablement au censeur, parce que le public de gens "haut placés et de jugement" ne fréquentait pas beaucoup les salles de vaudeville, et les critiques dramatiques des journaux en parlaient assez rarement. Il n'est donc pas erroné de croire que la résistance à la propagande pouvait se manifester dans le spectacle populaire; elle était probablement allusive plutôt qu'explicite, mais elle était lisible pour qui avait appris cette sorte de lecture. Le censeur qui avait le bras si long n'osait pas mettre les doigts partout . . .

Des partitions aveugles

Les films muets de la guerre appellent une forme de lecture particulière, non seulement contextuelle mais performative. Il faut comprendre qu'ils ne montraient pas la guerre mais en représentaient seulement l'aspect le moins rébarbatif; il faut supposer aussi qu'ils n'étaient pas toujours lus de cette façon par certains publics, qui en faisaient une lecture performative résistante, laquelle peut être réactualisée à travers les paratextes qui nous sont parvenus et reconstituent partiellement l'environnement sonore des films. Ces textes rapportent des propos jadis plus ou moins séditieux mais qui permettent de connaître une autre version du réel sur lequel les films gardaient et préservaient le silence.

Si le son du cinéma muet était fortement marqué par la performance, comme l'ont souligné Rick Altman et d'autres, il faut conclure qu'en contexte de conflit militaire les variantes de ces lectures performatives évoluent selon les contraintes extrêmement sévères de la guerre. Le cinéma de propagande est soutenu par des conférences de type naïf et épique, tandis que la performance résistante s'exprime en sourdine par des interventions paratextuelles comme celles que nous avons citées. Au double silence des représentations officielles correspondait le second degré de la lecture résistante.

Walter Benjamin a écrit qu'après cette guerre le silence s'imposait parce qu'il était impossible d'en raconter l'expérience: "Avec la Grande Guerre un processus devenait manifeste qui, depuis, ne devait plus s'arrêter. Ne s'est-on pas aperçu à l'armistice que les gens revenaient muets du front? non pas enrichis mais appauvris en expérience communicable. Et quoi d'étonnant à cela? Jamais expérience n'a été aussi foncièrement démentie que les expériences stratégiques par la guerre de position, matérielles par l'inflation, morales par les gouvernants."[19]

On pourrait croire que les autorités l'avaient compris car elles firent enfin des films où les fanfares n'étaient ni visibles ni audibles: "The Great Silence Filmed (. . .) most impressive vistas of the great multitude thronged round the base of the Cenotaph—hushed and silent in remembrance of the Glorious Dead."[20] Ce silence officiel n'était cependant pas de meilleure augure, il ne voulait en fait que continuer à taire l'horrible et rappeler l'épique, c'était le silence des trompettes et des fanfares succédant à celui des canons et des recruteurs.

L'histoire du cinéma muet ne doit donc pas se borner à faire parler l'image, puisque celle-ci n'était souvent que le reflet d'une expérience tue. L'expérience vécue et entendue est plutôt conservée dans la mémoire orale et les quelques textes rendant compte de celle-ci. S'il est vrai que les films dit muets devraient plutôt être appelés sourds, c'est face aux films de guerre que cet énoncé trouve tout son sens: des films sourds au fracas de la guerre, mais aussi des spectateurs sourds à ce silence complice autant qu'à un commentaire trop naïvement éloquent. L'histoire doit tenir compte de tous ces silences et de tous ces sons.

Notes

1. Film *Topical Budget* # 248-2 (27 May 1916): "The Blind Fiddler." Plusieurs autres films montraient les soldats aveugles: "Sightless Soldiers' Recreation" (# 247-2), "Blind Men's Boat Races" (# 255-1), "Blind Soldiers Typewriting" (# 271-2), etc. Ces renseigne-

ments nous ont été communiqués par l'historien anglais Luke McKernan, qui prépare une filmographie de la compagnie Topical Budget, à laquelle il a déjà consacré un ouvrage: *Topical Budget. The Great British News Film,* London: British Film Institute, 1992.

2. Film *Topical Budget* # 290–1 (14 March 1917): "Motor Volunteers Graphophone band."

3. Film *Topical Budget* # 208–1, 18 August 1915.

4. Anonyme, "Une jolie soirée au Monument," in *La Presse,* [Montréal] (8 octobre 1915), 2

5. Les films originaux furent détruits en 1967 dans l'incendie de l'entrepôt de l'Office national du film; des copies avaient été faites pour la collection de plans d'archives, mais leur origine fut oubliée et la majeure partie de la collection demeura invisible pendant quelques décennies. Voir à ce sujet l'article de Germain Lacasse, "Les films 'perdus' de la guerre oubliée," in *Canadian Journal of Film Studies* 7.1 (Spring 1998).

6. Film d'archives # FG-14-38, Office national du film, Montréal.

7. Ces notions sont développées dans notre thèse de doctorat: *Le bonimenteur et le cinéma oral. Le cinéma muet entre tradition et modernité,* Département de littérature comparée, Université de Montréal, 1996.

8. Rick Altman, "General Introduction: Cinema as Event," in Rick Altman, éd, *Sound Theory/Sound Practice* (New York and London: Routledge, 1992), 1–14.

9. Rick Altman, "The Silence of the Silents," *Musical Quarterly* 80.4 (Winter 1996), 688.

10. Publicité, "La guerre en France," in *La Presse,* 14 décembre 1915.

11. Paul Maroney, " 'The Great Adventure': The Context and Ideology of Recruiting in Ontario, 1914–17," *The Canadian Historical Review* 77 (March 1996), 75.

12. Chantal Hébert, *Le burlesque au Québec. Un divertissement populaire,* Montréal, Hurtubise HMH, 1981.

13. Armand Leclaire, "Le conscrit Baptiste," in *Le Passe-temps,* 8 septembre 1917.

14. Armand Leclaire, "La Valse des Piastres," in *Le Passe-Temps,* 10 mars 1917.

15. Paul Rosal, "Le Service National," in *Le Passe-Temps,* 27 janvier 1917.

16. Paul Rosal, "Nos braves conscriptionnistes," in *Le Passe-Temps,* 5 mai 1917.

17. Anonyme, "Dans nos théâtres," in *Le Pays,* 16 novembre 1918.

18. Ernest Chambers, "Rapport sur le service de la censure de la presse canadienne," reproduit dans les *Cahiers d'histoire politique* 2 (hiver 1996), 276.

19. Walter Benjamin, "Le narrateur. Réflexions à propos de l'oeuvre de Nicolas Leskov," in *Écrits français* (Paris, Gallimard, 1991), 206.

20. Film *Topical Budget* # 429–1, 13 November 1919.

Contributors

Richard Abel is Ellis and Nelle Levitt Professor of English at Drake University, where he teaches cinema/media/cultural studies. His most recent book is *The Red Rooster Scare: Making Cinema American, 1900–1910* (California, 1999), which was a finalist for the Kraszna-Krausz Moving Image Book Award. Currently he is editing the Routledge *Encyclopedia of Early Cinema.*

Rick Altman is Professor of Cinema and Comparative Literature at the University of Iowa. After publishing *Film/Genre* (British Film Institute, 1999), which won the SCS Katherine Singer Kovacs award, he edited a special issue of *Iris* 27 (Spring 1999) on the "State of Sound Studies." His current projects include a book on the silent cinema soundscape, a DVD devoted to illustrated song slides, and performances by his troupe, The Living Nickelodeon.

Edouard Arnoldy recently completed a doctoral thesis on the cultural history of sound practices in the cinema (1900–1930) at the Université de Liège.

Mats Björkin received his doctorate in cinema studies from Stockholm University with a dissertation on Americanism and film culture in Sweden during the 1920s. He is involved in a project to create a new archive for nonfiction films in Sweden, and currently is teaching film and television courses at the Department of Cinema Studies, Stockholm University.

Stephen Bottomore has been researching the early cinema for nearly two decades, while also working as a television documentary producer/director. His latest book is *I Want to See This Annie Mattygraph: A Cartoon History of the Coming of the Movies* (Le Giornate del Cinema Muto, 1995).

Marta Braun teaches at Ryerson Polytechnic University in Toronto. She is the author of *Picturing Time: The Work Of Etienne-Jules Marey* (Chicago, 1994).

Jean Châteauvert works as a film and television scriptwriter. He has published a book on voiceover narration, *Des mots à l'image: La voix over au cinéma* (Nuit blanche, 1996). Currently he also conducts research on intermediality in early cinema.

Ian Christie worked at the British Film Institute in various capacities, managing regional programming, distribution, and early cinema projects. Currently, he is Professor of Film and Media History, Birkbeck College, University of London. He has scripted a five-part series hosted by Terry Gilliam, *The Last Machine,* for BBC Television (1995) and is a regular broadcaster. Publications include *The Film Factory* (BFI, 1988) and other books on Russian cinema, co-edited with Richard Taylor, as well as essays on British and contemporary popular cinema.

Richard Crangle is a freelance researcher based in Exeter, U.K., working on the magic lantern and its relationship with the early moving picture. He was formerly Assistant Director of the Bill Douglas Centre for the History of Cinema and Popular Culture at the University of Exeter and is currently editor of the *Magic Lantern Journal,* published by the Magic Lantern Society.

John Fullerton is Associate Professor in the Department of Cinema Studies, Stockholm University. He has published many essays on early Swedish film, and edited *Celebrating 1895: The Centenary of Cinema* (1998). As Series Editor with Jan Olsson of Stockholm Studies in Cinema for John Libbey, he co-edited *Nordic Explorations: Film before 1930* (1999) and *Technologies of Moving Images* (1999), and is a contributor to *Allegories of Communication: Intermedial Concerns from Cinema to the Digital* (2000).

Jane Gaines is Associate Professor of Literature and English and Director of the Film and Video Program at Duke University. She has recently co-edited *Collecting Visible Evidence* (Minnesota, 1999) and completed *Fire and Desire: Mixed Race Movies in the Silent Era* (Chicago, 2001).

André Gaudreault is Professor of Art History at the Université de Montréal, where he serves as Director of GRAFICS (Groupe de recherche sur l'avènement et la formation des institutions cinématographique et scénique) as well as CRI (Centre de recherche sur l'intermédialité). He has published several books on film narratology and early cinema, among them *Le Récit cinématographique,* with François Jost (1991), *Pathé 1900: Fragments d'une filmographie analytique du cinéma des premiers temps* (1993), *Au pays des ennemis du cinéma,* with Germain Lacasse et Jean-Pierre Sirois-Trahan (1996), and *Du littéraire au filmique: Système du récit* (revised edition, 1999). He was the first President of Domitor and edits the scholarly journal *Cinémas.*

Tom Gunning teaches in the Art History and Cinema and Media Departments of the University of Chicago. He has published widely on early cinema, was a founding member of Domitor, and is now President of the organization. He is the author of *D. W. Griffith and the Origins of American Narrative Film* (Illinois, 1990) and *The Films of Fritz Lang* (BFI, 2000).

François Jost is a Professor at the Sorbonne Nouvelle Paris III where he serves as Director of CEISME (Centre d'Etudes sur l'Image et le Son Médiatiques). He is the author of many books on film narratology and theoretical television studies, among them *L'Oeil-caméra: Entre film et roman,* 2nd ed. (1987), *Le Récit cinématographique,* with André Gaudreault (1990), *Un Monde à notre image: Énonciation, Cinéma, Télévision* (1993), *Le Temps d'un regard: De l'image au specateur* (1998), *Penser la télévision* (1998), and *Introduction à analyse de la télévision* (1999). He also has written scripts and directed films, among them *La Mort du révolutionnaire hallucinée* (1979), and published a novel, *Les Thermes de Stabies* (1990).

Charlie Keil is assistant professor of cinema studies at the Graduate Centre for the Study of Drama, University of Toronto. He has published extensively on early cinema in journals including *Iris, Cinema Journal, Persistence of Vision,* and *Film History.* His book on American cinema of the transitional period is forthcoming from Columbia University Press.

Jeff Klenotic is Associate Professor of Communication at the University of New Hampshire at Manchester. His ongoing research on local film exhibition and the historical ethnography of movie-going most recently led to "Class Markers in the Mass Movie Audience (1926–32)," which appeared in the *Communication Review*. He is currently researching the link between film and advertising in early cinema.

Germain Lacasse is a historian who lives in Montreal and teaches at the Université du Québec. He has published books about early cinema in Quebec and is now writing a history of World War I Canadian films.

Neil Lerner received a Ph.D. in musicology from Duke University. He has published and presented essays on film music, Aaron Copland, Virgil Thomson, Theodor Adorno, Philip Glass, Dimitri Tiomkin, and documentary film. Currently he is assistant professor of music at Davidson College, where he teaches music history, American music, and film music.

Patrick Loughney is Head of the Moving Image Section of the Library of Congress Motion Picture, Broadcasting and Recorded Sound Division, Washington, D.C.

David Mayer and Helen Day-Mayer are theater historians and the founders of the Victorian and Edwardian Stage on Film Project at the University of Manchester (UK), where David Mayer is Emeritus Professor of Drama and Research and Helen Day-Mayer an adjunct lecturer in drama. David has written extensively on British and American popular entertainment, chiefly melodrama and pantomime. His books include *Playing Out the Empire: Ben-Hur and Other Toga Plays and Films* (Oxford, 1994). He also is a contributor to Le Giornate del cinema muto's *Griffith Project*.

Dominique Nasta received her Ph.D. from the Université Libre de Bruxelles (1989), where she now is in charge of the Film Studies Department and teaches film aesthetics and film analysis. She has published *Meaning in Film: Relevant Structures in Soundtrack and Narrative* (1991), as well as articles on film music, Michelangelo Antonioni, early melodrama, and postmodern auteurs. She is one of the editors of the *Revue belge du cinéma*.

Bernard Perron is an assistant professor of cinema at the Université de Montréal, and member of GRAFICS (Groupe de recherche sur l'avènement et le formation des institutions cinématographique et scénique). His research and writings concentrate on the advent of montage and on cognition, narration, and play in narrative cinema.

Jacques Polet is a Professor in the Department of Communication Studies at the Catholic University of Louvain as well as the Institute of Broadcasting Arts in Louvain-la-Neuve, where he teaches the history and theory of cinema. His essays on early cinema have appeared in many books and journals, among them *Les vingt premières années de cinema français* (Paris), *Revue belge du cinéma* (Brussels), and *Iris* (Iowa City).

Lauren Rabinovitz is Professor of American Studies and Film Studies at the University of Iowa. She is the author of *For the Love of Pleasure: Women, Movies, and Culture in Turn-of-the-Century Chicago* (Rutgers, 1998) as well as other books and articles on cinema and television. She also is a co-editor of *Iris: A Journal of Theory on Image and Sound*. Currently she is completing a computerized interactive turn-of-the-century amusement park.

Isabelle Raynauld is Associate Professor in film studies and film production at the Université de Montréal. She is also a screenwriter and film director. As an academic, her field of specialization is the history of screenwriting practices from early cinema to multimedia. She is particularly interested in the interrelationship between cinematic technologies and screenwriting rules.

Herbert Reynolds is a film historian with a special interest in the Kalem Company. He serves as General Editor of the George C. Pratt Reference Collection.

Gregory A. Waller teaches film studies in the Department of English at the University of Kentucky. His most recent book, *Main Street Amusements: Movies and Commercial Entertainment in a Southern City, 1896–1930* (Smithsonian, 1995), won both the Theatre Library Association award and the SCS Katherine Singer Kovacs book award. Currently he is working on a study of entertainment and the chautauqua movement.

Rashit M. Yangirov is a freelance scholar specializing in the relations between Russian artistic culture and film history.

Index

national identity, xiv, xvi*n*8; Anglophone Canada, 198–203; French Canada, 207–210; Germany, 154–155*n*48; United States, 150–151

Nationoscope (Montréal), xii

Nelson, Carol, 3, 122

Nelson Theater (Springfield, Massachusetts), 164*n*6

Newton and Company, 43

Nickel Theater (Manchester, New Hampshire), 159, *160, 161*

Nickelodeon (Ottumwa, Iowa), 146–147, *151*

nickelodeons, 130, 143–151, 233

999 Cuckolds [stage play] (Saburov), 111

"Nipper," 27–28, *28*

Le Noël de la fille perdue (1908), 97

Le Noël de Monsieur le Curé (1908), 97

Le Noël du pauvre hère (1908), 97

Nordisk Films Kompagni, 88, *88*, 89, *90, 92, 93*

Nye huslærer, Den [*The New Teacher*] (1910), 89, 91

Oderman, Stuart, 242–243

Ohmann, Richard, 154*n*46

opera, 32, 37

Orpheum (Chicago), xii

Ott, Fred, 17, *17*

Oxilia, Nino, 108*n*8

paintings: *L'Angélus,* 5, 10*n*16; *En écoutant du Schumann,* 5; *His Master's Voice,* 27–28, *28;* quotation of, in films, 189; *Stenka Razin, 112*

panoramas, 142*n*53

Parker, Lottie Blair, 221, 228–229

Pathé, Charles, 3

Pathé Frères company, 62–63, 79, 84, 97; action melodramas, 96–100; distribution in U.S., xiv, 150–151; "phono-cinematographic scenes," 59; sound events in screenplays, 69–70, 74

Pay Day (1907), 147, 150, *151*

Pearson, Roberta, 189

Pellerin, Hector, 208

Perret, Léonce, 104, *105, 106*

Petrov-Kraevsky, Yevgenii, 113, *114*

phonograph, 3–9, 13–29; to accompany films, 156–157, 234; for ballyhoo, 236; and [*Dickson Experimental Sound Film*], 215–217, *218;* and illustrated songs, 146; in Strindberg, 33–34, 36; used on movie sets, 54

Phonoscope, 14, 27

photography, 9

Pickford, Mary, 200

Polet, Jacques, 197*n*8

popular songs, 234, 237–239; and illustrated songs, 144–150; and national identity, 150–151, 200; in *'Way Down East,* 229; in World War I, 208

Porter, Edwin, 95, 221, 223, 227

projectionist, duties of, 235–236

Rabinovitz, Lauren, xv, 240*n*10

Radium Theater (Des Moines), 143, 145, *146,* 149

Raitt, Alan, 10*n*18

Ramsaye, Terry, 10*n*19

Rapsodia Satanica (1915), 108*n*8

Raynauld, Isabelle, 52, 82, 108*n*9

realism, 14; at *Hale's Tours,* 173, 175, 176, 178; sound effects and, 48, 237; and "talker pictures," 157–158, 161–163

reality effect, xiv, 193, 194

Reese, David, 242

Reynolds, Herbert, xv, xvi*n*10, 251*n*8

Riker, John, 156–157, 163–164

Riley Brothers, 40–44

Rilke, Rainer Maria, 9

Rimbaud, Arthur, 15, 29

Riot in St. Petersburg (1904), 144

Robertson, D. W., 122–126

Robinson, Bill "Bojangles," 228

Rogers, Will, 228

Rogin, Michael, 268*n*35

Romance of a Jewess, The (1908), 227–228

Ronell, Avital, 32, 38*n*7

Rosal, Paul, 208–209

Rosen, Charles, 11*n*23

Sacks, Oliver, 71, 73

Sadoul, Georges, 13, 142*n*57

Saint-Saëns, Camille, 50

Savigliano, Marta E., 267*n*21

Schaeffer, Pierre, 196

Schefer, Jean-Louis, 194

Schein, Louisa, xv

Schirren, Fernand, 194–195

score: for *The Battleship Potemkin,* 264; for *Birth of a Nation,* 252–265, *255, 257, 259, 261, 263;* for Kalem Company films, 241–250, *244;* for *Rapsodia Satanica,* 108*n*8; for *'Way Down East,* 229–230

Scott & Van Altena, 145, *145*

Selig, William, 130

www.ingramcontent.com/pod-product-compliance
Ingram Content Group UK Ltd.
Pitfield, Milton Keynes, MK11 3LW, UK
UKHW021849070225
454829UK00005B/191